THE JURISDICTION OF THE INTERNATIONAL CRIMINAL COURT OVER NATIONALS OF NON-STATES PARTIES

This book provides a systematic and comprehensive analysis of the ICC's jurisdiction over nationals of non-States Parties. It is within the context of developments at the Court in recent years that this work addresses the overarching question: On what legal basis is the ICC authorised to exercise jurisdiction over nationals of non-States Parties? Engaging with ICC jurisprudence and building upon arguments developed in legal scholarship, this book explores the theory of delegated jurisdiction and critically examines the idea that the Court might alternatively be exercising jurisdiction inherent to the international community. It argues that delegation of territorial jurisdiction and implied consent by virtue of UN membership provide a legal basis to allow the ICC to exercise jurisdiction over nationals of non-States Parties in almost all situations envisaged by the Rome Statute.

Monique Cormier is a Lecturer at the University of New England School of Law in New South Wales, Australia. She was previously a Research Fellow at Melbourne Law School and received her doctorate from the University of Melbourne.

THE JURISDICTION OF THE INTERNATIONAL CRIMINAL COURT OVER NATIONALS OF NON-STATES PARTIES

MONIQUE CORMIER
University of New England

CAMBRIDGE
UNIVERSITY PRESS

University Printing House, Cambridge CB2 8BS, United Kingdom

One Liberty Plaza, 20th Floor, New York, NY 10006, USA

477 Williamstown Road, Port Melbourne, VIC 3207, Australia

314–321, 3rd Floor, Plot 3, Splendor Forum, Jasola District Centre,
New Delhi – 110025, India

79 Anson Road, #06–04/06, Singapore 079906

Cambridge University Press is part of the University of Cambridge.

It furthers the University's mission by disseminating knowledge in the pursuit of
education, learning, and research at the highest international levels of excellence.

www.cambridge.org
Information on this title: www.cambridge.org/9781108499309
DOI: 10.1017/9781108588706

© Monique Cormier 2020

This publication is in copyright. Subject to statutory exception
and to the provisions of relevant collective licensing agreements,
no reproduction of any part may take place without the written
permission of Cambridge University Press.

First published 2020

A catalogue record for this publication is available from the British Library.

Library of Congress Cataloging-in-Publication Data
Names: Cormier, Monique (Law teacher) author.
Title: 'The Jurisdiction of the International Criminal Court over Nationals of Non-States
Parties' / Monique Cormier, University of New England, Australia.
Description: Cambridge, United Kingdom ; New York, NY, USA : Cambridge University
Press, 2020. | Based on author's thesis (doctoral – University of Melbourne, 2017). | Includes
bibliographical references and index.
Identifiers: LCCN 2020012176 (print) | LCCN 2020012177 (ebook) | ISBN 9781108499309
(hardback) | ISBN 9781108588706 (ebook)
Subjects: LCSH: International Criminal Court. | Criminal jurisdiction. | Jurisdiction
(International law)
Classification: LCC KZ7375 .C67 2020 (print) | LCC KZ7375 (ebook) | DDC 345/.0122–dc23
LC record available at https://lccn.loc.gov/2020012176
LC ebook record available at https://lccn.loc.gov/2020012177

ISBN 978-1-108-49930-9 Hardback

Cambridge University Press has no responsibility for the persistence or accuracy of
URLs for external or third-party internet websites referred to in this publication
and does not guarantee that any content on such websites is, or will remain,
accurate or appropriate.

CONTENTS

Foreword   *page* xi
Acknowledgements   xiii
Table of Cases   xv
Table of Treaties and Selected Other
Instruments   xxiii
List of Abbreviations   xxvii

1   Introduction   1
    1.1   The Jurisdiction Provisions   2
    1.2   Context and Aims   4
    1.3   Structure   7

2   Questions of State Consent and Sovereignty   11
    2.1   Introduction   11
    2.2   Does the ICC's Jurisdiction Infringe on the Sovereignty of Non-States Parties?   13
        2.2.1   The Rome Statute Violates the *Pacta Tertiis* Principle   14
        2.2.2   The Rome Statute Ignores the Importance of State Consent   18
        2.2.3   Complementarity as an Infringement on State Sovereignty   24
        2.2.4   Conclusion to Section 2.2   28
    2.3   The Rome Statute, Non-States Parties and Sovereignty   28
        2.3.1   Does the Rome Statute Infringe on State Sovereignty? Yes, No and Somewhat   29
        2.3.2   The Sovereignty Paradox   32
        2.3.3   What This Means for the ICC and Non-States Parties   34
    2.4   Conclusion   35

3 Delegation of Jurisdiction: The Concepts 36
3.1 Introduction 36
3.2 Delegation Debates in the Early Scholarship 40
    3.2.1 Is It Lawful to Delegate Criminal Jurisdiction without the Consent of the State of Nationality? 40
        3.2.1.1 Delegation of Jurisdiction among States 41
        3.2.1.2 Delegation of Jurisdiction to an International Court 44
    3.2.2 Delegation of Jurisdiction to an International Court Is Lawful 50
3.3 Delegation in International Law 50
    3.3.1 The ICC as an International Organisation 51
    3.3.2 How Do International Organisations Acquire Their Powers? 52
        3.3.2.1 Typology of Conferral 54
        3.3.2.2 Collective Conferral or Individual Delegation? 55
    3.3.3 The ICC as an Atypical International Organisation 57
3.4 Jurisdiction in International Law 57
    3.4.1 Jurisdiction to Prescribe (Adjudicate) and Enforce 59
    3.4.2 Principles of Criminal Jurisdiction under International Law 61
        3.4.2.1 Territoriality Principle 61
        3.4.2.2 Extraterritorial Jurisdiction 63
    3.4.3 Conclusion to Section 3.4 69
3.5 Conclusion 69

4 Delegation of Jurisdiction: Application and Limitations 71
4.1 Introduction 71
4.2 Is Delegation of Jurisdiction Affected by National Laws? 72
    4.2.1 *The* Lex Loci *of State Party X* 73
4.3 Is Delegation of Jurisdiction Affected by Customary Immunities? 76
    4.3.1 ICC Jurisdiction over Sitting Heads of Non-States Parties 76
    4.3.2 Prosecuting Sitting Heads of State: Background 77
        4.3.2.1 Head of State Immunity in Customary International Law 78
    4.3.3 Head of State Immunity and the ICC 81

        4.3.3.1   Articles 27 and 98 of the Rome Statute   81
        4.3.3.2   Consideration of Articles 27 and 98 in the Case of Al Bashir   84
    4.3.4   A Hypothetical Case Study: Can the ICC Exercise Jurisdiction over an Incumbent Head of State from a Non-State Party in a Situation Not Involving the Security Council?   91
        4.3.4.1   Is President X Immune from Arrest and Transfer?   91
        4.3.4.2   Does Delegation of Jurisdiction Provide a Legal Basis for ICC Jurisdiction over President X?   93
    4.3.5   Conclusion to Section 4.3   93
4.4   Is Delegation of Jurisdiction Affected by International Agreements?   94
    4.4.1   The Situation in Afghanistan   94
        4.4.1.1   Does the SOFA Limit Afghanistan's Ability to Delegate Jurisdiction?   96
        4.4.1.2   The Conflict between the Rome Statute and the SOFA   97
        4.4.1.3   Resolving the Conflict between the Statute and the SOFA   105
    4.4.2   The Situation in Palestine   106
        4.4.2.1   The Question of Statehood and Delegable Jurisdiction   108
        4.4.2.2   Restriction of Palestine's Judicial Jurisdiction via the Oslo Accords   109
        4.4.2.3   Does Delegation of Jurisdiction Provide a Legal Basis for ICC Jurisdiction over Israeli Nationals?   111
4.5   Conclusion   112

5   **The UN Security Council, the ICC and Nationals of Non-States Parties**   114
5.1   Introduction   114
5.2   The Role of the Security Council in the Rome Statute   116
5.3   The Negative Pillar: Excluding Jurisdiction   119
    5.3.1   Article 16: The Deferral Power   119
        5.3.1.1   Resolutions 1422 (2002) and 1487 (2003)   120
        5.3.1.2   The Validity of Resolution 1422   123
    5.3.2   Excluding Jurisdiction without Reference to the Rome Statute   125
        5.3.2.1   Resolution 1497 and Article 98(2) of the Rome Statute   127

- 5.3.2.2 Can Liberia Delegate Jurisdiction in Light of Resolution 1497?   128
- 5.3.3 Unorthodox and Unintended   130
- 5.4 The Positive Pillar: Enabling Jurisdiction   131
  - 5.4.1 Article 13(b): The Referral Power   131
    - 5.4.1.1 Resolution 1593: The Situation in Darfur   132
    - 5.4.1.2 Resolution 1970: The Situation in Libya   135
  - 5.4.2 Do Sudan and Libya Have Rights and Obligations under the Rome Statute?   137
  - 5.4.3 What Is the Legal Basis for ICC Jurisdiction over Situations Referred by the Security Council?   139
    - 5.4.3.1 The Security Council Empowers the Court   140
    - 5.4.3.2 What Empowers the Security Council?   141
  - 5.4.4 Implied Consent as a Legal Basis   151
- 5.5 The Hidden Pillar Revealed: The Crime of Aggression   152
  - 5.5.1 The Jurisdiction Trigger   153
  - 5.5.2 Determining the Existence of a Crime of Aggression   155
  - 5.5.3 A Mixed Role for the Security Council   157
- 5.6 Conclusion   158

6 Universality as a Legal Basis for ICC Jurisdiction   159
- 6.1 Introduction   159
- 6.2 What is Universal Jurisdiction?   161
  - 6.2.1 Three Types of Universal Jurisdiction   162
    - 6.2.1.1 Representative or Vicarious Jurisdiction   162
    - 6.2.1.2 Treaty-Based Universal Jurisdiction   162
    - 6.2.1.3 Universal Jurisdiction in Customary International Law   164
  - 6.2.2 'Universal Jurisdiction' in This Book   166
- 6.3 Universality and the Rome Statute   167
  - 6.3.1 Is the Principle of Universality Precluded by the Statute?   167
  - 6.3.2 Justiciability of Statute Crimes under Universal Jurisdiction   169
    - 6.3.2.1 Genocide   170
    - 6.3.2.2 Crimes Against Humanity   172
    - 6.3.2.3 War Crimes   174

               6.3.2.4 Aggression   177
        6.3.3 Conclusion to Section 6.3   181
   6.4 Universality as the Basis for ICC Jurisdiction   182
        6.4.1 Universal Jurisdiction as Belonging to States   182
               6.4.1.1 Delegation of Universal Jurisdiction   182
               6.4.1.2 The Limits of Delegated Universal
                        Jurisdiction   183
        6.4.2 Universal Jurisdiction as Inherent to the International
               Community   185
               6.4.2.1 The ICC as an Agent of the International
                        Community   186
               6.4.2.2 Inherent Universal Jurisdiction as a Legal Basis for
                        ICC Jurisdiction over Nationals of Non-States
                        Parties   188
               6.4.2.3 The Limits of Inherent Universal
                        Jurisdiction   190
        6.4.3 Two Shortcomings   193
   6.5 Conclusion   194

7 Concluding Remarks   196

   Bibliography   200
   Index   239

FOREWORD

Many of the past and present controversies surrounding the International Criminal Court proceed in some way from its jurisdiction over nationals of States not party to the Rome Statute, its constituent instrument. Preliminary examinations, investigations and cases involving alleged crimes by nationals of Israel, Myanmar, Russia, Sudan and the US have embroiled the Court in hotly disputed legal proceedings and exposed it to scathing and sometimes scandalous political attacks. In some of these instances, criticism of the Court has by no means been confined to non-States Parties.

To some, the ICC's jurisdiction over third-party nationals is the original sin from which other legal transgressions flow. To others, this same jurisdiction is but one legitimate incarnation of the '*jus puniendi* of the international community'. To others still, the Court's jurisdiction over nationals of non-States Parties is no lesser or greater than the respective jurisdictions over crimes on their territories enjoyed by States Parties to the Rome Statute or is justified in its exercise in situations referred to the Court by the Security Council by a non-State Party's consent as a member of the United Nations, by way of Article 25 of the UN Charter. What is instead potentially problematic to these last is the overlay of the ICC's jurisdiction over third-party nationals with other international legal issues, such as the immunities of State officials from foreign criminal jurisdiction.

In *The Jurisdiction of the International Criminal Court over Nationals of Non-States Parties*, Monique Cormier, with a view to a cogent rationalisation of the ICC's competence with respect to allegations of crimes by nationals of States not party to the Rome Statute, subjects to scrutiny these different schools of thought and the many and varied international legal questions thrown up one way or another by this competence. The result, the product of deep and broad study of the primary and secondary sources, is a rich, expansive and at times provocative study with implications for many points of law currently before or likely to come before the

Court. It deserves to be read, and will amply reward reading, by anyone interested in international criminal law, the law of international organisations, the law of treaties or international legal understandings of sovereignty.

Roger O'Keefe

Professor of International Law
Bocconi University, Milan

ACKNOWLEDGEMENTS

This book is a reviewed and updated version of my doctoral dissertation completed at the University of Melbourne, so the first vote of thanks must go to my PhD supervisors. Tim McCormack was an enthusiastic supporter of this project from the beginning and always willing to share his experience and insights on the situations before the International Criminal Court (ICC). Alison Duxbury was a dedicated supervisor and a supportive mentor and I particularly appreciated her expertise on international institutional law. I am also grateful for Alison's ongoing support during the preparation of my book manuscript. Thank you to Rain Liivoja, whose willingness to engage with the technicalities of international criminal jurisdiction assisted me greatly. The guidance, encouragement and good humour of my three supervisors sustained me throughout my candidature.

I am indebted to Roger O'Keefe and Roger Clark for examining my thesis and providing detailed and thoughtful comments that became a blueprint for revising and updating the text for publication. The reports from the anonymous Cambridge University Press reviewers were similarly invaluable.

The jurisdiction of the ICC over nationals of non-States Parties first caught my attention back in 2005 as an undergraduate at the University of Adelaide. I wrote my LLB Honours thesis on this topic under the dedicated supervision of Judith Gardam, unaware that I would still be preoccupied with this issue fifteen years later! I would also like to thank Gerry Simpson for introducing me to academia and encouraging me to pursue a PhD.

A number of colleagues read various versions of the manuscript, in whole or in part, and for that I would like to thank Cameron Moore and Samuli Haataja for their thoughts on specific chapters. Particular thanks must go to Carrie McDougall for her generous and detailed feedback on an earlier draft and to Rhys Ryan for his excellent research assistance.

The University of New England School of Law has been my academic home for the past three years and I would like to acknowledge the School and my UNE colleagues for their support while I finalised the manuscript.

I have presented aspects of this research at various conferences and workshops over a number of years and wish to express my appreciation broadly to the participants at the Australian International Criminal Law workshops; the Australian and New Zealand Society of International Law conferences; the 2015 American Society of International Law ICL Workshop; and the Harvard Law School Visiting Researchers Colloquium in 2016.

I am fortunate to be part of a supportive scholarly community of Melbourne PhD alumni and would like to thank Anna Hood, Madelaine Chiam, Simon McKenzie, Kobi Leins, Cait Storr and Sophie Rigney for their camaraderie, inspiration and good advice.

Finally, I thank my family for their unwavering support and encouragement.

TABLE OF CASES

Permanent Court of International Justice

SS Lotus (France v Turkey) (Judgment) [1927] PCIJ (Series A) No 10   49, 61, 63–64, 66–68

International Court of Justice

Accordance with International Law of the Unilateral Declaration of Independence in Respect of Kosovo (Advisory Opinion) [2010] ICJ Rep 403   151
Application of the Convention on the Prevention and Punishment of the Crime of Genocide (Bosnia and Herzegovina v Yugoslavia (Serbia and Montenegro)) (Preliminary Objections) [1996] ICJ Rep 595   171
Arrest Warrant of 11 April 2000 (Democratic Republic of the Congo v Belgium) (Judgment) [2002] ICJ Rep 3   22, 64, 67–68, 73, 77–78, 164–166
Certain Expenses of the United Nations (Advisory Opinion)[1962] ICJ Rep 151   142–143
Certain Questions of Mutual Assistance in Criminal Matters (Djibouti v France) (Judgment) [2008] ICJ Rep 177   80
East Timor (Portugal v Australia) (Judgment) [1995] ICJ Rep 90   13
Legality of the Use by a State of Nuclear Weapons in Armed Conflict (Advisory Opinion) [1996] ICJ Rep 66   52, 53
Military and Paramilitary Activities in and against Nicaragua (Nicaragua v US) (Merits) [1986] ICJ Rep 14   177
Monetary Gold Removed from Rome in 1943 (Italy v France) (Judgment) [1954] ICJ Rep 19   13, 23
Nottebohm Case (Liechtenstein v Guatemala) (Second Phase, Judgment) [1955] ICJ Rep 4   65
Questions of Interpretation and Application of the 1971 Montreal Convention Arising from the Aerial Incident at Lockerbie (Libyan Arab Jamahiriya v United States of America) (Preliminary Objections) [1998] ICJ Rep 115   148
Questions Relating to the Obligation to Prosecute or Extradite (Belgium v Senegal) (Judgment) [2012] ICJ Rep 422   163

TABLE OF CASES

Reparation for Injuries Suffered in the Service of the United Nations (Advisory Opinion)
    [1949] ICJ Rep 174   52–53, 56, 93, 192
*Reservations to the Convention on the Prevention and Punishment of the Crime of
    Genocide (Advisory Opinion)* [1951] ICJ Rep 15   170

International Criminal Tribunal for the Former Yugoslavia

*Prosecutor v Blaškić (Judgement on the Request for the Republic of Croatia for Review of
    the Decision of Trial Chamber II of 18 July 1997)* (International Criminal Tribunal for
    the former Yugoslavia, Appeals Chamber, Case No IT-95-14-AR-108,
    29 October 1997)   78
Prosecutor v Blaškić (Objection to the Issue of Subpoena Duces Tecum*)* (International
    Criminal Tribunal for the former Yugoslavia, Appeals Chamber, Case No IT-95-14-
    AR-108, 18 July 1997)   79
Prosecutor v Furundzija, (Judgement) (International Criminal Tribunal for the former
    Yugoslavia, Trial Chamber, Case No IT-95-17/I-T, 10 December 1998)   171
Prosecutor v Krnojelac (Judgement) (International Criminal Tribunal for the former
    Yugoslavia, Trial Chamber, Case No IT-97-25, 15 March 2002)   173
Prosecutor v Milošević (Indictment) (Office of the Prosecutor, International Criminal
    Tribunal for the former Yugoslavia, Case No IT-99-37, 22 May 1999)   150
Prosecutor v Milutinović (Decision on Motion Challenging Jurisdiction) (International
    Criminal Tribunal for the former Yugoslavia, Trial Chamber, Case No IT-99-37-PT,
    6 May 2003)   150–151
*Prosecutor v Tadić (Decision on the Defence Motion for Interlocutory Appeal on
    Jurisdiction)* (International Criminal Tribunal for the former Yugoslavia, Appeals
    Chamber II, Case No ICTY-94-1-AR72, 2 October 1995) 143, 147, 171, 177, 198
Prosecutor v Vasiljević (Judgement) (International Criminal Tribunal for the former
    Yugoslavia, Trial Chamber II, Case No IT-98-32-T, 29 November 2002)   173

International Criminal Tribunal for Rwanda

Prosecutor v Kanyabashi (Decision on the Defence Motion on Jurisdiction) (International
    Criminal Tribunal for Rwanda, Trial Chamber II, Case No ICTR-96-15 T,
    18 June 1997)   143
*Prosecutor v Ntuyahaga, (Decision on the Prosecutor's Motion to Withdraw the
    Indictment)* (International Criminal Tribunal for Rwanda, Trial Chamber I, Case No
    ICTR-90-40-T, 18 March 1999)   171

International Criminal Court

Decision Assigning the Situation in Uganda to Pre-Trial Chamber II (International
    Criminal Court, Presidency, Case No ICC-02/04, 5 July 2004)   135

TABLE OF CASES xvii

Decision on the constitution of Pre-Trial Chambers and on the assignment of the Democratic Republic of the Congo, Darfur, Sudan and Côte d'Ivoire situations (International Criminal Court, the Presidency, Case No ICC-Pres-01–12, 15 March 2012)   86

Prosecutor v Al Bashir (Decision on the Cooperation of the Democratic Republic of the Congo Regarding Omar Al Bashir's Arrest and Surrender to the Court) (Pre-Trial Chamber II, Case No ICC/02/05–01/09, 9 April 2014)   86, 137, 140

Prosecutor v Al Bashir (Decision pursuant to Article 87(7) of the Rome Statute on the Failure by the Republic of Malawi to Comply with the Cooperation Requests Issued by the Court with respect to the Arrest and Surrender of Omar Hassan Ahmad Al Bashir) (Pre-Trial Chamber I, Case No ICC/02/05–01/09, 12 December 2011)   85

Prosecutor v Al Bashir (Decision pursuant to Article 87(7) of the Rome Statute on the Failure by the Republic of Chad to Comply with the Cooperation Requests Issued by the Court with respect to the Arrest and Surrender of Omar Hassan Ahmad Al Bashir) (Pre-Trial Chamber I, Case No ICC/02/05–01/09, 13 December 2011)   85

Prosecutor v Al Bashir (Decision under article 87(7) of the Rome Statute on the non-compliance by Jordan with the request by the Court for the arrest and surrender of Omar Al-Bashir) (International Criminal Court, Pre-Trial Chamber II, Case No ICC/02/05–01/09, 11 December 2017)   87

Prosecutor v Al Bashir (Decision under article 87(7) of the Rome Statute on the non-compliance by South Africa with the request by the Court for the arrest and surrender of Omar Al-Bashir) (International Criminal Court, Pre-Trial Chamber II, Case No ICC/02/05–01/09, 6 July 2017)   87

Prosecutor v Al Bashir (Joint Concurring Opinion of Judges Eboe-Osuji, Morrison, Hofmański and Bossa) (International Criminal Court, Appeals Chamber, Case No ICC/02/05–01/09, 6 May 2019)   87–91, 184, 192

Prosecutor v Al Bashir (Judgment in the Jordan Referral re Al-Bashir Appeal) (International Criminal Court, Appeals Chamber, Case No ICC/02/05–01/09, 6 May 2019)   57, 87–90, 133, 137, 139, 193, 198

Prosecutor v Al Bashir (Order Regarding Omar Al-Bashir's Potential Visit to the Republic of Chad and to the State of Libya) (International Criminal Court, Pre-Trial Chamber II, Case No ICC-02/05–01/09, 15 February 2013)   86, 133

Prosecutor v Al Bashir (Warrant of Arrest) (International Criminal Court, Pre-Trial Chamber I, Case No ICC-02/05–01/09, 4 March 2009)   74, 82, 84, 133, 137–138, 152

Prosecutor v Gbagbo (Judgment on the Appeal of Mr Laurent Koudou Gbagbo against the Decision of Pre-Trial Chamber I on Jurisdiction and Stay of Proceedings) (International Criminal Court, Appeals Chamber, Case No ICC-02/11–01/11, 12 December 2012)   34

Prosecutor v Harun and Abd-Al-Rahman (Warrant of Arrest) (International Criminal Court, Pre-Trial Chamber I, Case No ICC-02/05–01/07, 27 April 2007)   20, 133

Prosecutor v Hussein (Warrant of Arrest) (International Criminal Court, Pre-Trial Chamber I, Case No ICC-02/05–01/12, 1 March 2012).   133

Prosecutor v Kenyatta (Decision on the Prosecutor's Application for Summonses to Appear for Francis Kirimi Muthaura, Uhuru Muigai Kenyatta and Mohammed Hussein Ali) (International Criminal Court, Pre-Trial Chamber II, Case No ICC-01/09–02/11, 8 March 2011). 83

Prosecutor v Kenyatta (Decision on the withdrawal of charges against Mr Kenyatta) (International Criminal Court, Trial Chamber V(B), Case No ICC-01/09–02/11, 13 March 2015) 83

Prosecutor v Lubanga (Decision on the Confirmation of Charges) (International Criminal Court, Pre-Trial Chamber I, Case No ICC-01/04–01/06, 29 January 2007) 176

Prosecutor v Lubanga (Judgment pursuant to Article 74 of the Statute) (International Criminal Court, Trial Chamber I, Case No ICC-01/04–01/06, 14 March 2012) 176

Prosecutor v Mahmoud Mustafa Busayf Al-Werfalli (Second Warrant of Arrest) (International Criminal Court, Pre-Trial Chamber I, Case No ICC-01/11–01/17, 4 July 2018) 136

Prosecutor v Muammar Gaddafi (Decision to Terminate the Case Against Muammar Mohammed Abu Minyar Gaddafi) (International Criminal Court, Pre-Trial Chamber I, Case No ICC-01/11–01/11, 22 November 2011) 83

Prosecutor v Muthauru, Kenyatta and Ali (Judgment on the appeal of the Republic of Kenya against the decision of Pre-Trial Chamber II of 30 May 2011 entitled 'Decision on the Application by the Government of Kenya Challenging the Admissibility of the Case Pursuant to Article 19(2)(b) of the Statute') (International Criminal Court, Appeals Chamber, Case No ICC-01/09–02/11 OA, 30 August 2011) 25

Prosecutor v Nourain (Warrant of Arrest) (International Criminal Court, Trial Chamber IV, Case No ICC-02/05–03/09, 11 September 2014) 133

Prosecutor v Ruto and Sang (Decision on Prosecutor's Application for Witness Summonses and resulting Request for State Party Cooperation) (International Criminal Court, Trial Chamber V (A), Case No ICC-01/09–01/11, 17 April 2014) 53

Prosecutor v Saif Al-Islam Gaddafi (Decision on the 'Admissibility Challenge by Dr Saif Al-Islam Gaddafi pursuant to Articles 17(1)(c), 19 and 20(3) of the Rome Statute') (International Criminal Court, Pre-Trial Chamber I, Case No ICC-01/11–01/11, 5 April 2019) 26, 136

Prosecutor v Saif Al-Islam Gaddafi and Abdullah Al-Senussi (Decision on the admissibility of the case against Saif Al-Islam Gaddafi) (International Criminal Court, Pre-Trial Chamber I, Case No ICC-01/11–01/11, 31 May 2013) 25–26, 136

Prosecutor v Saif Al-Islam Gaddafi and Abdullah Al-Senussi (Decision on the admissibility of the case against Abdullah Al-Senussi) (International Criminal Court, Pre-Trial Chamber I, Case No ICC-01/11–01/11, 11 October 2013) 25, 136, 138

Prosecutor v Saif Al-Islam Gaddafi and Abdullah Al-Senussi (Judgment on the appeal of Libya against the decision of Pre-Trial Chamber I of 31 May 2013) (International Criminal Court, Appeals Chamber, Case No ICC-01/11–01/11, 21 May 2014) 26, 136

TABLE OF CASES xix

Request under Regulation 46(3) of the Regulations of the Court (Decision on the 'Prosecution's Request for a Ruling on Jurisdiction under Article 19(3) of the Statute') (International Criminal Court, Pre-Trial Chamber I, Case No ICC-RoC46(3)-01/18, 6 September 2018)   17, 56

Situation in Bangladesh/Myanmar (Decision Pursuant to Article 15 of the Rome Statute on the Authorisation of an Investigation into the Situation in the People's Republic of Bangladesh/Republic of Myanmar) (International Criminal Court, Pre-Trial Chamber III, Case No. ICC-01/19, 14 November 2019)   37, 62, 76

Situation in Georgia (Decision on the Prosecutor's request for authorization of an investigation) (International Criminal Court, Pre-Trial Chamber I, Case No ICC-01/15, 27 January 2016)   27, 76

Situation in Libya (Warrant of Arrest for Al-Tuhamy Mohamed Khaled) (International Criminal Court, Pre-Trial Chamber I, Case No ICC-01/11–01/13, 18 April 2013)   136

Situation in Libya (Warrant of Arrest for Mahmoud Mustafa Busayf Al-Werfalli) (International Criminal Court, Pre-Trial Chamber I, Case No ICC-01/11–01/17, 15 August 2017)   136

Situation in the Islamic Republic of Afghanistan (Decision Pursuant to Article 15 of the Rome Statute on the Authorisation of an Investigation into the Situation in the Islamic Republic of Afghanistan) (International Criminal Court, Pre-Trial Chamber II, Case No ICC-02/17, 12 April 2019)   95

Situation in the Islamic Republic of Afghanistan (Judgment on the Appeal against the Decision on the Authorisation of an Investigation into the Situation in the Islamic Republic of Afghanistan) (International Criminal Court, Appeals Chamber, Case No ICC-02/17 OA4, 5 March 2020)

Situation in the Islamic Republic of Afghanistan (Request for Authorisation of an Investigation Pursuant to Article 15) (International Criminal Court, Office of the Prosecutor, Case No ICC-02/17-7-RED, 20 November 2017)   94

Situation in the Libyan Arab Jamahiriya (Warrant of Arrest for Abdullah Al Senussi) (International Criminal Court, Pre-Trial Chamber I, Case No ICC-01/11, 27 June 2011)   25, 136

Situation in the Libyan Arab Jamahiriya (Warrant of Arrest for Muammar Gaddafi) (International Criminal Court, Pre-Trial Chamber I, Case No ICC-01/11, 27 June 2011)   25, 83, 136

Situation in the Libyan Arab Jamahiriya (Warrant of Arrest for Saif Al-Islam Gaddafi) (International Criminal Court, Pre-Trial Chamber I, Case No ICC-01/11, 27 June 2011)   25, 136

Situation in the Republic of Burundi (Public Redacted Version of 'Decision Pursuant to Article 15 of the Rome Statute on the Authorization of an Investigation into the Situation in the Republic of Burundi') (International Criminal Court, Pre-Trial Chamber III, Case No ICC-01/17-X, 9 November 2017)   55

Situation in the Republic of Côte d'Ivoire (Decision Pursuant to Article 15 of the Rome Statute on the Authorisation of an Investigation into the Situation in the Republic of

Côte d'Ivoire) (International Criminal Court, Pre-Trial Chamber III, Case No ICC-02/11, 3 October 2011)   82
Situation in the Republic of Côte d'Ivoire (Warrant of Arrest for Laurent Koudou Gbagbo) (International Criminal Court, Pre-Trial Chamber III, Case No ICC-02/11, 23 November 2011)   83

International Military Tribunals

International Military Tribunal (Nuremberg), Judgment and Sentences, reproduced in 'Judicial Decisions' (1947) 41 *American Journal of International Law* 172   45–46, 178–179, 184
Röling, BVA and CF Rüter (eds), *The Tokyo Judgment: The International Military Tribunal for the Far East (IMTFE) 29 April 1946–2 November 1948* (APA – University Press, 1977)   178–179

Special Court for Sierra Leone

Prosecutor v Fofana (Decision on Preliminary Motion on Lack of Jurisdiction Materiae: Illegal Delegation of Powers by the United Nations) Special Court for Sierra Leone, Appeals Chamber, Case No SCSL-2004–14-AR72(E), 25 May 2004)   148
Prosecutor v Gbao (Decision on the Preliminary Motion on the Invalidity of the Agreement Between the United Nations and the Government of Sierra Leone on the Establishment of the Special Court) (Special Court for Sierra Leone, Appeals Chamber, Case No SCSL-2004–15-AR72(E), 25 May 2004)   48, 188
Prosecutor v Kallon and Kamara (Decision on Challenge to Jurisdiction: Lomé Accord Amnesty) (Special Court for Sierra Leone, Appeals Chamber, Case No SCSL-2004–15-AR72(E), 13 March 2004)   188
Prosecutor v Norman (Decision on Preliminary Motion Based on Lack of Jurisdiction (Child Recruitment)) (Special Court for Sierra Leone, Appeals Chamber, Case No SCSL 2004–14-AR72(E), 31 May 2004)   176
Prosecutor v Taylor (Decision on Immunity from Jurisdiction) (Special Court for Sierra Leone, Appeals Chamber, Case No SCSL-2003–01-I, 31 May 2004)   85

Special Tribunal for Lebanon

Prosecutor v Ayyash (Decision on the Defence Appeals Against the Trial Chamber's 'Decision on the Defence Challenges to the Jurisdiction and Legality of the Tribunal') (Special Tribunal for Lebanon, Appeals Chamber, Case No STL-11–01/PT/AC/AR90.1, 24 October 2012)   148

TABLE OF CASES xxi

European Court of Justice

van Gend & Loos v Nederlandse Administratie der Belastingen (C-26/62) [1963] ECR 1   52

Domestic Courts

Australia
Moti v The Queen (2011) 245 CLR 456   92
Giles v Tumminello [1963] SASR 96   66

Belgium
Prosecutor v Vincent Ntezimana, Alphonse Higaniro, Consolata Mukangango, and Julienne Mukabutera, [Brussels, Unreported] Cour d'Assises de l'Arrondissement Administratif Bruxelles, 8 June 2001   177

Israel
Attorney-General of the Government of Israel v Adolf Eichmann (1962) 36 ILR 5   66, 92, 164–165, 171, 185

Netherlands
Knezević, [Dutch Supreme Court] *Nederlandse Jurisprudentie* (1998) No 463, 11 November 1997   177

Switzerland
Grabež, [Swiss Military Tribunal] *Tribunal Militaire de Division I*, 18 April 1997   177

Ukraine
Opinion of the Constitutional Court on the Conformity of the Rome Statute with the Constitution of Ukraine, Case N 1–35/2001, 11 July 2001, summarised in ICRC, 'Issues Raised with Regard to the Rome Statute of the International Criminal Court by National Constitutional Courts, Supreme Courts and Councils of State' (January, 2003) icrc.org/eng/assets/files/other/issues_raised_with_regard_to_the_icc_statute.pdf   74

United Kingdom
Al Megrahi v Her Majesty's Advocate (Scotland) [1999] HCJT 1475   166
Naim Molvan, Owner of Motor Vessel 'Asya' v A-G (Palestine) [1948] AC 351   66
R v Bow Street Stipendiary Magistrate; Ex parte Pinochet Ugarte [1998] All ER 897   78
R v Bow Street Stipendiary Magistrate; Ex parte Pinochet Ugarte [No 2] [1999] 1 All ER 577   78, 180
R v Bow Street Stipendiary Magistrate; Ex parte Pinochet Ugarte [No 3] [2000] I AC 147   78

R v Jones [2006] UKHL 16   179–180

United States

US v Ali 718 F 3d 929 (DC Cir, 2013)   43–44
US v Newball 524 F Supp 715 (EDNY 1981)   66
US v Rezaq 134 F 3d 1121 (DC Cir, 1998)   43
US v Shi 525 F 3d 709 (9th Cir, 2008)   43
US v Yousef 327 F 2d 56 (2nd Cir, 2003)   43
US v Yunis 924 F 2d 1086 (DC Cir, 1991)   43

TABLE OF TREATIES AND SELECTED OTHER INSTRUMENTS

International Agreements

Agreement between the Government of the Transitional Islamic State of Afghanistan and the Government of the United States of America regarding the surrender of persons to the International Criminal Court (20 September 2002) law.georgetown.edu/library/research/guides/upload/Afghanistan03-119.pdf   96

Agreement between Liberia and the United Nations Concerning the Status of the United Nations Mission in Liberia (6 November 2003) unmil.unmissions.org/sites/default/files/unmil_status_of_forces_agreement_6_november_2003.pdf   129

Agreement between the North Atlantic Treaty Organization and the Islamic Republic of Afghanistan on the Status of NATO Forces and NATO Personnel Conducting Mutually Agreed NATO-Led Activities in Afghanistan (30 September 2014) mfa.gov.af/Content/files/SOFA%20ENGLISH.pdf   96

Agreement between the Parties to the North Atlantic Treaty Regarding the Status of Their Forces (19 June 1951) 199 UNTS 67   103

Agreement between the United Nations and the Government of Sierra Leone on the establishment of a Special Court for Sierra Leone, signed 16 January 2002, 2178 UNTS 137 (entered into force 12 April 2002)   48

Agreement between the United States of America and Romania Regarding the Status of United States Forces in Romania (signed 20 October 2001, entered into force 10 June 2002) TIAS 13170   103

Agreement for the Prosecution and Punishment of the Major War Criminals of the European Axis and Charter of the International Military Tribunal, 82 UNTS 279 (entered into force 8 August 1945)   45, 172, 178

Amendments on the crime of aggression to the Rome Statute of the International Criminal Court, Resolution RC/Res.6, adopted at the 13th plenary mtg (11 June 2010)   116, 152–158, 178, 193

Charter of the United Nations, opened for signature 26 June 1945, 1 UNTS XVI (entered into force 24 October 1945)

Coalition Provisional Authority Order No 17, Status of the Coalition, Foreign Liaison Missions, their Personnel and Contractors CPA/ORD/27 June 2004/17 (27 June 2004)   101

xxiv TABLE OF TREATIES AND SELECTED OTHER INSTRUMENTS

Convention against the Taking of Hostages, opened for signature 17 December 1979, 1316 UNTS 205 (entered into force 3 June 1983)   42–43, 66, 163

Convention against Torture and Other Cruel, Inhuman or Degrading Treatment or Punishment, opened for signature 10 December 1984, 1465 UNTS 85 (entered into force 26 June 1987)   42, 163

Convention for the Amelioration of the Condition of the Wounded and Sick in Armed Forces in the Field, opened for signature 12 August 1949, 75 UNTS 31 (entered into force 21 October 1950) ('Geneva Convention I')   175

Convention for the Amelioration of the Condition of the Wounded, Sick and Shipwrecked Members of Armed Forces at Sea, opened for signature 12 August 1949, 75 UNTS 85 (entered into force 21 October 1950) ('Geneva Convention II')   175

Convention for the Suppression of Unlawful Acts against the Safety of Maritime Navigation, opened for signature 10 March 1988, 1678 UNTS 221 (entered into force 26 June 1992)   42, 65

Convention for Suppression of Unlawful Seizure of Aircraft, opened for signature 16 December 1970, 860 UNTS 105 (entered into force 14 October 1971)   42, 163

Convention on the Prevention and Punishment of the Crime of Genocide, opened for signature 9 December 1948, 78 UNTS 277 (entered into force 12 January 1951)   170–171

Convention on Offences and Certain Other Acts Committed on Board Aircraft, opened for signature 14 September 1963, 704 UNTS 219 (entered into force 4 December 1969)   42, 65, 163

Convention on the Suppression and Punishment of the Crime of Apartheid, opened for signature 30 November 1973, 1015 UNTS 243 (entered into force 18 July 1976)   173

Convention Relative to Protection of Civilian Persons in Time of War, opened for signature 12 August 1949, 75 UNTS 287 (entered into force 21 October 1950) ('Geneva Convention IV')   175–176

Convention Relative to the Treatment of Prisoners of War, opened for signature 12 August 1949, 75 UNTS 135 (entered into force 21 October 1950) ('Geneva Convention III')   175

Convention respecting the Laws and Customs of War on Land, opened for signature 18 October 1907 (1908) 2 *American Journal of International Law Supplement* 90 (entered into force 26 January 1910) ('1907 Hague Convention IV')   174

Convention with respect to the Laws and Customs of War on Land, opened for signature 29 July 1899, (1907) 1 *American Journal of International Law Supplement* 129 (entered into force 4 September 1900) ('1899 Hague Convention II')   174

Declaration of Principles on Interim Self-Government Arrangements, Palestine Liberation Organisation – Israel (13 September 1993) ('Oslo I') unsco.org /Documents/Key/Declaration%20of%20Principles%20on%20Interim%20Self-Government%20Arrangements.pdf   110–111

Declaration regarding the defeat of Germany and the assumption of supreme authority with respect to Germany by the Governments of the United States of America, the Union of Soviet Socialist Republics, the United Kingdom and the Provisional

TABLE OF TREATIES AND SELECTED OTHER INSTRUMENTS xxv

Government of the French Republic ('Berlin Declaration'), signed 5 June 1945 avalon
.law.yale.edu/wwii/ger01.asp   46
European Convention on the Transfer of Proceedings in Criminal Matters, opened for
signature 15 May 1972, 865 UNTS 99 (entered into force 30 March 1978)   41–42
Instrument of Surrender, Germany, signed 4 May 1945 avalon.law.yale.edu/wwii/gs10
.asp   46
Instrument of Surrender, Japan, signed 2 September 1945 archives.gov/exhibits/fea
tured_documents/japanese_surrender_document   47
International Convention for the Suppression of the Financing of Terrorism, opened for
signature 9 December 1999, 2178 UNTS 197 (entered into force 10 April 2002)   42
Israeli–Palestinian Interim Agreement on the West Bank and the Gaza Strip, Palestinian
Liberation Organisation – Israel (28 September 1995) ('Oslo II')   8, 110–112
*Negotiated Relationship Agreement between the International Criminal Court and the
United Nations,* UN Doc A/58/874, Annex, 20 August 2004 (entered into force
4 October 2004)   114, 125, 148
Proclamation Defining the Terms for the Japanese Surrender, US-China-UK, signed
July 1945, 3 *Treaties and Other International Agreements of the United States of
America 1776–1949* 1204 ('Potsdam Proclamation')   47
*Protocol additional to the Geneva Conventions of 12 August 1949 and relating to the
Protection of Victims of International Armed Conflicts,* opened for signature
8 June 1977, 1125 UNTS 3 (entered into force 7 December 1978) ('Additional
Protocol I')   175–176
*Protocol additional to the Geneva Conventions of 12 August 1949 and relating to the
Protection of Victims of Non-International Armed Conflicts,* opened for signature
8 June 1977, 1125 UNTS 609 (entered into force 7 December 1978) ('Additional
Protocol II')   175, 177
Rome Statute of the International Criminal Court, opened for signature 17 July 1998,
2187 UNTS 90 (entered into force 1 July 2002)
*Security and Defense Cooperation Agreement between the Islamic Republic of
Afghanistan and the United States of America* (30 September 2014) justsecurity.org
/wp-content/uploads/2014/10/BSA-ENGLISH-AFG.pdf   96
United Nations Convention on the Law of the Sea 1982, opened for signature
10 December 1982, 1833 UNTS 3 (entered into force 16 November 1994)   62
Vienna Convention on Consular Relations 1963, opened for signature 24 April 1963, 596
UNTS 261 (entered into force 19 March 1967)   21
Vienna Convention on Diplomatic Relations, opened for signature 18 April 1961, 500
UNTS 95 (entered into force 24 April 1964)   78, 80, 96
Vienna Convention on the Law of Treaties, opened for signature 23 May 1969, 1155
UNTS 331 (entered into force 27 January 1980)   14–15, 52, 75, 111

United Nations Security Council Resolutions

SC Res 2479, UN SCOR, 8566th mtg, UN Doc S/RES/2479 (27 June 2019)   133

SC Res 1970, UN SCOR, 6491st mtg, UN Doc SC/RES/1970 (26 February 2011)   26, 83, 135–138
SC Res 1593, UN SCOR, 5158th mtg, UN Doc SC/Res/1593 (31 March 2005)   82, 132–140, 144
SC Res 1509, UN SCOR, 4830th mtg, UN Doc S/RES/1509 (19 September 2003)   128
SC Res 1497, UN SCOR, 4803rd mtg, UN Doc S/RES/1497 (1 August 2003)   125–130
SC Res 1487, UN SCOR, 4772nd mtg, UN Doc S/RES/1487 (12 June 2003)   120–121
SC Res 1422, UN SCOR, 4572nd mtg, UN Doc S/RES/1422 (12 July 2002)   120–126, 130
SC Res 955, UN SCOR, 3453rd mtg, UN Doc S/RES/955 (8 November 1994)   48, 143
SC Res 827, UN SCOR, 3217th mtg, UN Doc S/RES/827 (25 May 1993)   48, 143
SC Res 777, UN SCOR, 3116th mtg, UN Doc S/RES/777 (19 September 1992)   150
SC Res 713, UN SCOR, 3009th mtg, UN Doc SC/Res/713 (25 September 1991)   146
SC Res 409, UN SCOR, 2011th mtg, UN Doc SC/Res/409 (27 May 1977)   146

ABBREVIATIONS

DRC	Democratic Republic of the Congo
FRY	Federal Republic of Yugoslavia
ICC	International Criminal Court
ICJ	International Court of Justice
ICTR	International Criminal Tribunal for Rwanda
ICTY	International Criminal Tribunal for Yugoslavia
ILC	International Law Commission
ISAF	International Security Assistance Force
NATO	North Atlantic Treaty Organization
NGO	non-governmental organisation
PCIJ	Permanent Court of International Justice
PLO	Palestinian Liberation Organization
SCSL	Special Court for Sierra Leone
SFRY	Socialist Federal Republic of Yugoslavia
SOFA	Status of Forces Agreement
SOMA	Status of Mission Agreement
UK	United Kingdom
UN	United Nations
UNMIL	United Nations Mission in Liberia
US	United States
VCLT	Vienna Convention on the Law of Treaties

1

Introduction

In March 2005, the Acting United States (US) Representative to the United Nations (UN) issued a statement on the historic vote by the UN Security Council to refer the humanitarian situation in Darfur, Sudan, to the International Criminal Court (ICC). Ambassador Anne W Patterson explained that the US abstained from the vote because:

> [t]he United States continues to fundamentally object to the view that the ICC should be able to exercise jurisdiction over the nationals, including government officials, of states not party to the Rome Statute. This strikes at the essence of the nature of sovereignty.[1]

This statement effectively encapsulates the relationship between the ICC and certain States that are not party to its constitutive treaty, the Rome Statute.[2] There are particular circumstances in which the ICC can prosecute nationals of States that have not consented to the Court's jurisdiction, and as Ambassador Patterson acknowledged, this jurisdiction extends to senior State officials who would otherwise enjoy immunity from prosecution by foreign courts. An enduring belief exists among some States that there is no basis in international law for the ICC's jurisdiction where the State of nationality does not directly consent. While the US is perhaps the most high-profile non-State Party to object to the jurisdiction of the ICC over nationals of non-States Parties, it is by no means the only State to take this position. Since the adoption of the Rome Statute in 1998, the US has been joined in its objection to the jurisdiction of the ICC by a small but vocal chorus of non-States Parties some of which are, or have been, the focus of an ICC preliminary

---

[1] Ambassador Anne W Patterson, Acting US Representative to the United Nations, *Explanation of Vote on the Sudan Accountability Resolution*, in the Security Council, 31 March 2005.
[2] *Rome Statute of the International Criminal Court*, opened for signature 17 July 1998, 2187 UNTS 90 (entered into force 1 July 2002) (Rome Statute).

examination or investigation.[3] A number of States – parties and non-parties – have also been unhappy with the fact that the ICC does not recognise immunity for sitting Heads of State, arguing that the Statute conflicts with customary obligations on States to respect the immunity of foreign leaders.[4] It has been over twenty years since the Rome Statute was adopted, and to say that the Court's jurisdiction over nationals of non-States Parties remains legally and politically contentious might be an understatement.

1.1 The Jurisdiction Provisions

The story of the Rome Conference[5] negotiations over the ICC's jurisdiction provisions has been mythologised in countless retellings by those who were there.[6] The issue of the Court's personal jurisdiction has been

---

[3] Under Article 15 of the Rome Statute, the ICC Prosecutor may conduct a preliminary examination to determine whether there is sufficient evidence relating to the admissibility of crimes within the jurisdiction of the Court. If the conclusion is reached that there is a reasonable basis to open an investigation, the Prosecutor must then seek approval from the Pre-Trial Chamber to go ahead with the investigation.

Non-States Parties that have expressed opposition to the jurisdiction of the ICC over nationals of non-States Parties include China, India, Cuba, Pakistan, Iran, Russia, Myanmar, Israel, Sudan and Libya. The Court has examined or investigated situations in which nationals of the latter five States are accused of committing crimes. See Chapter 2 for an exploration of why these and other non-States Parties object to the jurisdiction of the ICC.

[4] See, eg, *Reports of the Secretary-General on the Sudan and South Sudan*, UN SCOR, 73rd sess, 8425th mtg, UN Doc S/PV.8425 (14 December 2018) statement of China p. 9, statement of Russian Federation p. 11, statement of Equatorial Guinea p. 12, statement of Kuwait p. 13; *Reports of the Secretary-General on the Sudan and South Sudan*, UN SCOR, 70th sess, 7478th mtg, UN Doc S/PV.7478 (15 June 2015) statement of Russian Federation p. 11, statement of Venezuela p. 14; *Reports of the Secretary-General on the Sudan and South Sudan*, UN SCOR, 72nd sess, 7963rd mtg, UN Doc S/PV.7963 (8 June 2017) statement of Egypt p. 7; *Report of the International Criminal Court*, UN GAOR, 65th sess, 41st mtg, Agenda Item 73, UN Doc A/65/PV.41 (29 October 2010) statement of Iran p. 24; *Report of the International Criminal Court*, UN GAOR, 68th sess, 42nd mtg, Agenda Item 75, UN Doc A/68/PV.42 (31 October 2013) statement of Rwanda p. 17.

[5] United Nations Diplomatic Conference of Plenipotentiaries on the Establishment of an International Criminal Court (Rome, 15 June–17 July 1998).

[6] See, eg, LN Sadat and SR Carden, 'The New International Criminal Court: An Uneasy Revolution' (1999) 88 *Georgetown Law Journal* 381 at 383–8; P Kirsch and D Robinson, 'Reaching Agreement at the Rome Conference' in A Cassese, P Gaeta, JRWD Jones (eds), *The Rome Statute of the International Criminal Court: A Commentary* (Oxford University Press, 2002) pp. 67–8; P Kirsch and JT Holmes, 'The Rome Conference on an International Court: The Negotiating Process' (1999) 93 *American Journal of International Law* 2.

described as 'the most important, politically the most difficult and therefore the most controversial question of the negotiations as a whole, in short: "the question of questions" of the entire project'.[7] The compromise on jurisdiction that was reached in the 'proverbial eleventh hour'[8] of the Conference enables the Court to prosecute individuals who are accused of committing Statute crimes[9] in situations where either the territorial State or the State of nationality have consented to the jurisdiction of the Court.[10] These 'preconditions to the exercise of jurisdiction' – codified in Article 12 of the Rome Statute – represented a deal breaker for States such as the US, which had lobbied for cumulative consent of both the territorial state *and* the state of nationality before the ICC could exercise jurisdiction.[11]

The Article 12 preconditions mean that the ICC can potentially exercise jurisdiction over nationals of non-States Parties who are accused of committing a Statute crime on the territory of a State Party[12] or on the territory of a State that has otherwise accepted the jurisdiction of the

---

[7] HP Kaul, 'Preconditions to the Exercise of Jurisdiction' in A Cassese, P Gaeta, JRWD Jones (eds), *The Rome Statute of the International Criminal Court: A Commentary* (Oxford University Press, 2002) p. 584.

[8] SA Williams, 'The Rome Statute on the International Criminal Court – Universal Jurisdiction or State Consent – To Make or Break the Package Deal' (2000) 75 *International Law Studies* 539 at 540. The Statute was adopted with 120 states voting in favour, seven voting against and twenty-one abstentions.

[9] 'Statute crimes' refer to those crimes within the jurisdiction of ICC: the crime of genocide; crimes against humanity; war crimes and the crime of aggression. Rome Statute, Article 5.

[10] For information and commentary on the negotiations of the jurisdiction provisions at the Rome Conference and on the historical negotiations prior to Rome, see generally MC Bassiouni, *The Legislative History of the International Criminal Court* (Transnational Publishers, 2005); C Tofan and R van der Wolf (eds), *The Long and Winding Road to ... Rome: A Brief History of the ICC* (International Courts Association by Wolf Legal Publishers, 2011); TLH McCormack and S Robertson, 'Jurisdictional Aspects of the Rome Statute for the New International Criminal Court' (1999) 23 *Melbourne University Law Review* 635; A Cassese, P Gaeta and JRWD Jones (eds), *The Rome Statute of the International Criminal Court: A Commentary* (Oxford University Press, 2002) pp. 3–91; W Schabas, *The International Criminal Court: A Commentary on the Rome Statute*, 2nd ed (Oxford University Press, 2016) pp. 345–50; W Schabas and G Pecorella, 'Article 12 Preconditions to the Exercise of Jurisdiction' in O Triffterer, K Ambos (eds), *Rome Statute of the International Criminal Court – A Commentary* (CH Beck Hart Nomos, 2016), p. 672; W Schabas and G Pecorella, 'Article 13 Exercise of Jurisdiction' in O Triffterer, K Ambos (eds), *Rome Statute of the International Criminal Court – A Commentary* (CH Beck Hart Nomos, 2016), p. 690.

[11] D Scheffer, Ambassador-At-Large for War Crimes Issues, *Remarks before the 6th Committee of the 53rd General Assembly* (21 October 1998).

[12] Rome Statute, Article 12(2).

4   INTRODUCTION

Court on an ad hoc basis.[13] Upon satisfaction of one of the preconditions, Articles 13(a) and (c) of the Rome Statute then activate the Court's jurisdiction when a situation is referred to the Court by a State Party,[14] or when the ICC Prosecutor has initiated an investigation *proprio motu*.[15] Article 13(b) provides that the ICC may also exercise its jurisdiction when a situation is referred to the Court by the UN Security Council acting under Chapter VII of the UN Charter.[16] The Article 12 preconditions do not apply to a Security Council referral, which means that the ICC can potentially exercise jurisdiction over crimes committed on the territory of any State, irrespective of the nationality of the accused.

Furthermore, the Rome Statute prevents accused individuals from relying on any immunities or amnesties.[17] This blanket ban on individual exemptions to the ICC's personal jurisdiction was not contentious at the Rome Conference but has proven to be divisive in the years since the Court began operations.

1.2 Context and Aims

Since the ICC's establishment in 2003, there have been quite a few situations subject to either a preliminary examination or an investigation that involve nationals of non-States Parties,[18] and in this book I use select

---

[13] Rome Statute, Article 12(3).
[14] Rome Statute, Article 13(a).
[15] Rome Statute, Article 13(c).
[16] *Charter of the United Nations*, opened for signature 26 June 1945, 1 UNTS XVI (entered into force 24 October 1945) (UN Charter).
[17] Rome Statute, Article 27.
[18] Crimes committed by the following non-State Party nationals have been considered by the ICC: US nationals (in the Afghanistan situation), Myanmarese nationals (in the Bangladesh/Myanmar situation), Sudanese nationals (in the Darfur situation), Russian nationals (in the Georgia and Ukraine situations), Libyan nationals (in the Libya situation) North Korean nationals (in the Republic of Korea situation) and Israeli nationals (in the Palestine situation and the situation concerning the registered vessels of Comoros, Greece and Cambodia).

In 2014 the ICC Prosecutor closed the preliminary examination into the situation in the Republic of Korea given insufficient grounds on which to seek an investigation: Office of the Prosecutor, 'Statement of the Prosecutor of the International Criminal Court, Fatou Bensouda, on the conclusion of the preliminary examination of the situation in the Republic of Korea' (Press Release, 23 June 2014). The Prosecutor also declined to open an investigation into the situation concerning the registered vessels of Comoros, Greece and Cambodia on the grounds that any case arising would not meet the gravity threshold for admission: *Situation on the Registered Vessels of the Union of the Comoros, the Hellenic Republic and the Kingdom of Cambodia (Final decision of the Prosecutor concerning the*

examples to illustrate particular legal issues or to inform hypothetical scenarios.[19] The fact that there are situations under either preliminary examination or investigation that involve nationals of non-States Parties – including from several powerful States – reflects the ongoing significance of the issue of the ICC's jurisdiction over such individuals. These situations have given rise to numerous questions about State sovereignty and consent, delegation of powers, State Party obligations, customary immunities, treaty conflicts, Security Council powers and the nature of international criminal jurisdiction. It is not surprising then that the jurisdiction provisions of the Rome Statute have attracted a considerable amount of scholarly attention. This book is an attempt to bring some coherence to the growing body of scholarship and emerging ICC jurisprudence on this topic.

Throughout the book I argue that the ICC itself needs to identify and explain the assumptions that underpin its reasoning in cases involving nationals of non-States Parties in more detail than it has to date. The ICC has not been especially comprehensive or consistent in its jurisprudence relating to jurisdiction over such nationals, and its expanding catalogue of examinations and investigations mean that this issue will not be disappearing any time soon. In particular, it will be imperative for the Court to articulate the legal basis for its jurisdiction and, I argue, ensure that this basis is grounded in State consent.

In reflecting on the literature, State practice and ICC jurisprudence since the Court's establishment, this book explores whether and how the ICC can lawfully exercise its jurisdiction over nationals of non-States Parties in the circumstances provided for by the Rome Statute. Non-States Parties, by their very definition, have not agreed to the Rome Statute and are not bound by its provisions. To simply assert that the ICC can exercise jurisdiction over nationals of non-States Parties because

---

'Article 53(1) Report' (ICC-01/13-6-AnxA), dated 6 November 2014) (International Criminal Court, Office of the Prosecutor, Case No ICC-01/13, 2 December 2019).

The situation in the Democratic Republic of the Congo (DRC) also involves nationals of non-States Parties; several Rwandan nationals have been charged with crimes committed on the territory of the DRC. The DRC is a State Party to the Rome Statute, and Rwanda is not. While Rwanda has been highly critical of the ICC's jurisdiction more generally, it has not objected to the Court's exercise of jurisdiction over these particular nationals in this situation. This is likely because the charged individuals (Sylvestra Mudacumura and Bosco Ntaganda [a dual citizen]) are members of rebel groups. See, Stephen Lamony, 'Rwanda and the ICC: Playing Politics with Justice', *African Arguments* (21 October 2013).

[19] The information in this book is current as at March 2020.

the Rome Statute provides for such, is therefore an unsatisfactory explanation for states that have not consented to the Statute's terms. There must instead be an underlying basis for the ICC's jurisdiction that complies with the broader principles of international law. Without a legal basis to underpin the Statute, the Court runs the risk of exceeding its competence. Without a legal basis that gives due regard to the principle of State consent, the Court risks further damage to an already fragile reputation.[20]

A general consensus has emerged among international criminal law scholars (with a few notable exceptions) that in situations referred by States Parties or investigations initiated by the Prosecutor, the legal basis for the ICC's jurisdiction over nationals of non-States Parties is framed as 'delegation of jurisdiction'.[21] Prima facie, delegation of jurisdiction is a straightforward concept whereby a State with the right to prosecute foreign nationals for crimes committed on its territory, delegates this right to the ICC by ratifying the Rome Statute. The theory that the ICC's authority over nationals of non-States Parties is predicated on delegation of jurisdiction from States Parties has prevailed in the literature, and I take it as the starting point for my inquiry. I conduct a systematic conceptual analysis of what it means to say that States Parties are delegating jurisdiction to the ICC, before considering how this legal basis would work in practice. In particular, I focus on questions that arise in situations complicated by customary or treaty-based immunities. For example, how can the Rome Statute's rejection of immunities be reconciled with the absolute personal immunity enjoyed by incumbent Heads of State under customary international law? Can a State Party delegate jurisdiction to the ICC where the State's own jurisdiction is limited by a bilateral agreement? Ultimately I argue that in situations referred to the Court by States Parties or investigations initiated by the Prosecutor, the delegation theory provides a relatively comprehensive legal basis for the ICC's jurisdiction.

With respect to situations referred to the ICC by the UN Security Council, there does not seem to be as much concern among either scholars or States about the legal basis for the Court's jurisdiction over nationals of non-States Parties. Often the Article 13(b) referral mechanism is glossed over in discussions about the Court's jurisdiction, with

---

[20] For a snapshot of some of the criticisms directed at the Court, see UK Statement by Andrew Murdoch, Legal Director to the International Criminal Court Assembly of States Parties, *Seventeenth Session of the Assembly of States Parties to the Rome Statute of the International Criminal Court* (5 December 2018).
[21] See 3.2 for a review of the relevant scholarship.

only a brief reference to the Security Council's powers under Chapter VII of the UN Charter as an explanation for the Council's role in the Statute. But the fact that the Council has a mandate to maintain international peace and security under the Charter does not, on its own, explain why the ICC – an independent international court established by treaty – can exercise criminal jurisdiction over nationals of States that have not consented to the terms of the Rome Statute.

I undertake a holistic examination of the Security Council's relationship with the ICC to detangle the complex web of State obligations that are created when the two institutions interact. For instance, does a non-State Party referred to the ICC become a de facto State Party to the Rome Statute as a consequence of the UN Security Council resolution? Is the ICC itself legally bound by Security Council resolutions? I argue that in any referral to the ICC, the Security Council resolution must be *intra vires* the Charter and consistent with the Rome Statute before there is a legal basis for the ICC's jurisdiction. Where referrals meet these conditions, the ICC's jurisdiction over nationals of non-States Parties is indirectly grounded in State consent by virtue of the referred State's membership of the UN.

1.3 Structure

The book is divided into five substantive chapters, and I begin in Chapter 2 by providing a contextual discussion of why certain non-States Parties object to the jurisdiction of the ICC. In this chapter I engage with the allegation that the Rome Statute infringes on the sovereignty of non-States Parties by allowing the ICC to prosecute their nationals in certain circumstances. This involves an analysis of how the Statute affects non-States Parties and an evaluation of whether such effects amount to an infringement of State sovereignty. How sovereignty interacts with international law is largely a matter of perspective, and how States perceive sovereignty shapes their views of whether there is a legal basis for the Rome Statute's jurisdiction provisions. I argue that the ICC will need to recognise such concerns and formulate the legal basis for its jurisdiction in a way that maximises the role of State consent.

Chapter 3 then turns to analyse the prevailing theory that the ICC's jurisdiction is based on delegation from States Parties. I undertake a review of scholarship published in the years following the adoption of the Rome Statute and adopt one of the principal conclusions from this early debate: that States may lawfully delegate jurisdiction to an international court. This chapter then proceeds to undertake a conceptual analysis of what delegation of jurisdiction actually entails in the context of the ICC. I explore how the concept of delegation is understood in international institutional law, which provides a framework for understanding how international institutions receive and exercise their powers. This is directly relevant for the ICC as an international organisation. The second part of this chapter demonstrates the utility of describing jurisdiction as 'the legal right to exercise powers'. No study on jurisdiction would be complete without an overview of the principles of international law under which a State may exercise jurisdiction extraterritorially, and I explain how these apply to the Rome Statute jurisdiction regime. I argue that delegation of jurisdiction is, in theory, a sound legal basis for the ICC's jurisdiction when either the territorial State or the State of nationality has consented to the Statute.

In Chapter 4, I test this theory by applying it to a number of hypothetical case studies based on past and present situations before the ICC. Specifically, I use scenarios that potentially involve legal immunities to explore whether delegation of jurisdiction provides a legal basis for the ICC's jurisdiction in such situations that come before the Court via a State referral or Prosecutor-initiated investigation. The first case study is a hypothetical scenario in which a sitting Head of State from a non-State Party is wanted by the ICC for the commission of crimes on the territory of a State Party. Certain incumbent senior officials are immune from prosecution in foreign domestic courts, which raises the question of how States Parties can be said to delegate jurisdiction to the ICC, when such jurisdiction has been curtailed domestically. The second and third case studies use the examples of Palestine and Afghanistan. Each of these situations raises particular legal obstacles relating to domestic jurisdiction that could affect whether the ICC is able to lawfully prosecute nationals of non-States Parties. For example, in the Afghanistan situation, I examine whether Status of Forces Agreements and bilateral non-surrender agreements would affect the ICC's jurisdiction over US nationals for crimes committed on the territory of Afghanistan. In the situation in Palestine I explore how the Oslo Accords[22] and questions of statehood might affect the ICC's potential jurisdiction over Israeli nationals. I conclude that delegation of

---

[22] *Declaration of Principles on Interim Self-Government Arrangements*, Palestine Liberation Organisation – Israel (13 September 1993) (Oslo I); *Israeli–Palestinian Interim Agreement on the West Bank and the Gaza Strip*, Palestinian Liberation Organisation – Israel (28 September 1995) (Oslo II).

jurisdiction provides a legal basis for the ICC's jurisdiction over nationals of non-States Parties in most situations. Uncertainty remains, however, as to whether there would be a legal basis for ICC jurisdiction over a sitting Head of a non-State Party accused of committing crimes on the territory of a State Party without a Security Council referral.

Chapter 5 then focuses on the ICC's relationship with the UN Security Council. Under the Rome Statute, the Council has two important roles: Article 13(b) provides that the Security Council may trigger the jurisdiction of the Court (the 'referral power'), and under Article 16 the Council may halt any ICC investigation for twelve months at a time (the 'deferral power'). In the 2010 Kampala Amendments, the Security Council was also given a third role to play with respect to the Court's jurisdiction over the crime of aggression.[23] In the first part of Chapter 5 I critically examine the ways in which the Council has used Article 16 in an attempt to limit the jurisdiction of the Court. In particular, I analyse Resolutions 1422 and 1487 in which the Security Council purported to exempt certain non-party nationals from the jurisdiction of the ICC,[24] before concluding that it is unlikely that Resolution 1422 is consistent with the Rome Statute. I then discuss the Article 13(b) referral power by using the Darfur and Libya situations as case studies for my analysis. I argue that the legal basis for the ICC's authority in those situations is grounded in the implied consent of Sudan and Libya to the jurisdiction of the Court by virtue of their membership of the UN. The final part of Chapter 5 considers the role of the Security Council with respect to the crime of aggression and the consequences of this for States not party to the Rome Statute.

Chapter 6 addresses an alternative theory to delegation of territorial jurisdiction and implied consent. I explore whether the concept of universal jurisdiction can provide a coherent legal basis for the ICC's jurisdiction in the various situations allowed by the Rome Statute. I take two different approaches to the possibility that universal jurisdiction provides a foundation for the ICC's authority over nationals of non-States Parties. First is the idea that States are delegating universal jurisdiction to the ICC, along with jurisdiction based on territoriality and nationality. I also discuss a second approach to universality as a legal

---

[23] *Amendments on the crime of aggression to the Rome Statute of the International Criminal Court,* Resolution RC/Res.6, adopted at the 13th plenary mtg (11 June 2010); International Criminal Court, *Activation of the jurisdiction of the Court over the crime of aggression,* Resolution ICC-ASP/16/Res.5 (adopted 14 December 2017).

[24] SC Res 1422, UN SCOR, 4572nd mtg, UN Doc S/RES/1422 (12 July 2002); SC Res 1487, UN SCOR, 4772nd mtg, UN Doc S/RES/1487 (12 June 2003).

basis for ICC jurisdiction; one that envisages universal jurisdiction as inherent to the international community and exercisable by the ICC as an agent of this community. Ultimately I argue that the limitations in both the delegated and inherent universal jurisdiction approaches mean that there is no advantage to conceiving of the legal basis for the ICC's jurisdiction as predicated on universal jurisdiction.

In Chapter 7 I draw together the key arguments and analysis raised throughout this book and offer some observations on the importance of articulating a legal basis for the ICC's jurisdiction over nationals of non-States Parties.

While the focus of this book is on particular legal issues relating to the ICC's jurisdiction, it is essential to bear in mind the political context in which such legal questions arise. The ICC was created by States and despite the rhetoric surrounding the prosecutorial and judicial independence of the Court, international criminal justice is an inherently political project.[25] Identifying an appropriate legal basis for the ICC's jurisdiction in contentious political situations is not, in and of itself, going to appease all those who object to the Court's jurisdiction over nationals of non-States Parties. But given that many of the objections to the ICC's jurisdiction over nationals of non-States Parties are framed as issues of legality, addressing these in a comprehensive and consistent manner should nevertheless be a priority for the ICC regardless of whether there are broader political motives behind such claims.

---

[25] See, H Cullen, P Kastner and S Richmond, 'Introduction: The Politics of International Criminal Law' (2018) 18 *International Criminal Law Review* 907.

2

Questions of State Consent and Sovereignty

2.1 Introduction

The classic conception of sovereignty provides that a State has exclusive rights within its territory and remains free from external interference. States that are not party to the Rome Statute claim that the ICC does not sufficiently respect their freedom from external interference. An understanding of why non-States Parties object to the jurisdiction provisions of the Rome Statute is an essential first step in the process of clarifying the legal basis for the Court's jurisdiction over nationals of non-States Parties. By taking the main concerns of non-States Parties into account, the legal basis can be formulated in a way that addresses such concerns and reduces the strength of the arguments against the Court's jurisdiction. This chapter focuses on one of the most common accusations levelled against the Court: in allowing the prosecution of nationals of non-States Parties, the Statute infringes on the sovereignty of the State of nationality. The purpose of this chapter is not to provide a comprehensive account of how the ICC affects sovereignty for non-States Parties, nor is it to remedy the relative under-theorisation of the relationship between sovereignty and international criminal justice.[1] Instead, it provides necessary context and lays some of the conceptual groundwork required for the analysis in later chapters.

The chapter begins in Section 2.2 with a discussion of the major claims that many non-States Parties make in objection to the jurisdiction provisions of the Rome Statute. In particular, I examine attitudes of high-profile non-States Parties such as China, India and the US, as well as the grounds for opposing jurisdiction raised by Sudan and Libya in the wake of the UN Security Council referrals of situations in those non-States Parties.[2]

---

[1] R Cryer, 'International Criminal Law vs State Sovereignty: Another Round?' (2005) 16 *European Journal of International Law* 979 at 980.
[2] SC Res 1593, UN SCOR, 5158th mtg, UN Doc SC/Res/1593 (2005); SC Res 1970, UN SCOR, 6491st mtg, UN Doc SC/RES/1970 (2011).

I outline the three main contentions that have been directed against the ICC's exercise of jurisdiction over non-party nationals. First, that the Rome Statute contravenes Article 34 of the Vienna Convention on the Law of Treaties[3] (VCLT); second, that it ignores the importance of State consent in international law; and third, that the principle of complementarity infringes on sovereignty by allowing the Court to evaluate the competence of a non-State Party's judicial system. In analysing whether there is any merit to these allegations, I focus on whether the Rome Statute does affect non-States Parties in the manner claimed. In particular, this section explores whether a State has the right to object to the prosecution of its nationals abroad, and how the principle of complementarity affects non-States Parties.

Section 2.3 examines to what extent such effects amount to an infringement on the sovereignty of non-States Parties, and whether any such infringement is, nevertheless, justifiable. The strength of the arguments in this part very much depends on the preferred underlying characterisation of sovereignty. For example, is a State's sovereignty absolute in nature and inherent to the existence of the State? Or is it flexible, conditional and subject to international law? There has been a significant shift in the conception of sovereignty since the end of World War II[4] away from the Bodin-inspired absolutist sovereignty of the Westphalian era and towards a definition that allows for the evolution of a 'cosmopolitical social contract'.[5] But even as the latter characterisation has gained in popularity, the former has not entirely disappeared. States and commentators remain free to conceptualise sovereignty in different ways. Such theorisation is relevant for later chapters where I focus on jurisdiction.[6] For the purposes of this chapter I argue that the question of whether non-States Parties are prepared to accept that there is a legal

---

[3] *Vienna Convention on the Law of Treaties*, opened for signature 23 May 1969, 1155 UNTS 331 (entered into force 27 January 1980).

[4] D Grimm, *Sovereignty: The Origin and Future of a Political Concept* (Columbia University Press, 2015) [trans of Souveränität: Herkunft und Zukunft eines Schlüsselbegriffs, first published 2009] p. 82.

[5] F Mégret, 'Epilogue to an Endless Debate: The International Criminal Court's Third Party Jurisdiction and the Looming Revolution of International Law' (2001) 12 *European Journal of International Law* 247 at 266.

[6] Separating the analysis of 'sovereignty' and 'jurisdiction' in different chapters is not intended to imply that the concepts are entirely distinct from one another. Clearly, sovereignty and jurisdiction are inextricably linked. This chapter discusses sovereignty in broad terms, which is reflective of how a number of non-States Parties frame their objections to the Rome Statute. Subsequent chapters delve into a specific aspect of a State's sovereignty: criminal jurisdiction.

basis for the ICC's prosecution of their nationals is influenced by their interpretation of the concept of sovereignty.

Throughout this chapter I use the term 'infringe on' where there is an element of unwanted intrusiveness into a State's sovereign sphere of liberty and the Rome Statute can be said to have an impact on a State's sovereign rights and obligations. Whether the Statute 'affects' or 'has an effect on' sovereignty refers to any consequences for a State's broader legal and political interests.[7] The question of whether such an infringement or effect is 'acceptable' asks whether there is an underlying rationale that makes theoretical sense for such an infringement/effect. It does not mean that the argument or proposition must be accepted by all States or commentators.

2.2 Does the ICC's Jurisdiction Infringe on the Sovereignty of Non-States Parties?

More than twenty years on from the adoption of the Rome Statute, over a third of the world's nations remain non-States Parties. These States have declined to accede to the Statute for a variety of reasons[8] but this

---

[7] I have adopted the language used by the ICJ, which distinguishes between a State's rights and obligations, and its interests. See, eg, *East Timor (Portugal v Australia) (Judgment)* [1995] ICJ Rep 90; *Monetary Gold Removed from Rome in 1943 (Italy v France) (Judgment)* [1954] ICJ Rep 19.

[8] Other common grounds for opposing the Statute include the expansion of the list of acts considered to be crimes against humanity or war crimes (China, Israel), the inclusion of the crime of aggression (China), the exclusion of the use of nuclear weapons as a crime (India, Egypt), the exclusion of the crime of terrorism (India, Cuba), the fact that the Prosecutor has *proprio motu* powers (China, Israel, Pakistan) and the fact that the UN Security Council can trigger the Court's jurisdiction (India, Pakistan; Egypt). See, generally, *Summary Record of the 9th Meeting*, UN GAOR, 6th Comm, 53rd sess, 9th mtg, Agenda Item 153, UN Doc A/C.6/53/SR.9 (4 November 1998); *Summary Record of the 11th Meeting*, UN GAOR, 6th Comm, 53rd sess, 11th mtg, Agenda Item 153, UN Doc A/C.6/53/SR.11 (3 November 1998); *Summary Record of the 12th Meeting*, UN GAOR, 6th Comm, 53rd sess, 12th mtg, Agenda Item 153, UN Doc A/C.6/53/SR.12 (19 December 1998).

For discussion of other reasons why some States have not ratified the Statute, see L Jianping and W Zhixiang, 'China's Attitude towards the ICC' (2005) 3 *Journal of International Criminal Justice* 608; S Huikuri, 'Empty Promises: Indonesia's Non-Ratification of the Rome Statute of the International Criminal Court' (2016) 30 *The Pacific Review* 74; J Thirawat, 'To Join or Not to Join the International Criminal Court: The Thai Dilemma' (2005) 1 *Asia-Pacific Yearbook of International Humanitarian Law* 168; R Banerjee, 'Rome Statute and India: An Analysis of India's Attitude towards the International Criminal Court' (2011) 4 *Journal of East Asia and International Law* 457; H Takemura, 'The Asian Region and the International Criminal Court' in Y Nakanishi (ed), *Contemporary Issues in Human Rights Law – Europe and Asia* (Springer Open, 2018);

section will focus on grounds that relate directly to the jurisdiction of the Court over nationals from non-States Parties. As mentioned in Chapter 1, the question of the Court's jurisdiction was the most contentious aspect of the negotiations and has remained controversial since the adoption of the ICC's jurisdiction regime in Articles 12 and 13 of the Statute. This section will analyse the principal objections raised by non-States Parties that oppose the possibility of ICC jurisdiction over their nationals. For clarity of analysis I am separating the objections into three categories although in reality there is significant overlap among them. All three fall under the umbrella criticism of 'ICC jurisdiction infringes on the sovereignty of non-States Parties'.

2.2.1 The Rome Statute Violates the Pacta Tertiis Principle

One of the earliest objections raised by States unhappy with the final version of the Rome Statute is also one of the easiest to dismiss. In the aftermath of the Statute's adoption, a number of States were quick to claim that the provisions giving the ICC jurisdiction over nationals of non-States Parties were in contravention of the customary *pacta tertiis nec nocent nec prosunt* principle embodied in Article 34 of the VCLT.[9] Article 34 provides that 'a treaty does not create either obligations or rights for a third State without its consent'. In India's explanation of its negative vote on the adoption of the Statute, the Head of the Delegation declared that:

> [The Statute] makes a mockery of the distinction between States Parties and those who choose not to be bound by a treaty. It is truly unfortunate that a Statute drafted for an institution to defend the law should start out straying so sharply from established international law. Before it tries its first criminal, the ICC would have claimed a victim of its own – the Vienna Convention on the Law of Treaties.[10]

The former US Ambassador-at-Large for War Crimes Issues, David Scheffer, summarised his country's objections to the Statute in similar terms:

U Ramanathan, 'India and the ICC' (2005) 3 *Journal of International Criminal Justice* 627; H Abtahi, 'The Islamic Republic of Iran and the ICC' (2005) 3 *Journal of International Criminal Justice* 635.

[9] For a comprehensive overview of the *pacta tertiis* principle, see M Fitzmaurice, 'Third Parties and the Law of Treaties' (2002) 6 *Max Planck Yearbook of United Nations Law* 37; DJ Bederman, 'Third Party Rights and Obligations in Treaties' in DB Hollis (ed), *The Oxford Guide to Treaties* (Oxford University Press, 2012).

[10] Explanation of vote by Mr Dilip Lahiri, Head of Delegation of India, on the adoption of the Statute of the International Criminal Court (17 July 1998).

2.2 INFRINGING ON JURISDICTION OF NON-STATES PARTIES 15

[T]he treaty purports to establish an arrangement whereby US armed forces operating overseas could be conceivably prosecuted by the international court even if the United States has not agreed to be bound by the treaty.... [T]his is contrary to the most fundamental principles of treaty law.[11]

In the decades since the adoption of the Statute, the allegation that the Court's jurisdiction over nationals of non-States Parties violates the *pacta tertiis* principle has endured. It is routinely raised by non-States Parties involved in situations that are under examination or investigation by the ICC Prosecutor. The Sudanese government, for example, has repeatedly asserted that any exercise of the Court's jurisdiction over the situation in Darfur would contravene the VCLT.[12] When the US grew concerned about a possible ICC investigation into its nationals for war crimes committed in Afghanistan, it doubled down on the claim that 'it is a fundamental principle of international law that a treaty is binding only on its parties and that it does not create obligations for non-parties without their consent'.[13] When Myanmar faced the prospect of an ICC investigation into a potential crime against humanity committed against the Rohingya ethnic group, the Myanmarese government issued a public statement asserting that 'the actions of the Prosecutor constitute an attempt to circumvent the spirit of article 34 of the Vienna Convention'.[14]

The overwhelming majority of commentators who write on questions relating to the relationship between the ICC and non-States Parties agree that such claims are without merit.[15] In cases where the ICC has

---

[11] Statement of David Scheffer, *Hearing Before the Subcommittee on International Operations of the Senate Committee on Foreign Relations of the United States Senate*, 23 July 1998, 105th Congress, 2nd sess, S Rep No 105 724, 13.

[12] See, eg, *Report of the International Criminal Court*, UN GAOR, 63rd sess, 35th mtg, Agenda Item 69, UN Doc A/63/PV.35 (31 October 2008) pp. 25–6; *Report of the International Criminal Court*, UN GAOR, 72nd sess, 37th mtg, Agenda Item 76, UN Doc A/72/PV.37 (30 October 2017) pp. 21–3.

[13] United States of America, *Statement on behalf of the United States of America*, 16th Session of the Assembly of States Parties (8 December 2017).

[14] Government of the Republic of the Union of Myanmar Ministry of the Office of the State Counsellor (Press Release, 9 August 2018).

[15] See, eg, D Akande, 'The Jurisdiction of the International Criminal Court over Nationals of Non-Parties: Legal Basis and Limits' (2003) 1 *Journal of International Criminal Justice* 618 at 620; GM Danilenko, 'The Statute of the International Criminal Court and Third States' (1999) 21 *Michigan Journal of International Law* 445 at 448; M Morris, 'High Crimes and Misconceptions: The ICC and Non-Party States' (2001) 64 *Law and Contemporary Problems* 13 at 26; MP Scharf, 'The ICC's Jurisdiction over the Nationals of Non-Party States: A Critique of the U.S. Position' (2001) 64 *Law and Contemporary Problems* 67 at

jurisdiction over a national of a non-State Party on the basis of Article 13 (a) or (c), the State of the accused's nationality incurs neither rights nor obligations under the Rome Statute. The State of nationality is under no legal obligation to cooperate with the Court, which means, for example, that it does not have to surrender the accused to the ICC if the charged individual is in the custody of the State of nationality. Where the ICC has jurisdiction over nationals of a non-State Party by virtue of Article 13(b), it is the Security Council resolution that imposes rights and obligations on the State in question.[16] Statements such as those by India, Sudan, the US and Myanmar represent a conflation of *pacta tertiis* with the question of whether the ICC can prosecute non-party nationals without the consent of the State of nationality, which is a separate issue that I address in Section 2.2.2.

While the Rome Statute does not create obligations or rights for non-States Parties, it may nevertheless affect the interests of such States in a variety of ways. Under the George W. Bush administration, for example, the US government was famously hostile to the ICC and, after 'unsigning' the Rome Statute, enacted the *American Servicemembers' Protection Act* of 2002.[17] This federal statute prohibits US governments and agencies from assisting the ICC and authorises the president 'to use all means necessary and appropriate' to secure the release of any American citizen detained by the Court.[18] It further requires the president to withdraw military support from any State that ratifies the Rome Statute unless it signs a bilateral agreement promising not to transfer American personnel to the Court.[19] Despite its rejection of the Rome Statute, the US was sufficiently concerned about the Statute's possible effects for it to take such measures.[20]

98; JA Rutigliano Jr, 'Fundamental Concerns: Why the US Government Should Not Accede to the Rome Statute' (2014) 63 *Naval Law Review* 92 at 95.

[16] See further discussion in Chapter 5.

[17] Letter from John R Bolton, US Under Secretary of State for Arms Control and International Security to Kofi Annan, UN Secretary General (6 May 2002); *American Servicemembers' Protection Act*, Public Law Number 107–206, 116 Stat. 899, 22 USC §§7421–33 (2002).

[18] *American Servicemembers' Protection Act* §7427. This broad authority led to the provision being dubbed the 'Hague Invasion' clause.

[19] Ibid., §7423.

[20] Such measures are analysed in more detail in Chapter 4. For discussion of the US's relationship with the ICC over the years, see BS Brown, 'US Objections to the Statute of the International Criminal Court: A Brief Response' (1999) 31 *International Law and Politics* 855; D Scheffer, 'The United States and the International Criminal Court' (1999)

2.2 INFRINGING ON JURISDICTION OF NON-STATES PARTIES

Similarly, in September 2014, Israel announced that it would be investigating and prosecuting allegations of misconduct by Israeli soldiers during the 2014 Gaza conflict. The announcement came only two weeks after the end of the conflict and was viewed as 'a swift effort to preempt an investigation' by the ICC.[21] The Office of the Prosecutor opened a preliminary examination of the situation in Palestine only four months later,[22] but prior to that, the mere possibility of the ICC getting involved was likely a motivating factor in Israel's expedited investigations.

Pre-Trial Chamber I has recognised that one of the ways that non-States Parties are affected by the ICC's activities is by choosing to cooperate with the Court:

> Such cooperation may concern, for instance, the arrest and surrender of suspects, the explicit approval of Security Council resolutions referring situations to the ICC, refraining from exercising the veto power, participating as observers in the works of the Assembly of States Parties, or consenting to outreach activities.[23]

Non-States Parties including the US, Israel, Russia, China and India have all cooperated with the ICC in one way or another at some stage in the Court's history.[24]

---

93 *American Journal of International Law* 12; R Wedgwood, 'The International Criminal Court: An American View' (1999) 10 *European Journal of International Law* 93; J Stephens, 'Don't Tread on Me: Absence of Jurisdiction by the International Criminal Court over the U.S. and Other Non-Signatory States' (2005) 52 *Naval Law Review* 151; P McEvoy, 'Reflections on US Opposition to the International Criminal Court' (2006) 6 *Hibernian Law Journal* 33; A Bogdan, 'The United States and the International Criminal Court: Avoiding Jurisdiction through Bilateral Agreements in Reliance on Article 98 (2008) 8 *International Criminal Law Review* 1; Rutigliano Jr, 'Fundamental Concerns'.

[21] I Kershner, 'Israeli Government Watchdog Investigates Military's Conduct in Gaza War', *New York Times* (20 January 2015).

[22] Office of the Prosecutor, 'The Prosecutor of the International Criminal Court, Fatou Bensouda, opens a preliminary examination of the situation in Palestine' (Press Release, ICC-OTP-20150116-PR1083, 16 January 2015).

[23] *Request under Regulation 46(3) of the Regulations of the Court (Decision on the 'Prosecution's Request for a Ruling on Jurisdiction under Article 19(3) of the Statute')* (International Criminal Court, Pre-Trial Chamber I, Case No ICC-RoC46(3)-01/18, 6 September 2018) para 47.

[24] Some examples of cooperation with the Court include the 2013 US facilitation of the transfer of Bosco Ntaganda to the ICC after he surrendered himself to the US embassy in Rwanda; Israel's acceptance of a visiting delegation from the Office of the Prosecutor in 2016; the US, Russia and China's participation as observer States at sessions of the Assembly of States Parties; and in 2011, Security Council permanent members Russia, the US and China, and non-permanent members India and Lebanon, voted in favour of referring the situation in Libya to the ICC. See *Request under Regulation 46(3) of the Regulations of the Court (Decision on the 'Prosecution's Request for a Ruling on Jurisdiction*

Furthermore, the Statute's wide ratification is likely to have some broader influence on the development of international criminal law, and any normative consequences of the Rome Statute will not be limited to States Parties. Just as international criminal law affects all States by 'prohibiting behaviour perhaps previously outside of the purview of international law',[25] the definitional standardisation of genocide, war crimes and crimes against humanity will likely have far-reaching effects. Most States Parties have implemented the substantive definitions of the Statute crimes into their domestic legislation, and Article 88 of the Statute requires States Parties to enact procedures in their national law to facilitate cooperation with the Court. The fact that more than 120 States have so far ratified the Rome Statute means that it has the potential to generate new customary law, particularly with respect to the elements of the crimes elaborated in the Statute.[26] This will affect domestic enforcement of international criminal law and interstate cooperation in international criminal matters.

2.2.2 The Rome Statute Ignores the Importance of State Consent

Although the Rome Statute does not explicitly create positive obligations or rights for non-States Parties, one of the primary objections to the Court's jurisdiction is that prosecution of non-party nationals without the consent of the State of nationality takes something away from that State's sovereign domain. For example, in a statement following the adoption of the Rome Statute in 1998, China asserted that States 'would no longer be able to invoke their non-acceptance of the Court's jurisdiction in order to prevent the Court's interference with their judicial sovereignty'.[27] In the UN General Assembly, Cuba has repeatedly asserted that '[t]he Court must respect the principle of law regarding consent of a State to be bound by a treaty' and 'reiterated its serious concern about ... the Court's decisions to initiate criminal trials against

---

under Article 19(3) of the Statute') (International Criminal Court, Pre-Trial Chamber I, Case No ICC-RoC46(3)-01/18, 6 September 2018) para 47 and attendant footnotes.

[25] Cryer, 'International Criminal Law vs State Sovereignty', 985.
[26] Danilenko, 'The Statute of the International Criminal Court and Third States', 448–9.
[27] Statement of China, *Summary Record of the 9th Meeting*, UN GAOR, 6th Comm, 53rd sess, 9th mtg, Agenda Item 153, UN Doc A/C.6/53/SR.9 (4 November 1998) para 33. See also Statement of India, *Summary Record of the 11th Meeting*, UN GAOR, 6th Comm, 53rd sess, 11th mtg, Agenda Item 153, UN Doc A/C.6/53/SR.11 (3 November 1998) para 29.

2.2 INFRINGING ON JURISDICTION OF NON-STATES PARTIES

nationals of States that are not party to the Rome Statute'.[28] Both China and Cuba have remained non-parties and, despite some warming of attitudes towards the Court, maintain their objection to the Statute on the basis that it allows the ICC to prosecute non-party nationals without first obtaining consent from the State of the accused's nationality.[29]

Perhaps more than any other non-State Party, the US has continually objected to the jurisdiction of the ICC on the basis that it disrespects the principle of State consent. While US relations with the Court have waxed and waned over the years depending on which administration was in office, the spectre of an investigation and potential prosecution of US nationals in the situation in Afghanistan has ensured a consistent response to the Court's jurisdiction over nationals of non-States Parties. Under the Obama administration, when relations between the US and the ICC were at its warmest,[30] the government continued to frame its objection to the Court's jurisdiction over its nationals as a matter of consent:

> We do not believe that an ICC examination or investigation with respect to the actions of US personnel in relation to the situation in Afghanistan is warranted or appropriate. As we previously noted, the United States is not a party to the Rome Statute and has not consented to ICC jurisdiction.[31]

The Trump administration saw the resurgence of general anti-ICC rhetoric[32] and reaffirmed US rejection of the Court's jurisdiction:

> The United States reiterates its continuing and long-standing principled objection to any assertion of ICC jurisdiction over nationals of States that

---

[28] See, eg, *Report of the International Criminal Court,* UN GAOR, 64th sess, 29th mtg, Agenda Item 75, UN Doc A/64/PV.29 (29 October 2009) p. 13; *Report of the International Criminal Court,* UN GAOR, 68th sess, 42nd mtg, Agenda Item 75, UN Doc A/68/PV.42 (31 October 2013) p. 26.

[29] Jianping and Zhixiang, 'China's Attitude Towards the ICC', 611–12; J Wuthnow, 'China and the ICC', *The Diplomat* (7 December 2012); Cuba, Statement by HE Mrs Soraya Alvarez Núñez, Ambassador of Cuba in the Kingdom of the Netherlands, *Eighteenth Assembly of the States Parties to the Rome Statute of the International Criminal Court* (2–7 December 2019).

[30] D Bosco, *Rough Justice: The International Criminal Court in a World of Power Politics* (Oxford University Press, 2014) p. 175.

[31] US Department of State, *Daily Briefing,* 15 November 2016 (Elizabeth Trudeau).

[32] See, eg, Speech given by former National Security advisor John Bolton to the Federalist Society in Washington DC on 10 September 2018 in which Bolton went so far as to threaten criminal prosecution against ICC judges and personnel. For a transcript of the speech, see 'Full Text of John Bolton's Speech to the Federalist Society', *Al Jazeera* (11 September 2018).

are not party to the Rome Statute, including the United States and Israel, without a Security Council referral or the consent of such a State.[33]

While it is perhaps not surprising that a non-State Party facing a possible ICC investigation into conduct of its nationals should be strident in its criticism of the Court, the US has been outspoken about its belief in the importance of State consent since before the adoption of the Statute.[34]

Other non-States Parties joined this particular bandwagon a little later on. After the Security Council referred the situations in Sudan and Libya to the Court, both States used the absence of their consent to the Statute as the primary reason for refusing to recognise ICC authority over their nationals. Upon announcement of arrest warrants for two senior Sudanese government officials,[35] one of the indicted – Minister Ahmad Harun – declared that there was 'no jurisdiction to take action on this issue for the simple reason that the government of Sudan did not approve the ICC basic law'.[36] Similarly, Libya also invoked lack of consent as the grounds for its refusal to hand over former officials Saif Al-Islam Gaddafi and Abdullah Al-Senussi to the ICC: 'Libya is not a signatory to the Rome Statute that establishes the ICC's authority . . . We insist on trying Sayf-al-Islam in accordance with provisions that are well established in the Libyan law and cannot be overlooked. It is a matter of sovereignty'.[37]

States and scholars alike have claimed that the ICC's prosecution of nationals from non-States Parties represents a flagrant disrespect for the 'fundamentally important' principle of State consent in international

---

[33] *The Situation in Libya*, UN SCOR, 73rd sess, 8250th mtg, UN Doc S/PV.8250 (9 May 2018) p. 8.

[34] See generally, 'Is a U.N. International Criminal Court in the U.S. National Interest?', *Hearing before the Subcommittee on International Operations of the Committee on Foreign Relations of the United States Senate*, S HRG 105–724 (23 July 1998).

[35] *Prosecutor v. Harun and Abd-Al-Rahman (Warrant of Arrest for Ahmad Harun and Ali Muhammad Ali Abd-Al-Rahman)* (International Criminal Court, Pre-Trial Chamber I, Case No ICC-02/05-01/07, 27 April 2007).

[36] 'Sudan Rejects ICC Ruling on Darfur', *Al Jazeera* (28 February 2007). The Sudanese government has further claimed that its stance against the ICC is 'in line with international law because Sudan is not a member of the treaty that founded this jurisdiction': 'Sudan Rejects ICC Arrest Warrants', *Sudan Tribune* (2 May 2007).

[37] Abd-al-Qadir al-Minsaz (a member of the ruling National Transitional Council in charge of legal affairs) quoted in 'Trial of Sayf-al-Islam in Libya is question of sovereignty – NTC official', *BBC Monitoring Middle East* (9 April 2012) cited in *Prosecutor v. Saif Al-Islam Gaddafi and Abdullah Al-Senussi (Addendum to Request for Finding of Non-Compliance)* (International Criminal Court, Pre-Trial Chamber I, Case No ICC-01/11-01/11, 18 June 2013) fn 5.

law.[38] But how important is it for the State of nationality to consent before its nationals can be prosecuted for crimes committed on foreign territory? Under customary international law, States do not have unfettered authority over their citizens at all times. Individuals travelling abroad are bound by the laws of the territorial State, subject to certain basic human rights standards guaranteed by customary international law.[39] Under the principle of territorial jurisdiction,[40] the territorial State may prosecute a foreigner for a crime committed on its territory and in this situation consent of the accused's State of nationality is not required. The State of nationality may intervene diplomatically and the accused is entitled to consular assistance but consent of the State of nationality is not necessary for the foreign domestic prosecution to go ahead.[41] Only where there is an international agreement in place between States to specifically exempt nationals from prosecution by foreign courts does a State have the exclusive right to jurisdiction over its nationals.[42]

Given that consent of the State of nationality is not required for foreign prosecutions in domestic courts, it would seem that such objections of non-States Parties to ICC prosecution of their nationals are largely unfounded. However, as argued by Madeline Morris in her often-cited article critiquing the relationship between the ICC and non-States Parties, prosecution by an international court may have greater political and legal consequences for the State of the accused than prosecution by a foreign domestic court.[43] This would particularly be the case for situations before the ICC which involve Heads of State.

Under customary international law sitting Heads of State and certain senior State officials are immune from prosecution in foreign domestic

---

[38] Rutigliano Jr, 'Fundamental Concerns', 95; LA Casey and DBJ Rivkin, 'The Limits of Legitimacy: The Rome Statute's Unlawful Application to Non-State Parties' (2003) 44 *Virginia Journal of International Law* 63 at 64; Statement of David Scheffer, *Hearing Before the Subcommittee on International Operations of the Senate Committee on Foreign Relations of the United States Senate*, S HRG 105–724 (23 July 1998), p. 13.

[39] Casey and Rivkin, 'Limits of Legitimacy', 84.

[40] This, and other principles of jurisdiction, will be discussed in detail in Chapter 3.

[41] See, eg, Article 5(i) Vienna Convention on Consular Relations, which provides that consular functions include 'subject to the practices and procedures obtaining in the receiving State, representing or arranging appropriate representation for nationals of the sending State before the tribunals and other authorities of the receiving State': *Vienna Convention on Consular Relations 1963*, opened for signature 24 April 1963, 596 UNTS 261 (entered into force 19 March 1967).

[42] Whether international agreements between States affect the jurisdiction of the ICC is analysed in later chapters.

[43] Morris, 'High Crimes and Misconceptions: The ICC and Non-Party States', 30.

courts.[44] Any attempt to prosecute would be a violation of international law. Under Article 27 of the Rome Statute, however, sitting Heads of State are not immune from prosecution by the ICC.[45] Morris argues that the prosecution of senior officials amounts to prosecution of the State by proxy, as crimes committed by such individuals in their official capacity generally occur pursuant to State policy.[46] Even the perception that the ICC is prosecuting States – particularly States that have not ratified the Rome Statute – will likely have significant political consequences.[47]

There is also a concern that the ICC could become a de facto adjudicator in interstate disputes involving a non-State Party,[48] which is a distinct possibility in any litigation involving Palestine and Israel. Palestine acceded to the Rome Statute in January 2015 and Israel remains a non-State Party. The investigation into the situation in Palestine is in relation to crimes committed 'in the West Bank, including East Jerusalem, and the Gaza Strip',[49] and will almost certainly involve an examination of the legality of Israel's occupation policies.[50] Israel's Attorney General has warned that the investigation will 'draw the ICC

---

[44] *Arrest Warrant of 11 April 2000 (Congo v Belgium) (Judgment)* [2002] ICJ Rep 3, paras 51–4.

[45] The question of whether there is a legal basis for ICC prosecution of Heads of State from non-States Parties will be discussed in detail in Section 4.3.

[46] Morris, 'High Crimes and Misconceptions: The ICC and Non-Party States', 25.

[47] The ICC's prosecution of Kenya's president Uhuru Kenyatta, for example, drew significant ire from the African Union, which claimed the prosecution of a Head of State 'could undermine the sovereignty' of Kenya and other African Union Member States: Assembly of the African Union, *Decision on Africa's Relationship with the International Criminal Court*, Extraordinary Session, Ext/Assembly/AU/Dec. 1 (12 October 2013), 1.

The ICC has struggled with the perception that it is unfairly targeting African countries, compounded by arrest warrants issued for Heads of State in the situations in Kenya and Darfur in particular. See, eg, AS Knottnerus, 'The AU, the ICC, and the Prosecution of African Presidents' in KM Clarke, AS Knottnerus and E de Volder (eds), *Africa and the ICC – Perceptions of Justice* (Cambridge University Press, 2016).

[48] Morris, 'High Crimes and Misconceptions: The ICC and Non-Party States', 16–18.

[49] *Situation in the State of Palestine (Prosecution request pursuant to article 19(3) for a ruling on the Court's territorial jurisdiction in Palestine)* (International Criminal Court, Office of the Prosecutor, Case No ICC-01/18, 20 December 2019). See also, Palestinian National Authority, Referral by the State of Palestine Pursuant to Articles 13(a) and 14 of the Rome Statute (15 May 2018).

[50] The Prosecutor discussed the illegality of the Israeli settlements in the West Bank in her request to Pre-Trial Chamber I for a ruling on jurisdiction: *Situation in the State of Palestine (Prosecution request pursuant to article 19(3) for a ruling on the Court's territorial jurisdiction in Palestine)* (International Criminal Court, Office of the Prosecutor, Case No ICC-01/18, 20 December 2019) paras 157–77.

2.2 INFRINGING ON JURISDICTION OF NON-STATES PARTIES

into core political aspects of the Israeli-Palestinian conflict'.[51] As Morris points out, '[t]he political repercussions of [the ICC] determining that a State's acts or policies were unlawful would be substantial indeed, and categorically different from the repercussions of the same verdict rendered by a national court'.[52]

Under the consent principle of international adjudication, an international tribunal only has jurisdiction when both parties to the dispute have agreed to be bound by the tribunal's decision.[53] In the *Monetary Gold* case, the International Court of Justice (ICJ) further held that it was precluded from exercising jurisdiction where the legal interests of a third State formed 'the very subject matter of the decision'.[54] There is some suggestion that the *Monetary Gold* principle is a broader principle of international law, applicable beyond the ICJ.[55] It is conceivable that an ICC case involving an interstate dispute or the prosecution of a Head of State could mean that the interests of a non-State Party form the very subject matter of the decision. There is not, however, any precedent for applying the *Monetary Gold* principle to international criminal tribunals exercising jurisdiction over individuals.[56] Furthermore, Article 25(4) of the Rome Statute confirms that 'no provision in the Statute relating to individual criminal responsibility shall affect the responsibility of States under international law'. Undoubtedly there may well be ICC cases in which the *political* interests of a third State form the very subject matter of the decision, but any consequences for that State's legal interests would be indirect.

---

[51] State of Israel Office of the Attorney General, 'The International Criminal Court's lack of jurisdiction over the so-called "situation in Palestine"' (20 December 2019), p. 1. The Israeli Attorney-General also claimed that 'nothing could be more harmful to the credibility and legitimacy of a court of law than compromising its judicial character and appearing to over-reach. This would especially be the case where consent to jurisdiction has not been given (such as where the conduct of a State not Party to the Rome Statute is concerned)', p. 34.

[52] Morris, 'High Crimes and Misconceptions: The ICC and Non-Party States', 30.

[53] CF Amerasinghe, *Jurisdiction of International Tribunals* (Kluwer Law International, 2003) pp. 69–100.

[54] *Monetary Gold Removed from Rome in 1943 (Italy v France) (Judgment)* [1954] ICJ Rep 1954, 32.

[55] See, eg, International Law Commission Commentary to Article 16 (Articles on State Responsibility) [2001] II(2) *Yearbook of the International Law Commission* para 11; D Akande, 'Prosecuting Aggression: The Consent Problem and the Role of the Security Council' (Working Paper, Oxford Institute for Ethics, Law and Armed Conflict, May 2010) 18-20.

[56] C McDougall, *The Crime of Aggression under the Rome Statute of the International Criminal Court* (Cambridge University Press, 2013) pp. 245–6.

2.2.3 Complementarity as an Infringement on State Sovereignty

In addition to the underlying complaint that the Rome Statute's jurisdiction provisions ignore the importance of State consent in international law, some non-States Parties have claimed that the principle of complementarity embedded in the Rome Statute only serves as a further infringement on their sovereignty. Ironically, complementarity was included in the Statute to respect the sovereign right of States to prosecute crimes within their domestic jurisdiction, with Article 1 of the Statute emphasising that the Court is intended to be 'complementary to national criminal jurisdictions'.[57] Article 17 provides that the Court may decide admissibility of a particular case by determining whether a State with jurisdiction over it is 'unwilling or unable genuinely to carry out an investigation or prosecution'.[58] At Rome, India was concerned that complementarity would mean that:

> all nations must constantly prove the viability of their judicial structures or find these overridden by the ICC. Certainly, it is inconceivable to India, as it is to many other countries, that States with well established and functioning judicial and investigative systems should be subjected to a Star Chamber procedure.[59]

Not long after the Statute's adoption, China also expressed concern that giving the ICC the power to judge whether a State is willing or able to properly prosecute its own nationals means that the Court has become a 'supra-national organ'.[60] Indonesia stressed that the principle of complementarity is 'of paramount importance' and that the Court 'must not become a mechanism for interfering in State's internal affairs'.[61]

---

[57] 'The most apparent underlying interest that the complementarity regime of the Court is designed to protect and serve is the *sovereignty* both of State parties and third states': M Benzing, 'The Complementarity Regime of the International Criminal Court: International Criminal Justice between State Sovereignty and the Fight against Impunity' (2003) 7 *Max Planck Yearbook of United Nations Law* 591 at 595 (emphasis original).

[58] Rome Statute, Art 17(1)(a).

[59] *Statement by Mr Dilip Lahiri, Head of the Indian Delegation at the United Nations Diplomatic Conference of Plenipotentiaries on the Establishment of an International Criminal Court* (Rome, 16 June 1998) para 8.

[60] Jianping and Zhixiang, 'China's Attitude Towards the ICC', 611. See also, *Summary Record of the 9th Meeting*, UN GAOR, 6th Comm, 53rd sess, 9th mtg, Agenda Item 153, UN Doc A/C.6/53/SR.9 (4 November 1998) para 32.

[61] *Summary Record of the 14th Meeting*, UN GAOR, 6th Comm, 54th sess, 14th mtg, Agenda Item 158, UN Doc A/C.6/54/SR.14 (10 November 1999) para 12.

2.2 INFRINGING ON JURISDICTION OF NON-STATES PARTIES 25

The ICC has held that the burden in admissibility challenges is on the applicant State to prove that the case is inadmissible before the Court.[62] In 2011 the Court issued arrest warrants for Saif Al-Islam Gaddafi and Abdullah Al-Senussi for crimes committed in Libya.[63] In May 2013 Pre-Trial Chamber I decided that the case against Gaddafi was admissible before the ICC because Libya was 'unable genuinely to carry out the investigation or prosecution against Mr Gaddafi'.[64] In a lengthy appeal submission, representatives for the Libyan government invoked Libya's sovereignty on numerous occasions and declared the Pre-Trial Chamber's decision 'an unwarranted intrusion upon the right of a sovereign state to determine its own domestic procedures'.[65]

Libya's 2013 admissibility challenge in the Gaddafi case provides a good example of what this involves for a challenging State. In brief, Pre-Trial Chamber I had to 'assess whether the Libyan authorities are capable of investigating or prosecuting Mr Gaddafi in accordance with the substantive and procedural law applicable in Libya'.[66] To make this assessment, the Court undertook a detailed examination of Libya's relevant legislation and reviewed evidence of Libya's ongoing investigation

---

[62] *Prosecutor v Francis Kirimi Muthauru, Uhuru Muigai Kenyatta and Mohammed Hussein Ali (Judgment on the appeal of the Republic of Kenya against the decision of Pre-Trial Chamber II of 30 May 2011 entitled 'Decision on the Application by the Government of Kenya Challenging the Admissibility of the Case Pursuant to Article 19(2)(b) of the Statute')* (International Criminal Court, Appeals Chamber, Case No ICC-01/09-02/11 OA, 30 August 2011) para 61.

[63] *Situation in the Libyan Arab Jamahiriya (Warrant of Arrest for Saif Al-Islam Gaddafi)* (International Criminal Court, Pre-Trial Chamber I, Case No ICC-01/11, 27 June 2011); *Situation in the Libyan Arab Jamahiriya (Warrant of Arrest for Abdullah Al Senussi)* (International Criminal Court, Pre-Trial Chamber I, Case No ICC-01/11, 27 June 2011).

[64] The Pre-Trial Chamber recognised the procedural fairness safeguards of Libya's Code of Criminal Procedure but concluded that the national judicial system remained 'unavailable': *Prosecutor v Saif Al-Islam Gaddafi and Abdullah Al-Senussi (Decision on the admissibility of the case against Saif Al-Islam Gaddafi)* (International Criminal Court, Pre-Trial Chamber I, Case No ICC-01/11-01/11, 31 May 2013) paras 199–205. In October 2013, Pre-Trial Chamber I held that the case against Al-Senussi was inadmissible before the ICC under Article 17(1)(a): *Prosecutor v Saif Al-Islam Gaddafi and Abdullah Al-Senussi (Decision on the admissibility of the case against Abdullah Al-Senussi)* (International Criminal Court, Pre-Trial Chamber I, Case No ICC-01/11-01/11, 11 October 2013).

[65] *Prosecutor v Saif Al-Islam Gaddafi and Abdullah Al-Senussi (Document in support of the Government of Libya's Appeal against the 'Decision on the admissibility of the case against Saif Al-Islam Gaddafi')* (International Criminal Court, Appeals Chamber, Case No ICC-01/11-01/11, 24 June 2013) para 165.

[66] *Prosecutor v Saif Al-Islam Gaddafi and Abdullah Al-Senussi (Decision on the admissibility of the case against Saif Al-Islam Gaddafi)* (International Criminal Court, Pre-Trial Chamber I, Case No ICC-01/11-01/11, 31 May 2013) para 200.

into crimes allegedly committed by Gaddafi.[67] It considered whether the Libyan government could ensure adequate protection for witnesses and provide a lawyer for the defendant, and whether the government had sufficient control over the detention facilities in which Gaddafi was being held.[68] Ultimately, Pre-Trial Chamber I held that there was not 'evidence of a sufficient degree of specificity and probative value' to find that Libya was able genuinely to prosecute Gaddafi.[69] Despite Libya's request to submit further evidence, it was denied by the Pre-Trial Chamber, whose decision was upheld on appeal.[70]

Although Libya is obliged to cooperate with the Court by virtue of Security Council Resolution 1970, there is nothing in the Rome Statute itself to compel a non-State Party to respect an ICC decision on admissibility.[71] Indeed, Libya did not surrender Gaddafi to the ICC and instead proceeded with a trial of its own. In June 2018 Libya submitted another admissibility challenge on the grounds that Gaddafi had since been tried and convicted by the Tripoli Criminal Court for 'substantially the same conduct' as alleged in the ICC proceedings against him. Pre-Trial Chamber I again considered the relevant Libyan laws and judicial processes before concluding that the case against Gaddafi remained admissible as the Tripoli Court's verdict did not have the required '*res judicata* effect' and could be appealed.[72]

---

[67] Ibid., paras 107–37.
[68] Ibid., paras 185–89, 209–10.
[69] Ibid., para 135.
[70] Ibid., paras 136–7; *Prosecutor v Saif Al-Islam Gaddafi and Abdullah Al-Senussi (Judgment on the appeal of Libya against the decision of Pre-Trial Chamber I of 31 May 2013)* (International Criminal Court, Appeals Chamber, Case No ICC-01/11-01/11, 21 May 2014).
[71] See Chapter 5 for discussion about whether the Rome Statute applies to non-States Parties referred to the Court by the Security Council.

For a discussion of how complementarity operates with respect to Security Council referrals, see generally A Bishop, 'Failure of Complementarity: The Future of the International Criminal Court Following the Libyan Admissibility Challenge' (2013) 22 *Minnesota Journal of International Law* 388; J Pichon, 'The Principle of Complementarity in the Cases of the Sudanese Nationals Ahmad Harun and Ali Kushayb before the International Criminal Court' (2008) 8 *International Criminal Law Review* 185 at 188–90. For further information about complementarity, see C Stahn and M El Zeidy (eds), *The International Criminal Court and Complementarity: From Theory to Practice* (Cambridge University Press, 2011).

[72] *Prosecutor v Saif Al-Islam Gaddafi (Decision on the 'Admissibility Challenge by Dr Saif Al-Islam Gaddafi pursuant to Articles 17(1)(c), 19 and 20(3) of the Rome Statute)* (International Criminal Court, Pre-Trial Chamber I, Case No ICC-01/11-01/11, 5 April 2019) para 36.

2.2 INFRINGING ON JURISDICTION OF NON-STATES PARTIES 27

At the time of writing, there have not been any situations outside of a Security Council referral in which a non-State Party has officially challenged the admissibility of an ICC case under Article 19. But there are two scenarios in which this could occur. The first is in a situation where a national of a non-State Party commits a Statute crime on the territory of a State Party. For example, in 2016 the ICC authorised an investigation into crimes committed on the territory of Georgia.[73] Nationals from both Georgia and Russia have been accused of committing Statute crimes. Georgia is a party to the Statute, Russia is not. In accordance with the principle of complementarity, the ICC respects that Russia may assert jurisdiction over any accused Russian nationals based on the nationality principle of jurisdiction.[74] Under Article 19(2)(b) of the Rome Statute, Russia would be able to challenge the admissibility of any future ICC case against a Russian national.

The second scenario is where a national of a State Party commits a Statute crime on the territory of a non-State Party. The preliminary examination into crimes committed in Iraq represents an example of this.[75] Nationals from the UK, which is a State Party, are accused of committing Statute crimes in Iraq, which is not a party. Should this examination proceed to the investigation stage, Iraq could exercise jurisdiction over the accused UK nationals based on the territoriality principle and would be able to challenge the admissibility of any cases that come before the ICC.

In either the Georgia or the Iraq/UK situations, the non-State Party would likely experience 'extraordinary pressure to carry out its own investigation'[76] if the ICC decided to proceed with an official investigation. If Russia and Iraq challenged admissibility, both States would then

---

[73] *Situation in Georgia (Decision on the Prosecutor's request for authorization of an investigation)* (International Criminal Court, Pre-Trial Chamber I, Case No ICC-01/15, 27 January 2016).

[74] See Chapter 3 for a discussion of the customary principles of jurisdiction.

[75] Office of the Prosecutor, 'Prosecutor of the International Criminal Court, Fatou Bensouda, re-opens the preliminary examination of the situation in Iraq' ('Statement', 13 May 2014).

[76] R Wedgwood, 'The Irresolution of Rome' (2001) 64 *Law and Contemporary Problems* 193 at 199. It should be noted that the States Parties involved in such situations (eg, Georgia and the UK) would also face pressure to investigate and prosecute, and the UK has warned that '[t]he Court is not there to second guess, still less to review, the decisions of competent, functioning national systems of justice': UK Statement by Andrew Murdoch, Legal Director to the International Criminal Court Assembly of States Parties, *Seventeenth Session of the Assembly of States Parties to the Rome Statute of the International Criminal Court* (5 December 2018).

be subject to a review by the ICC under Article 17 to determine whether they are willing and able genuinely to prosecute.

No matter the outcome of an admissibility decision, the very fact that the complementarity regime empowers the ICC to review a non-State Party's investigative and judicial processes in such detail, and then make a final decision as to admissibility, is a clear-cut example of how the ICC can have a significant effect on non-States Parties.

2.2.4 Conclusion to Section 2.2

Non-States Parties frequently frame their objections to the ICC's jurisdiction in terms of sovereignty and State consent. While the Rome Statute does not create obligations or rights for non-States Parties, as demonstrated above, the Court's activities may nevertheless have various direct or indirect effects on such States. Whether such effects amount to an infringement on State sovereignty and whether such infringement is morally and legally justifiable very much depends on how modern sovereignty is characterised. The next section will examine how different interpretations of sovereignty can significantly alter the validity of non-State Party objections to the Statute.

2.3 The Rome Statute, Non-States Parties and Sovereignty

Many non-States Parties object to the Rome Statute on the grounds that any effect on their interests constitutes an unacceptable infringement on their sovereign rights. The basis for this objection ultimately arises out of the fact that the ICC exercises criminal jurisdiction, long considered 'one of the most sacred areas of State sovereignty'.[77] But there is no singular understanding of the concept of sovereignty,[78] which in turn means that there is no universal agreement about what might be considered a 'sacred' aspect of it. In this section, I examine the various ways that international criminal law scholars have interpreted the relationship

---

[77] A Cassese, 'On the Current Trends towards Criminal Prosecution and Punishment of Breaches of International Humanitarian Law' (1998) 9 *European Journal of International Law* 2 at 11; HP Kaul, 'Preconditions to the Exercise of Jurisdiction' in A Cassese, P Gaeta and JRWD Jones (eds), *The Rome Statute of the International Criminal Court: A Commentary* (Oxford University Press, 2002) p. 585.

[78] Grimm, *Sovereignty*, p. 4; M Koskenniemi, *From Apology to Utopia: The Structure of International Legal Argument: Reissue with a New Epilogue* (Cambridge University Press, 2005) p. 242.

between the ICC and State sovereignty, demonstrating divergence of opinions even among academic advocates of the Court. In the section that follows, I analyse whether such diverse views on the issue of the Rome Statute's relationship with State sovereignty can be reconciled, which involves a brief examination of the theoretical foundations of sovereignty. The analysis in these sections is a necessary simplification of what is an immensely complex issue.[79] For the purposes of this book, however, understanding and accepting the contradictions inherent in the concept of sovereignty goes some way to explaining the diversity of answers to the question 'does the Rome Statute infringe on State sovereignty?' and allows for the recognition of conflicting arguments as mutually valid.

2.3.1 Does the Rome Statute Infringe on State Sovereignty? Yes, No and Somewhat

Scholars have responded to the claim that the Rome Statute represents an unacceptable infringement on State sovereignty with a diverse range of views. At one end of the broad spectrum of opinions is the argument that the ICC does not represent any significant challenge to the concept of sovereignty. For example, M Cherif Bassiouni concludes that 'the ICC neither infringes upon national sovereignty nor overrides national legal systems capable of and willing to carry out their international legal obligations'.[80] Bassiouni sees the jurisdiction of the Court as representative of the collective will of States, and the existence of the complementarity regime as a sufficient safeguard for the sovereignty of non-States Parties. Bruce Broomhall is similarly convinced that 'the institution of sovereignty, at least in the areas relevant to international criminal law, is

---

[79] For a more detailed analysis of modern sovereignty, particularly as it interacts with international criminal justice, see JN Maogoto, *State Sovereignty and International Criminal Law: Versailles to Rome* (Transnational Publishers, 2003); SH Hashmi (ed), *State Sovereignty: Change and Persistence in International Relations* (Pennsylvania State University Press, 1997); Grimm, *Sovereignty*; T Jacobsen, CJG Sampford and RC Thakur (eds), *Re-Envisioning Sovereignty: The End of Westphalia?* (Ashgate, 2008); K Hessler, 'State Sovereignty as an Obstacle to International Criminal Law' in L May and Z Hoskins (eds), *International Criminal Law and Philosophy* (Cambridge University Press, 2010); J Crawford, 'Sovereignty as a Legal Value' in J Crawford and M Koskenniemi (eds), *The Cambridge Companion to International Law* (Cambridge University Press, 2012); L May, *Crimes Against Humanity: A Normative Account* (Cambridge University Press, 2004) pp. 8–20.

[80] MC Bassiouni, 'The Permanent International Criminal Court' in M Lattimer and P Sands (eds), *Justice for Crimes Against Humanity* (Hart Publishing, 2003) p. 181.

in no danger of being replaced or of its importance being radically diminished in the foreseeable future'.[81]

At the other end of the spectrum is the claim that the establishment of the ICC embodies a transformation of global politics and a new era in international law. Antonio Cassese declared the ICC to be 'a revolutionary institution that intrudes into state sovereignty by subjecting states' nationals to an international criminal jurisdiction'.[82] Leila Sadat takes the idea of the ICC as a revolutionary institution further, to argue that the Rome Statute is having a transformative effect on international law by challenging the Westphalian model of State sovereignty:

> The process by which the Statute was adopted, the Court's ultimate institutional structure, and the fact that it [has] jurisdiction over individuals, not traditionally considered subjects of international law, all suggest an important shift in the substructure of international law upon which the Court's establishment is premised.[83]

Situated somewhere in between these contrasting positions are scholars who remain sceptical about the alleged transformative impact of the ICC on State sovereignty and yet do not necessarily agree that the institution of sovereignty will remain completely unscathed by the activities of the ICC. Robert Cryer, for example, does not see the ICC as a threat to sovereignty's existence or integrity but argues that the Court does inevitably have some effect on the sovereignty of all States, party and non-party.[84] He emphasises the importance of acknowledging the role that sovereignty played in the creation of the Court, and the role that it continues to play when States exercise their sovereign prerogative to ratify the Rome Statute and respect decisions of the Court.[85] Cryer claims that '[n]on-party states have not had their sovereignty limited in any additional way by this concession made by states parties'.[86]

This small cross-section of opinions suggests that there does not appear to be a consensus among international criminal law scholars on the question of whether the Rome Statute infringes on State sovereignty.

---

[81] B Broomhall, *International Justice and the International Criminal Court: Between Sovereignty and the Rule of Law* (Oxford University Press, 2003) p. 5.
[82] A Cassese, 'The Statute of the International Criminal Court: Some Preliminary Reflections' (1999) 10 *European Journal of International Law* 144 at 145.
[83] LN Sadat, *The International Criminal Court and the Transformation of International Law: Justice for the New Millennium* (Transnational Publishers, 2002) p. 79.
[84] Cryer, 'International Criminal Law vs State Sovereignty', 983–5.
[85] Ibid., 985.
[86] Ibid., 985–6.

2.3 ROME STATUTE, NON-STATES PARTIES & SOVEREIGNTY 31

There is, however, general agreement among them that any effect, infringement or transformation would be entirely acceptable, even if this involves non-States Parties.[87] Although it may be an oversimplification to say that 'international criminal law scholars see sovereignty as the enemy ... thwarting international criminal justice at every turn',[88] they do tend to prioritise the goals of international criminal justice over the preservation of State sovereignty. The notion that any limitation of sovereignty by the ICC is legally and morally justifiable is the main point of divergence from the position of non-States Parties and their supporters who argue that any infringement on sovereignty is unacceptable.

So why do some scholars consider ICC infringement on State sovereignty to be an acceptable, even desirable, development? The argument is predicated on the notion that international crimes represent 'a formal limit to a State's legitimate exercise of its sovereignty, and so in principle justify a range of international responses'[89] including prosecution by an international court.[90] This is part of a broader evolution of the understanding of the concept of 'sovereignty as control' to 'sovereignty as responsibility'. This reconceptualisation of sovereignty manifests most palpably in the Responsibility to Protect doctrine and the idea that the international community has a responsibility to act when a State is unwilling or unable to protect its citizens from 'avoidable catastrophe'.[91] Any breach of this responsibility may be grounds for international prosecution of those most responsible for the harm, on the basis that sovereignty cannot be used to shield perpetrators of international crimes.[92]

Yet, as Bassiouni observes, 'state sovereignty remains an obstacle to international criminal justice ... because it is interpreted and used as a means of achieving goals that contradict those of international justice'.[93]

---

[87] See, eg, Cassese, 'The Statute of the International Criminal Court: Some Preliminary Reflections', 171; Cassese, 'On the Current Trends towards Criminal Prosecution and Punishment of Breaches of International Humanitarian Law', 16.
[88] Cryer, 'International Criminal Law vs State Sovereignty', 980.
[89] Broomhall, *International Justice and the International Criminal Court*, p. 43.
[90] A Altman and CH Wellman, *A Liberal Theory of International Justice* (Oxford University Press, 2009) pp. 73, 78, 95.
[91] International Commission on Intervention and State Sovereignty, *The Responsibility to Protect* (International Development Research Centre, December 2001) p. viii.
[92] See, generally, M Benzing, 'Sovereignty and the Responsibility to Protect in International Criminal Law' in D König, PT Stoll, V Röben and N Matz-Lück (eds), *International Law Today: New Challenges and the Need for Reform?* (Springer Berlin Heidelberg, 2008).
[93] MC Bassiouni, 'Foreword' in Maogoto, *State Sovereignty and International Criminal Law*, p. x.

32   QUESTIONS OF STATE CONSENT AND SOVEREIGNTY

On the one hand we have a number of States not party to the Rome Statute using sovereignty as the main legal, political and moral rationale for their objection to the jurisdiction of the ICC. On the other are advocates for international criminal justice who argue that it is legally, politically and morally justifiable to disregard sovereignty in circumstances where a State fails in its responsibility. To better appreciate why this dichotomy exists, and how it might affect the legal basis for the ICC's jurisdiction over nationals of non-States Parties, the next section provides a brief analysis of the theoretical foundations of modern sovereignty.

2.3.2   The Sovereignty Paradox

As mentioned in the introduction to this chapter, there has been a shift away from characterising sovereignty in absolutist Westphalian terms towards an understanding that better reflects the evolving role of States in a global community. Traditionally, sovereignty gives States unfettered and exclusive authority over their territory. International law exists because States are free to consent to be bound in relation to each other. Martti Koskenniemi identifies this as the 'ascending' perspective on statehood, because rights and responsibilities of international law ascend from the inherent freedom of States.[94] Koskenniemi associates this understanding with Carl Schmitt who viewed sovereignty as 'external to international law, a normative fact with which the law must accommodate itself'.[95] Counter to this construction is the 'descending' perspective, which Koskenniemi attributes to Hans Kelsen and HLA Hart.[96] The concept of descending sovereignty explains the recent conception of sovereignty as responsibility. Under this approach, sovereignty is a product of – or descends from – international law which allocates liberties and competencies to the States.[97]

International criminal lawyers tend to employ the descending approach to sovereignty as justification for the existence of international criminal law and its intrusive nature. Georg Schwarzenberger, for

---

[94] Koskenniemi, *From Apology to Utopia*, p. 225.
[95] Ibid., p. 231. See also C Schmitt, *Political Theology: Four Chapters on the Concept of Sovereignty* (MIT Press, 1985).
[96] Koskenniemi, *From Apology to Utopia*, p. 229.
[97] Ibid., pp. 229–30.

example, argued that sovereignty 'only exists within the limits drawn at any time by international law'.[98] By characterising sovereignty in this manner, any limits that international criminal law places on a State's liberty have an acceptable theoretical basis, and 'interference with sovereignty' does not hold up as a legitimate objection. In contrast, those States that maintain their objection to the ICC's jurisdiction over nationals of non-States Parties do so on an understanding of sovereignty as ascending. The US in particular remains 'one of the most tenacious advocates of Westphalian notions of State sovereignty'[99] and its continuing opposition to the Rome Statute's Article 12 jurisdiction preconditions is framed in terms of sovereignty and State consent. Similarly, as discussed in Section 2.2.2, Libya and Sudan predicate their objections on the basis of the sanctity of sovereignty and the illegitimacy of the ICC prosecuting their nationals without explicit State consent. This is a justifiable position in light of the ascending view of sovereignty.

The fact that these perspectives on sovereignty give rise to conflicting claims is a result of the 'constant oscillation' of the doctrine of modern sovereignty between competing viewpoints.[100] Neither the ascending nor the descending approach is unimpeachable, and so the uneasy co-existence of both means that 'in the end, the debate turns on what one chooses to understand by the term sovereignty'.[101] Not all arguments based on differing conceptual foundations of sovereignty will have equal merit. But the fact that there is not necessarily a common response to the question of whether the Rome Statute represents an unacceptable infringement on the sovereignty of non-States Parties provides the ICC with the flexibility it needs to navigate the myriad political, diplomatic and legal concerns that come before it. As Koskenniemi emphasises, 'indeterminacy is an absolutely central aspect of international law's acceptability'.[102]

---

[98] G Schwarzenberger, 'The Problem of an International Criminal Law' (1950) 3 *Current Legal Problems* 263 at 275. See also Altman and Wellman, *A Liberal Theory of International Justice*, p. 295.
[99] JG Ralph, *Defending the Society of States: Why America Opposes the International Criminal Court and its Vision of World Society* (Oxford University Press, 2007) p. 2.
[100] Koskenniemi, *From Apology to Utopia*, p. 225.
[101] A Clapham, 'National Action Challenged: Sovereignty, Immunity and Universal Jurisdiction before the International Court of Justice' in M Lattimer and P Sands (eds), *Justice for Crimes against Humanity* (Hart Publishing, 2003) p. 312. See also Mégret, 'Epilogue to an Endless Debate', 265.
[102] Koskenniemi, *From Apology to Utopia*, p. 591.

2.3.3 What This Means for the ICC and Non-States Parties

Of the main objections to the Rome Statute analysed in Section 2.2, the issue of whether the Statute's complementarity mechanism represents an unacceptable infringement on the sovereignty of non-States Parties is the one most likely to turn on the chosen conceptualisation of sovereignty. For example, the ICC's review of Libya's investigative and judicial processes and subsequent decisions rejecting the Gaddafi admissibility challenges could undoubtedly be construed as an infringement on Libya's sovereignty. For an international court to appraise a State's judicial system, particularly when the State in question has not consented to this action, is arguably an intrusion into the State's sovereign domain.[103] Adopting an ascending perspective on sovereignty, the outcome of the Court's admissibility consideration matters less than the fact that the ICC had authority to conduct the review of Libya's judicial system in the first place.

Conversely, the existence of the review mechanism in Article 19 of the Statute and the ICC's application of this in the Gaddafi case amounts to an entirely acceptable infringement on State sovereignty when viewed through the lens of a descending interpretation of sovereignty. International law places limits on sovereignty to prevent impunity for international crimes. The principle of complementarity respects the sovereign right of States to exercise criminal jurisdiction but, as the Rome Statute makes clear, if a State is unable or unwilling to prosecute, then the ICC will step in. This also means that Libya's objections to the ICC's admissibility decision on the grounds of sovereignty are not justifiable under the descending paradigm of sovereignty.

Ultimately, the conceptual indeterminacy of sovereignty means that the ICC will make its decisions in light of the Court's purpose and the aims of international criminal justice more generally.[104] While this means that the ICC will likely conceptualise sovereignty in a manner that allows for a State's sovereign liberty to be limited in particular circumstances, the Court also needs to demonstrate due respect to the genuine concerns that States have about the potentially extensive reach of the Rome Statute.

---

[103] Whether the Security Council referral operates as an acceptable substitute for State consent will be discussed in Chapter 5.

[104] See, eg, *Prosecutor v Gbagbo (Judgment on the Appeal of Mr Laurent Koudou Gbagbo against the Decision of Pre-Trial Chamber I on Jurisdiction and Stay of Proceedings)* (International Criminal Court, Appeals Chamber, Case No ICC-02/11-01/11, 12 December 2012) para 83.

2.4 Conclusion

A number of vocal non-States Parties continue to object to the potential for ICC jurisdiction over their nationals on the grounds that it represents an unacceptable infringement on their sovereignty. Of the various objections raised by non-States Parties, there are two that identify some genuine issues with respect to the Statute's impact on sovereignty. First is the fact that Heads of State from non-States Parties may be prosecuted by the ICC while still in office.[105] This could very well be perceived as a prosecution of the State by proxy and would likely have significant political and legal ramifications for the States involved. The second issue arises when a non-State Party has primary jurisdiction over a case before the ICC and challenges admissibility under Article 19(2)(b) of the Statute. The Court is then authorised to review the State's investigative processes and judicial structures and make a final determination as to whether the case is admissible.

Whether such an infringement on the sovereignty of a non-State Party is considered acceptable or not ultimately comes down to how one chooses to conceptualise sovereignty. The dichotomy of the ascending/ descending theory of sovereignty allows for competing, yet mutually valid, claims about the ICC's relationship with non-States Parties. The availability of interpretive choices and the continual oscillation between them goes some way towards explaining why the Rome Statute, as a product of compromise, is viewed with disappointment both by those who feel that it goes too far in its constraint of State sovereignty,[106] and those who believe it does not go far enough.[107] It also demonstrates the importance of grounding the legal basis for ICC jurisdiction in State consent and accepted international legal principles. The following chapters explore how the ICC can accomplish this.

---

[105] Whether there is a legal basis for the ICC to prosecute incumbent Heads of States from non-States Parties will be the focus of Section 4.3.

[106] See, eg, Kaul, 'Preconditions to the Exercise of Jurisdiction', pp. 613–15; Cassese, 'The Statute of the International Criminal Court: Some Preliminary Reflections', 161.

[107] See generally, D Scheffer, 'The International Criminal Court: The Challenge of Jurisdiction' (1999) 93 *American Society of International Law Proceedings* 68; Wedgwood, 'The Irresolution of Rome'; Morris, 'High Crimes and Misconceptions: The ICC and Non-Party States'.

3

Delegation of Jurisdiction: The Concepts

3.1 Introduction

In scholarship focusing on the ICC, a general consensus appears to have developed with respect to the legal basis for the Court's jurisdiction. The prevailing theory is that the ICC is lawfully able to exercise criminal jurisdiction because such jurisdiction is delegated to the Court by States Parties.[1] Delegation of jurisdiction, it is argued, explains how and why the ICC can lawfully exercise jurisdiction over nationals of non-States Parties in certain circumstances. If a foreign national commits a Statute crime on the territory of State X, State X has the right to prosecute the foreign national without the consent of his or her State of nationality. If State X has agreed to the jurisdiction of the ICC, and the case is otherwise admissible under the Rome Statute, State X is said to have delegated its own right to prosecute such a foreign national accused to the ICC. It is a seemingly coherent explanation designed to address accusations that the ICC's jurisdiction over nationals of non-States Parties is unlawful without the consent of the State of nationality.[2] The ICC itself appears to

---

[1] See, eg, S Williams, *Hybrid and Internationalised Criminal Tribunals: Selected Jurisdictional Issues* (Hart Publishing, 2012) pp. 305–8; I Cameron, 'Jurisdiction and Admissibility Issues under the ICC Statute' in D McGoldrick, P Rowe and E Donnelly (eds), *The Permanent International Criminal Court: Legal and Policy Issues* (Hart Publishing, 2004) pp. 412–13; O Bekou and R Cryer, 'The International Criminal Court and Universal Jurisdiction: A Close Encounter' (2007) 56 *International and Comparative Law Quarterly* 49 at 50; Y Shany, 'In Defence of Functional Interpretation of Article 12(3) of the Rome Statute: A Response to Yaël Ronen' (2010) 8 *Journal of International Criminal Justice* 329 at 330; S Wallerstein, 'Delegation of Powers and Authority in International Criminal Law' (2015) 9 *Criminal Law and Philosophy* 124; KJ Heller, 'What Is an International Crime: (A Revisionist History)' (2017) 58 *Harvard International Law Journal* 353 at 375; M Vagias, *The Territorial Jurisdiction of the International Criminal Court* (Cambridge University Press, 2014) p. 86; EC Barbour and MC Reid, The International Criminal Court (ICC): Jurisdiction, Extradition, and US Policy (Congressional Research Service Report for Congress, 16 March 2010) pp. 17–18.

[2] See Chapter 2 for further discussion of some of the accusations levelled at the Court by non-States Parties.

have recognised the relevance of delegation in relation to its authority in at least one decision.[3]

Delegation of jurisdiction was not always the presumed legal basis for ICC jurisdiction. As I mentioned in Chapter 1, a significant amount of scholarship was produced in the years after the adoption of the Rome Statute that debated whether or not a legal basis for ICC jurisdiction over nationals of non-States Parties even existed.[4] A sizeable portion of this commentary was devoted to the question of whether delegation of jurisdiction from States Parties was an acceptable explanation for how and why the ICC could lawfully prosecute nationals of non-States Parties in the circumstances prescribed by the Rome Statute. Arguably the capstone to this debate was Dapo Akande's influential article of 2003, which seemed to tip the scales in favour of delegation as the prevailing theory for ICC jurisdiction over nationals of non-States Parties.[5]

---

[3] '[W]hen States delegated authority to an international organisation they transfer all the powers necessary to achieve the purposes for which the authority was granted to the organisation': *Situation in Bangladesh/Myanmar (Decision Pursuant to Article 15 of the Rome Statute on the Authorisation of an Investigation into the Situation in the People's Republic of Bangladesh/Republic of the Union of Myanmar)* (International Criminal Court, Pre-Trial Chamber III, Case No ICC-01/19, 14 November 2019) para 60. See also, *Situation in the State of Palestine (Prosecution request pursuant to article 19(3) for a ruling on the Court's territorial jurisdiction in Palestine)* (International Criminal Court, Office of the Prosecutor, Case No ICC-01/18, 20 December 2019) paras 183–5, in which the Prosecutor discusses whether Palestine can delegate jurisdiction to the ICC. At the time of writing, the ICC has not, however, properly articulated the legal basis for its jurisdiction.

[4] M Morris, 'The Jurisdiction of the International Criminal Court over Nationals of Non-Party States (Conference Remarks)' (1999) 6 *ILSA Journal of International & Comparative Law* 363; GM Danilenko, 'The Statute of the International Criminal Court and Third States' (1999) 21 *Michigan Journal of International Law* 445; E La Haye, 'The Jurisdiction of the International Criminal Court: Controversies over the Preconditions for Exercising its Jurisdiction' (1999) 46 *Netherlands International Law Review* 1; M Morris, 'High Crimes and Misconceptions: The ICC and Non-Party States' (2001) 64 *Law and Contemporary Problems* 13; MP Scharf, 'The ICC's Jurisdiction over the Nationals of Non-Party States: A Critique of the U.S. Position' (2001) 64 *Law and Contemporary Problems* 67; JJ Paust, 'The Reach of ICC Jurisdiction over Non-Signatory Nationals' (2000) 33 *Vanderbilt Journal of Transnational Law* 1; F Mégret, 'Epilogue to an Endless Debate: The International Criminal Court's Third Party Jurisdiction and the Looming Revolution of International Law' (2001) 12 *European Journal of International Law* 247; M Inazumi, 'The Meaning of the State Consent Precondition in Article 12(2) of the Rome Statute of the International Criminal Court: A Theoretical Analysis of the Source of International Criminal Jurisdiction' (2002) 49 *Netherlands International Law Review* 159; LA Casey and DBJ Rivkin, 'The Limits of Legitimacy: The Rome Statute's Unlawful Application to Non-State Parties' (2003) 44 *Virginia Journal of International Law* 63.

[5] D Akande, 'The Jurisdiction of the International Criminal Court over Nationals of Non-Parties: Legal Basis and Limits' (2003) 1 *Journal of International Criminal Justice* 618.

Missing from this early scholarship, and from much of the growing body of literature that deals with questions surrounding ICC jurisdiction and non-States Parties,[6] is a clear conceptual analysis of 'jurisdiction' and 'delegation'.[7] In this chapter I address this lacuna by undertaking an exploration of what is meant by jurisdiction and what it means to say that this jurisdiction is being delegated to the ICC. The aim of this chapter, therefore, is to provide a detailed conceptual analysis of delegation of jurisdiction with a view to demonstrating how and why it works as an appropriate legal basis for the ICC's jurisdiction. While the delegation theory was developed in response to the issue of ICC jurisdiction over nationals of non-States Parties, I argue that delegation of jurisdiction provides an overarching foundation to explain how a treaty-based international court can exercise powers of criminal jurisdiction traditionally reserved to States. To this end, international institutional law provides a useful framework for exploring how the ICC, as an international organisation, acquires its powers from States Parties.

---

[6] This body of scholarship analyses particular features of the ICC's jurisdiction, including aspects of its relationship with non-States Parties, but little focuses specifically on the legal basis for the Court's jurisdiction over nationals from such States. See, eg, R Cryer, 'The International Criminal Court and its Relationship to Non-Party States' in G Sluiter and C Stahn (eds), *The Emerging Practice of the International Criminal Court* (Martinus Nijhoff Publishers, 2009) p. 260; M Milanović, 'Is the Rome Statute Binding on Individuals? (And Why We Should Care)' (2011) 9 *Journal of International Criminal Justice* 25; D Robinson, 'The Controversy over Territorial State Referrals and Reflections on ICL Discourse' (2011) 9 *Journal of International Criminal Justice* 355; G Sluiter, 'Obtaining Cooperation from Sudan – Where is the Law?' (2008) 6 *Journal of International Criminal Justice* 871; J Stephens, 'Don't Tread on Me: Absence of Jurisdiction by the International Criminal Court over the U.S. and Other Non-Signatory States' (2005) 52 *Naval Law Review* 151; R Cryer, 'The ICC and its Relationship to Non-States Parties' in C Stahn (ed), *The Law and Practice of the International Criminal Court* (Oxford University Press, 2015) pp. 260–80.

[7] This is not to imply that there has not been significant theoretical analysis of either 'jurisdiction' or 'delegation' in international law (and international criminal law) more broadly, but that in the doctrinal literature that deals specifically with ICC jurisdiction over nationals of non-States Parties, 'delegation of jurisdiction' is often presented as a legal basis with limited consideration of what this actually entails. For comprehensive analyses of jurisdiction and delegation in different contexts see, eg, A Chehtman, *The Philosophical Foundations of Extraterritorial Punishment* (Oxford University Press, 2010); C Ryngaert, *Jurisdiction in International Law*, 2nd ed (Oxford University Press, 2015); CF Amerasinghe, *Jurisdiction of International Tribunals* (Kluwer Law International, 2003); M. Akehurst, 'Jurisdiction in International Law' (1972) 46 *British Year Book of International Law* 145; D Sarooshi, *International Organizations and their Exercise of Sovereign Powers* (Oxford University Press, 2005); CA Bradley and JG Kelley (eds), 'Special Issue: The Law and Politics of International Delegation' (2008) 71 *Law and Contemporary Problems* 1; DG Hawkins et al., *Delegation and Agency in International Organizations* (Cambridge University Press, 2006).

3.1 INTRODUCTION

Section 3.2 begins by summarising the arguments and issues raised in the early scholarship, which focused on the question of whether States can lawfully delegate their powers of criminal jurisdiction over foreign nationals to an international court without the consent of the accused's State of nationality. I outline the existing arguments about whether, prior to the ICC, there was any precedent for States delegating their criminal jurisdiction over foreign nationals to an international court, and whether delegation might nevertheless be lawful as an innovation. A review of this literature demonstrates how international criminal law scholars arrived at the broadly accepted conclusion that the legal basis for the ICC's authority is delegated jurisdiction.

In Section 3.3 I take a step back from the arguments presented in the narrow context of the legal basis for the ICC's jurisdiction to discuss some of the basic tenets of international institutional law. In particular, I explore how and why States confer their sovereign powers on international organisations. This involves an analysis of the doctrine of attributed powers and a discussion of the unique features of multilateral treaties as constituent documents.

Section 3.4 breaks down the concept of jurisdiction in international law and attempts to make sense of the tapestry of terminology and principles that exist with respect to criminal jurisdiction in international law. I provide an overview of the principles under which a State may exercise jurisdiction in customary international law and explain how these apply in the context of the ICC. I distinguish between powers of criminal jurisdiction and the right to exercise them, and argue why this distinction is especially relevant for any discussion of the ICC's jurisdiction.

Clarifying the foundational concepts of 'delegation' and 'jurisdiction' requires a certain amount of descriptive exposition that is essential for understanding what it means to say that delegation of jurisdiction is the legal basis that allows the ICC to prosecute nationals of non-States Parties. The purpose of this chapter is to test the coherence of the delegation of jurisdiction theory before applying it in the following chapters to situations involving nationals of non-States Parties. I argue that delegation provides a defensible legal basis for the ICC's jurisdiction, but that 'delegation of jurisdiction' is a more complex theory than usually acknowledged by scholars who write about the ICC. An understanding of the foundational concepts of 'delegation' and 'jurisdiction' is necessary to explain how, why, or even whether the ICC may lawfully exercise criminal jurisdiction in the various circumstances envisaged by the Statute.

3.2 Delegation Debates in the Early Scholarship

Delegation of jurisdiction was raised soon after the Rome Statute's adoption as a theory that purported to explain how the ICC can lawfully prosecute nationals of non-States Parties within the parameters of Article 12(2). In the early years of the Statute's existence, scholars and other commentators who were interested in issues of ICC jurisdiction focused their discussions on whether delegation of criminal jurisdiction to an international court is lawful. In particular, the emphasis was on whether States could lawfully delegate criminal jurisdiction exercisable over foreign nationals without consent of the State of nationality. The existing scholarship has covered this question quite comprehensively, and here I provide a concise review of the main issues and arguments that were debated in the literature to demonstrate the possible legal foundations for the delegation of jurisdiction theory in the ICC context. The majority of the analysis on this question was produced between 1999 and 2003; collectively I refer to it as the 'early scholarship'.[8]

3.2.1 Is It Lawful to Delegate Criminal Jurisdiction without the Consent of the State of Nationality?

Two main issues were commonly addressed in the early scholarship with respect to the 'lawfulness of delegation' question. The first was whether States are generally entitled to delegate their criminal jurisdiction to each other without the consent of the State of the accused's nationality. The second issue dealt with the argument that even if States can lawfully delegate their criminal jurisdiction to other States without agreement from the State of the accused's nationality, it remains unlawful to delegate such jurisdiction to an international court. The following outlines the essence of each of these debates.

---

[8] See, eg, Morris, 'The Jurisdiction of the International Criminal Court over Nationals of Non-Party States (Conference Remarks)'; R Wedgwood, 'The International Criminal Court: An American View' (1999) 10 *European Journal of International Law* 93; D Scheffer, 'The International Criminal Court: The Challenge of Jurisdiction' (1999) 93 *American Society of International Law Proceedings* 68; Danilenko, 'The Statute of the International Criminal Court and Third States'; Paust, 'The Reach of ICC Jurisdiction over Non-Signatory Nationals'; Morris, 'High Crimes and Misconceptions: The ICC and Non-Party States'; Scharf, 'ICC's Jurisdiction over the Nationals of Non-Party States'; R Wedgwood, 'The Irresolution of Rome' (2001) 64 *Law and Contemporary Problems* 193; Mégret, 'Epilogue to an Endless Debate'; Casey and Rivkin, 'Limits of Legitimacy'; Akande, 'The Jurisdiction of the International Criminal Court over Nationals of Non-Parties: Legal Basis and Limits'.

3.2.1.1 Delegation of Jurisdiction among States

It was, by and large, accepted in the early scholarship that States have the right to prosecute non-nationals on the basis of criminal jurisdiction delegated from other States.[9] States can and do prosecute foreign nationals via delegated criminal jurisdiction without the consent of the State of the suspect's nationality. There are numerous examples of multilateral treaties that provide for delegation among States Parties. Typically such treaties involves agreement that the State of custody will either extradite the offender to the State with primary jurisdiction, or prosecute on the basis of delegated jurisdiction.

One such example of State-to-State delegation of criminal jurisdiction that was frequently mentioned in the early scholarship is the European Convention on the Transfer of Proceedings in Criminal Matters.[10] This Convention allows any State Party to prosecute a crime on behalf of another State Party that would otherwise have jurisdiction.[11] The Convention provides the prosecuting State with jurisdiction by creating 'a legal fiction allowing the [prosecuting] state to treat the offense as if it had been committed in its own territory'.[12] Madeline Morris, a vocal critic of the delegation of jurisdiction theory in the ICC context, conceded that the European Convention does represent an example of State-to-State delegation of jurisdiction. But she argued that the Convention does not represent an example of delegation of jurisdiction exercisable without consent from the State of the accused's nationality.[13] Michael Scharf challenged Morris's contention, claiming that 'the Convention does in fact permit transfer of proceedings in the absence of consent of

---

[9] 'The fact that the overwhelming majority of states have been prepared to delegate and to accept delegations of jurisdiction, even in cases where the state of nationality of the offender has not given its consent, is evidence that states generally take the view that such delegations of jurisdiction are lawful.' Akande, 'The Jurisdiction of the International Criminal Court over Nationals of Non-Parties: Legal Basis and Limits', 624. Contra Casey and Rivkin, 'Limits of Legitimacy', 88.

[10] *European Convention on the Transfer of Proceedings in Criminal Matters*, opened for signature 15 May 1972, 865 UNTS 99 (entered into force 30 March 1978).

[11] This is also known as 'vicarious' jurisdiction. Article 2(1) of the Convention provides: 'For the purposes of applying this Convention, any Contracting State shall have competence to prosecute under its own criminal law any offence to which the law of another Contracting State is applicable'. There are twenty-five States Parties to this Convention (at November 2019).

[12] MC Bassiouni, 'Introduction to Transfer of Criminal Proceedings' in MC Bassiouni (ed), *International Criminal Law* (Martinus Nijhoff Publishers, 2008) p. 516.

[13] Morris, 'High Crimes and Misconceptions: The ICC and Non-Party States', 44.

the state of nationality'.[14] Based on an examination of the Convention's legislative history and an interview conducted with one of the drafters of the Council of Europe's 1985 Explanatory Report on the European Convention, Scharf demonstrated that consent from the State of the accused's nationality is not required when transferring criminal proceedings.[15] Indeed, there does not seem to be anything in either the Convention or the Explanatory Report[16] to suggest that a national from a non-State Party could not be prosecuted by a State Party with custody of the accused for a crime committed on the territory of another State Party.

The agreements collectively known as the anti-terrorism treaties[17] were widely cited in the early scholarship as further examples of State-to-State delegation of criminal jurisdiction.[18] Such treaties specify a list of States with primary jurisdiction over the proscribed acts and an 'extradite or prosecute' clause for the custodial State.[19] None of these treaties require the State of the offender's nationality to consent to prosecution,

---

[14] Scharf, 'ICC's Jurisdiction over the Nationals of Non-Party States', 113.

[15] MP Scharf, Interview with A Klip, Associate Professor at the University of Utrecht, (Siracusa Sicily, 15 September 1999) in Scharf, 'ICC's Jurisdiction over the Nationals of Non-Party States', 114.

[16] *Explanatory Report to the European Convention on the Transfer of Proceedings in Criminal Matters*, ETS 73 (1972).

[17] Examples of such treaties include the *Convention on Offences and Certain Other Acts Committed on Board Aircraft*, opened for signature 14 September 1963, 704 UNTS 219 (entered into force 4 December 1969); *Convention for Suppression of Unlawful Seizure of Aircraft*, opened for signature 16 December 1970, 860 UNTS 105 (entered into force 14 October 1971); *Convention against the Taking of Hostages*, opened for signature 17 December 1979, 1316 UNTS 205 (entered into force 3 June 1983); *Convention against Torture and Other Cruel, Inhuman or Degrading Treatment or Punishment*, opened for signature 10 December 1984, 1465 UNTS 85 (entered into force 26 June 1987); *Convention for the Suppression of Unlawful Acts against the Safety of Maritime Navigation*, opened for signature 10 March 1988, 1678 UNTS 221 (entered into force 26 June 1992); *International Convention for the Suppression of the Financing of Terrorism*, opened for signature 9 December 1999, 2178 UNTS 197 (entered into force 10 April 2002).

[18] See, eg, Scharf, 'ICC's Jurisdiction over the Nationals of Non-Party States', 99–103; Morris, 'High Crimes and Misconceptions: The ICC and Non-Party States', 61–6; Akande, 'The Jurisdiction of the International Criminal Court over Nationals of Non-Parties: Legal Basis and Limits', 622–33. These treaties are also often cited as providing States with universal jurisdiction over such crimes (see Section 6.2.1.2 for a discussion of treaty-based universal jurisdiction).

[19] States with primary jurisdiction usually include the territorial State, the State of the accused's nationality and the State of the victim's nationality. For a detailed analysis of these treaties and the *aut dedere aut judicare* principle, see L Reydams, *Universal Jurisdiction: International and Municipal Legal Perspectives* (Oxford University Press, 2003) pp. 43–80.

3.2 DELEGATION DEBATES IN THE EARLY SCHOLARSHIP

and there have been cases where nationals of States not party to the particular anti-terrorism treaty have been prosecuted in the custodial or territorial State without the State of nationality's consent. The US has on multiple occasions prosecuted foreign nationals for crimes committed outside US territory, using jurisdiction granted by anti-terrorism treaties.[20] This has occurred even where such crimes did not affect US nationals or interests.

For example, in 2013, the US Court of Appeals for the DC Circuit addressed the question of prosecuting a non-US national for crimes committed extra-territorially in the case of *US v Ali*.[21] Ali Mohamed Ali, a Somali national, was arrested in the US and charged with offences relating to piracy and hostage-taking. Ali was accused of aiding and abetting the capture of a Danish-owned merchant ship that was flying a Bahamian flag with a crew consisting of eleven Russians, one Georgian and one Lithuanian. In conformity with the Convention against the Taking of Hostages (Hostage Convention), the American implementing legislation provides for jurisdiction over non-nationals found in the US who have committed the crime of taking hostages outside the US, even where there is no other nexus to the US aside from custody.[22] In accordance with Article 5(1)(a) of the Hostage Convention, the Bahamas, as a party to the Convention and as the flag State of the ship on board which the hostages were taken, would have had primary jurisdiction over Ali. So too would Russia, Lithuania and Georgia, as the hostages' States of nationality, under Article 5(1)(d). As the custodial State, the US can be said to have been exercising jurisdiction delegated from those States of primary jurisdiction.[23] The fact that Somalia was not a party to the Hostage Convention and, as argued by Ali, had therefore not consented

---

[20] *US v Yunis* 924 F 2d 1086 (DC Cir, 1991); *US v Rezaq* 134 F 3d 1121 (DC Cir, 1998); *US v Yousef* 327 F 2d 56 (2nd Cir, 2003); *US v Shi* 525 F 3d 709 (9th Cir, 2008); *US v Ali* 718 F 3d 929 (DC Cir, 2013). See also the discussion in Scharf, 'ICC's Jurisdiction over the Nationals of Non-Party States', 101–3; Akande, 'The Jurisdiction of the International Criminal Court over Nationals of Non-Parties: Legal Basis and Limits', 623–4.

[21] 718 F 3d 929 (DC Cir, 2013).

[22] 18 USC §1203 (1985).

[23] Alternatively, the court could be said to have been exercising universal jurisdiction, given that hostage-taking is considered a 'crime under national law of international concern' and arguably subject to universal jurisdiction in customary international law: Amnesty International, *Universal Jurisdiction – Strengthening This Essential Tool of International Justice* (2012) 7. Universal jurisdiction will be addressed below and explored in detail in Chapter 6.

to US jurisdiction over a Somali national, was not considered to be relevant.[24]

In summary, State-to-State delegation of criminal jurisdiction is generally uncontroversial, and consent of the State of the accused's nationality is not usually required. This was the conclusion reached in the early scholarship which also grappled with the more contentious question of whether such jurisdiction could be delegated to an international court.

3.2.1.2 Delegation of Jurisdiction to an International Court

Regardless of how jurisdiction may be delegated among States, critics of the Rome Statute maintained in the early scholarship that conferral of criminal jurisdiction on an international court is unlawful, particularly when it is to be exercised without consent from the State of the accused's nationality.[25] As discussed in Chapter 2, those who object to the ICC's jurisdiction over nationals of non-States Parties argue that although it may be acceptable for a State to prosecute a non-national without consent in certain circumstances, the political ramifications of such a prosecution by an international court would be far greater.[26] This is of particular concern in cases where the crimes arise from official State policy. However, potentially adverse political consequences of ICC prosecution do not mean that the Court's jurisdiction is unlawful.

The early scholarship on this issue debated whether any precedents exist among historical and contemporary international criminal tribunals for the notion that States can delegate criminal jurisdiction to an international court without the consent of the State of nationality. The International Military Tribunal established at Nuremberg after World War II (Nuremberg Tribunal) is a case study frequently used in the early scholarship to argue both for and against delegation of criminal jurisdiction to an international court without the consent of the accused's State of nationality. Scharf and Gennady Danilenko, for example, argued that

---

[24] *US v Ali* 718 F 3d 929, 944 (DC Cir, 2013). The Court held that the existence of the Hostage Convention provides non-nationals with sufficient notice that hostage-taking is prosecutable by any State Party.

[25] Morris, 'High Crimes and Misconceptions: The ICC and Non-Party States', 29–47; Scheffer, 'International Criminal Court', 69; Wedgwood, 'The Irresolution of Rome', 198–200.

[26] Morris, 'High Crimes and Misconceptions: The ICC and Non-Party States', 25–6.

3.2 DELEGATION DEBATES IN THE EARLY SCHOLARSHIP 45

in establishing the Tribunal via the Agreement for the Prosecution and Punishment of the Major War Criminals of the European Axis,[27] the victorious Allied nations could be said to have delegated their individual rights to prosecute the Nazi leadership to the Nuremberg Tribunal.[28] Morris, on the other hand, argued that after the war the Allies were acting as the German sovereign, and that consent from the accused's State of nationality was therefore unnecessary in establishing the Nuremberg Tribunal as essentially a national court.[29]

The Nuremberg judgment itself does not shed any light on which of these theories – delegated jurisdiction or Allies as sovereign – provides the basis for the Tribunal's authority to prosecute German nationals. The most relevant passage in the judgment was cited somewhat selectively in the early scholarship, but I set it out here in full:

> The making of the Charter was the exercise of the sovereign legislative power by the countries to which the German Reich unconditionally surrendered; and the undoubted right of these countries to legislate for the occupied territories has been recognized by the civilized world. The Charter is not an arbitrary exercise of power on the part of the victorious nations, but in the view of the Tribunal, as will be shown, it is the expression of international law existing at the time of its creation; and to that extent is itself a contribution to international law.
>
> The Signatory Powers created this Tribunal, defined the law it was to administer, and made regulations for the proper conduct of the Trial. In doing so, they have done together what any one of them might have done

---

[27] *Agreement for the Prosecution and Punishment of the Major War Criminals of the European Axis and Charter of the International Military Tribunal*, 82 UNTS 279 (signed and entered into force 8 August 1945).

[28] The right of the Allied nations to prosecute the German major war criminals was based on the permissive jurisdiction principles of territoriality, passive personality and possibly the protective principle. These will be discussed in Section 3.4.2. Scharf, 'ICC's Jurisdiction over the Nationals of Non-Party States', 103–6; Danilenko, 'The Statute of the International Criminal Court and Third States', 465.

[29] Morris, 'High Crimes and Misconceptions: The ICC and Non-Party States', 38–42. In support of her argument Morris relied on post-war scholarship by Frederick A Mann and Georg Schwarzenberger: FA Mann, 'The Present Legal Status of Germany' (1947) 1 *International Law Quarterly* 314 at 330; G Schwarzenberger, 'The Problem of an International Criminal Law' (1950) 3 *Current Legal Problems* 263 at 290–1. Alternatively, consent was entirely irrelevant because Germany had ceased to exist as a State: H Kelsen, 'The Legal Status of Germany According to the Declaration of Berlin' (1945) 39 *American Journal of International Law* 518 at 525. For a further discussion on whether *debellatio* was applicable to post-war Germany, see KJ Heller, *The Nuremberg Military Tribunals and the Origins of International Criminal Law* (Oxford University Press, 2011) pp. 113–16.

singly; for it is not to be doubted that any nation has the right thus to set up special courts to administer law.[30]

The second paragraph of this passage was highlighted by those who viewed the Nuremberg Tribunal as a precedent for delegation of jurisdiction to an international court, exercisable over nationals of a State that has not consented to such prosecution.[31] Conversely, the first sentence of the first paragraph was emphasised by those who claim that jurisdiction of the Tribunal was based on the fact that the Allied nations were acting as the sovereign (effective or actual) of Germany at the time.[32] Support for this interpretation is based on the German Instrument of Surrender and the Berlin Declaration through which the Allied governments '[assumed] supreme authority with respect to Germany, including all the powers possessed by the German Government, the High Command and any State, municipal, or local government or authority'.[33] Critics of the delegation theory argued that the sovereign theory overcomes the perceived problem of consent, particularly if the prosecutions could be considered an exercise of national jurisdiction by the Allies in their capacity as German sovereign.[34]

The UN Secretary General's 1949 Memorandum on the Nuremberg Tribunal discusses both the possibility that the Tribunal was based on collective exercise of delegated jurisdiction and the prospect that the Tribunal was validly established and imbued with jurisdiction by the Allied nations acting as the German sovereign.[35] Early scholarship

---

[30] International Military Tribunal (Nuremberg), Judgment and Sentences, reproduced in 'Judicial Decisions' (1947) 41 *American Journal of International Law* 172 at 216.

[31] Danilenko, 'The Statute of the International Criminal Court and Third States', 465; Paust, 'The Reach of ICC Jurisdiction over Non-Signatory Nationals', 4; Scharf, 'ICC's Jurisdiction over the Nationals of Non-Party States', 104.

[32] Morris, 'High Crimes and Misconceptions: The ICC and Non-Party States', 40. See also Scheffer, 'International Criminal Court', 71.

[33] Instrument of Surrender, Germany, signed 4 May 1945; *Declaration regarding the defeat of Germany and the assumption of supreme authority with respect to Germany by the Governments of the United States of America, the Union of Soviet Socialist Republics, the United Kingdom and the Provisional Government of the French Republic* ('Berlin Declaration'), signed 5 June 1945.

[34] Morris, 'High Crimes and Misconceptions: The ICC and Non-Party States', 40. Kevin Jon Heller views this argument as 'particularly unseemly: the idea that the Allies using their defeat of Germany to consent on Germany's behalf to the prosecution of German war criminals is more than a little redolent of victor's justice': Heller, *The Nuremberg Military Tribunals and the Origins of International Criminal Law*, p. 133.

[35] Memorandum submitted by the Secretary-General, *The Charter and Judgment of the Nürnberg Tribunal History and Analysis*, UN Doc A/CN.4/5 (1949) 79–80.

3.2 DELEGATION DEBATES IN THE EARLY SCHOLARSHIP 47

proponents of both the delegation and sovereign theories cited the Memorandum as authority for each interpretation.[36] The Memorandum, however, acknowledges that '[t]he Court seems to have perceived two different grounds of jurisdiction' and does not come to a definitive conclusion as to which is more persuasive.[37] Indeed, it appears that the legal basis for the establishment of the Nuremberg Tribunal and its authority over the Nazi leadership remains somewhat indeterminate. As such, the most useful conclusion that can be drawn from Nuremberg may be that articulated by Akande: 'one cannot rely with any certainty on the Nuremberg Tribunal as a precedent for delegation without the consent of the State of nationality'.[38]

There is less uncertainty surrounding the jurisdictional basis of the International Military Tribunal for the Far East (Tokyo Tribunal).[39] Unlike Germany, Japan retained a functioning government at the conclusion of World War II, and under the terms of the Potsdam Proclamation and the Japanese Instrument of Surrender, acceded to the jurisdiction of the Tokyo Tribunal over its nationals.[40] The Tokyo Tribunal is therefore generally not considered to be a precedent for the exercise of delegated jurisdiction by an international court over nationals of a State that does not consent to prosecution.[41]

Some of the early scholarship also examined whether the International Criminal Tribunal for the former Yugoslavia (ICTY); the International Criminal Tribunal for Rwanda (ICTR) and the Special Court for Sierra Leone (SCSL) could be held up as precedents for the delegation of jurisdiction to an international court without the consent of the State

---

[36] Danilenko, 'The Statute of the International Criminal Court and Third States', 465; Morris, 'High Crimes and Misconceptions: The ICC and Non-Party States', 40–1; Scharf, 'ICC's Jurisdiction over the Nationals of Non-Party States', 104.
[37] Memorandum submitted by the Secretary-General, *The Charter and Judgment of the Nürnberg Tribunal History and Analysis*, UN Doc A/CN.4/5 (1949) 79.
[38] Akande, 'The Jurisdiction of the International Criminal Court over Nationals of Non-Parties: Legal Basis and Limits', 627.
[39] Morris, 'High Crimes and Misconceptions: The ICC and Non-Party States', 37; Scharf, 'ICC's Jurisdiction over the Nationals of Non-Party States', 106.
[40] Proclamation Defining the Terms for the Japanese Surrender, US-China-UK, signed July 1945, 3 *Treaties and Other International Agreements of the United States of America 1776–1949* 1204 ('*Potsdam Proclamation*'); Instrument of Surrender, Japan, signed 2 September 1945.
[41] Given the coerced nature of Japan's consent, however, it may be possible to draw some parallels between this and the ICC's exercise of jurisdiction in situations referred by the Security Council, which is discussed in Chapter 5.

of nationality.[42] Akande argued that the ICTY, ICTR and SCSL provided 'evidence of extensive practice of States delegating part of their criminal jurisdiction over non-nationals' to international tribunals.[43] Given the involvement of the UN Security Council in the establishment of the ICTY and ICTR,[44] their precedential value for the ICC is arguably limited to cases where the Security Council refers nationals of non-States Parties to the Court. Neither can the SCSL be conclusively held up as an example of an international court exercising delegated criminal jurisdiction.[45] The SCSL is a *sui generis* court' having been established by a treaty between the UN and Sierra Leone.[46] Despite academic arguments to the contrary,[47] the SCSL Appeals Chamber held that the Special Court 'does not operate on the basis of transferred jurisdiction but is a new jurisdiction operating in the sphere of international law'.[48]

Notwithstanding the confidence in some of the early scholarship that precedent exists for delegation of jurisdiction over foreign nationals to an international court, there is enough uncertainty about the jurisdictional basis of previous international tribunals to render them unpersuasive as precedents.[49] More persuasive is the alternative argument put

---

[42] Scharf, 'ICC's Jurisdiction over the Nationals of Non-Party States', 108; Akande, 'The Jurisdiction of the International Criminal Court over Nationals of Non-Parties: Legal Basis and Limits', 628–31.

[43] Akande, 'The Jurisdiction of the International Criminal Court over Nationals of Non-Parties: Legal Basis and Limits', 633. Akande also uses lesser-known examples including the preliminary reference procedure of the European Court of Justice and the Caribbean Court of Justice, 632–3.

[44] SC Res 827, UN SCOR, 3217th mtg, UN Doc S/RES/827 (25 May 1993); SC Res 955, UN SCOR, 3453rd mtg, UN Doc S/RES/955 (8 November 1994).

[45] Even if it was evident that the SCSL is an example of an international court exercising delegated jurisdiction over a foreign national (President Charles Taylor of Liberia), the SCSL was established in 2002, three and a half years after the adoption of the Rome Statute. It would not, strictly speaking, be considered a precedent to the ICC.

[46] *Report of the Secretary-General on the Establishment of a Special Court for Sierra Leone*, UN Doc S/2000/915 (4 October 2000) 3; *Agreement between the United Nations and the Government of Sierra Leone on the establishment of a Special Court for Sierra Leone*, signed 16 January 2002, 2178 UNTS 137 (entered into force 12 April 2002).

[47] Sarah Williams argues that Sierra Leone has delegated territorial jurisdiction to the SCSL: Williams, *Hybrid and Internationalised Criminal Tribunals: Selected Jurisdictional Issues*, pp. 303–5.

[48] *Prosecutor v Gbao (Decision on the Preliminary Motion on the Invalidity of the Agreement Between the United Nations and the Government of Sierra Leone on the Establishment of the Special Court)* (Special Court for Sierra Leone, Appeals Chamber, Case No SCSL-2004-15-AR72(E), 25 May 2004) para 6. The idea of 'a new jurisdiction operating in the sphere of international law' will be discussed further in Chapter 6.

[49] For a detailed analysis of the legal bases and jurisdictional complexities of the various international tribunals, see Williams, *Hybrid and Internationalised Criminal Tribunals:*

forward by Scharf and Frédéric Mégret, which contends that a permissive rule of international law (ie, customary precedent or treaty) is not needed to validate delegation of jurisdiction to an international court. As long as delegation does not violate an existing rule of international law, it is a perfectly lawful jurisdictional arrangement.[50] The principle that international law gives States 'a wide measure of discretion' to exercise their jurisdiction unless there is a prohibitive rule against such exercise was recognised by the Permanent Court of International Justice (PCIJ) in the 1927 *Lotus* case.[51] Applying this to the ICC, Scharf argued that States are free to collectively establish an international court that will exercise criminal jurisdiction over nationals of non-States Parties because there is no rule in customary international law that prevents them from doing so.[52] In his view, '[t]he continued growth and evolution of international criminal law requires a permissive legal culture, which encourages State experimentation with new forms of collective international jurisdictional arrangements'.[53] Given that the *Lotus* principle has attracted significant criticism since it was first pronounced, caution should be exercised with respect to its application.

Mégret suggested that even if there is some question about the applicability of the *Lotus* principle in the ICC context, the fact that a State can, under customary international law, exercise criminal jurisdiction over foreign nationals for crimes committed on their territory is a sufficient permissible rule.[54] He argued that 'customary international law deals only with the existence and establishment of territorial jurisdiction, not the technical modalities of its use'.[55] In other words, the delegation of jurisdiction to an international court comes within the purview of the permissible rule that allows States to exercise jurisdiction under the principle of territoriality.

The *Lotus* case and the permissible principles of jurisdiction (including territoriality) will be discussed in detail in Section 3.4.2.2. For now, it is worth noting that underneath the numerous and complex arguments in the early scholarship on the question of whether States can lawfully

Selected Jurisdictional Issues, pp. 253–320. Williams sees the ICC as an original precedent for the delegation of jurisdiction to an international court, at 306.
[50] Mégret, 'Epilogue to an Endless Debate', 252–4; Scharf, 'ICC's Jurisdiction over the Nationals of Non-Party States', 72–4.
[51] *SS Lotus (France v Turkey) (Judgment)* [1927] PCIJ (Series A) No 10, 19.
[52] Scharf, 'ICC's Jurisdiction over the Nationals of Non-Party States', 73.
[53] Ibid., 74.
[54] Mégret, 'Epilogue to an Endless Debate', 252–3.
[55] Ibid., 253.

delegate their criminal jurisdiction to an international court, there does not appear to be any convincing legal reason for why this is not a valid action. As discussed in Chapter 2, an international court exercising delegated criminal jurisdiction over nationals of non-States Parties may very well have negative *political* consequences, but this does not necessarily preclude the legality of delegation.[56]

3.2.2 Delegation of Jurisdiction to an International Court Is Lawful

It is significant that in more recent ICC scholarship, delegated jurisdiction has largely become the presumed legal basis for the Court's jurisdiction.[57] By examining State practice in which criminal jurisdiction appears to have been delegated, the early scholarship made the case that such action is lawful. Missing from this analysis, however, is a proper conceptualisation of what delegation of jurisdiction actually entails. Understanding what is being delegated by States to the ICC and the processes through which delegation occurs is essential for determining whether delegation of jurisdiction works as a legal basis for ICC jurisdiction over nationals of non-States Parties in all circumstances envisaged by the Statute. The rest of this chapter therefore addresses two conceptual questions: What is delegation? And what is jurisdiction?

3.3 Delegation in International Law

So far, my consideration of delegation has been limited by the parameters of the discussion in the early scholarship. This literature – written predominantly by international criminal law specialists – consistently acknowledges the *sui generis* nature of the ICC as a permanent, independent, international criminal court established by a multilateral treaty. What it does not sufficiently recognise, however, is the fact that the theory of delegation has its origins in international institutional law, and that the elements that make the ICC unique among international

---

[56] Ibid., 254.
[57] See, eg, Shany, 'In Defence of Functional Interpretation of Article 12(3) of the Rome Statute: A Response to Yaël Ronen', 330; Williams, *Hybrid and Internationalised Criminal Tribunals: Selected Jurisdictional Issues*, pp. 305–8; Wallerstein, 'Delegation of Powers and Authority in International Criminal Law'; E Kontorovich, 'Israel/Palestine – The ICC's Uncharted Territory' (2013) 11 *Journal of International Criminal Justice* 979 at 989; Heller, 'What Is an International Crime', 375.

criminal tribunals are classic characteristics of international organisations. In this section I explore the theory of delegation in its international institutional law context and argue that viewing the ICC as an international organisation can provide a useful framework for understanding the source and scope of the Court's authority.[58]

3.3.1 The ICC as an International Organisation

Henry Schermers and Niels Blokker identify three defining features of an international organisation.[59] The first is that an international organisation is founded by an international agreement, commonly a multilateral treaty.[60] The second feature is that it should have 'at least one organ with a will of its own', meaning that the organisation is not simply a forum for Member States, but can make decisions and take action independently of its members.[61] The third defining feature of an international organisation is that it must be established under international law. Schermers and Blokker clarify that this third criterion can be assumed where the organisation is founded by an international agreement, unless the agreement specifies that the organisation should be established under a domestic legal system.[62]

Under this definition, the ICC is a clear example of an international organisation.[63] The ICC's establishment by multilateral treaty

---

[58] The analysis in this part is necessarily limited to the most basic elements of international institutional law. For a more comprehensive treatment of the field see, eg, J Klabbers, *An Introduction to International Institutional Law*, 2nd ed (Cambridge University Press, 2009) pp. 60–103; HG Schermers and N Blokker, *International Institutional Law: Unity within Diversity*, 6th ed (Brill Nijhoff, 2018) pp. 163–76; F Seyersted, *Common Law of International Organizations* (Martinus Nijhoff Publishers, 2008) pp. 65–70; DG Hawkins, DA Lake, DL Nielson and MJ Tierney (eds), *Delegation and Agency in International Organizations* (Cambridge University Press, 2006). For an international relations perspective on delegation, see Bradley and Kelley, 'Special Issue: The Law and Politics of International Delegation'.

[59] See also V Engström, *Constructing the Powers of International Institutions* (Brill, 2012) p. 11.

[60] Schermers and Blokker, *International Institutional Law*, pp. 41–7.

[61] Ibid., pp. 48–50.

[62] Ibid., pp. 50–1.

[63] The ICC has been recognised as an international organisation in international institutional law scholarship. See, eg, P Sands and P Klein, *Bowett's Law of International Institutions*, 6th ed (Sweet & Maxwell, 2009) pp. 385–90; Klabbers, *An Introduction to International Institutional Law*, p. 241; AS Muller, 'Setting Up the International Criminal Court: Not One Moment but a Series of Moments' (2004) 1 *International Organizations Law Review* 189.

distinguishes it from other international criminal tribunals, and fulfils the first and third criteria for its characterisation as an international organisation. Importantly, international law recognises that constituent treaties are in a special category of treaty owing to their nature as 'conventional and at the same time institutional'.[64] Article 5 of the VCLT acknowledges that '[t]he present Convention applies to any treaty which is the constituent instrument of an international organization and to any treaty adopted within an international organization without prejudice to any relevant rules of the organization'. Practice suggests that constituent treaties are often interpreted by favouring a teleological approach over the traditional textual interpretation.[65]

With respect to the second feature – an organ with a will of its own – the Rome Statute specifically provides that the ICC has international legal personality,[66] and the Statute further recognises the independence of the Office of the Prosecutor as a separate organ from the rest of the Court.[67] Given the ICC's status as an international organisation, therefore, the question of how the Court acquires its jurisdiction can be explored through the principles of international institutional law.

3.3.2 How Do International Organisations Acquire Their Powers?

The notion that international organisations are established on a functional basis is the leading theory to explain why an organisation is able to exercise certain powers traditionally reserved to States: organisations

---

[64] *Legality of the Use by a State of Nuclear Weapons in Armed Conflict (Advisory Opinion)* [1996] ICJ Rep 66, 75. See also C Brölmann, 'Specialized Rules of Treaty Interpretation: International Organizations' in DB Hollis (ed), *The Oxford Guide to Treaties* (Oxford University Press, 2012) pp. 510–19; A Aust, *Modern Treaty Law and Practice*, 3rd ed (Cambridge University Press, 2013) pp. 342–62.

[65] Klabbers, *An Introduction to International Institutional Law*, pp. 86–90; Brölmann, 'Specialized Rules of Treaty Interpretation: International Organizations', pp. 512–15. Examples of teleological interpretations of constituent treaties include *Reparation for Injuries Suffered in the Service of the United Nations (Advisory Opinion)* [1949] ICJ Rep 174, 179; *Legality of the Use by a State of Nuclear Weapons in Armed Conflict (Advisory Opinion)* [1996] ICJ Rep 66, 79–80; and *van Gend & Loos v Nederlandse Administratie der Belastingen* (C-26/62) [1963] ECR 1, 12.

[66] Rome Statute, Article 4(1). See also Sands and Klein, *Bowett's Law of International Institutions*, p. 386; Klabbers, *An Introduction to International Institutional Law*, pp. 38–9.

[67] The independence of the Office of the Prosecutor is enshrined in Article 42(1) of the Rome Statute, which specifically provides that 'a member of the office shall not seek or act on instructions from any external source'.

need to have the ability to fulfil their functions.[68] In this context, the term 'powers' is used to describe any number of wide-ranging actions that an organisation might legally take,[69] and how an organisation acquires its powers is widely considered to be by attribution from States.[70] In its *Legality of the Use of Nuclear Weapons Advisory Opinion*, the ICJ describes the attributed competence of international organisations in the following terms:

> [I]nternational organizations are subjects of international law which do not, unlike States, possess a general competence. International organizations are governed by the 'principle of specialty', that is to say, they are invested by the States which create them with powers, the limits of which are a function of the common interests whose promotion those States entrust to them.[71]

The rationale behind the doctrine of attributed, or conferred, powers is 'the manifest will of the founders', which ensures that an organisation's powers are limited to what is required to fulfil its functions.[72] Founding States confer express powers on an international organisation through the establishing treaty, which also becomes the organisation's constituent instrument. It is generally accepted that international organisations are also granted certain implied powers, limited to those that are necessary for the exercise of express powers and incidental to the fulfilment of the organisations' functions.[73] The following section briefly sets out the conceptual

---

[68] J Klabbers, *International Law* (Cambridge University Press, 2013) p. 98. For Klabbers' critique of functionalism, see J Klabbers, 'The Transformation of International Organizations Law' (2015) 26 *European Journal of International Law* 9.

[69] V Engström, 'Reasoning on Powers of Organizations' in J Klabbers and Å Wallendahl (eds), *Research Handbook on the Law of International Organizations* (Edward Elgar, 2011) p. 56. See also Engström, *Constructing the Powers of International Institutions*.

[70] Schermers and Blokker, *International Institutional Law*, pp. 164–71.

[71] *Legality of the Use by a State of Nuclear Weapons in Armed Conflict (Advisory Opinion)* [1996] ICJ Rep 66, 78.

[72] Klabbers, *An Introduction to International Institutional Law*, p. 64.

[73] Ibid., pp. 58–9; Schermers and Blokker, *International Institutional Law*, pp. 194–202. See also *Reparation for Injuries Suffered in the Service of the United Nations (Advisory Opinion)* [1949] ICJ Rep 174, 196 (Judge Hackworth). The ICC has held that it has certain implied powers necessary 'for the exercise of its primary jurisdiction or the performance of its essential duties and functions' such as the power to subpoena witnesses: *Prosecutor v Ruto and Sang (Decision on Prosecutor's Application for Witness Summonses and resulting Request for State Party Cooperation)* (International Criminal Court, Trial Chamber V(A), Case No ICC-01/09-01/11, 17 April 2014) paras 61–87, 81. The implied powers of an international organisation should not be confused with the *inherent* power of an international judicial body to determine its own jurisdiction pursuant to the principle of *compétence de la compétence*. See P Gaeta, 'Inherent

parameters of conferred powers (particularly delegation) as understood in international institutional law, and as applicable to the ICC.[74]

3.3.2.1 Typology of Conferral

Dan Sarooshi laments that the '[f]ailure to distinguish between different types of conferrals of power confuses analysis of the differing legal consequences of these conferrals and obfuscates the domestic policy debates that surround their conferral'.[75] Indeed, in much of the literature dealing with the legal basis for ICC jurisdiction, terms such as 'delegation' and 'transfer' are used interchangeably.[76] In an attempt to clarify this state of affairs, Sarooshi has undertaken one of the more comprehensive examinations of how attributed powers are acquired by international organisations.[77] For the purposes of this book, it is therefore appropriate to adopt Sarooshi's typology of conferral that categorises and explains the variables involved in the attribution of powers from States to international organisations. Sarooshi envisions a spectrum on which there are three main ways that a State can confer powers on an international organisation: agency, delegation and transfer.[78] In the case of agency, the powers conferred on the international organisation are revocable, and the conferring State retains control over how the powers are exercised by the organisation. The State further retains the right to exercise the conferred powers concurrently with the organisation.[79] At the opposite end of Sarooshi's spectrum is transfer, whereby a State

---

Powers of International Courts and Tribunals' in LC Vohrah, F Pocar, Y Featherstone, O Fourmy, C Graham, J Hocking and N Robson (eds), *Man's Inhumanity to Man: Essays on International Law in Honour of Antonio Cassese* (Kluwer Law International, 2003) p. 353.

[74] This section reproduces some material published in M Cormier, 'Can the ICC Exercise Jurisdiction over US Nationals for Crimes Committed in the Afghanistan Situation?' (2018) 5 *Journal of International Criminal Justice* 1043. Reproduced with permission from Oxford University Press.

[75] D Sarooshi, 'Conferrals by States of Powers on International Organizations: The Case of Agency' (2004) 74 *British Yearbook of International Law* 291 at 294.

[76] See, eg, Williams, *Hybrid and Internationalised Criminal Tribunals: Selected Jurisdictional Issues*, pp. 306, 314; D Akande, 'Prosecuting Aggression: The Consent Problem and the Role of the Security Council' (Working Paper, Oxford Institute for Ethics, Law and Armed Conflict, May 2010) 7. Danilenko, 'The Statute of the International Criminal Court and Third States', 452.

[77] Sarooshi, 'Conferrals by States of Powers on International Organisations'; D Sarooshi, 'Some Preliminary Remarks on the Conferral by States of Powers on International Organizations' (2003) *Jean Monnet Working Paper*; Sarooshi, *International Organizations and their Exercise of Sovereign Powers*.

[78] Sarooshi, *International Organizations and their Exercise of Sovereign Powers*, pp. 28–32.

[79] Sarooshi, 'Conferrals by States of Powers on International Organizations', 296.

3.3 DELEGATION IN INTERNATIONAL LAW

irrevocably cedes powers to an international organisation and relinquishes all claims to further use of such powers.[80] Somewhere between agency and transfer is delegation. Powers conferred by delegation are revocable, and the conferring State retains the right to exercise such powers concurrently. It differs from agency in that the State does not have any control over how delegated powers are used by the organisation.[81]

This is a simplified overview of Sarooshi's typology, but it is sufficient to see that his characterisation of delegation is broadly applicable to the ICC. Through a constituent treaty (the Rome Statute) States Parties confer powers on an international organisation (the ICC). Under Article 127 of the Statute, States can withdraw from the Statute, meaning that the power is revocable,[82] and the principle of complementarity embedded in the Statute ensures that States Parties not only retain their powers to prosecute international crimes but are given primacy to do so. Finally, States Parties do not preserve authority to control how the ICC uses its powers once conferred via the Rome Statute. It would therefore appear that the ICC represents a relatively archetypal example of an international organisation exercising delegated powers.

3.3.2.2 Collective Conferral or Individual Delegation?

Sarooshi also underscores the importance of distinguishing between the notion of individual and collective conferral.[83] Individual delegation occurs when States delegate powers that they possess in their individual capacity to an international organisation. Collective conferral occurs when a group of States collectively confer a power or powers that they do not possess individually.[84] For example, individually, States are unable to provide an authoritative interpretation of a multilateral treaty but collectively they may confer on an international tribunal the power to do so. The

---

[80] Sarooshi, *International Organizations and their Exercise of Sovereign Powers*, pp. 31–2.
[81] Ibid., p. 54.
[82] Although Article 127(2) provides that a withdrawing State is still obliged to cooperate with the Court with respect to continuing matters that were underway while the State was a party. At the time of writing, two States with situations before the Court have withdrawn from membership of the ICC: Burundi in October 2017 and The Philippines in March 2019. Pre-Trial Chamber III authorised an investigation into the situation in Burundi after its withdrawal took effect: *Situation in the Republic of Burundi (Public Redacted Version of "Decision Pursuant to Article 15 of the Rome Statute on the Authorization of an Investigation into the Situation in the Republic of Burundi")* (International Criminal Court, Pre-Trial Chamber III, Case No ICC-01/17-X, 9 November 2017) paras 22–6.
[83] Sarooshi, 'Conferrals by States of Powers on International Organizations', 297–8.
[84] Ibid.; Engström, *Constructing the Powers of International Institutions*, p. 103.

rationale behind collective conferral is that 'the powers which can be exercised – and hence conferred – by the collective totality of sovereign States is greater than the sum of the individual powers of these States'.[85] In the *Reparations for Injuries Suffered in the Service of the United Nations* case, the ICJ held that the UN had capacity to bring an international claim because its Member States had, via collective conferral of powers, established an organisation with international legal personality:

> [T[he Court's opinion is that fifty States, representing the vast majority of the Members of the international community, had the power, in conformity with international law, to bring into being an entity possessing objective international personality, and not merely personality recognised by them alone .[86]

The idea that 'the vast majority' of the international community may collectively confer powers on an international organisation is an imprecise metric. It would presumably be sufficient to prevent two or three States from attempting to establish an external entity with international legal personality,[87] but there is no way to definitively identify an acceptable minimum number of States that would possess this collective conferral power. With respect to the ICC, this is arguably not such an issue given that 120 States voted in favour of adopting the Rome Statute in 1998 and the 60 ratifications required for its entry into force was a stipulation that States agreed upon at Rome.[88] Referencing the ICJ's *Reparations* dicta, Pre-Trial Chamber I affirmed that

> it is the view of the Chamber that more than 120 States, representing the vast majority of the members of the international community, had the power, in conformity with international law, to bring into being an entity called the 'International Criminal Court', possessing objective international personality, and not merely personality recognized by them alone together with the capacity to act against impunity for the most serious crimes of concern to the international community as a whole and which is complementary to national criminal jurisdictions.[89]

---

[85] Sarooshi, 'Conferrals by States of Powers on International Organizations', 297 n 13.
[86] *Reparation for Injuries Suffered in the Service of the United Nations (Advisory Opinion)* [1949] ICJ Rep 174, 185.
[87] Sarooshi, 'Conferrals by States of Powers on International Organizations', 297 n 13.
[88] Rome Statute, Article 126. For a related discussion on what constitutes 'the international community' see Section 6.4.2.3.
[89] *Request under Regulation 46(3) of the Regulations of the Court (Decision on the 'Prosecution's Request for a Ruling on Jurisdiction under Article 19(3) of the Statute')* (International Criminal Court, Pre-Trial Chamber I, Case No ICC-RoC46(3)-01/18, 6 September 2018) para 48.

Characterising the ICC's establishment as a collective conferral of powers by the vast majority of the international community is unlikely to be seriously contested. Beyond the conferral of objective legal personality, however, the Pre-Trial Chamber seems to infer that the rest of the Court's powers are also a result of collective conferral. I would argue that they are better characterised as a matter of individual delegation because they reflect the powers that States possess in their individual capacities. This would ensure that the Court is not tempted to expand its jurisdictional reach beyond the limits of what States Parties themselves may do.[90]

3.3.3 The ICC as an Atypical International Organisation

Viewing the ICC as an international organisation exercising conferred powers provides a useful way to understand how delegation operates as a legal basis for the ICC's jurisdiction. As an independent international court, however, the ICC is an atypical international organisation in that it exercises criminal jurisdiction.[91] The remainder of this chapter deals with the second half of the conceptual 'delegation of jurisdiction' question by exploring what jurisdiction means in this context.

3.4 Jurisdiction in International Law

While the early scholarship described in Section 3.2 produced convincing arguments as to why States can lawfully delegate their criminal jurisdiction, what 'delegated jurisdiction' actually is remains

---

[90] For a discussion of the theory that collective conferrals can create an 'objective regime' in which legal obligations may be imposed on States not party to the establishing treaty, see DJ Bederman, 'Third Party Rights and Obligations in Treaties' in DB Hollis (ed), *The Oxford Guide to Treaties* (Oxford University Press, 2012) pp. 341–5. It is beyond the scope of this book to discuss objective regimes in more detail.
    The ICC Appeals Chamber has stated that '[International courts] do not act on behalf of a State or States. Rather, international courts act on behalf of the international community as a whole'. But it is not clear whether it sees the Court's legal basis as individual delegation or collective conferral, or something different entirely: *Prosecutor v Al Bashir (Judgment in the Jordan Referral re Al-Bashir Appeal)* (International Criminal Court, Appeals Chamber, Case No ICC/02/05-01/09, 6 May 2019) para 115. This decision will be discussed further in Chapters 4 and 6.
[91] Pre-Trial Chamber I described the ICC as 'a legal-judicial-institutional entity': *Request under Regulation 46(3) of the Regulations of the Court (Decision on the "Prosecution's Request for a Ruling on Jurisdiction under Article 19(3) of the Statute")* (International Criminal Court, Pre-Trial Chamber I, Case No ICC-RoC46(3)-01/18, 6 September 2018) para 48.

under-conceptualised. By necessity, an analysis of delegated jurisdiction must begin with some basic consideration of the concept of jurisdiction itself, which, unsurprisingly, is difficult to define with any precision. In international law scholarship and jurisprudence there is a veritable labyrinth of sub-concepts and terminology that needs to be navigated in order to reach an understanding of what is meant by jurisdiction.[92] Until now, I have been deliberately general in my use of the word 'jurisdiction' in this book, but the rest of this chapter will demonstrate why the term needs to be clarified and why its interpretation matters when talking about delegation of jurisdiction to the ICC.

At the outset it is necessary to differentiate between two distinct applications of the term 'jurisdiction', both of which are relevant to the ICC. The first relates to a State's general legal competence to exercise authority over territory and persons by virtue of its sovereignty.[93] One of the most helpful explanations of this type of jurisdiction comes from Frederick A Mann's 1964 Hague lectures on 'The Doctrine of Jurisdiction in International Law':

> Jurisdiction involves a state's *right* to exercise certain of its powers. It is a problem, accordingly, that is entirely distinct from that of internal power or constitutional capacity or, indeed, sovereignty. There is, of course, no doubt that, as a matter of internal law, a State is free to legislate in whatever manner and for whatever purpose it chooses. But like all other attributes of sovereignty this liberty is subject to the overriding question of entitlement. The existence in fact or in municipal law of the State's power to do a particular act does not by any means imply its international right to do so.[94]

In other words, jurisdiction in this context concerns the question of whether a State has the right under international law to exercise certain powers. 'Powers' refers broadly to those 'public powers of government or administration [that] derive from the sovereignty of a State', including

---

[92] Amerasinghe, *Jurisdiction of International Tribunals*, p. 52; FA Mann, 'The Doctrine of Jurisdiction in International Law' (1964) 111 *Recueil des Cours de l'Academie de Droit Internationale* 1 at 9; Ryngaert, *Jurisdiction in International Law*; F Berman, 'Jurisdiction: The State' in SV Konstadinidis, MD Evans and P Capps (eds), *Asserting Jurisdiction: International and European Legal Approaches* (Hart Publishing, 2003) pp. 3–4. For a concise overview of the various ways in which the term 'jurisdiction' is used, see R Liivoja, 'The Criminal Jurisdiction of States – A Theoretical Primer' (2010) 7 *No Foundations* 25 at 25–7.

[93] J Crawford and I Brownlie, *Principles of Public International Law*, 8th ed (Oxford University Press, 2012) p. 456.

[94] Mann, 'The Doctrine of Jurisdiction in International Law', 9. Emphasis original.

3.4 JURISDICTION IN INTERNATIONAL LAW

powers relating to criminal justice.[95] This distinction between 'powers' and the legal right to exercise those powers is essential, and for the purposes of this book, I will refer broadly to a State's international legal right to exercise certain powers as its 'sovereign jurisdiction'.

The second use of 'jurisdiction' is much narrower and largely concerns the exercise of judicial powers by courts and associated entities of the domestic judicial system.[96] Courts represent a mechanism through which a State exercises certain of its sovereign powers over persons and territory.[97] Courts are given particular judicial competences by a State's domestic legal framework. To say that a court has jurisdiction over someone or over a particular geographical area means that it has the legal right to exercise certain judicial powers over that person or that territory. The question of whether a court has such 'judicial jurisdiction' is a matter of procedure.[98]

Distinguishing between sovereign jurisdiction and judicial jurisdiction is useful for discussing jurisdiction in the context of the ICC. When reference is made to 'the jurisdiction of the ICC' this describes its judicial jurisdiction. Determining what is meant by delegation of jurisdiction, however, involves an analysis of both the judicial and sovereign jurisdiction of States Parties. The relevance of this distinction will become further apparent in later chapters. The rest of this part explores aspects of a State's jurisdiction over criminal matters, and where applicable, it also explains how particular terms apply to the ICC.

3.4.1 Jurisdiction to Prescribe (Adjudicate) and Enforce

When discussing jurisdiction in international law, the majority of scholars appear to have followed the influential 1987 Restatement (Third) of the Foreign Relations Law of the United States which identified three subcategories of sovereign jurisdiction that concern the power of a State to prescribe, to adjudicate and to enforce laws.[99] According to the

---

[95] Sarooshi, 'Conferrals by States of Powers on International Organizations', 291.
[96] A Cassese, 'When May Senior State Officials Be Tried for International Crimes? Some Comments on the Congo v. Belgium Case' (2002) 13 *European Journal of International Law* 853 at 858.
[97] Liivoja, 'The Criminal Jurisdiction of States – A Theoretical Primer', 35.
[98] M Hirst, *Jurisdiction and the Ambit of the Criminal Law* (Oxford University Press, 2003) p. 10.
[99] *Restatement of the Law Third, Foreign Relations Law of the United States* (American Law Institute, 1987) §401; Akehurst, 'Jurisdiction in International Law', 145; Brownlie, *Principles of Public International Law*, p. 299; Ryngaert, *Jurisdiction in International Law*, pp. 9–10; LN Sadat and SR Carden, 'The New International Criminal Court: An Uneasy Revolution' (1999) 88 *Georgetown Law Journal* 381 at 406.

Restatement, jurisdiction to prescribe relates to the authority to make laws 'applicable to the activities, relations, or status of persons, or the interests of persons';[100] jurisdiction to adjudicate describes the power of a State 'to subject persons or things to the process of its courts or administrative tribunals';[101] and jurisdiction to enforce refers to powers 'to induce or compel compliance or to punish noncompliance with its laws or regulations'.[102] Not all writers subscribe to the tripartite division of jurisdiction, with some preferring a twofold distinction between legislative and prerogative jurisdiction,[103] or between the jurisdiction to prescribe and to apply.[104] The totality of the jurisdictional powers remains the same no matter whether they are divided among two or three categories, but scholars who promote a twofold distinction are not always in agreement about how these powers should be divided.[105] For the purposes of this book, it is useful to apply a two-part division between prescriptive and enforcement jurisdiction and to adopt Roger O'Keefe's interpretation of such.[106] O'Keefe is not the first to advocate for this particular split; his argument builds on the conceptualisation of twofold jurisdiction adopted by others.[107] But O'Keefe's scholarship provides one of the more comprehensive explanations of the distinct aspects of jurisdiction, particularly as they relate to criminal matters.

According to O'Keefe's description, jurisdiction to prescribe in the criminal context encompasses a State's right to enact laws proscribing particular conduct as criminal, and to apply those laws to certain persons

---

[100] *Restatement of the Law Third, Foreign Relations Law of the United States* (American Law Institute, 1987) §401.
[101] Ibid.
[102] Ibid. These descriptions have remained the same in the Fourth Restatement: *Restatement of the Law Fourth, Foreign Relations Law of the United States* (American Law Institute, 2017) §401.
[103] Mann, 'The Doctrine of Jurisdiction in International Law', 13.
[104] R Higgins, 'The Legal Bases of Jurisdiction' in CJ Olmstead (ed), *Extra-Territorial Application of Laws and Responses Thereto* (International Law Association in association with ESC, 1984) p. 4. See also Crawford and Brownlie, *Brownlie's Principles of Public International Law*, p. 456.
[105] Adjudicative jurisdiction is sometimes included as part of prescriptive jurisdiction and other times as part of enforcement jurisdiction. Liivoja, 'The Criminal Jurisdiction of States – A Theoretical Primer', 31.
[106] R O'Keefe, 'Universal Jurisdiction: Clarifying the Basic Concept' (2004) 2 *Journal of International Criminal Justice* 735 at 737.
[107] See, eg, Mann, 'The Doctrine of Jurisdiction in International Law', 13; Brownlie, *Principles of Public International Law*, p. 299; Higgins, 'The Legal Bases of Jurisdiction', p. 4; MN Shaw, *International Law*, 7th ed (Cambridge University Press, 2014) p. 469.

and territory.[108] This includes the application of criminal law by a State's criminal courts.[109] Jurisdiction to enforce comprises a State's powers to investigate and collect evidence, to issue subpoenas, to arrest and retain custody over defendants, to convene a criminal trial, to incarcerate, etc.[110] '[I]n short, to exercise any or all of the usual range of police, prosecutorial, judicial and related executive powers in relation to criminal justice.'[111] This division is also suitable for describing the jurisdiction of the ICC. Ascribing aspects of prescriptive and enforcement jurisdiction to the ICC does not mean that the Court has the power to make laws or to enforce them in the sense that it can compel compliance. But the Court does have elements of prescriptive jurisdiction to the extent that it has the right to apply law to certain persons and territory. It has limited enforcement jurisdiction in that it is empowered to, inter alia, investigate crimes, issue arrest warrants and keep suspects in custody.

3.4.2 Principles of Criminal Jurisdiction under International Law

Under customary international law there are five accepted principles under which a State has the right to exercise its powers over criminal matters: territoriality, nationality, passive personality, protection and universality. A recitation of these principles of jurisdiction is almost mandatory in any discussion of criminal jurisdiction in international law. It is indeed necessary to set them out here to explain where they fit within the broader context of jurisdiction as a concept, and to clarify how they are applicable to the delegation theory for ICC jurisdiction. I deal first with territorial jurisdiction before examining the grounds on which a State may exercise jurisdiction extraterritorially.

3.4.2.1   Territoriality Principle

At its essence, territorial jurisdiction is a manifestation of State sovereignty[112] and is considered to be of fundamental importance in the international legal system.[113] In criminal matters, jurisdiction exercisable under the territoriality principle allows a State to prescribe and enforce with respect to crimes committed on its territory. The *locus*

---

[108] R O'Keefe, *International Criminal Law* (Oxford University Press, 2015) p. 6.
[109] O'Keefe, 'Universal Jurisdiction', 737.
[110] O'Keefe, *International Criminal Law*, p. 29.
[111] Ibid.
[112] Ibid., p. 9.
[113] *SS Lotus (France v Turkey)* [1927] PCIJ (Series A) No 10, 20.

delicti commissi is generally the *forum conveniens* due to the ease and expediency of gathering evidence and locating witnesses. Prosecuting international crimes where they were committed can also have a significant psychological impact on the affected community, providing some sense of resolution and justice.[114]

The assertion of territorial jurisdiction over criminal matters is not without its challenges. There may be questions as to what constitutes territory within a State's sovereign authority. For example, an aircraft in international airspace or a ship on the high seas may be considered analogous to the territory of the flag State for the purposes of jurisdiction,[115] but foreign vessels in territorial waters will be subject to criminal jurisdiction of the coastal State in most circumstances.[116] Issues may further arise where a crime is planned in one State and committed in another, giving rise to a potential conflict of territorial jurisdictions.[117] There is no uniform practice among States as to which jurisdiction has priority in such a scenario.[118] Despite such uncertainties, territorial jurisdiction maintains a particular significance in matters of international criminal law due to the high value that States place on the

---

[114] A Cassese and P Gaeta (eds), *Cassese's International Criminal Law*, 3rd ed (Oxford University Press, 2013) pp. 274–5.

[115] See, eg, the earlier ICC preliminary examination into the situation on the vessel *Mavi Marmara*, which was registered to the Union of the Comoros, a State Party to the Rome Statute. Under Article 12(2)(a) of the Statute, the *Mavi Marmara* is considered territory of the Comoros: Office of the Prosecutor, Situation on Registered *Vessels of Comoros, Greece and Cambodia Article 53(1) Report* (6 November 2014) 13. While the ICC would have had jurisdiction over this situation on that basis, the Prosecutor declined to proceed with an investigation: *Situation on the Registered Vessels of the Union of the Comoros, the Hellenic Republic and the Kingdom of Cambodia (Final decision of the Prosecutor concerning the 'Article 53(1) Report'* (ICC-01/13-6-AnxA), dated 6 November 2014) (International Criminal Court, Office of the Prosecutor, Case No ICC-01/13, 2 December 2019).

[116] Article 27 *United Nations Convention on the Law of the Sea 1982*, opened for signature 10 December 1982, 1833 UNTS 3 (entered into force 16 November 1994).

[117] For a detailed analysis of the complexities of territorial jurisdiction, see generally Vagias, *The Territorial Jurisdiction of the International Criminal Court*; Ryngaert, *Jurisdiction in International Law*, pp. 49–100. See also, the ICC investigation into the situation in Bangladesh/Myanmar. The Prosecutor is investigating allegations that officials of Myanmar (a non-State Party) have committed crimes against humanity by deporting members of the Rohingya ethnic group to Bangladesh (a State Party). The Appeals Chamber authorised the Prosecutor to investigate crimes 'committed at least in part on the territory of Bangladesh'. *Situation in Bangladesh/Myanmar (Decision Pursuant to Article 15 of the Rome Statute on the Authorisation of an Investigation into the Situation in the People's Republic of Bangladesh/Republic of Myanmar)* (International Criminal Court, Pre-Trial Chamber III, Case No. ICC-01/19, 14 November 2019) para 124.

[118] Cassese and Gaeta, *Cassese's International Criminal Law*, p. 276.

principles of sovereign equality and non-intervention. There are, however, limited circumstances in which a State can extend its prescriptive jurisdiction extraterritorially.

3.4.2.2 Extraterritorial Jurisdiction

Cedric Ryngaert advises that the word extraterritorial 'might best be avoided' in relation to jurisdiction because it is often inaccurately deployed as a shorthand for 'not *exclusively* territorial'.[119] Ryngaert further reasons that even where a State is asserting jurisdiction over a crime with no territorial link to the prosecuting State, such jurisdiction is still exercised territorially in the courts of the prosecuting State.[120] This is technically true, but given the pervasiveness of the term extraterritorial jurisdiction and the absence of any appropriate alternative, I will continue to apply it in this book to situations where the crime being prosecuted was committed entirely outside the territory of the prosecuting State.

***Lotus* Case** The 1927 PCIJ *Lotus* case is the 'inescapable starting point'[121] for any discussion of the legality of extraterritorial criminal jurisdiction.[122] The case originated from a collision that occurred on the high seas between the French steamer *SS Lotus* and a Turkish collier. The Turkish vessel sank causing the deaths of eight crewmembers and passengers. When the *SS Lotus* docked in Turkey, its officer of the watch was charged and convicted of involuntary manslaughter under Turkish law. France objected to Turkey exercising criminal jurisdiction over a French national for a crime that did not occur on Turkish territory.[123] The majority of the PCIJ found in favour of Turkey, reasoning that international law does not prohibit a State from exercising jurisdiction in its own territory, over acts that occurred outside its territory. Contrary to what was argued by France, the PCIJ held that Turkey did not need to identify a permissive rule of international law in order for it to be allowed to prosecute the French officer for the Lotus collision. Instead, the majority found that when it comes to the extraterritorial application of jurisdiction, international law gives States:

---

[119] Ryngaert, *Jurisdiction in International Law*, p. 8. Emphasis original.
[120] Ibid.
[121] Cassese and Gaeta, *Cassese's International Criminal Law*, p. 272.
[122] *SS Lotus (France v Turkey) (Judgment)* [1927] PCIJ (Series A) No 10.
[123] Ibid., 7.

a wide measure of discretion which is only limited in certain cases by prohibitive rules; as regards other cases, every State remains free to adopt the principles which it regards as best and most suitable. ... In these circumstances, all that can be required of a State is that it should not overstep the limits which international law places upon its jurisdiction; within these limits, its title to exercise jurisdiction rests in its sovereignty.[124]

In Judge Loder's dissenting opinion, His Excellency summarised the majority's reasoning in a pithy one line: 'under international law, every door is open unless it is closed by treaty or by established custom'.[125] Described decades later in an ICJ joint separate opinion as the 'high water mark of *laissez-faire* in international relations',[126] the *Lotus* case has received significant criticism in international law scholarship, with many commentators concluding that it no longer represents good law.[127] Instead, the prevailing opinion among scholars is that a State can only exercise prescriptive jurisdiction over crimes committed outside of its territory where one of four recognised principles of extraterritorial jurisdiction applies: nationality; passive personality; the protective principle; and universality. I return to the *Lotus* decision later in the chapter to discuss its continuing relevance for the exercise of extraterritorial jurisdiction in modern international law. First, however, I will provide a brief overview of each of the permissive principles of extraterritorial jurisdiction.

Permissive Principles of Extraterritorial Jurisdiction
Nationality Principle

The nationality principle, sometimes referred to as the active personality principle, is one of two principles of personal jurisdiction (the other being passive personality, discussed below. The nationality principle allows a State to exercise prescriptive jurisdiction over its own nationals for conduct occurring outside the State of nationality's

---

[124] Ibid., 19.
[125] Ibid., 34 (Judge Loder).
[126] *Arrest Warrant of 11 April 2000 (Congo v Belgium)* [2002] ICJ Rep 2001 (Joint Separate Opinion of Judges Higgins, Kooijmans and Buergenthal) para 51.
[127] See, eg, Crawford and Brownlie, *Brownlie's Principles of Public International Law*, p. 478; GD Triggs, *International Law: Contemporary Principles and Practices* (LexisNexis Butterworths, 2006) p. 349. In 1964 Mann wrote '[i]t can be confidently asserted that [the *Lotus* reasoning has] been condemned by the majority of the immense number of writers who have discussed [it]': Mann, 'The Doctrine of Jurisdiction in International Law', 35. Although see O'Keefe, *International Criminal Law*, p. 7.

territory.[128] While many States have limited their exercise of jurisdiction on the basis of nationality to serious crimes only, international law does not limit the nationality principle in this way.[129] Furthermore, it is not necessary for the conduct being prosecuted to be criminalised by the *lex loci delicti commissi*. It is sufficient for the conduct to constitute a crime under the *lex fori*.[130] Problems with respect to the assertion of jurisdiction based on the nationality principle may arise where an accused is a dual national, or where there has been a change of nationality in the period between the commission of the crime and its prosecution.[131]

Passive Personality Principle

Passive personality allows a State to assert prescriptive jurisdiction over criminal acts that take place outside its territory where one or more of its nationals is a victim of the crime. Unlike the nationality principle which is a non-controversial basis for extraterritorial jurisdiction, passive personality (or passive nationality) has been criticised as 'an excess of jurisdiction'.[132] In particular it raises issues with respect to defendants' rights, particularly when defendants subject to a claim of passive personality jurisdiction may be ignorant of the foreign law, and unaware of its applicability to their actions.[133]

Under the various anti-terrorism treaties, States Parties are given jurisdiction over acts of terrorism committed extraterritorially where 'the offence has been committed by or against a national or permanent resident of such State'.[134] In customary international law, however, there

---

[128] Under Division 272 of Australia's *Criminal Code Act 1995* (Cth), for example, it is a criminal offence for Australian citizens to participate in child sex tourism overseas.
[129] 'Harvard Research in International Law, Jurisdiction with Respect to Crime' (1935) 29 *Supplement to the American Journal of International Law* 435 at 531.
[130] Cassese and Gaeta, *Cassese's International Criminal Law*, p. 276.
[131] Crawford and Brownlie, *Brownlie's Principles of Public International Law*, p. 460; Z Deen-Racsmany, 'The Nationality of the Offender and the Jurisdiction of the International Criminal Court' (2001) 95 *American Journal of International Law* 606. For a discussion of nationality in international law more generally, see Crawford and Brownlie, *Brownlie's Principles of Public International Law*, pp. 509–26; *Nottebohm Case (Liechtenstein v Guatemala) (Second Phase, Judgment)* [1955] ICJ Rep 4.
[132] Mann, 'The Doctrine of Jurisdiction in International Law', 92.
[133] Ryngaert, *Jurisdiction in International Law*, pp. 110–11.
[134] See, eg, *Convention on Offences and Certain Other Acts Committed on Board Aircraft*, opened for signature 14 September 1963, 704 UNTS 219 (entered into force 4 December 1969), Article 4(b). Other examples include Article 6(2)(b) of the *Convention for the Suppression of Unlawful Acts against the Safety of Maritime*

is some question as to whether a permissive rule allowing for jurisdiction based on passive personality does actually exist. Ryngaert posits that passive personality jurisdiction may instead fall under the legal umbrella of the *Lotus* case, enabling such jurisdiction in the absence of a prohibitive rule to the contrary.[135]

Protective Principle

Under the protective principle of jurisdiction, a State may assert prescriptive jurisdiction over the extraterritorial acts of non-nationals if they threaten the national security or key interests of the prosecuting State. Despite the potentially broad nature of this jurisdictional basis, the invocation of the protective principle has not been particularly controversial. It has been used for offences such as drug smuggling[136] and illegal immigration,[137] for example. More questionable was the District Court of Jerusalem's application of the protective principle in *Israel v Eichmann*,[138] given the fact that the State of Israel did not exist at the time the offences were committed.[139]

Universality Principle

The final principle of extraterritorial jurisdiction is universality, which gives rise to universal jurisdiction. This allows for a State to extend its laws to any individual, of any nationality, for certain crimes committed anywhere in the world. According to some commentators, 'true' or 'pure' universal jurisdiction is only exercised where the prosecuting State does not have any nexus whatsoever to the crime, including custody of the

---

Navigation, opened for signature 10 March 1988, 1678 UNTS 221 (entered into force 26 June 1992); Article 5(d) of the *Convention against the Taking of Hostages*, opened for signature 17 December 1979, 1316 UNTS 205 (entered into force 3 June 1983). See also Division 115 of Australia's *Criminal Code Act 1995* (Cth) which gives Australia criminal jurisdiction over crimes that harm Australians abroad.

[135] Ryngaert, *Jurisdiction in International Law*, p. 112.
[136] *United States v Newball* 524 F Supp 715 (EDNY 1981): 'Drug smuggling threatens the security and sovereignty of the United States by affecting its armed forces, contributes to widespread crime, and circumvents federal customs and laws' at 720.
[137] *Naim Molvan, Owner of Motor Vessel 'Asya' v A-G (Palestine)* [1948] AC 351 [UK]; *Giles v Tumminello* [1963] SASR 96 [Australia].
[138] *Attorney-General of the Government of Israel v Adolf Eichmann* (1962) 36 ILR 5, 54–7. The application of the protective principle was accepted by the Supreme Court, at 304. I return to this case in Chapter 6.
[139] Crawford and Brownlie, *Brownlie's Principles of Public International Law*, p. 462.

accused.[140] Given that universal jurisdiction only gives States the right to prescribe laws that extend universally; States cannot enforce these laws unless they also have custody of the defendant.[141] But due to the significant procedural problems and human rights concerns of conducting a trial *in absentia*, States generally do not prosecute without first acquiring custody of the accused.[142] How universal jurisdiction may or may not be applicable to the ICC will be the focus of Chapter 6.

Prohibitive vs Permissive Rules I return now to examine the current status of extraterritorial jurisdiction in international law as there is still some question about how the prohibitive rule of the *Lotus* case can be reconciled with the existence of permissive principles. Are States only allowed to exercise extraterritorial jurisdiction when they can demonstrate a permissive rule based on the nationality, protective, passive personality or universality principles? Or, in accordance with the *Lotus* case, are States allowed to exercise jurisdiction extraterritorially in whatever manner they choose as long as there is no prohibitive rule to the contrary?

Despite the controversy over the *Lotus* decision, it remains central to the analysis of extraterritorial jurisdiction. As James Crawford and Ian Brownlie point out, it is the only decision by an international court that directly deals with this aspect of jurisdiction.[143] Rather than insisting on either the *Lotus* approach or the permissive rules approach as the only correct interpretation of extraterritorial jurisdiction in international law, a more nuanced view acknowledges the legitimacy of both.[144] Cassese, for example, recognises that the divergence between the two approaches is the result of 'one's own understanding of sovereignty and of the role and function of international law in a society whose primary subjects are sovereign states'.[145] Directly applicable here, is Martti Koskenniemi's

---

[140] See, eg, A Cassese, 'Is the Bell Tolling for Universality? A Plea for a Sensible Notion of Universal Jurisdiction' (2003) 1 *Journal of International Criminal Justice* 589 at 592; G Abi-Saab, 'The Proper Role of Universal Jurisdiction' (2003) 1 *Journal of International Criminal Justice* 596 at 601; Reydams, *Universal Jurisdiction*, p. 38. See also Section 6.2.
[141] Crawford and Brownlie, *Brownlie's Principles of Public International Law*, p. 478.
[142] *Arrest Warrant of 11 April 2000 (Congo v Belgium)* [2002] ICJ Rep 2001 (declaration of Judge Ranjeva) 55–7; (separate opinion of Judge ad hoc Bula-Bula) 121–6.
[143] Crawford and Brownlie, *Brownlie's Principles of Public International Law*, p. 477. See also Ryngaert, *Jurisdiction in International Law*, pp. 30–2.
[144] P Weil, 'International Law Limitations on State Jurisdiction' in CJ Olmstead (ed), *Extra-Territorial Application of Laws and Responses Thereto* (Internaional Law Association in association with ESC, 1984) p. 33; Ryngaert, *Jurisdiction in International Law*, p. 29.
[145] Cassese and Gaeta, *Cassese's International Criminal Law*, pp. 272–3.

acknowledgment of sovereignty as 'ascending' and/or 'descending', discussed in Chapter 2.[146] It is unsurprising that most scholars of international law and jurisdiction should be so insistent on the permissive rules approach to extraterritorial jurisdiction, given their natural preference for the descending perspective on sovereignty. As articulated by Prosper Weil,

> [t]he prevailing view – from Bourgin and Basdevant to Brierly, from Sir Gerald Fitzmaurice to Rousseau – is that state jurisdiction is not limited, but rather conferred, by international law. International law, in their view, is the source of state jurisdiction; states exercise their jurisdiction by delegation, as it were, of international law.[147]

Conversely, supporters of the *Lotus* approach view sovereignty as inherent to States, and State jurisdiction only limited by international law where necessary to prevent interference with a foreign State's sovereignty.[148] This corresponds to the ascending perspective on sovereignty. Although there is a preference for the permissive rules approach among scholars and the judiciary, the majority reasoning in the *Lotus* case continues to survive.[149] Ryngaert observes that a State's preference for either the *Lotus* approach or the permissive rules approach may depend on whether a State is asserting extraterritorial jurisdiction or opposing another State's claim to jurisdiction.[150] For example, the asserting State might claim the *Lotus* approach in order to shift the burden of proof to the opposing State to demonstrate that there is a rule of international law prohibiting such jurisdiction. The opposing State might prefer the permissive rules approach to require the asserting State to show that its behaviour is in compliance with one of the four principles of extraterritorial jurisdiction.[151]

---

[146] M Koskenniemi, *From Apology to Utopia: The Structure of International Legal Argument: Reissue with a New Epilogue* (Cambridge University Press, 2005) pp. 225–30.
[147] Weil, 'International Law Limitations on State Jurisdiction', p. 32. See also, Mann who asserts that '[t]he existence of the State's right to exercise jurisdiction is exclusively determined by *public international law*' (emphasis original): Mann, 'The Doctrine of Jurisdiction in International Law', 10–11.
[148] Mégret, 'Epilogue to an Endless Debate', 252; Weil, 'International Law Limitations on State Jurisdiction', p. 33.
[149] The ICJ did little to clarify the status of *Lotus* in *Arrest Warrant of 11 April 2000 (Congo v Belgium)* [2002] ICJ Rep 2001 (Joint Separate Opinion of Judges Higgins, Kooijmans and Buergenthal, paras 50–1; Separate Opinion of Judge Guillaume, para 14).
[150] Ryngaert, *Jurisdiction in International Law*, p. 29.
[151] Ibid., p. 21.

For the purposes of this chapter, it is unnecessary to discuss the divergence between the *Lotus* approach and the permissive rules approach any further. The delegation of jurisdiction theory is compatible with either approach, although delegation does tend to be associated with the permissive rules approach given the explicit reference to territoriality and nationality in the Rome Statute.

3.4.3   Conclusion to Section 3.4

To summarise, under international law, States have the right to exercise their sovereign powers by prescribing and enforcing laws on the basis of certain permissive principles. These laws form the domestic legal framework that regulates how the State's powers are exercised internally. Under the domestic legal framework a State's courts are empowered with particular judicial competences, which allow them to exercise judicial jurisdiction.

Under the Rome Statute, the ICC has the power to, inter alia, conduct investigations; issue orders and warrants for arrest; confirm charges; convene criminal trials; pronounce on guilt or innocence; and apply penalties.[152] The Statute also sets out the circumstances in which the ICC may use these powers; analogous to how a State's domestic legal framework regulates the internal exercise of the State's sovereign powers.[153] The jurisdiction provisions of the Statute are what give the Court the right to exercise its powers with respect to particular conduct; over specified territory; in relation to certain individuals and within a limited timeframe.[154] These Statute provisions mean that the ICC is strictly limited in its authority; it cannot go beyond what the Rome Statute provides.

3.5   Conclusion

The purpose of this chapter was to examine the notion that the jurisdiction of the ICC is predicated on delegation from States Parties. The debates in the early scholarship show that there is nothing to legally prevent States from delegating their powers of criminal justice to an

---

[152] See, eg, Rome Statute, Articles 53–8; 61–4; 66(3); 76–8.
[153] D Sarooshi, 'The Essentially Contested Nature of the Concept of Sovereignty: Implications for the Exercise by International Organizations of Delegated Powers of Government' (2003) 25 *Michigan Journal of International Law* 1107 at 1122.
[154] See, eg, Rome Statute, Articles 5–8; 11–13.

international court. What has been lacking in the literature is a conceptual analysis of what 'delegation of jurisdiction' actually means in the context of the ICC. Such an analysis, I argued, is a necessary precursor to determining whether and how this theory provides a legal basis for the Court's jurisdiction in all circumstances allowed by the Rome Statute.

Jurisdiction is essentially the legal right to exercise power, whether it is the State's right to exercise sovereign power or a court's right to exercise judicial powers. In international institutional law, when the term 'delegation' is used, it is in the context of delegation of powers. In adopting the Rome Statute, States at Rome agreed to establish an international organisation and delegate to it certain powers of prescription and enforcement that each State possesses by virtue of its sovereignty. The ICC's right to exercise these powers under the Rome Statute reflects the right of States themselves to exercise their powers of criminal justice in accordance with the customary principles of territoriality and nationality.[155]

Conceiving of the legal basis for such jurisdiction as delegation from States Parties addresses the perceived problem of State consent when nationals from non-States Parties come within the jurisdiction of the Court. States may prosecute foreign nationals for crimes committed on their territory, and the consent of the State of nationality is not required under international law. In the abstract, therefore, delegation of jurisdiction is a sound theory to explain how and why the ICC is lawfully empowered to exercise jurisdiction over nationals of non-States Parties. Whether the delegation theory provides a legal basis for ICC authority in different situations involving non-party nationals will be analysed in the following chapters.

---

[155] Although this does not include situations involving a UN Security Council referral, in which case some commentators talk about the ICC as exercising 'universal jurisdiction'. This notion will be discussed in Chapters 5 and 6.

4

Delegation of Jurisdiction: Application and Limitations

4.1 Introduction

This chapter explores whether delegation of jurisdiction provides a legal basis for the ICC to prosecute nationals of non-States Parties in situations that have been referred to the ICC by a State Party, or where investigations have been initiated *proprio motu* by the ICC Prosecutor.[1] Specifically I analyse whether restrictions on a State's judicial jurisdiction[2] can affect the legal basis for the ICC's jurisdiction in certain circumstances. For example, are States Parties delegating only such jurisdiction as is exercisable in their domestic legal systems, or are they delegating territorial and nationality jurisdiction unaffected by limitations on domestic judicial jurisdiction? The question is important because there are situations and cases in which the ICC's jurisdiction is potentially complicated by immunities and other limitations that affect a State Party's domestic jurisdiction. If such limitations affect a State's delegable jurisdiction, this would in turn affect the legal basis for the ICC's jurisdiction. The analysis in this chapter is limited to the legal basis for ICC jurisdiction in situations that do not involve the UN Security Council. Chapter 5 will explore the Security Council's relationship with the ICC.

Section 4.2 of this chapter begins by addressing whether a State's domestic legal framework has any effect on what a State Party can delegate to the ICC. It demonstrates that the parameters of a State's delegable jurisdiction are defined by international, not domestic, law. On the basis of this conclusion the rest of the chapter then focuses on whether there are any restrictions on delegable jurisdiction under international law.

In Section 4.3 I investigate whether personal immunities under customary international law have any bearing on delegation of jurisdiction

---

[1] This chapter is primarily addressing situations that come before the Court via the Article 13(a) or 13(c) avenues. It does not deal with situations referred by the UN Security Council in accordance with Article 13(b), unless otherwise stated.
[2] For the difference between 'judicial' and 'sovereign' jurisdiction, see Section 3.4.

to the ICC. I use a hypothetical scenario in which a sitting Head of State from a non-State Party is wanted by the ICC. This section begins with some necessary background discussion on the status of Head of State immunity before the ICC. Here, I examine judicial consideration of this issue by the ICC itself, which has left a number of questions unsettled. Uncertainty remains, for example, over whether the Court can lawfully issue a request for the arrest and transfer of a foreign Head of a non-State Party in circumstances that do not involve a Security Council referral. Ultimately I argue that delegation of jurisdiction would not provide a legal basis for the ICC to prosecute such an individual considering that States Parties are precluded under customary international law from exercising jurisdiction over foreign incumbent Heads of State.

Section 4.4 uses the examples of Afghanistan and Palestine to further explore the possible limitations on delegable jurisdiction under international law. Each of these situations raise unique legal obstacles that could affect whether the ICC is able to exercise jurisdiction over certain nationals of non-States Parties on the basis of delegated jurisdiction. I use the Afghanistan situation as a case study to examine whether bilateral immunities contained in status of forces agreements (SOFAs) would affect the jurisdiction of the ICC. With respect to the situation in Palestine, I discuss how the question of Palestinian statehood and the existence of the Oslo Accords might affect Palestine's ability to delegate jurisdiction.

I establish that where a State's own jurisdiction is restricted, its delegable jurisdiction will only be affected by limitations contained in customary international law. A State's delegable jurisdiction will not be affected by the *lex loci* nor will it be limited by any immunities contained in a bilateral or multilateral agreement. Conceptualising delegation of jurisdiction in this way will allow the ICC to lawfully exercise its powers over nationals of non-States Parties in almost all circumstances provided for in the Rome Statute.

4.2 Is Delegation of Jurisdiction Affected by National Laws?

Recalling the discussion in Chapter 3, a State's judicial jurisdiction refers to the actual powers of jurisdiction exercisable by courts and associated entities in a State's domestic justice system. The parameters of this judicial jurisdiction are defined by the domestic legal framework. In this section I briefly address the question of whether a State Party's legal framework – the *lex loci* – affects State delegation of jurisdiction to the ICC.

4.2.1 The *Lex Loci* of State Party X

Consider the following hypothetical example: The Pre-Trial Chamber approves the Prosecutor's request to open an investigation *proprio motu* into the situation in State Party X. Charges are laid under Article 8(2)(b)(xxvi) of the Rome Statute against a national of State X for the war crime of conscripting or enlisting children under the age of fifteen into the armed forces. State X has not criminalised the conscription of child soldiers in its domestic law, meaning that State X's own courts do not have domestic judicial jurisdiction over such conduct.[3] How, then, can State X be said to have delegated its jurisdiction to the ICC when such jurisdiction does not exist in the *lex loci*? Conceptualising a State's delegable jurisdiction more broadly than its domestic judicial jurisdiction would overcome this hurdle.

Under customary international law, a sovereign State has the right to exercise wide-ranging powers of criminal justice over its territory and its nationals, and may choose for itself the specific parameters that its jurisdiction will take within that territory.[4] In the *Arrest Warrant* case, the ICJ recognised that:

> national legislation reflects the circumstances in which a State provides in its own law the ability to exercise jurisdiction. But a State is not required to legislate up to the full scope of jurisdiction allowed by international law.[5]

Returning to the example in the previous paragraph, just because State X has not criminalised the conscription of child soldiers does not mean that it does not possess the right to do so under international law. It is State X's right to empower its legal system with jurisdiction over such acts (on the basis of territoriality, nationality etc.) that comprises its delegable jurisdiction. The argument for rejecting a narrow characterisation of delegable jurisdiction is further strengthened by considering the sheer diversity of the criminal laws and criminal justice systems among States

---

[3] There was some question during the drafting of the Rome Statute about whether conscription and enlistment of child soldiers was a war crime or a human rights issue: H von Hebel and D Robinson, 'Crimes within the Jurisdiction of the Court' in RS Lee (ed), *The International Criminal Court – The Making of the Rome Statute* (Kluwer Law International, 1999) p. 117; M Morris, 'High Crimes and Misconceptions: The ICC and Non-Party States' (2001) 64 *Law and Contemporary Problems* 13 at 28. See further discussion of this issue in Chapter 6.

[4] FA Mann, 'The Doctrine of Jurisdiction in International Law' (1964) 111 *Recueil des Cours de l'Academie de Droit Internationale* 1 at 9.

[5] *Arrest Warrant of 11 April 2000 (Congo v Belgium)* [2002] ICJ Rep 2001 para 45 (Joint Separate Opinion of Judges Higgins, Kooijmans and Buergenthal).

Parties.[6] It would be entirely unworkable if the jurisdiction of the ICC were subject to the vagaries of the *lex loci* of delegating States Parties.[7] Furthermore, the ICC's status as an entity with international legal personality means that the Court is exercising its own jurisdiction, not that of States Parties. The legal basis for such jurisdiction may be delegation from States Parties, but the ICC is not merely their agent.[8]

An interesting case study on the *lex loci* issue involves the question of Ukraine's ratification of the Rome Statute. In 2001 Ukraine's Constitutional Court held that ratification of the Rome Statute would be unconstitutional.[9] At the time, Article 124 of Ukraine's Constitution provided that administration of justice in Ukraine was to be undertaken only by its courts, and specifically prohibited delegation of any judicial functions to other entities.[10] This led the government of Ukraine to claim that it was unable to ratify the Rome Statute without an amendment to the Constitution because the delegation of any judicial powers was prohibited.[11] This constitutional

---

[6] See generally, K Heller and M Dubber (eds), *Handbook of Comparative Criminal Law* (Stanford University Press, 2010). That book contains a comparative analysis of the criminal laws in sixteen countries, nine of which are States Parties to the Rome Statute.

[7] See also, RK Woetzel, *The Nuremberg Trials in International Law with a Postlude on the Eichmann Case* (Steven & Sons Ltd, 1962) pp. 60–1. Note that Article 21(1)(c) of the Rome Statute does recognise, as a source of applicable law, 'general principles of law derived by the Court from national laws of legal systems of the world including, as appropriate, the national laws of States that would normally exercise jurisdiction over the crime'. Such principles are subsidiary to the Rome Statute, Elements of Crimes, Rules of Procedure, applicable treaties and principles of international law. Furthermore, Pre-Trial Chamber I has held that recourse to principles of law derived from national laws can only be had where there is a lacuna in the Rome Statute and Elements of Crimes: *Prosecutor v Al Bashir (Warrant of Arrest)* (International Criminal Court, Pre-Trial Chamber I, Case No ICC-02/05-01/09, 4 March 2009) para 126. See also, 'Article 21' in W Schabas, *The International Criminal Court: A Commentary on the Rome Statute*, 2nd ed (Oxford University Press, 2016) p. 515; G Bitti, 'Article 21 of the Statute of the International Criminal Court and the Treatment of Sources of Law in the Jurisprudence of the ICC' in G Sluiter and C Stahn (eds), *The Emerging Practice of the International Criminal Court* (Brill, 2008) pp. 281–304; M Vagias, 'The Territorial Jurisdiction of the International Criminal Court – A Jurisdictional Rule of Reason for the ICC?' (2012) 59 *Netherlands International Law Review* 43 at 101–30.

[8] On the difference between delegation and agency, see the discussion in Section 3.3.2.1.

[9] *Opinion of the Constitutional Court on the Conformity of the Rome Statute with the Constitution of Ukraine*, Case N 1-35/2001, 11 July 2001, summarised in ICRC, 'Issues Raised with Regard to the Rome Statute of the International Criminal Court by National Constitutional Courts, Supreme Courts and Councils of State' (January, 2003) 10.

[10] Ibid. In 2016, Ukraine's parliament amended Article 124 of the Constitution to recognise the jurisdiction of the ICC. The amendment came into force on 1 July 2019.

[11] International Criminal Court Press and Media, 'President of the Assembly of States Parties visit to Ukraine' (Press Release, ICC-ASP-20141009-PR1048, 9 October 2014).

prohibition notwithstanding, Ukraine nevertheless lodged declarations under Article 12(3) of the Rome Statute accepting ICC jurisdiction over its territory on an ad hoc basis.[12] Assuming delegation as the underlying basis on which the ICC exercises its powers, any State acceptance of ICC jurisdiction – even acceptance on an ad hoc basis under Article 12(3) – would involve an act of delegation.[13] It is entirely within a State's sovereign prerogative to restrict delegation of its powers under domestic law, but this does not affect the State's right to delegate under international law. It is therefore likely that Ukraine's Article 12(3) declarations were invalid under Ukraine's unamended Constitution but perfectly valid under the Rome Statute and customary international law.[14] It is another example of how the *lex loci* of a State does not affect the jurisdiction of the ICC.[15]

Ultimately, the jurisdiction of the ICC may not reflect the domestic judicial jurisdiction of a State's courts. As long as the State has the right, under international law, to empower its courts, then that jurisdiction is lawfully delegable to the ICC. To say that the ICC is exercising jurisdiction based on delegation from States Parties is without regard to the actual judicial jurisdiction of individual States' domestic courts.

While the *lex loci* does not influence delegation of jurisdiction, there may nevertheless be restrictions on delegable jurisdiction imposed by international law. The following examples explore how delegation of jurisdiction might be restricted by the application of international legal immunities, and whether that in turn would affect the legality of the ICC's jurisdiction over nationals of non-States Parties in certain circumstances.

---

[12] International Criminal Court Press and Media, 'Ukraine accepts ICC jurisdiction over alleged crimes committed between 21 November 2013 and 22 February 2014' (Press Release, ICC-CPI-20140417-PR997, 17 April 2014); *Declaration by Ukraine lodged under Article 12(3) of the Rome Statute* (8 September 2015).

[13] KJ Heller, 'Thoughts on the Ukraine Ad Hoc Self-Referral', *Opinio Juris* (18 April 2014).

[14] See also Article 46 of the Vienna Convention on the Law of Treaties which specifies that 'A State may not invoke the fact that its consent to be bound by a treaty has been expressed in violation of a provision of its internal law regarding competence to conclude treaties as invalidating its consent unless that violation was manifest and concerned a rule of its internal law of fundamental importance': *Vienna Convention on the Law of Treaties*, opened for signature 23 May 1969, 1155 UNTS 331 (entered into force 27 January 1980).

[15] For a discussion of how entering into treaties can affect domestic constitutions, see generally, TM Franck (ed), *Delegating State Powers: The Effect of Treaty Regimes on Democracy and Sovereignty* (Transnational Publishers, 2000).

4.3 Is Delegation of Jurisdiction Affected by Customary Immunities?

Under customary international law, incumbent senior State officials and diplomats accredited to a foreign State are immune from prosecution in foreign domestic courts. The Rome Statute, however, provides that immunities 'under national or international law' do not apply before the ICC.[16] This section examines whether delegation of jurisdiction provides a legal basis for ICC prosecution of incumbent presidents from non-States Parties in situations where crimes have been committed on the territory of a State Party.

4.3.1 ICC Jurisdiction over Sitting Heads of Non-States Parties

Aside from the two Security Council referrals, there have been a number of situations at the ICC which involve crimes allegedly committed by nationals of non-States Parties on the territory of States Parties. At the time of writing, the situations in Georgia,[17] Bangladesh/Myanmar,[18] Palestine[19] and Afghanistan[20] are under investigation, and there is a preliminary examination in Ukraine.[21] In the Georgian and Ukraine situations, it is alleged that Russian armed forces have been involved in committing Statute crimes; in Afghanistan, there are accusations of crimes committed by US soldiers; the situation in Palestine involves crimes allegedly committed by Israeli soldiers in the occupied Palestinian territories; and the Prosecutor is examining crimes committed against the Rohinghya by Myanmarese nationals, of which at least one element can

---

[16] Rome Statute, Article 27(2).
[17] *Situation in Georgia (Decision on the Prosecutor's request for authorization of an investigation)* (International Criminal Court, Pre-Trial Chamber I, Case No ICC-01/15, 27 January 2016).
[18] *Situation in Bangladesh/Myanmar (Decision Pursuant to Article 15 of the Rome Statute on the Authorisation of an Investigation into the Situation in the People's Republic of Bangladesh/Republic of Myanmar)* (International Criminal Court, Pre-Trial Chamber III, Case No. ICC-01/19, 14 November 2019).
[19] *Situation in the State of Palestine (Prosecution request pursuant to article 19(3) for a ruling on the Court's territorial jurisdiction in Palestine)* (International Criminal Court, Office of the Prosecutor, Case No ICC-01/18, 20 December 2019).
[20] *Situation in the Islamic Republic of Afghanistan (Judgment on the Appeal against the Decision on the Authorisation of an Investigation into the Situation in the Islamic Republic of Afghanistan)* (International Criminal Court, Appeals Chamber, Case No ICC-02/17 OA4, 5 March 2020).
[21] As mentioned above, Ukraine is not yet a State Party but has accepted the jurisdiction of the ICC under Article 12(3).

be said to have occurred in neighbouring Bangladesh.[22] Russia, the US, Israel and Myanmar are not party to the Rome Statute. Whether and how these particular examinations or investigations progress, the fact that the ICC has asserted jurisdiction over crimes allegedly committed by nationals of non-States Parties raises the possibility that the Court could indict Heads of State or other senior officials from such non-parties, even while they remain in office. To say that such an action would be controversial is an understatement, which is why it is necessary to examine whether the ICC could lawfully prosecute a sitting Head of State from a non-State Party in situations not involving a Security Council referral. Before analysing whether delegation of jurisdiction provides a legal basis for prosecution in such a case, it is useful to briefly discuss the doctrine of Head of State immunity and its exceptions.

4.3.2 *Prosecuting Sitting Heads of State: Background*

There is an almost overwhelming amount of scholarship[23] and judicial consideration[24] on the topic of individual and State immunities in

---

[22] I emphasise that nationals of Russia, the US and Israel are not the only ones accused of committing crimes in these situations.

[23] See, eg, J Foakes, *The Position of Heads of State and Senior Officials in International Law* (Oxford University Press, 2014); R Pedretti, *Immunity of Heads of State and State Officials for International Crimes* (Brill Nijhoff, 2015); SA Watts, 'The Legal Position in International Law of Heads of State, Heads of Government and Foreign Ministers' (1994) 247 *Recueil des Cours de l'Academie de Droit Internationale* 9; D Akande and S Shah, 'Immunities of State Officials, International Crimes, and Foreign Domestic Courts' (2010) 21 *European Journal of International Law* 815; R van Alebeek, *The Immunity of States and Their Officials in International Criminal Law and International Human Rights Law* (Oxford University Press, 2008); JC Barker, C Warbrick, and D McGoldrick, 'The Future of Former Head of State Immunity after ex parte Pinochet' (1999) 48 *The International and Comparative Law Quarterly* 937; G Buzzini, 'Lights and Shadows of Immunities and Inviolability of State Officials in International Law: Some Comments on the Djibouti v. France Case' (2009) 22 *Leiden Journal of International Law* 455; A Cassese, 'When May Senior State Officials Be Tried for International Crimes? Some Comments on the Congo v. Belgium Case' (2002) 13 *European Journal of International Law* 853; H Fox, 'The Resolution of the Institute of International Law on the Immunities of Heads of State and Government' (2002) 51 *International and Comparative Law Quarterly* 119; MA Tunks, 'Diplomats or Defendants? Defining the Future of Head-of-State Immunity' (2002) 52 *Duke Law Journal* 651; S Zappalà, 'Do Heads of State in Office Enjoy Immunity from Jurisdiction for International Crimes? The Ghaddafi Case Before the French Cour de Cassation' (2001) 12 *European Journal of International Law* 595; EH Franey, 'Immunity from the Criminal Jurisdiction of National Courts' in A Orakhelashvili (ed), *Research Handbook on Jurisdiction and Immunities in International Law* (Edward Elgar Publishing, 2015) p. 205.

[24] See, eg, *Arrest Warrant of 11 April 2000 (Congo v Belgium) (Judgment)* [2002] ICJ Rep 3; *R v Bow Street Stipendiary Magistrate; Ex parte Pinochet Ugarte* [1998] All ER 897

international law, indicative of the complexity of the issue. The discussion contained in this section can only scratch the surface of the legal issues surrounding Head of State immunity, but it is sufficient for the purposes of this book. I begin by providing an overview of Head of State immunity in foreign domestic courts before turning to discuss the prosecution of incumbent Heads of State by the ICC.[25]

4.3.2.1 Head of State Immunity in Customary International Law

The rationale behind conferring certain State officials with immunity from the jurisdiction of foreign domestic courts is to facilitate stable international relations.[26] Senior State officials who travel to foreign countries have unique diplomatic responsibilities, the performance of which is necessarily protected by the principle of immunity.[27] In customary international law, the doctrine of immunity comprises two distinct applications: immunity *ratione materiae* (functional immunity) and immunity *ratione personae* (personal or private immunity). Only the latter is relevant for my hypothetical case study, but I will first provide a brief summary of functional immunity in order to contextualise the relevance of personal immunity for the ICC.

Functional immunity attaches to all official acts attributable to the State and it is the State that bears responsibility for them rather than the

---

('*Pinochet I*'); *R v Bow Street Stipendiary Magistrate; Ex parte Pinochet Ugarte [No 2]* [1999] 1 All ER 577 ('*Pinochet II*'); *R v Bow Street Stipendiary Magistrate; Ex parte Pinochet Ugarte [No 3]* [2000] I AC 147 ('*Pinochet III*'); *Prosecutor v Blaškić (Judgement on the Request for the Republic of Croatia for Review of the Decision of Trial Chamber II of 18 July 1997)* (International Criminal Tribunal for the former Yugoslavia, Appeals Chamber, Case No IT-95-14-AR-108, 29 October 1997).

[25] The discussion in this section is limited to Heads of State and certain other senior officials, but it should be noted that diplomats also enjoy immunity from certain foreign domestic jurisdictions. This is a rule of customary international law that has been codified in the *Vienna Convention on Diplomatic Relations,* opened for signature 18 April 1961, 500 UNTS 95 (entered into force 24 April 1964) Article 31(1). See, generally, I Roberts, 'Privileges and Immunities of Diplomatic Agents' in I Roberts (ed), *Satow's Diplomatic Practice* (Oxford University Press, 2009) p. 121. See also, fn 30.

[26] C Wickremasinghe, 'Immunities Enjoyed by Officials of States and International Organizations' in MD Evans (ed), *International Law* (Oxford University Press, 2010) p. 380.

[27] See *Arrest Warrant of 11 April 2000 (Congo v Belgium) (Judgment)* [2002] ICJ Rep 3, 85 para 75 (Judges Higgins, Kooijmans and Buergenthal): 'immunities are granted to high State officials to guarantee proper functioning of the network of mutual inter-State relations, which is of paramount importance for a well-ordered and harmonious international system'.

4.3 DELEGATION AND CUSTOMARY IMMUNITIES

individual who performed the acts in his or her official capacity.[28] This type of immunity is based on the nature of the conduct rather than the status of the individual who carried out the act.[29] As such, it may be relied on by former officials (including Heads of State) for acts undertaken during their tenure in office as well as by individuals who perform acts on behalf of the State even if they are not State officials.[30] It has been argued that this type of immunity provides a substantive defence to any criminal charges, in the sense that functional immunity prevents legal responsibility from attaching to the individual, and instead shifts it to the State itself.[31] There is, however, a move towards recognising an exception to functional immunity for individuals accused of international crimes in both foreign domestic and international courts.[32]

---

[28] Pedretti, *Immunity of Heads of State and State Officials for International Crimes*, pp. 14–20.

[29] For a detailed discussion of what constitutes 'acts performed in an official capacity', see Foakes, *The Position of Heads of State and Senior Officials in International Law*, pp. 142–75.

[30] See, eg, Wickremasinghe, 'Immunities Enjoyed by Officials of States and International Organizations', p. 383; HF Van Panhuys, 'In the Borderland between the Act of State Doctrine and Questions of Jurisdictional Immunities' (1964) 13 *International and Comparative Law Quarterly* 1193 at 1201.

[31] See *Prosecutor v Blaškić (Objection to the Issue of Subpoena Duces Tecum)* (International Criminal Tribunal for the Former Yugoslavia, Appeals Chamber, Case No IT-95-14-AR-108, 18 July 1997) para 38. Contra, Foakes, *The Position of Heads of State and Senior Officials in International Law*, p. 10.

[32] Akande and Shah, 'Immunities of State Officials, International Crimes, and Foreign Domestic Courts', 828–51; Cassese, 'When May Senior State Officials Be Tried for International Crimes?', 865; S Wirth, 'Immunity for Core Crimes? The ICJ's Judgment in the Congo v. Belgium Case' (2002) 13 *European Journal of International Law* 877; Foakes, *The Position of Heads of State and Senior Officials in International Law*, pp. 149–60; Pedretti, *Immunity of Heads of State and State Officials for International Crimes*, pp. 307–8. Since 2007, the International Law Commission (ILC) has included the topic of 'Immunity of State Officials From Foreign Criminal Jurisdiction' in its programme of work. In July 2017, by a vote of twenty-one to eight (with one abstention) the ILC adopted draft Article 7 which provides that:

1. Immunity *ratione materiae* from the exercise of foreign criminal jurisdiction shall not apply in respect of the following crimes under international law:
   (a) crime of genocide;
   (b) crimes against humanity;
   (c) war crimes;
   (d) crime of *apartheid*;
   (e) torture;
   (f) enforced disappearance.

There is still significant resistance to the idea that there is a customary exception to function immunity before foreign domestic jurisdictions, although there is more acceptance of the

Irrespective of whether functional immunity applies, sitting Heads of State also enjoy personal immunity as an absolute bar against being subjected to foreign criminal jurisdiction while they remain in office. Personal immunity can be invoked by a limited group of State officials, whose freedom of action is essential to the functioning of their State. There is some contention over precisely which senior officials attract personal immunity, but there is no doubt that incumbent Heads of State, Heads of Government and Foreign Ministers are protected.[33] It should be noted that personal immunity is procedural in nature and does not exempt a person from criminal responsibility. It provides a temporary bar from prosecution in a foreign court for the duration of the individual's official status.[34] Despite some suggestion that there might be an erosion of personal immunity in order to allow for the prosecution of sitting Heads of State accused of committing international crimes,[35] State

notion that such an exception exists before an international court: International Law Commission, *Report of the International Law Commission*, 69th sess, UN Doc A/72/10 (1 May–2 June; 3 July–4 August 2017) 163–92; *Report of the International Law Commission on the work of its sixty-ninth session – Topical summary of the discussion held in the Sixth Committee of the General Assembly during its seventy-second session*, UN GAOR, UN Doc A/CN.4/713 (26 February 2018) paras 29–44. See also, R O'Keefe, 'An "International Crime" Exception to the Immunity of State Officials from Foreign Criminal Jurisdiction: Not Currently, Not Likely' (2015) 109 *AJIL Unbound* 167; I Wuerth, 'Pinochet's Legacy Reassessed' (2012) 106 *American Journal of International Law* 731.

[33] *Certain Questions of Mutual Assistance in Criminal Matters (Djibouti v France) (Judgment)* [2008] ICJ Rep 177, para 170; *Arrest Warrant of 11 April 2000 (Congo v Belgium) (Judgment)* [2002] ICJ Rep 3, 20–1 para 51; Draft article 3, International Law Commission, *Draft articles on immunity of State Officials from foreign criminal jurisdiction*, UN Doc A/CN.4/L.814 (4 June 2014). For arguments in favour of widening the category of individuals to whom immunity *ratione personae* applies, see Akande and Shah, 'Immunities of State Officials, International Crimes, and Foreign Domestic Courts', 820–5; Foakes, *The Position of Heads of State and Senior Officials in International Law*, pp. 128–33.

For the purposes of this book, any reference to 'Head of State immunity' is taken to include other senior State officials who enjoy customary immunity *ratione personae*. Although diplomats are also immune from foreign criminal jurisdiction, unlike immunity for senior State officials, diplomats only enjoy immunity *ratione personae* while on the territory of the receiving State, with some limited exceptions. Diplomats are not automatically immune from arrest while travelling outside the receiving State. For example, in 2014, the Italian ambassador to Turkmenistan was arrested while on holiday in Manila on suspicion of child abuse. The ambassador's diplomatic immunity did not apply in the Philippines: 'Italian Diplomat Faces Child Abuse Charges in Philippines', *Agence France Presse* (26 May 2014). See also, *Vienna Convention on Diplomatic Relations*, Articles 31, 39–40.

[34] Cassese, 'When May Senior State Officials Be Tried for International Crimes?', 863.
[35] Tunks, 'Diplomats or Defendants?', 659–63; KC O'Neill, 'A New Customary Law of Head of State Immunity? Hirohito and Pinochet' (2002) 38 *Stanford Journal of International*

practice does not yet support such an exception in foreign domestic courts.[36] Whether there is a customary exception to personal immunity applicable in *international* courts is a more difficult question, and one that has direct relevance to the jurisdiction of the ICC over incumbent Heads of State.[37] This will be addressed in the next section.

4.3.3 Head of State Immunity and the ICC

4.3.3.1 Articles 27 and 98 of the Rome Statute

Article 27 of the Rome Statute provides:

(1) This Statute shall apply equally to all persons without any distinction based on official capacity. In particular, official capacity as a Head of State or Government, a member of a Government or parliament, an elected representative or a government official shall in no case exempt a person from criminal responsibility under this Statute, nor shall it, in and of itself, constitute a ground for reduction of sentence.
(2) Immunities or special procedural rules which may attach to the official capacity of a person, whether under national or international law, shall not bar the Court from exercising its jurisdiction over such a person.

This provision was adopted at Rome without controversy and amounts to a clear rejection of all immunities, including functional immunity and personal immunity for sitting Heads of State.[38] It is not the only

---

Law 289 at 317. See discussion in Section 4.3.3.2 on the ICC Appeals Chamber's view of personal immunities for Heads of State.

[36] In 2018, for example, the Australian Attorney-General refused to give consent for a privately initiated prosecution against Aung San Suu Kyi to go ahead because of her 'complete immunity ... under customary international law': B Doherty, 'Aung San Suu Kyi cannot be prosecuted in Australia, Christian Porter says', *The Guardian* (17 March 2018). For a comprehensive review of State practice on this question, see Pedretti, *Immunity of Heads of State and State Officials for International Crimes*, pp. 138–55, 190–1. See also, Concepción Escobar Hernández, Special Rapporteur, *Fifth report on the immunity of State Officials from foreign criminal jurisdiction*, UN Doc A/CN.4/701 (14 June 2016) 24–54.

[37] See, Pedretti, *Immunity of Heads of State and State Officials for International Crimes*, pp. 232–71; P Gaeta, 'Official Capacity and Immunities' in A Cassese, P Gaeta and JRWD Jones (eds), *The Rome Statute of the International Criminal Court: A Commentary* (Oxford University Press, 2002) p. 975.

[38] O Triffterer and C Burchard, 'Article 27 Irrelevance of official capacity' in O Triffterer and K Ambos (eds), *Rome Statute of the International Criminal Court – A Commentary* (CH Beck Hart Nomos, 2016) p. 1048; 'Article 27', Schabas, *The International Criminal Court: A Commentary*, p. 595.

provision that must be considered when discussing jurisdiction of the ICC over Heads of State from States not party to the Statute. Article 98(1) provides that:

> [t]he Court may not proceed with a request for surrender or assistance which would require the requested State to act inconsistently with its obligations under international law with respect to the State or diplomatic immunity of a person or property of a third State, unless the Court can first obtain the cooperation of that third State for the waiver of the immunity.

Article 98(1) is ambiguous with respect to a number of questions that relate to sitting Heads of State: What is the relationship between this provision and Article 27? Does the reference to a 'third State' apply only to non-States Parties or to States Parties as well? Is the ICC precluded from even issuing an arrest warrant for a non-party Head of State? How does a Security Council referral affect this provision? Such questions have been debated extensively in academic commentary,[39] and the ICC's consideration of Articles 27 and 98(1) has proven to be somewhat inconsistent.

The ICC has dealt with a number of situations involving accused Heads of State, including Sudanese President Omar Al Bashir;[40] Laurent Gbagbo, the former president of the Côte d'Ivoire;[41] Kenyan President Uhuru

---

[39] See, eg, D Akande, 'International Law Immunities and the International Criminal Court' (2004) 98 *American Journal of International Law* 407; P Gaeta, 'Does President Al Bashir Enjoy Immunity from Arrest?' (2009) 7 *Journal of International Criminal Justice* 315; AG Kiyani, 'Al-Bashir & the ICC: The Problem of Head of State Immunity' (2013) 12 *Chinese Journal of International Law* 467; S Papillon, 'Has the United Nations Security Council Implicitly Removed Al Bashir's Immunity?' (2010) 10 *International Criminal Law Review* 275; M Ssenyonjo, 'The International Criminal Court Arrest Warrant Decision for President Al Bashir of Sudan' (2010) 59 *International & Comparative Law Quarterly* 205.

[40] The situation in Darfur, Sudan was referred to the ICC by the Security Council in 2005: SC Res 1593, UN SCOR, 5158th mtg, UN Doc SC/Res/1593 (31 March 2005). In 2009, Pre-Trial Chamber I issued a warrant of arrest for Omar Al Bashir: *Prosecutor v Omar Hassan Ahmad Al Bashir (Warrant of Arrest)* (International Criminal Court, Pre-Trial Chamber I, Case No ICC-02/05-01/09, 4 March 2009).

[41] In December 2010, the Côte d'Ivoire, not a party to the Rome Statute at that stage, reaffirmed its earlier 2003 acceptance of ICC jurisdiction under Article 12(3) of the Statute. See *Situation in the Republic of Côte d'Ivoire (Decision Pursuant to Article 15 of the Rome Statute on the Authorisation of an Investigation into the Situation in the Republic of Côte d'Ivoire)* (International Criminal Court, Pre-Trial Chamber III, Case No ICC-02/11, 3 October 2011). In November 2011, Pre-Trial Chamber III issued an arrest warrant for Gbagbo, who was president until his arrest and transfer to The Hague: *Situation in the Republic of Côte d'Ivoire (Warrant of Arrest for*

4.3 DELEGATION AND CUSTOMARY IMMUNITIES

Kenyatta;[42] and Colonel Muammar Gaddafi of Libya.[43] Of the four of these, at the time of writing, only the case against Al Bashir remains before the Court.[44] Gbagbo was acquitted in January 2019[45] and, as a former Head of State at the time of his arrest, could not claim personal immunity to protect him from criminal proceedings. Even if he had still been in power when an arrest warrant was issued, the Côte d'Ivoire had previously accepted the jurisdiction of the ICC on an ad hoc basis and, in doing so, accepted the scope of the Rome Statute including the Article 27(2) exclusion. Similarly, before the charges against President Kenyatta were withdrawn in March 2015,[46] there was no question about whether the ICC could exercise jurisdiction over him, as Kenya is a State Party to the Rome Statute. The Gaddafi case was terminated in November 2011 following his death.[47]

The case against Omar Al Bashir is therefore the only one in which there has been any judicial consideration of ICC jurisdiction

---

Laurent Koudou Gbagbo) (International Criminal Court, Pre-Trial Chamber III, Case No ICC-02/11, 23 November 2011). His trial began on 28 January 2016: International Criminal Court Press and Media, 'Trial of Laurent Gbagbo and Charles Blé Goudé opens at International Criminal Court' (Press Release, ICC-CPI -20160128-PR1184, 28 January 2016).

[42] Uhuru Kenyatta was summoned to appear before the ICC in March 2011: *Prosecutor v Kenyatta (Decision on the Prosecutor's Application for Summonses to Appear for Francis Kirimi Muthaura, Uhuru Muigai Kenyatta and Mohammed Hussein Ali)* (International Criminal Court, Pre-Trial Chamber II, Case No ICC-01/09-02/11, 8 March 2011). Kenyatta became President of Kenya in March 2013 while the ICC case against him was still in progress.

[43] The situation in Libya was referred to the ICC in 2011: SC Res 1970, UN SCOR, 6491st mtg, UN Doc SC/RES/1970 (26 February 2011). An arrest warrant was issued for Muammar Gaddafi in June 2011: *Situation in the Libyan Arab Jamahiriya (Warrant of Arrest for Muammar Gaddafi)* (International Criminal Court, Pre-Trial Chamber I, Case No ICC-01/11, 27 June 2011).

[44] Although Omar Al Bashir is no longer President of Sudan after being deposed in April 2019: 'Sudan's military seizes power from President Omar al-Bashir', *Al Jazeera* (12 April 2019).

[45] Laurent Gbagbo was acquitted of all charges in January 2019: International Criminal Court Press and Media, 'ICC Trial Chamber I acquits Laurent Gbagbo and Charles Blé Goudé from all charges' (Press Release, ICC-CPI-20190115-PR1427, 15 January 2019).

[46] All charges against Kenyatta were withdrawn on 13 March 2015: *Prosecutor v Kenyatta (Decision on the withdrawal of charges against Mr Kenyatta)* (International Criminal Court, Trial Chamber V(B), Case No ICC-01/09-02/11, 13 March 2015).

[47] *Prosecutor v Muammar Gaddafi (Decision to Terminate the Case Against Muammar Mohammed Abu Minyar Gaddafi)* (International Criminal Court, Pre-Trial Chamber I, Case No ICC-01/11-01/11, 22 November 2011).

and Head of State immunities. Although the situation in Darfur was referred to the ICC by the UN Security Council, Sudan is not a party to the Rome Statute and the judicial analysis of the various Chambers in Al Bashir's case has direct relevance for potential ICC prosecutions of Heads of State from non-States Parties in situations that do not involve the Security Council.

4.3.3.2 Consideration of Articles 27 and 98 in the Case of Al Bashir

In March 2009, Pre-Trial Chamber I approved the Prosecutor's application for an arrest warrant against Al Bashir, holding that 'the current position of Omar Al Bashir as Head of a State which is not party to the Statute, has no effect on the Court's jurisdiction over the present case'.[48] The Chamber gave the following four reasons for its pronouncement, which I summarise as follows:

1. The Preamble to the Rome Statute provides that one of the ICC's core goals is to end impunity for international crimes.
2. The provisions of Article 27 of the Statute clearly provide that neither official capacity nor immunities shall prevent the Court from exercising its jurisdiction.
3. Under Article 21, resort to other sources of law (such as customary international law) can only be had where there is a lacuna in the Statute, Elements of Crimes and Rules.
4. By referring the situation in Darfur to the ICC under Article 13(b), the Security Council accepted that any prosecution arising from the referral would 'take place in accordance with the statutory framework provided for in the Statute'.[49]

This fragmented reasoning attracted criticism for being vague and legally unconvincing.[50] It was, however, only the beginning of the Court's attempts to justify its authority over President Al Bashir. Two and a half years later, Al Bashir remained at large, and the question of whether a sitting Head of State from a non-State Party enjoys immunity from arrest by States Parties under Article 98(1) came before Pre-Trial

---

[48] *Prosecutor v Al Bashir (Decision on the Prosecution's Application for a Warrant of Arrest against Omar Hassan Ahmad Al Bashir)* (International Criminal Court, Pre-Trial Chamber I, Case No ICC-02/05-01/09, 4 March 2009) para 41.
[49] Ibid., paras 42–5.
[50] See, eg, Gaeta, 'Does President Al Bashir Enjoy Immunity from Arrest?', 323–4.

4.3 DELEGATION AND CUSTOMARY IMMUNITIES

Chamber I. The Republic of Malawi and the Republic of Chad, both States Parties to the Rome Statute, and both accused of failing to comply with cooperation requests by the ICC to arrest Al Bashir, argued that such action would conflict with their legal obligations under customary international law to respect the personal immunity of a foreign incumbent Head of State.[51] In its rejection of Malawi and Chad's arguments, Pre-Trial Chamber I reconsidered the position of Head of State immunity vis-à-vis the ICC, and after examining the practice of previous international courts,[52] concluded that:

> the principle in international law is that immunity of either former or sitting Heads of State cannot be invoked to oppose a prosecution by an international court. This is equally applicable to former or sitting Heads of States not Parties to the Statute whenever the Court may exercise jurisdiction. ... [T]he Chamber finds that customary international law creates an exception to Head of State immunity when international courts seek a Head of State's arrest for the commission of international crimes.[53]

In essence, the Pre-Trial Chamber found there to be two customary exceptions to personal immunity. The first prevents a sitting Head of State from relying on immunities before international courts, and the second allows national authorities to arrest and transfer a foreign Head of State to an international court.

---

[51] *Prosecutor v Al Bashir (Decision pursuant to Article 87(7) of the Rome Statute on the Failure by the Republic of Malawi to Comply with the Cooperation Requests Issued by the Court with respect to the Arrest and Surrender of Omar Hassan Ahmad Al Bashir)* (International Criminal Court, Pre-Trial Chamber I, Case No ICC/02/05-01/09, 12 December 2011); *Prosecutor v Al Bashir (Decision pursuant to Article 87(7) of the Rome Statute on the Failure by the Republic of Chad to Comply with the Cooperation Requests Issued by the Court with respect to the Arrest and Surrender of Omar Hassan Ahmad Al Bashir)* (International Criminal Court, Pre-Trial Chamber I, Case No ICC/02/05-01/09, 13 December 2011).

[52] Notably, the Pre-Trial Chamber relied on the Special Court for Sierra Leone Appeals Chamber decision in *Prosecutor v Taylor (Decision on Immunity from Jurisdiction)* (Special Court for Sierra Leone, Appeals Chamber, Case No SCSL-2003-01-I, 31 May 2004).

[53] *Prosecutor v Al Bashir (Decision pursuant to Article 87(7) of the Rome Statute on the Failure by the Republic of Malawi to Comply with the Cooperation Requests Issued by the Court with respect to the Arrest and Surrender of Omar Hassan Ahmad Al Bashir)* (International Criminal Court, Pre-Trial Chamber I, Case No ICC/02/05-01/09, 12 December 2011) paras 36, 43; *Prosecutor v Al Bashir (Decision pursuant to Article 87(7) of the Rome Statute on the Failure by the Republic of Chad to Comply with the Cooperation Requests Issued by the Court with respect to the Arrest and Surrender of Omar Hassan Ahmad Al Bashir)* (International Criminal Court, Pre-Trial Chamber I, Case No ICC/02/05-01/09, 13 December 2011) para 13.

Despite Pre-Trial Chamber I's proclamation, Al Bashir remained unarrested and continued to travel outside Sudan with seeming impunity. In 2012, the ICC Presidency reassigned the situation in Darfur to Pre-Trial Chamber II.[54] From February 2013 to April 2014, this chamber was provided with numerous notifications of Al Bashir's travel plans.[55] It responded to all of these by simply holding that States Parties are obliged under the Rome Statute to arrest and surrender Al Bashir to the Court. Conversely, Pre-Trial Chamber II acknowledged that non-States Parties are not under such an obligation, although Security Council Resolution 1593 urges the cooperation of all States.[56] The Chamber did not at any time consider the question of Al Bashir's immunity.

In February 2014 the Prosecutor notified the Court of Al Bashir's intent to travel to the Democratic Republic of the Congo (DRC). In response to the DRC's non-cooperation with the arrest warrant, Pre-Trial Chamber II finally gave some more substantive consideration to the question of whether Al Bashir's customary immunity as a Head of State conflicts with the Rome Statute obligations on States Parties to effect his arrest and surrender.[57] The Chamber did not acknowledge the reasoning of Pre-Trial Chamber I in the Chad and Malawi decisions, and did not even address the possibility of a customary international law exception to Head of State immunity for the arrest and transfer or prosecution by an international court. Instead, it simply held that Al Bashir does not enjoy immunity from arrest in a foreign State because the Security Council referral 'implicitly waived the immunities granted to Omar Al Bashir under international law and attached to his position as a Head of State'.[58]

The next judicial consideration of Head of State immunities came in 2017 after South Africa failed to arrest Al Bashir when he attended an African Union summit in Johannesburg in 2015. This time, a differently

---

[54] *(Decision on the constitution of Pre-Trial Chambers and on the assignment of the Democratic Republic of the Congo, Darfur, Sudan and Côte d'Ivoire situations)* (International Criminal Court, The Presidency, Case No ICC-Pres-01-12, 15 March 2012).

[55] Al Bashir's travel during this period – actual and intended – included to Chad, Libya, Nigeria, USA, Ethiopia, Saudi Arabia and Kuwait.

[56] *Prosecutor v Al Bashir (Order Regarding Omar Al-Bashir's Potential Visit to the Republic of Chad and to the State of Libya)* (International Criminal Court, Pre-Trial Chamber II, Case No ICC-02/05-01/09, 15 February 2013) paras 10–13. See Chapter 5 for further discussion.

[57] *Prosecutor v Al Bashir (Decision on the Cooperation of the Democratic Republic of the Congo Regarding Omar Al Bashir's Arrest and Surrender to the Court)* (International Criminal Court, Pre-Trial Chamber II, Case No ICC/02/05-01/09, 9 April 2014).

[58] Ibid., para. 29. This concept will be discussed in more detail in Chapter 5.

4.3 DELEGATION AND CUSTOMARY IMMUNITIES 87

constituted Pre-Trial Chamber II essentially rejected the reasoning of Pre-Trial Chamber I in the 2011 Malawi and Chad decision by finding that there was no exception to Head of State immunity under customary international law for the arrest, transfer and prosecution of a Head of State by an international court.[59] By virtue of Security Council Resolution 1593, however, the Pre-Trial Chamber found that 'for the limited purpose of the situation in Darfur, Sudan has rights and duties analogous to those of States Parties to the Statute'.[60] This meant that Article 27(2) of the Statute rendered Al Bashir's immunity inapplicable before the ICC and that Article 98(1) was therefore not relevant.[61]

Five months later, in December 2017, Pre-Trial Chamber II applied its reasoning from the South Africa decision to another case of non-compliance; this time concluding that Jordan's failure to arrest and surrender Al Bashir warranted referral to the Assembly of States Parties and the UN Security Council.[62] Jordan appealed this decision and in May 2019 the ICC Appeals Chamber upheld the Pre-Trial Chamber's decision that Jordan had failed to comply with its obligations to cooperate with the Court but overturned Jordan's referral to the Assembly of States Parties and UN Security Council.[63] The Appeals Chamber Judgment is not especially noteworthy for its ultimate conclusion, but it is significant for its analysis and interpretation of Head of State immunity under international law.

In its Judgment and Joint Concurring Opinion, the Appeals Chamber held that customary international law has never recognised Head of State immunity before an international court exercising jurisdiction over crimes under international law.[64] Given that the ICC's jurisdiction was

---

[59] *Prosecutor v Al Bashir (Decision under article 87(7) of the Rome Statute on the non-compliance by South Africa with the request by the Court for the arrest and surrender of Omar Al-Bashir)* (International Criminal Court, Pre-Trial Chamber II, Case No ICC/02/05-01/09, 6 July 2017) para 68.

[60] Ibid., para 88.

[61] Ibid., para 93.

[62] *Prosecutor v Al Bashir (Decision under article 87(7) of the Rome Statute on the non-compliance by Jordan with the request by the Court for the arrest and surrender of Omar Al-Bashir)* (International Criminal Court, Pre-Trial Chamber II, Case No ICC/02/05-01/09, 11 December 2017).

[63] *Prosecutor v Al Bashir (Judgment in the Jordan Referral re Al-Bashir Appeal)* (International Criminal Court, Appeals Chamber, Case No ICC/02/05-01/09, 6 May 2019).

[64] *Prosecutor v Al Bashir (Judgment in the Jordan Referral re Al-Bashir Appeal)* (International Criminal Court, Appeals Chamber, Case No ICC/02/05-01/09, 6 May 2019); *Prosecutor v Al Bashir (Joint Concurring Opinion of Judges Eboe-Osuji, Morrison, Hofmański and Bossa)* (International Criminal Court, Appeals Chamber, Case No ICC/02/05-01/09, 6 May 2019).

properly triggered by Security Council Resolution 1593, Al Bashir is unable to rely on any immunities before the Court. The Appeals Chamber reasoned that it was not a question of Sudan or the Security Council 'waiving' Al Bashir's immunity, because such immunity does not exist before an international court.[65] To that end, Article 27 is essentially a reflection of custom.[66]

The Appeals Chamber applied the same logic to its explanation of why Article 98(1) would not prevent Jordan or other States Parties from arresting and transferring Al Bashir to the ICC. When acting upon a request by the Court for the arrest and transfer of a Head of State, a State 'is not proceeding to arrest the Head of State in order to prosecute him or her before the courts of the requested State Party: it is only lending assistance to the Court in the exercise of its proper jurisdiction'.[67] If immunities do not exist before an international court, they cannot be asserted before domestic authorities who are merely assisting the ICC in the exercise of its jurisdiction. The Chamber went further in its Joint Concurring Opinion to say that States Parties arresting a foreign Head of State wanted by the ICC 'should not be seen as exercising their own criminal jurisdiction. They are merely acting as jurisdictional surrogates of the ICC, for the purposes of enabling it to exercise its jurisdiction effectively as authorised by the Security Council resolution in question'.[68]

The series of decisions on Al Bashir's immunity by four differently constituted chambers of the ICC over a period of ten years resulted in a rather fragmented body of jurisprudence on Head of State immunities before the Court. While consistently holding that Al Bashir's immunity does not apply before the ICC and does not prevent States Parties from arresting and transferring him to the Court, the legal reasoning for why this is so varied significantly. It is not surprising then that these attempts to clarify the Head of State immunity have been widely criticised in

---

[65] *Prosecutor v Al Bashir (Judgment in the Jordan Referral re Al-Bashir Appeal)* (International Criminal Court, Appeals Chamber, Case No ICC/02/05-01/09, 6 May 2019) paras 113–17; *Prosecutor v Al Bashir (Joint Concurring Opinion of Judges Eboe-Osuji, Morrison, Hofmański and Bossa)* (International Criminal Court, Appeals Chamber, Case No ICC/02/05-01/09, 6 May 2019) paras 76–174, 414–18.

[66] *Prosecutor v Al Bashir (Judgment in the Jordan Referral re Al-Bashir Appeal)* (International Criminal Court, Appeals Chamber, Case No ICC/02/05-01/09, 6 May 2019) para 103.

[67] Ibid., para 127.

[68] *Prosecutor v Al Bashir (Joint Concurring Opinion of Judges Eboe-Osuji, Morrison, Hofmański and Bossa)* (International Criminal Court, Appeals Chamber, Case No ICC/02/05-01/09, 6 May 2019) para 445. See Chapter 6 for further discussion.

scholarly commentary, with different aspects of the Chambers' legal reasoning coming under fire.[69]

Causing particular uncertainty was Pre-Trial Chamber I's declaration of the existence of a customary exception to personal immunity and then, more than seven years later, the Appeals Chamber's assertion that customary international law has never recognised immunities before an international court. There is little consensus among scholars as to whether there is sufficient State practice to support a customary exception for the prosecution of sitting Heads of State by international courts.[70] The Appeals Chamber's determination that customary international law has never recognised immunities before an international court is essentially a reconceptualisation of the customary exception line of

---

[69] See, eg, Kiyani, 'Al-Bashir & the ICC'; N Boschiero, 'The ICC Judicial Finding on Non-Cooperation Against the DRC and No Immunity for Al-Bashir Based on UNSC Resolution 1593' (2015) 13 *Journal of International Criminal Justice* 625; Pedretti, *Immunity of Heads of State and State Officials for International Crimes*, pp. 285–99; D Tladi, 'The ICC Decisions on Chad and Malawi' (2013) 11 *Journal of International Criminal Justice* 199; D Akande, 'ICC Issues Detailed Decision on Bashir's Immunity (... At Long Last...) But Gets the Law Wrong', *EJIL: Talk!* (15 December 2011); WA Schabas, 'Obama, Medvedev and Hu Jintao may be Prosecuted by International Criminal Court, Pre-Trial Chamber Concludes', *PhD Studies in Human Rights* (15 December 2011); P Gaeta, 'Guest Post: The ICC Changes Its Mind on the Immunity from Arrest of President Al Bashir, But It Is Wrong Again', *Opinio Juris* (23 April 2014); A de Hoogh and A Knottnerus, 'ICC Issues New Decision on Al Bashir's Immunities – But Gets the Law Wrong ... Again', *EJIL: Talk!* (18 April 2014); A Knottnerus, 'The Immunity of al-Bashir: The Latest Turn in the Jurisprudence of the ICC', *EJIL: Talk!* (15 November 2017); A Kiyani, 'Elisions and Omissions: Questioning the ICC's Latest Bashir Immunity Ruling', *Just Security* (8 May 2019); D Akande, 'ICC Appeals Chamber Holds that Heads of State Have No Immunity Under Customary International Law Before International Tribunals', *EJIL: Talk!* (6 May 2019).

[70] Cassese, 'When May Senior State Officials Be Tried for International Crimes?', 865–6; Akande, 'International Law Immunities and the International Criminal Court', 416–17; Kiyani, 'Al-Bashir & the ICC', 487–9; Pedretti, *Immunity of Heads of State and State Officials for International Crimes*, pp. 304–7; D Jacobs, 'The Frog that Wanted to Be an Ox: The ICC's Approach to Immunities and Cooperation' in C Stahn (ed), *The Law and Practice of the International Criminal Court* (Oxford University Press, 2015) p. 288; CE Hernández, Special Rapporteur, *Fifth report on the immunity of State Officials from foreign criminal jurisdiction*, UN Doc A/CN.4/701 (14 June 2016) para 248. But see, C Kreß, 'Preliminary Observations on the ICC Appeals Chamber's Judgment of 6 May 2019 in the Jordan Referral re Al-Bashir Appeal (Occasional Paper Series No 8, Torkel Opsahl Academic Epublisher, May 2019) 7–8; Sadat, 'The Uneasy Revolution Continues', 33; Gaeta, 'Does President Al Bashir Enjoy Immunity from Arrest?', 320–1. Gaeta argues that there is a customary exception to Head of State immunity before international courts, but such an exception does not extend to the national level with respect to arrest and transfer of an accused Head of State to an international court.

reasoning, and early commentary has likewise been sceptical.[71] Several non-States Parties have also raised doubts about the Appeals Chamber's reasoning on immunities before international courts. At the 2019 Assembly of States Parties, China, for example, expressed

> concerns ... regarding several controversial judgements and denying immunity by various Chambers of the Court, for weaknesses of those judgements including, inter alia, their not well-grounded-reasoning and, in particular, lack of consistency among each other's reasonings, therefore lacking the most basic feature in building the authority of the Court's jurisprudence.[72]

In the Security Council, the US specifically noted its

> disagreement with a number of aspects of the ICC Appeals Chamber's recent decision in the Jordan appeal, including the analysis and conclusions regarding customary international law and the interpretation of Security Council resolutions.[73]

The most controversial aspect of conceiving the non-application of Head of State immunities before the ICC as rooted in custom relates to Heads of States wanted by the ICC in situations not involving the UN Security Council. If personal immunities do not apply in cases where an international court seeks arrest and transfer of a sitting Head of State, this means that the ICC is not precluded under Article 98(1) from issuing a request for cooperation to a non-State Party. Article 98(1) would essentially be rendered meaningless as there would not be any competing obligations under international law to prevent a non-State Party from arresting and transferring a visiting foreign Head of State to the ICC if the State chose to do so. As highlighted by France:

> [T]he immunity enjoyed by representatives of States under customary international law, which is crucial to the good conduct of international relations and to which there can be no exception, can be removed only by an express renunciation of the States concerned, just like the one to which

---

[71] B Batros, 'A Confusing ICC Appeals Judgment on Head-of-State Immunity', *Just Security* (7 May 2019); K Anderson, 'ICC Appeals Chamber resurrects controversial customary international law argument to find Al-Bashir has no immunity before international courts', *ILA Reporter* (May 2019).

[72] Statement by Mr Hu Bin, Head of the Chinese Observer Delegation and Deputy Director-General of the Department of Treaty and Law, Ministry of Foreign Affairs of China, *Eighteenth Session of the Assembly of States Parties to the Rome Statute of the International Criminal Court* (The Hague, 3 Dec 2019).

[73] *Reports of the Secretary-General on the Sudan and South Sudan*, UN SCOR, 8554th mtg, UN Doc S/PV.8554 (19 June 2019) p. 13. See also, statements of Russia and Sudan.

the States parties to the Rome Statute consented, which applies also to non-States parties *whose situation has been referred to the Court by the Security Council.*[74]

The default absence of any immunities before international courts raises a number of issues, not least of which is the question of what constitutes an international court.[75] The next section builds on the analysis of the ICC's jurisprudence in the Al Bashir case to determine whether the ICC could lawfully exercise jurisdiction over a sitting head of a non-State Party in a situation that does not involve a Security Council referral.

4.3.4 A Hypothetical Case Study: Can the ICC Exercise Jurisdiction over an Incumbent Head of State from a Non-State Party in a Situation Not Involving the Security Council?

In this section I use a hypothetical case involving the ICC prosecution of a sitting Head of State from Non-State Party X (President X) for crimes committed on the territory of State Party Y. This hypothetical case is based on four important assumptions:

1. That crimes have been committed on the territory of State Party Y that reach the gravity threshold required by the Rome Statute.
2. That these crimes were committed by nationals of Non-State Party X.
3. That there is evidence that President X is criminally responsible.
4. That the Court's jurisdiction is triggered by a State Party referral or *proprio motu* investigation by the Prosecutor.

4.3.4.1 Is President X Immune from Arrest and Transfer?

Applying the Appeals Chamber's reasoning and assuming that Article 27(2) reflects customary international law, President X cannot assert Head of State immunity before the ICC. If President X is travelling on the territory of State Party Z, that State would be obliged to arrest

---

[74] *Reports of the Secretary-General on the Sudan and South Sudan*, UN SCOR, 8554th mtg, UN Doc S/PV.8554 (19 June 2019) p. 7. Emphasis added.

[75] Jacobs, 'The Frog that Wanted to Be an Ox: The ICC's Approach to Immunities and Cooperation', p. 288. But see, the ICC Appeals Chamber's discussion on what constitutes an international court: *Prosecutor v Al Bashir (Joint Concurring Opinion of Judges Eboe-Osuji, Morrison, Hofmański and Bossa)* (International Criminal Court, Appeals Chamber, Case No ICC/02/05-01/09, 6 May 2019) paras 56–64. See also, Gaeta, 'Does President Al Bashir Enjoy Immunity from Arrest?', 322. See Chapter 6 for further analysis of the idea that the legal basis for the ICC's jurisdiction is a *jus puniendi* inherent in the international community, exercisable by an international court.

President X and transfer him to the Court. In accordance with the Appeals Chamber's reasoning, Article 98(1) does not apply because State Party Z is not exercising its own criminal jurisdiction in arresting President X, it is merely a surrogate for the ICC's jurisdiction. State Party Z will therefore not be acting inconsistently with its obligations under international law by exercising its jurisdiction over a foreign Head of State. Conceiving State Party Z's exercise of enforcement jurisdiction over President X as belonging to the ICC would make it easier, legally speaking, for the Court to gain custody of an accused incumbent Head of a non-State Party by removing the procedural barrier of personal immunity in foreign domestic jurisdictions. But the idea that a State Party can – or must – act as a surrogate of the ICC is far-fetched and does not have any basis in State practice.[76]

Assuming instead that State Party Z would need to exercise its own enforcement jurisdiction to arrest and transfer President X to the ICC, it could not do so without violating President X's personal immunity. The ICC would therefore be precluded under Article 98(1) from requesting State Party Z to arrest President X while he or she remains in office.

Hypothetically speaking, if the ICC were to somehow gain custody of such an accused Head of State,[77] this would clear only the immunity hurdle at the domestic level. There would still be a question of whether

---

[76] Indeed, even scholars who are of the view that Article 27(2) reflects customary international law do not agree that it renders Article 98(1) inapplicable. See, eg, *Prosecutor v Al Bashir (Observations by Professor Paola Gaeta as amicus curiae on the merits of the legal questions presented in Jordan's appeal against the 'Decision under Article 87(7) of the Rome Statute on the non-compliance by Jordan with the request by the Court for the arrest and surrender of Omar Al-Bashir' of 12 March 2018)* (International Criminal Court, Appeals Chamber, Case No ICC/02/05-01/09 OA2, 18 June 2018) pp. 9–11.

[77] Conceivably, an accused could turn him or herself into the ICC, or a foreign State could arrest and transfer the accused president to the ICC in violation of its customary international law obligations to respect personal immunities. In *Israel v Eichmann,* the Supreme Court held the fact that Eichmann was abducted from Argentina was not a bar to the jurisdiction of the Israeli Court: Attorney-General of the Government of Israel v Adolf Eichmann (1962) 36 ILR 5, 308. It is possible, however, that the ICC would hold that an unlawful transfer of an accused to the ICC constituted an abuse of process, notwithstanding the fact that the Court would have jurisdiction to prosecute. This scenario occurred in the Australian High Court case of *Moti v The Queen,* in which the Australian defendant was charged with the offence of engaging in sexual intercourse with a person under the age of 16 years whilst outside Australia (s. 50BA of the *Crimes Act 1914* [Cth]). The High Court held that it would be an abuse of process to prosecute Mr Moti in Australia because an Australian official facilitated his deportation from the Solomon Islands, which was unlawful under Solomon Islands law: *Moti v The Queen* (2011) 245 CLR 456.

the ICC could exercise jurisdiction over President X. That will depend on whether 'delegation of jurisdiction' constitutes an appropriate legal basis in this instance.

4.3.4.2 Does Delegation of Jurisdiction Provide a Legal Basis for ICC Jurisdiction over President X?

The nature of personal immunity as an absolute procedural bar to prosecution of sitting Heads of State in all foreign domestic jurisdictions means that no State Party to the ICC has the right to exercise its powers of criminal justice over President X. The absence of this jurisdiction at the domestic level would appear to preclude its lawful delegation to the ICC, as States Parties do not possess an internationally recognised right to prosecute foreign Heads of State in their individual capacities. It might be possible, however, to conceive of ICC jurisdiction over President X as based on collective conferral. Recalling the discussion in Chapter 3, the idea of collective conferral is that where the 'vast majority' of States act together, they can confer certain powers on an international organisation that, individually, they do not have.[78] But this characterisation of the legal basis for ICC jurisdiction over Heads of State from non-States Parties is only sustainable if customary international law does not recognise Head of State immunity before international courts.[79] If, for example, future ICC cases follow the Appeals Chamber's reasoning in the Jordan decision and hold that the customary international law of personal immunity for incumbent Heads of State does not apply to international courts, then it would follow that the ICC can exercise jurisdiction over President X on the basis of collectively conferred jurisdiction. As mentioned above, however, whether or not a Head of State's personal immunity applies before international courts is far from a settled matter of customary law.

4.3.5 Conclusion to Section 4.3

At present, how Article 27, Article 98(1) and the doctrine of Head of State immunity in customary international law interact with each other remains contentious and may never be resolved to the satisfaction of all States and all commentators. The Court has not yet had the opportunity

---

[78] *Reparation for Injuries Suffered in the Service of the United Nations (Advisory Opinion)* [1949] ICJ Rep 174, 185. See Section 3.3.2 for further discussion of collective conferral.

[79] Either as an exception to the customary international law rule of personal immunity or based on an absence of any customary rule of personal immunity applicable to international courts.

to consider how these legal issues would play out in a case against a sitting Head of State from a non-State Party in a situation not involving a Security Council referral. Beyond the issue of whether States are precluded from arresting and transferring a foreign head of a non-State Party to the ICC, the Court must still be able to provide a legal basis for jurisdiction if it intends to prosecute. As the above analysis has demonstrated, it remains uncertain as to whether customary international law renders personal immunity inapplicable before an international court. Without a clear customary exception, neither individual delegation nor collective conferral would provide a legal basis for ICC jurisdiction over an incumbent Head of State from a State not party to the Rome Statute.[80]

4.4 Is Delegation of Jurisdiction Affected by International Agreements?

This section explores whether bilateral agreements that provide procedural immunities for foreign nationals affect a State Party's delegable jurisdiction, and whether this in turn affects the legal basis for the ICC's jurisdiction. Here, I use as examples two situations that are under investigation at the ICC: Afghanistan and Palestine. Both situations potentially involve nationals of non-States Parties, and both raise unique legal issues that could have an impact upon delegation of jurisdiction as a legal basis for ICC prosecution.

4.4.1 The Situation in Afghanistan

On 20 November 2017, the ICC Prosecutor requested authorisation to proceed with an investigation into crimes alleged to have been committed on the territory of Afghanistan since 1 May 2003.[81] This decision to seek judicial approval to open an investigation was preceded by a preliminary examination that lasted more than ten years. The request confirmed that the Prosecutor intended to investigate Afghan government forces, Taliban affiliates and members of the US armed forces and Central Intelligence Agency (CIA) for allegedly committing war crimes and crimes against humanity in connection with the situation in

---

[80] For a discussion on whether there is a legal basis for ICC prosecution of sitting Heads of State from non-States Parties in situations referred by the Security Council, see Chapter 5.
[81] *Situation in the Islamic Republic of Afghanistan (Request for authorisation of an investigation pursuant to Article 15)* (Office of the Prosecutor, Case No ICC-02/17-7-RED, 20 November 2017) ('Prosecutor Request for Authorisation of an Investigation').

4.4 DELEGATION AND INTERNATIONAL AGREEMENTS   95

Afghanistan. While Pre-Trial Chamber II initially declined to authorise an investigation,[82] in March 2020 that decision was overturned by the Appeals Chamber and the Prosecutor was duly authorised to open an investigation into the situation in Afghanistan.[83] The situation provides an interesting and complex example of competing jurisdictional arrangements, and the main issue that arises is whether the SOFAs between the US and Afghanistan have any bearing on whether the ICC could exercise jurisdiction in the Afghanistan situation.[84]

US forces have made up a significant proportion of foreigners operating in Afghanistan since the 2001 intervention, as part of the International Security Assistance Force (ISAF) under the control of the North Atlantic Treaty Organization (NATO) since 2003[85] and as part of Operation Enduring Freedom under US command. The ICC Prosecutor has specified that her office intends to investigate and prosecute crimes committed on the territory of Afghanistan 'principally in the 2003–2004 period',[86] and during this time there were two main agreements regulating the status of US forces in Afghanistan. The first was the Military Technical Agreement between ISAF and the Interim Administration of Afghanistan, which entered into force on 4 April 2002. The annex to this agreement provides that all ISAF personnel are subject 'under all circumstances and at all times' to the exclusive criminal and disciplinary jurisdiction of their home States.[87] The second agreement was the Exchange of Notes between the

---

[82] *Situation in the Islamic Republic of Afghanistan (Decision Pursuant to Article 15 of the Rome Statute on the Authorisation of an Investigation into the Situation in the Islamic Republic of Afghanistan)* (International Criminal Court, Pre-Trial Chamber II, Case No ICC-02/17, 12 April 2019). The Pre-Trial Chamber controversially held that an investigation would not serve the interests of justice as required by Article 53(1)(c) of the Statute.

[83] *Situation in the Islamic Republic of Afghanistan (Judgment on the Appeal against the Decision on the Authorisation of an Investigation into the Situation in the Islamic Republic of Afghanistan)* (International Criminal Court, Appeals Chamber, Case No ICC-02/17 OA4, 5 March 2020).

[84] This section reproduces some material published in M Cormier, 'Can the ICC Exercise Jurisdiction over US Nationals for Crimes Committed in the Afghanistan Situation?' (2018) 5 *Journal of International Criminal Justice* 1043. Reproduced with permission of Oxford University Press.

[85] The ISAF mission ended on 28 December 2014 and was replaced by the non-combat Resolute Support Mission.

[86] Prosecutor Request for Authorisation of an Investigation, para. 4.

[87] *Military Technical Agreement between the International Security Assistance Force and the Interim Administration of Afghanistan,* UN Doc S/2002/117 Annex A – Arrangements regarding the status of the international security assistance force, Section 1(2) ('the Military Technical Agreement'). This was superseded by the NATO-Afghanistan Exchange of Letters (5 September 2004, 22 November 2004), which was eventually

US and the Transitional Islamic State of Afghanistan, which entered into force on 12 December 2002.[88] Under this agreement, US military and civilian personnel of the US Department of Defense were 'accorded a status equivalent to that accorded to the administrative and technical staff of the Embassy of the United States of America under the Vienna Convention on Diplomatic Relations'.[89] This agreement essentially gave Department of Defense personnel immunity from Afghanistan's criminal jurisdiction.[90] Such arrangements giving the US exclusive jurisdiction over its service members led at least one commentator to allege that any attempt by the ICC to exercise jurisdiction over US soldiers would be unlawful, and that it would also 'undermine the basic tenets of established treaty law'.[91]

The claim that the ICC cannot assert jurisdiction over US nationals in the Afghanistan situation is predicated on the argument that the US–Afghanistan SOFA precludes Afghanistan from delegating jurisdiction to the ICC. In its request to the Pre-Trial Chamber to authorise an investigation, the Prosecutor essentially dismissed these allegations in a single sentence stating that a SOFA 'does not affect the Court's jurisdiction'.[92] But the question of whether the US–Afghanistan SOFA would preclude the ICC from exercising jurisdiction is complex.

4.4.1.1 Does the SOFA Limit Afghanistan's Ability to Delegate Jurisdiction?

Under the SOFA, Afghanistan has agreed that the US retains exclusive jurisdiction over US soldiers for crimes committed on Afghan territory. Michael Newton contends that Afghanistan has, for all intents and purposes, relinquished its jurisdiction over US nationals and therefore

---

superseded by the *Agreement between the North Atlantic Treaty Organization and the Islamic Republic of Afghanistan on the Status of NATO Forces and NATO Personnel Conducting Mutually Agreed NATO-Led Activities in Afghanistan* (30 September 2014).

[88] Exchange of notes between the Embassy of the United States of America and the Transitional Islamic State of Afghanistan (26 September 2002, 12 December 2002, 28 May 2003) ('2002 Exchange of Notes'). This was eventually superseded by *Security and Defense Cooperation Agreement between the Islamic Republic of Afghanistan and the United States of America* (30 September 2014) ('bilateral security agreement'). For the remainder of this section, I will refer to any applicable SOFAs in force at the time of the alleged crimes as the singular 'US-Afghanistan SOFA'.

[89] Ibid.

[90] *Vienna Convention on Diplomatic Relations*, Article 37(2).

[91] MA Newton, 'How the International Criminal Court Threatens Treaty Norms' (2016) 49 *Vanderbilt Journal of Transnational Law* 371 at 374–5.

[92] Prosecutor Request for Authorisation of an Investigation, para 46. The Prosecutor elaborates slightly in footnote 47, which I discuss later in this section.

4.4 DELEGATION AND INTERNATIONAL AGREEMENTS

Afghanistan no longer possesses such jurisdiction to delegate to the ICC.[93] While Afghanistan has essentially agreed not to exercise its judicial jurisdiction over US nationals, its rights and powers of sovereign jurisdiction nevertheless remain unaffected by the SOFA and may therefore be delegated to the ICC. As discussed in Chapter 3 and as articulated by Roger O'Keefe, 'jurisdiction is not a quantity[, i]t is a complex – a complex of rights, and of rights the existence of which is not to be confused with their exercise'.[94] In her request to the Pre-Trial Chamber the Prosecutor endorsed this characterisation of jurisdiction, arguing – in a footnote – that 'while a SOFA might constitute a decision by a State to not to exercise its enforcement jurisdiction, such an agreement does not extinguish a State's prescriptive and enforcement jurisdiction, which serve as inherent attributes of State sovereignty'.[95] I would go further than this and argue that in ratifying the SOFA, Afghanistan has simply promised not to exercise its powers of enforcement over US service members. Under international law, Afghanistan retains the right to exercise those powers over foreign nationals in accordance with the principle of territoriality, even if it has agreed via the SOFA not to assert that right in limited circumstances. Afghanistan can therefore be said to have lawfully delegated to the ICC its customary rights to exercise certain enforcement powers on the basis of territoriality and nationality. In turn, the ICC has the right to exercise those powers in accordance with the Rome Statute. Whether the ICC's exercise of jurisdiction over US soldiers for crimes committed in Afghanistan would nevertheless 'undermine international law' by 'overriding preexisting agreements between sovereign states'[96] is discussed in the next section.

4.4.1.2 The Conflict between the Rome Statute and the SOFA

In pursuing an investigation into crimes allegedly committed by US soldiers, the ICC stands accused of 'erasing the traditional jurisdictional arrangements between states'.[97] When Afghanistan became a State Party to the Rome Statute, it agreed, via delegation, to allow the ICC to exercise jurisdiction over international crimes committed on its territory by persons of any nationality. It also agreed 'to cooperate fully with the

---

[93] Newton, 'How the International Criminal Court Threatens Treaty Norms', 398.
[94] R O'Keefe, 'Quid Not Quantum: A Comment on How the International Criminal Court Threatens Treaty Norms' (2016) 49 *Vanderbilt Journal of Transnational Law* 433 at 436.
[95] Prosecutor Request for Authorisation of an Investigation, para 47 fn 47.
[96] Newton, 'How the International Criminal Court Threatens Treaty Norms', 379.
[97] Ibid., 391.

Court in its investigation and prosecution of crimes within the jurisdiction of the Court'.[98] As far as the US is concerned, this state of affairs gives rise to two potential issues. The first is that Afghanistan will be obliged to cooperate with the ICC in any prosecution of US soldiers, which would conflict with Afghanistan's SOFA obligations that give procedural immunity to members of the US armed forces for crimes committed in Afghanistan. The second issue is that even if the ICC gains custody of a US suspect without any assistance from Afghanistan, any exercise of the ICC's jurisdiction over that suspect will still be in contravention of the SOFA. From the US's perspective, if the ICC exercises jurisdiction over US service members for crimes committed in Afghanistan, it is not really any different from Afghanistan exercising such jurisdiction contrary to the SOFA. Any action on the part of the ICC essentially prevents Afghanistan from guaranteeing the US exclusive jurisdiction over its nationals for any crimes committed in Afghanistan.

In consenting to be bound by the SOFA, Afghanistan has agreed not to assert its right to prosecute US soldiers for crimes committed on its territory. The practical effect of this is that Afghanistan cannot lawfully exercise domestic judicial jurisdiction over US soldiers, but Afghanistan's ratification of the Rome Statute does not interfere with this. In fact, Article 98(2) was inserted into the Rome Statute to ensure that States Parties would not be required 'to act inconsistently with its obligations' under certain international agreements. The full text of this article provides that:

> The Court may not proceed with a request for surrender which would require the requested State to act inconsistently with its obligations under international agreements pursuant to which the consent of a sending State is required to surrender a person of that State to the Court, unless the Court can first obtain the cooperation of the sending State for the giving of consent for the surrender.

Between 2002 and 2006, the US concluded 100 bilateral agreements with foreign governments for the purpose of ensuring that members of the US armed forces would not be surrendered to the ICC without the 'express consent' of the US.[99] While the US–Afghanistan SOFA is arguably an

---

[98] Rome Statute, Article 86.
[99] In many of these agreements, the US purported to include government officials, employees and contractors, military personnel and even nationals as a blanket category of people subject to the agreement's provisions. David Scheffer argues that this goes beyond what Article 98(2) was intended to cover, namely personnel subject to a SOFA or status

4.4 DELEGATION AND INTERNATIONAL AGREEMENTS 99

agreement that would be covered by Article 98,[100] the US entered into a separate Article 98 agreement with Afghanistan in 2002, stipulating that Afghanistan would not surrender US nationals to the ICC without the consent of the US government. The existence of both the SOFA and the Article 98 agreement means that the ICC is prevented from requesting Afghanistan's assistance with arresting and surrendering any US suspects to the Court because Afghanistan's cooperation in such matters would violate the terms of either agreement.

As identified by the Prosecutor in her request for authorisation, and acknowledged by Newton, Article 98(2) does not, however, have any bearing on whether the ICC may lawfully exercise jurisdiction over US nationals; it merely prevents the ICC from requesting Afghanistan's assistance with arrest and surrender.[101] This means that if the ICC is able to somehow gain custody of accused US nationals,[102] exercising jurisdiction over them is not necessarily precluded.[103]

---

of mission agreement: D Scheffer, 'Article 98(2) of the Rome Statute: America's Original Intent' (2005) 3 *Journal of International Criminal Justice* 333 at 339.

The strategy of concluding Article 98 agreements was used somewhat selectively after some US allies refused to enter into such arrangements. See, *European Union Guiding Principles concerning Arrangements between a State Party to the Rome Statute of the International Criminal Court and the United States Regarding the Conditions to Surrender of Persons to the Court* [2002] 12488/1/02 COJUR 10 USA 37 PESC 374. Those Article 98 Agreements that are publicly available can be found at Georgetown Law Library website: Georgetown Law Library, *International Criminal Court – Article 98 Agreements Research Guide* (5 February 2018) available at guides.ll.georgetown.edu /article_98.

[100] C Kreß and K Prost, 'Article 98 Cooperation with Respect to Waiver of Immunity and Consent to Surrender' in O Triffterer, K Ambos (eds), *Rome Statute of the International Criminal Court – A Commentary* (CH Beck Hart Nomos, 2016) p. 2143.

[101] Prosecutor Request for Authorisation of an Investigation, para 46; Newton, 'How the International Criminal Court Threatens Treaty Norms', 393.

[102] Via a self-surrender, for example. In 2013, Bosco Ntaganda became the first person to surrender himself voluntarily to the ICC: Office of the Prosecutor, 'Bosco Ntaganda in the ICC's custody' (Press Release, ICC-CPI-20130322-PR888, 22 March 2013).

[103] Article 98(2) would make it more difficult for the ICC to pursue a prosecution of a US national accused of committing a crime in Afghanistan if that suspect was still on the territory of Afghanistan. Given the significant time lapse between the alleged commission of the crimes in 2003–4 and any future cases before the ICC, it is highly unlikely that any American suspects would still be in Afghanistan.

For further analysis of the relationship between Article 98(2) and SOFAs, see A Bogdan, 'The United States and the International Criminal Court: Avoiding Jurisdiction through Bilateral Agreements in Reliance on Article 98' (2008) 8 *International Criminal Law Review* 1; E Rosenfeld, 'Application of U.S. Status of Forces Agreements to Article 98 of the Rome Statute' (2003) 2 *Washington University Global Studies Law Review* 273; J Crawford, P Sands and R Wilde, 'In the Matter of the

Article 98(2) is not the only provision in the Rome Statute designed to make it more difficult for the ICC to exercise jurisdiction. Under the principle of complementarity enshrined in Article 17, a case is inadmissible before the ICC if it 'is being investigated or prosecuted by a State which has jurisdiction over it, unless the State is unwilling or unable genuinely to carry out the investigation or prosecution'.[104] As the territorial state, Afghanistan would usually have priority over the ICC to prosecute US nationals for crimes committed on its territory. Courtesy of the SOFA, however, Afghanistan has agreed not to exercise domestic judicial jurisdiction over members of the US armed forces, meaning that the ICC would likely consider Afghanistan unwilling to prosecute. As the state of nationality, the US would also be considered a State with primacy of jurisdiction, but the Prosecutor has disputed the adequacy of US investigations and proceedings.[105] While Article 17 gives the US the opportunity to challenge the admissibility of any cases against its nationals, the Court may agree with the Prosecutor and hold that the US has not demonstrated sufficient willingness to carry out investigations or prosecutions. Much like Article 98(2), Article 17 provides a procedural hurdle that could make it more difficult for the ICC to exercise jurisdiction over US nationals. Neither provision requires Afghanistan to prosecute US soldiers in contravention of the SOFA, yet the fact that it remains possible for the ICC to exercise jurisdiction over US nationals for crimes committed in Afghanistan may nevertheless conflict with a key provision in the SOFA.

As mentioned previously, Afghanistan has agreed that the US retains 'exclusive jurisdiction' over US soldiers for crimes committed on Afghan territory.[106] This is broader than simply promising that Afghanistan will not exercise its jurisdiction over US nationals, and in theory it appears to prevent not only Afghanistan but any other State or entity from exercising jurisdiction over US soldiers for crimes committed in Afghanistan.[107]

Statute of the International Criminal Court and In the Matter of Bilateral Agreements Sought by the United States under Article 98(2) of the Statute' (Joint Legal Opinion, 5 June 2003).

[104] Rome Statute, Article 17(1).
[105] Prosecutor Request for Authorisation of an Investigation, paras 290–335.
[106] While the 2002 Exchange of Notes does not use such language, the Annex to the Military Technical Agreement does at Section 1(3), as does the more recent bilateral security agreement at Article 13(1).
[107] For detailed analysis of the concept of exclusive jurisdiction in the context of a SOFA, see R Liivoja, *Criminal Jurisdiction over Armed Forces Abroad* (Cambridge University Press, 2017) pp. 125–38.

4.4 DELEGATION AND INTERNATIONAL AGREEMENTS

Completely exclusive jurisdiction, however, is not something that can be implemented by a bilateral treaty. This agreement would have no effect on a third State purporting to exercise jurisdiction over US nationals for crimes committed in Afghanistan under the principles of universality or passive personality. For example, in 2008 the Italian Court of Cassation held that it had jurisdiction under the principle of passive personality to prosecute a US soldier for killing an Italian military intelligence officer in Iraq, notwithstanding the fact that the relevant SOFA at the time gave sending states exclusive jurisdiction over their nationals.[108] The Italian court held that the provision of such immunity only applies between the sending and receiving States, not between two sending States.[109]

Arguably, the US would still be able to claim exclusive jurisdiction over any of its service members wanted by the ICC for crimes committed in Afghanistan because the ICC's jurisdiction in such a case would be based on territoriality, delegated by Afghanistan. There is nothing in the Statute, however, that allows for an exception to the Court's jurisdiction in circumstances where the territorial state has restricted its own judicial jurisdiction through a bilateral treaty. Article 120 of the Statute specifically prohibits States Parties from making reservations to the treaty, meaning that when Afghanistan ratified the Statute, there was no option for carving out an exception for ICC jurisdiction over US soldiers because of the SOFA.

By agreeing to be bound by the Rome Statute, Afghanistan has provided the ICC with jurisdiction over US service members for crimes committed on Afghan territory. This appears to conflict with Afghanistan's promise under the SOFA that the US shall retain exclusive jurisdiction over its armed forces. Does the existence of this conflict mean that the onus is on the ICC to ensure it does not exercise jurisdiction in a way that contradicts the US–Afghanistan SOFA?

By not taking the SOFA into account when assessing whether the ICC could exercise its jurisdiction over the situation in Afghanistan, the Prosecutor has been accused of 'usurping domestic jurisdiction'.[110]

---

[108] Coalition Provisional Authority Order No 17, Status of the Coalition, Foreign Liaison Missions, their Personnel and Contractors CPA/ORD/27 June 2004/17 (27 June 2004) Section 2(4).
[109] *Mario Luiz Lozano v Italy* [Italian Supreme Court of Cassation] Judgment No 31171/2008, 24 July 2008 discussed in A Sari, 'The Status of Foreign Armed Forces Deployed in Post-Conflict Environments: A Search for Basic Principles' in C Stahn, JS Easterday and J Iverson (eds), *Jus Post Bellum: Mapping the Normative Foundations* (Oxford University Press, 2014) pp. 492–5.
[110] Newton, 'How the International Criminal Court Threatens Treaty Norms', 380.

Newton claims that the Court is undermining international treaty norms and its own Statute by not considering whether the Statute's jurisdiction provisions are compatible with existing jurisdictional agreements. He argues that the ICC ought to 'seek interpretations that harmonize the two sets of treaties'[111] so as to ensure the exclusive jurisdiction clause in the SOFA remains intact. While the Court was designed to be complementary to the domestic jurisdiction of States, this does not mean it should accommodate every alternative international jurisdictional arrangement that may be inconsistent with the Statute.

Requiring the ICC to consider treaty arrangements of States Parties in order to minimise jurisdictional conflicts between States would be unsustainable and unnecessary. It would mean that the Court would be obliged to review any number of international agreements entered into by both States Parties and non-parties. As Sarooshi writes, 'there cannot be a presumption that [a] treaty is to be applied in a different way to member States depending on their domestic public or administrative law systems and the way in which the conferred governmental power or an analogous power is treated under these various systems'.[112] Similarly, there should not be a presumption that the Rome Statute is to be applied in a different way to States Parties depending on how they have limited their domestic judicial jurisdiction under a different treaty.

To expect the ICC to refrain from exercising jurisdiction if it conflicts with a State's prior claim to exclusive jurisdiction would essentially amount to the importation of an additional admissibility criterion into the Statute. Furthermore, the consequences of modifying the ICC's jurisdiction on the basis of the US–Afghanistan SOFA could prove to be particularly incongruous in the Afghanistan situation because of the complex mix of territories, jurisdictional arrangements and the two different US groups involved in the conflict.

The Prosecutor's preliminary examination found evidence of war crimes allegedly committed by, inter alia, members of the US armed forces and the CIA on the territories of Afghanistan, Poland, Romania and Lithuania. All four states were early ratifiers of the Rome Statute,[113] and all four had CIA-operated 'black site' detention facilities on their territory for a period of time in the mid-2000s, as part of the armed

---

[111] Ibid., 422.
[112] D Sarooshi, 'The Role of Domestic Public Law Analogies in the Law of International Organizations' (2008) 5 *International Organizations Law Review* 237 at 238.
[113] The Rome Statute entered into force for Afghanistan in May 2003, Poland and Romania in July 2002, and Lithuania in August 2003.

4.4 DELEGATION AND INTERNATIONAL AGREEMENTS   103

conflict in Afghanistan.[114] The Prosecutor alleged that US nationals committed acts of torture, outrages upon personal dignity and sexual violence in each of these detention facilities against detainees who were suspected members of the Taliban and Al Qaeda.[115] Members of the US armed forces are accused of committing such acts on the territory of Afghanistan, and members of the CIA are accused of committing such acts in Afghanistan and the three European states.[116]

Assume a hypothetical state of affairs in which the ICC is obliged to refrain from exercising jurisdiction in situations where to do so would conflict with a bilateral jurisdictional arrangement between states. In such a scenario, the ICC would not exercise jurisdiction over any members of the US armed forces accused of committing war crimes on Afghan territory in deference to Afghanistan's SOFA commitment that the US retains exclusive jurisdiction over its armed forces. The CIA, however, is not subject to any of the SOFAs that were in force at the time of the alleged crimes because such agreements are only applicable to the US armed forces and associated civilian personnel subject to the authority of the Department of Defense. Any CIA officials accused of committing war crimes in Afghanistan are therefore not covered by the exclusive jurisdiction arrangement in the SOFA, meaning that there are no grounds on which the US could claim exclusive jurisdiction over them. Similarly, in relation to the European black sites, any SOFAs between the US and Lithuania, Poland or Romania do not apply to members of the CIA.[117] There is evidence to suggest that secret bilateral agreements were in place between the US and each of the three European states, to ensure that the CIA detention programmes '[remained] absolutely

---

[114] Prosecutor Request for Authorisation of an Investigation, paras 202–3.
[115] Ibid., paras 191–203.
[116] The Prosecutor Request for Authorisation does not suggest that there was any involvement of the US armed forces in crimes allegedly committed in the European detention facilities.
[117] The SOFA in force at the time to regulate the status of US armed forces in Poland and Lithuania was the NATO SOFA, which recognises shared jurisdiction between the sending and receiving States but gives priority to the sending state in relation to 'offences arising out of any act or omission done in the performance of official duty': *Agreement between the Parties to the North Atlantic Treaty Regarding the Status of Their Forces* (19 June 1951) 199 UNTS 67, Art. VII(3)(a)(i). Under the SOFA in force at the time between the US and Romania, Romania waived its primary right to exercise criminal jurisdiction over US service members: *Agreement between the United States of America and Romania Regarding the Status of United States Forces in Romania* (signed 20 October 2001, entered into force 10 June 2002) TIAS 13170, Art III.

outside of the mechanisms of civilian oversight'.[118] The contents of any such agreements are classified, however, meaning that the ICC would be unable to take these secret jurisdiction arrangements into account, leading to a problematic scenario in which only publicly available bilateral agreements would affect the exercise of the ICC's jurisdiction.

Ultimately, the fact that members of the CIA are not covered by any publicly available jurisdictional agreements means that the ICC would be free to exercise jurisdiction over any accused CIA official in the Afghanistan situation. This could lead to a state of affairs in which an American CIA official allegedly responsible for war crimes against Afghan nationals in a detention facility in Lithuania, Poland or Romania would be subject to the ICC's jurisdiction, but an American military official accused of the same acts against Afghan nationals in a detention facility in Afghanistan would be exempt because of the SOFAs. More problematic would be a case in which a CIA official accused of committing war crimes in a black site detention facility in Afghanistan would be subject to prosecution by the ICC, but an American military official accused of committing the same crimes in the same facility would be procedurally immune from the Court's jurisdiction because of the SOFA. Stretching this hypothetical scenario further, if former US president George W Bush was charged by the ICC as someone with superior responsibility for crimes committed in the Afghanistan situation, he would theoretically only be subject to the Court's jurisdiction in relation to the CIA's crimes, even though he was also commander-in-chief of the armed forces.[119]

For the ICC to defer to the bilateral jurisdiction arrangements made by States would result in an inconsistent and potentially unfair exercise of the Court's jurisdiction. It could lead to impunity for some individuals as there is no guarantee that those subject to the exclusive jurisdiction of the sending State would be prosecuted. In the Afghanistan situation, certain US nationals would, in effect, be exempt from the ICC's jurisdiction on the basis of their official capacity as members of the armed forces. Such a result could arguably come into conflict with Article 27(2) of the

---

[118] D Marty, Rapporteur, Council of Europe Parliamentary Assembly Committee on Legal Affairs and Human Rights, *Secret detentions and illegal transfers of detainees involving Council of Europe member states: second report*, para 168.

[119] While an argument could be made that SOFAs do not apply to such senior officials, Bush is a former Head of State and therefore cannot rely on personal immunity under customary international law. See discussion in Section 4.3.2.1.

Rome Statute, which makes clear that 'the Statute shall apply equally to all persons without any distinction based on official capacity'.

There is nothing in the Statute that requires the ICC to consider any external treaty-based jurisdictional arrangements when it is deciding whether a case is admissible, and, for reasons outlined above, no such consideration should be made. This means that the incompatibility between the Rome Statute and the US–Afghanistan SOFA cannot be resolved by the ICC, but, as I argue in the next section, it is not the ICC's responsibility to resolve such conflicts.

4.4.1.3 Resolving the Conflict between the Statute and the SOFA

By virtue of its ratification of the Rome Statute, Afghanistan has agreed to allow the ICC to exercise jurisdiction over certain crimes committed by any national on Afghan territory. Under the SOFA, Afghanistan has agreed to allow the US to exercise exclusive jurisdiction over all crimes committed by US service members on Afghan territory. Given that members of the US armed forces are suspected of committing war crimes on Afghan territory, honouring both agreements appears impossible, which means Afghanistan is facing a classic treaty conflict.[120] It is beyond the scope of this chapter to explore in detail how the complex doctrine of treaty conflict might apply to the Afghanistan situation.[121] In cases like this one where there is no commonality of parties,[122] it is sufficient to acknowledge that 'neither the VCLT nor the customary canons of treaty construction offer a ready solution to such conflicts'.[123] It may be that in this situation, Afghanistan has essentially resorted to the principle of political decision, which Jan Klabbers describes as applying where 'the state concerned simply has to make a political decision which commitment to prefer'.[124] Some observers may baulk at the indeterminacy of

---

[120] CJ Borgen, 'Treaty Conflicts and Normative Fragmentation' in DB Hollis (ed), *The Oxford Guide to Treaties* (Oxford University Press, 2012) p. 455.
[121] For a comprehensive treatment on the law of treaty conflict, see generally J Klabbers, *Treaty Conflict and the European Union* (Cambridge University Press, 2009); See also, A Aust, *Modern Treaty Law and Practice*, 3rd ed (Cambridge University Press, 2013) pp. 192–204.
[122] Afghanistan is the only party to both treaties.
[123] Borgen, 'Treaty Conflicts and Normative Fragmentation', p. 456. This difficulty is likely compounded by the special nature of the Rome Statute as the constituent treaty of an international organisation.
[124] Klabbers, *Treaty Conflict and the European Union*, p. 88. The term 'political decision' was originally coined by Manfred Zuleeg in 'Vertragskonkurrenz im Völkerrecht. Teil I:

allowing Afghanistan to simply choose to honour its obligation under the Rome Statute over its promise to the US, but as Klabbers argues, 'it is precisely the indeterminacy of the principle of political decision that allows for flexible and responsive politics'.[125] Afghanistan's decision to enter into the SOFA and to voluntarily restrict its own judicial jurisdiction by bestowing procedural immunity on US soldiers was a quintessentially sovereign act. Ratifying the Rome Statute and agreeing to allow the ICC to exercise jurisdiction over Afghan territory was also a sovereign act. The consequences of entering into conflicting agreements are therefore a matter for Afghanistan, not the ICC. As long as Afghanistan remains a party to the Rome Statute, if an investigation into the situation were to eventuate, the ICC could lawfully exercise jurisdiction over acts committed by US soldiers on the territory of Afghanistan.

4.4.2 The Situation in Palestine

The ICC's consideration of the Palestine situation began in January 2009 when the Palestinian National Authority lodged an Article 12(3) declaration accepting the jurisdiction of the ICC over 'acts committed on the territory of Palestine since 1 July 2002'.[126] The Prosecutor opened a preliminary examination but eventually decided that Palestine could not be considered a State for the purposes of Article 12(3), and therefore was unable to accept the jurisdiction of the ICC. The Prosecutor reasoned that the 'competence for determining the term "State" within the meaning of article 12 rests, in the first instance with the United Nations Secretary General who, in case of doubt, will defer to the guidance of [the] General Assembly'.[127]

In November 2012, the UN General Assembly elevated Palestine from observer to 'non-member observer State status at the United Nations' in a resolution that was adopted by 138 votes in favour, with 9 against and 41 abstentions.[128] In 2014, the Office of the Prosecutor

---

Verträge zwischen souveränen Staaten', 20 *German Yearbook of International Law* (1977) 246–76.

[125] Klabbers, *Treaty Conflict and the European Union*, p. 90. For further discussion of the principle of political decisions, see S Ranganathan, *Strategically Created Treaty Conflicts and the Politics of International Law* (Cambridge University Press, 2014) pp. 56–61.

[126] Palestinian National Authority, *Declaration recognizing the Jurisdiction of the International Criminal Court* (21 January 2009).

[127] Office of the Prosecutor, 'Situation in Palestine' (Statement, 3 April 2012) para 5.

[128] *Status of Palestine in the United Nations*, GA Res 67/19, UN GAOR, 67th sess, 44th plen mtg, UN Doc A/Res/67/19 (29 November 2012).

4.4 DELEGATION AND INTERNATIONAL AGREEMENTS

released a statement acknowledging the General Assembly resolution as sufficient recognition of Palestinian statehood for the purposes of the ICC.[129] The Prosecutor declared that Palestine could accede to the Statute or lodge another Article 12(3) declaration and the Court would potentially be able to exercise jurisdiction over crimes committed on Palestinian territory after 29 November 2012.[130] On 1 January 2015, Palestine lodged a declaration under Article 12(3) accepting the jurisdiction of the ICC over crimes allegedly committed 'in the occupied Palestinian territory, including East Jerusalem, since June 13, 2014'. The following day Palestine acceded to the Rome Statute,[131] and two weeks later the Office of the Prosecutor announced that it would be opening a preliminary examination into crimes committed in the territory during the time period specified by Palestine in its declaration.[132] In December 2019, the Prosecutor decided to open an investigation into crimes committed 'in the West Bank, including East Jerusalem, and the Gaza Strip'.[133] Crimes in this situation are alleged to have been committed by both Palestinian and Israeli nationals.[134] Israel is not a State Party to the Rome Statute.

Should this investigation progress to the point where the ICC Prosecutor is pursuing active cases against Israeli nationals, two potential issues may arise with respect to delegation of jurisdiction as the legal basis for such action. The first relates to the question of Palestine's statehood and the extent of its delegable jurisdiction. The second issue concerns the

---

[129] Office of the Prosecutor, 'The Prosecutor of the International Criminal Court, Fatou Bensouda, opens a preliminary examination of the situation in Palestine' (Press Release, ICC-OTP-20150116-PR1083, 16 January 2015).

[130] Ibid.

[131] International Criminal Court Press and Media, 'The State of Palestine accedes to the Rome Statute' (Press Release, ICC-ASP-20150107-PR1082, 7 January 2015).

[132] Office of the Prosecutor, 'The Prosecutor of the International Criminal Court, Fatou Bensouda, opens a preliminary examination of the situation in Palestine' (Press Release, ICC-OTP-20150116-PR1083, 16 January 2015). Furthermore, in May 2018, Palestine submitted a referral to the Court, requesting the Prosecutor 'to investigate, in accordance with the temporal jurisdiction of the Court, past, ongoing and future crimes within the court's jurisdiction committed in all parts of the territory of the State of Palestine': Palestinian National Authority, *Referral by the State of Palestine Pursuant to Articles 13 (a) and 14 of the Rome Statute* (15 May 2018) para 9.

[133] *Situation in the State of Palestine (Prosecution request pursuant to article 19(3) for a ruling on the Court's territorial jurisdiction in Palestine)* (International Criminal Court, Office of the Prosecutor, Case No ICC-01/18, 20 December 2019).

[134] Office of the Prosecutor, *Report on Preliminary Examination Activities (2016)* (International Criminal Court, 14 November 2016) 25.

ability of Palestine to delegate jurisdiction in light of certain immunities provided under the Oslo Accords.[135]

4.4.2.1 The Question of Statehood and Delegable Jurisdiction

Despite the General Assembly resolution and Palestine's subsequent accession to the Rome Statute, there are still some who doubt whether Palestine is really a State in the traditional sense, with the full gamut of sovereign powers.[136] As it stands, 137 States recognise the State of Palestine,[137] and the Palestinian government has joined numerous international organisations either as a member[138] or an observer.[139] Palestine has not, however, been able to secure a recommendation from the Security Council, which is required for admission to the UN as a Member State. And as David Luban has observed, 'the Palestinian effort to bootstrap itself into statehood by joining international organisations backhandedly concedes that its statehood claim needs buttressing'.[140] The question of whether Palestine is or is not a State does not fall within the scope of this chapter.[141] It is, however, necessary to acknowledge that some ambiguity remains with respect to Palestinian statehood.[142] By

---

[135] The Palestine/Israel situation is extraordinarily complex and while I recognise that there are myriad political and legal issues that would undoubtedly arise in the course of any ICC investigation, this section is necessarily limited to a broad brush strokes account of the situation. See, eg, H Jöbstl, 'An Unlikely Day in Court? Legal Challenges for the Prosecution of Israeli Settlements under the Rome Statute' (2018) 51 *Israel Law Review* 339.

[136] See, eg, 'Letter to the Editor from Former Deputy Legal Adviser to Israel's Permanent Mission to the United Nations', *Just Security* (8 April 2014). See also, J Magid, 'Attorney General: ICC Can't Rule on Conflict as There Is No Palestinian State', *The Times of Israel* (27 November 2018); State of Israel Office of the Attorney General, 'The International Criminal Court's Lack of Jurisdiction over the So-Called "Situation in Palestine"' (20 December 2019), pp. 6–16.

[137] Diplomatic Relations, *Permanent Observer Mission of the State of Palestine to the United Nations New York* palestineun.org/about-palestine/diplomatic-relations/.

[138] For example, Palestine is a member of the Arab League, the Group of 77 and the United Nations Educational, Cultural and Scientific Organisation.

[139] Palestine has observer status at the World Health Organisation, the Universal Postal Union and the International Telecommunications Union, among others.

[140] D Luban, 'Palestine and the ICC – Some Legal Questions', *Just Security* (2 January 2015).

[141] For background on the issue of statehood in international law, see, eg, J Crawford and I Brownlie, *Brownlie's Principles of Public International Law*, 8th ed (Oxford University Press, 2012) pp. 127–42; K Knop, 'Statehood: Territory, People, Government' in J Crawford, M Koskenniemi (eds), *The Cambridge Companion to International Law* (Cambridge University Press, 2012) pp. 95–116.

[142] Y Ronen, 'Recognition of the State of Palestine: Still too much too soon?' in C Chinkin and F Baetens (eds), *Sovereignty, Statehood and State Responsibility: Essays in Honour of James Crawford* (Cambridge University Press, 2015) pp. 229–47.

becoming a non-member observer State at the UN, Palestine met the statehood threshold criterion set by the ICC Prosecutor for the purposes of acceding to the Rome Statute, but its uncertain status beyond the ICC may nevertheless have implications for Palestine's ability to delegate jurisdiction.[143]

Given that sovereign jurisdiction is the right under international law of a State to exercise certain of its sovereign powers,[144] the question arises as to whether Palestine possesses sufficient sovereign powers to delegate. In particular, can Palestine empower the ICC to prosecute Israeli nationals on the basis of delegated jurisdiction? As James Crawford points out:

> [O]nce a State is generally recognised – evidenced most obviously by admission to the United Nations – then a new situation arises, a category divide is established, marked by the legal category of statehood. The new state *is* 'sovereign', *has* 'sovereignty'; and this is true, no matter how fragile its condition, how diminutive its resources.[145]

If Palestine is considered a State, then it is sovereign and possesses sovereign powers of criminal justice exercisable under international law over foreign nationals for crimes committed on Palestinian territory.[146] Such jurisdiction would be delegable to the ICC, and would provide the basis for the Court to lawfully prosecute Israeli nationals for crimes committed on the territory of Palestine. Even assuming Palestinian statehood, however, there is another legal issue that could potentially affect Palestine's ability to delegate jurisdiction to the ICC: the existence of the Oslo Accords.

4.4.2.2 Restriction of Palestine's Judicial Jurisdiction via the Oslo Accords

The Oslo Accords comprise two agreements between the government of Israel and the Palestine Liberation Organisation (PLO), concluded in

---

[143] For a discussion about the possible implications of the ICC's recognition of Palestine as a State, see H Lee, 'Defining "State" for the Purpose of the International Criminal Court: The Problem Ahead after the Palestine Decision' (2016) 77 *University of Pittsburgh Law Review* 345. See also, MN Shaw, 'The Article 12(3) Declaration of the Palestinian Authority, the International Criminal Court and International Law' (2011) 9 *Journal of International Criminal Justice* 301 at 309–17.

[144] See Section 3.4.

[145] J Crawford, 'Sovereignty as a Legal Value' in J Crawford and M Koskenniemi (eds), *The Cambridge Companion to International Law* (Cambridge University Press, 2012) p. 117. Emphasis original.

[146] There is of course the significant question of what constitutes 'Palestinian territory'. See, eg, E Kontorovich, 'Israel/Palestine – The ICC's Uncharted Territory' (2013) 11 *Journal of International Criminal Justice* 979 at 983–8.

1993 and 1995, respectively.[147] The Accords are considered the 'cornerstone' of the peace process.[148] They created the Palestinian Authority and Oslo II divided the West Bank into three areas: Area A, over which Palestinians were to be given full control; Area B, which would give Palestinians control over civilian matters and Palestine and Israel joint control over security matters; and Area C, over which Israel has full control. Of particular relevance for the question of Palestine's ability to delegate jurisdiction to the ICC is the Protocol Concerning Legal Affairs. This is contained in Annex IV to Oslo II and provides that Israel has sole criminal jurisdiction over offences committed by Israelis in all areas.[149]

Politically, the Oslo Accords are essentially defunct, but their provisions continue to regulate daily life in the Palestinian territories despite some recent attempts to disregard them.[150] For example, shortly after Palestine's accession to the Rome Statute, a judge in the criminal department of the Jenin Magistrates Court in the West Bank declared that the Oslo Accords were no longer in effect, meaning that Israeli nationals were no longer exempt from prosecution in Palestinian courts.[151] Less than a week after this decision, the judge was transferred out of the criminal division of the Jenin court, with the Palestinian High Judicial Council releasing a statement affirming that the continuing validity of the Oslo Accords 'is a political matter to be decided by the Palestinian leadership, not a judicial body of any form'.[152]

---

[147] *Declaration of Principles on Interim Self-Government Arrangements*, Palestine Liberation Organisation – Israel (13 September 1993); *Israeli–Palestinian Interim Agreement on the West Bank and the Gaza Strip*, Palestinian Liberation Organisation – Israel (28 September 1995) ('Oslo I' and 'Oslo II').

[148] J Rudoren, 'What the Oslo Accords Accomplished', *The New York Times* (30 September 2015). For a thorough analysis of the status of the Oslo Accords under international law, see GR Watson, *The Oslo Accords: International Law and the Israeli–Palestinian Peace Agreements* (Oxford University Press, 2000). For the purposes of my argument, it is assumed that the Oslo Accords represent, at a minimum, a binding agreement between international legal subjects.

[149] Oslo II, Art I(2)(b).

[150] D Luban, 'Palestine and the ICC – Some Legal Questions', *Just Security* (2 January 2015). See also, Y Sayigh and S Erekat, 'Who Killed the Oslo Accords?', *Al Jazeera* (1 October 2015).

[151] N Nazzal, 'Jenin Judge Reassigned over Unilateral Move', *Gulf News* (19 January 2015); 'In the Name of the Palestinian People: Court Abrogates Oslo Accords', *The Legal Agenda* (24 February 2015).

[152] 'In the Name of the Palestinian People: Court Abrogates Oslo Accords', *The Legal Agenda* (24 February 2015), citing Jenin Magistrates Court, case 855, 11 January 2015 [trans].

4.4 DELEGATION AND INTERNATIONAL AGREEMENTS

Nine months later, 'the Palestinian leadership' set out the political position on the issue. In his speech to the UN General Assembly in September 2015, Palestinian President Mahmoud Abbas declared that Palestinians were no longer bound by the terms of the Oslo Accords.[153] But his declaration has not been followed by any implementing measures, and observers remain sceptical that Abbas will implement the 'concrete action' needed to truly dismantle the systems put in place by the Oslo Accords.[154] As such, the Protocol Concerning Legal Affairs remains applicable and Israeli nationals continue to be immune from prosecution in Palestinian courts, even for crimes committed on Palestinian territory.

4.4.2.3 Does Delegation of Jurisdiction Provide a Legal Basis for ICC Jurisdiction over Israeli Nationals?

The circumstances of Palestine and Oslo II are similar to the situation with Afghanistan and the SOFA discussed in Section 4.4.1. Both Palestine and Afghanistan have entered into agreements that provide procedural immunity to certain foreign nationals. But unlike the SOFA, the Oslo Accords are arguably not treaties in the traditional sense because they were not concluded between States.[155] At best, the PLO could be considered a non-State subject of international law, meaning that the Oslo Accords still have binding force between the two parties.[156] Complicating the status of the Accords further is the fact that they were concluded by the PLO, which has essentially been succeeded by the Palestinian Authority as the main governing body of the State of Palestine.[157]

Assuming, for the purposes of this analysis, that Oslo II remains in effect between Palestine and Israel, it does not affect the sovereign ability of Palestine to delegate its jurisdiction to the ICC. By ratifying the Rome Statute, however, Palestine has created a conflict between its obligations to delegate territorial jurisdiction to the ICC without reservation and its obligations to provide procedural immunity to Israeli nationals. As with the Afghanistan–US situation, Palestine's choice to restrict its own

---

[153] Permanent Observer Mission of the State of Palestine to the United Nations, 'Statement by HE Mr Mahmoud Abbas President of the State of Palestine at the General Debate of the United Nations General Assembly at its 70th Session' (30 September 2015).
[154] R Gladstone and J Rudoren, 'Mahmoud Abbas, at UN, Says Palestinians Are No Longer Bound by Oslo Accords', *The New York Times* (30 September 2015).
[155] Aust, *Modern Treaty Law and Practice*, pp. 58–9; Watson, *The Oslo Accords*, pp. 57–74.
[156] Watson, *The Oslo Accords*, pp. 91–102. See *Vienna Convention on the Law of Treaties*, Article 3.
[157] Y Ronen, 'Israel, Palestine and the ICC – Territory Uncharted but Not Unknown' (2014) 12 *Journal of International Criminal Justice* 7 at 23.

judicial jurisdiction should not affect the ICC's jurisdiction. The ICC operates on the assumption that States Parties are validly delegating jurisdiction in accordance with the Rome Statute. To assume otherwise would create an untenable onus on the Court to review a State Party's international agreements to ensure there are no restrictions on its delegable jurisdiction. More importantly it would significantly impair the uniform application of the ICC's jurisdiction provisions to States Parties.

Ultimately, Palestine has made a political decision to delegate jurisdiction to the ICC. Whether this is in contravention of Oslo II depends on whether Palestine still considers itself bound by the Accords. In any event, any irreconcilable conflict between Palestine and Israel about delegation of territorial jurisdiction is Palestine's issue to resolve, not the ICC's.[158] As long as Palestine can be considered a State under international law, it can delegate jurisdiction to the ICC, and the ICC's jurisdiction is not affected by the Oslo Accords.[159]

4.5 Conclusion

Under the Rome Statute, the ICC may exercise its jurisdiction over nationals of non-States Parties for crimes committed on the territory of States Parties. There are no allowances in the Statute for variations to this by way of immunities or other jurisdictional limitations. In ratifying the Rome Statute, a State is delegating jurisdiction to the ICC on the understanding that the Court will act in accordance with the preconditions and jurisdictional provisions contained in the Statute. It would be somewhat antithetical if the existence of a treaty limiting the exercise of domestic judicial jurisdiction over particular persons could then also further limit the jurisdiction of the ICC. The ICC is not an agent of any individual State Party, and it therefore would be incongruous for a State's decision to enter into international agreements to impede the ICC's jurisdiction.

---

[158] For alternative arguments as to why the Oslo Accords do not affect Palestine's ability to delegate jurisdiction to the ICC, see Ronen, 'Israel, Palestine and the ICC – Territory Uncharted but not Unknown', 21–4.

[159] But see, Y Shany, 'In Defence of Functional Interpretation of Article 12(3) of the Rome Statute: A Response to Yaël Ronen' (2010) 8 *Journal of International Criminal Justice* 329 at 339–42. Shany's arguments are based on the assumption that Palestine is not a State with 'full sovereignty [and] comprehensive criminal jurisdiction over [its] territory and nationals' at 339; State of Israel Office of the Attorney General, 'The International Criminal Court's Lack of Jurisdiction over the So-Called "Situation in Palestine"' (20 December 2019).

4.5 CONCLUSION

At present, delegation of jurisdiction may not, however, provide the Court with a legal basis for jurisdiction over incumbent Heads of State and other senior officials from non-States Parties. Such individuals are likely to be able to claim personal immunity as a procedural bar to ICC jurisdiction, despite the existence of Article 27(2). Given that Head of State immunity is a rule of customary international law, it is a matter for custom to provide exceptions to such immunity (unless a State has agreed to the waiver of its own Head of State immunity by virtue of its ratification of the Statute).

In summary, where a situation is referred to the ICC by States Parties or an investigation is initiated by the Prosecutor, delegation of jurisdiction provides the Court with a legal basis to prosecute nationals of non-States Parties for crimes committed on the territory of a State Party. The only exception to this is where the accused non-party national is an incumbent Head of State. In the next chapter I explore the legal basis for ICC jurisdiction over nationals of non-States Parties in situations referred to the Court by the Security Council.

5

The UN Security Council, the ICC and Nationals of Non-States Parties

5.1 Introduction

Chapter 4 focused almost exclusively on situations in which the ICC's jurisdiction is triggered by a State Party referral or by the initiation of an investigation by the Prosecutor. This chapter turns to examine the role of the UN Security Council in both activating and limiting the jurisdiction of the Court, particularly as it relates to nationals of non-States Parties.

The Preamble of the Rome Statute recognises that the crimes within the jurisdiction of the ICC 'threaten the peace, security and well-being of the world'. The maintenance of international peace and security is the *raison d'être* of the UN, and the primary responsibility of the Security Council.[1] The drafters of the Rome Statute recognised this potential overlap between the ICC's mandate and the UN's, and worked to ensure it would result in collaboration rather than conflict. There are references throughout the Rome Statute to the UN[2] and in 2004 the two institutions concluded the *Negotiated Relationship Agreement between the International Criminal Court and the United Nations* (ICC–UN Relationship Agreement) in which the UN and the ICC agreed to 'respect each other's status and mandate' and to cooperate on matters of mutual concern.[3] There are no circumstances in which this need for respect and cooperation is more important than the relationship between the ICC and the Security Council.

As mentioned in previous chapters, the Rome Statute provides the Security Council with two significant avenues of intervention into the Court's processes. The first is in Article 13(b) which gives the Council the power to trigger the Court's jurisdiction over a particular situation, and the second is in Article 16 which allows the Council to defer an

---

[1] UN Charter, Articles 1 and 24.
[2] See, eg, Rome Statute, Articles 2; 8(b)(iii); 115(b); 121; 125.
[3] *Negotiated Relationship Agreement between the International Criminal Court and the United Nations*, UN Doc A/58/874, Annex, 20 August 2004 (entered into force 4 October 2004) Articles 2(3), 3.

5.1 INTRODUCTION

investigation or prosecution for twelve months at a time. Both provisions stipulate that the Security Council must be acting under Chapter VII of the UN Charter when taking such actions as recognised by the Rome Statute. Chapter VII of the Charter sets out the measures that the Council may authorise 'with respect to threats of the peace, breaches of the peace and acts of aggression'.[4] Under Article 25 of the Charter, the Council's decisions are binding on UN Member States. Decisions are made by an affirmative vote of at least nine of the fifteen Council members, as long as none of the permanent five members have used their veto.[5]

Of particular relevance to this book are the issues that arise when, in exercising its referral powers under the Rome Statute, the Security Council affects the jurisdiction of the ICC over nationals of non-States Parties. Article 13(b) of the Statute is not subject to the territorial limit that applies to the other two Article 13 trigger mechanisms, meaning that the Council can extend the jurisdiction of the ICC to crimes committed on the territory of non-States Parties. Conversely, the Council has attempted to exempt nationals of non-States Parties from the jurisdiction of the Court using both the referral and deferral powers. This chapter explores the parameters of the Security Council's powers in Article 13(b) and Article 16 of the Statute and examines how the Council has utilised these powers in practice. Despite the existence of the ICC–UN Relationship Agreement, the 'partly overlapping mandates' of the Court and the Security Council have caused some tensions between the two.[6] The aim of this chapter is to examine the validity of some of the actions the Security Council has taken since the Statute entered into force, as well as to analyse the legal basis for ICC jurisdiction over Council-referred situations in non-States Parties. While delegation of jurisdiction provides a basis for the ICC's authority in situations where either the territorial State or the State of nationality are parties to the Rome Statute, it is not sufficient for situations involving non-States Parties that are referred to the Court by the Security Council. I argue that the legal basis for the ICC's jurisdiction in such Council-referred situations nevertheless remains anchored in the consent of the territorial State, implied by virtue of

---

[4] UN Charter, Article 39.
[5] UN Charter, Article 27. Of the permanent members, France and the UK are also States Parties to the Rome Statute. China, Russia and the US remain staunchly opposed to ratifying the Rome Statute.
[6] N White and R Cryer, 'The ICC and the Security Council: An Uncomfortable Relationship' in J Doria, HP Gasser and MC Bassiouni (eds), *The Legal Regime of the International Criminal Court* (Martinus Nijhoff Publishers, 2009) p. 456.

that State's membership of the UN and its obligations under the UN Charter.

Section 5.2 provides a brief overview of the negotiations for a permanent international criminal court in which delegates waxed and waned on the powers to be granted to the Security Council under the draft Statute. The rest of this chapter then focuses on each of the different roles given to the Council; beginning in Section 5.3 with the Article 16 power of deferral, which was invoked by the Council almost immediately after the Statute's entry into force. In this section I canvass the Council's early attempts to shield nationals of non-States Parties from the jurisdiction of the Court, arguing that such action is a misuse of the Council's power under the Statute.

In Section 5.4, I focus on the Security Council's role in referring situations to the ICC under Article 13(b) of the Rome Statute. Using the situations in Sudan and Libya, I argue that these States have implicitly consented to the jurisdiction of the Court over their nationals by virtue of their membership of the UN. In this part, I also touch upon whether the Council's power to refer situations to the ICC is intra or ultra vires the UN Charter and the effect that this would have on the legal basis for the ICC's jurisdiction.

In the final substantive section of this chapter, I turn to discuss the role to be played by the Security Council in the Court's jurisdiction over the crime of aggression. The 2010 Kampala Amendments[7] provide the Council with an additional (albeit limited) role in determining the existence of an act of aggression, and the amendments also provide some limitations on the Court's jurisdiction over non-States Parties.

5.2 The Role of the Security Council in the Rome Statute

What role the Security Council should play with respect to the ICC was a question that plagued the various preparatory committees tasked with drafting a statute for a permanent international criminal court. Early on, the International Law Commission (ILC) envisioned a relatively minor role for the Security Council. The only power allocated to the Council

---

[7] *Amendments on the crime of aggression to the Rome Statute of the International Criminal Court,* Resolution RC/Res.6, adopted at the 13th plenary mtg (11 June 2010) ('Kampala Amendments'). The Amendments entered into force in July 2018: International Criminal Court, *Activation of the jurisdiction of the Court over the crime of aggression,* Resolution ICC-ASP/16/Res.5 (14 December 2017).

5.2 ROLE OF SECURITY COUNCIL IN THE ROME STATUTE 117

under the 1991 Draft Code of Crimes against the Peace and Security of Mankind was the ability to override any prima facie determination by the court that an act of aggression had been committed.[8] Such a limited role for the Security Council reflected the prevailing view at the time that the maintenance of international peace and security was incompatible with judicial criminal proceedings.[9] This attitude changed markedly after the Council's establishment of the ad hoc criminal tribunals in 1993 and 1994, with the ILC's 1994 Draft Statute for an International Criminal Court incorporating a much greater role for the Security Council. Importantly, the 1994 Draft Statute provided that the Council may, acting under Chapter VII of the UN Charter, refer a matter involving any State to the court (as opposed to matters involving only States Parties to the proposed statute).[10] The rationale behind giving the Security Council broad referral power was to provide an alternative to establishing any more ad hoc tribunals.[11] In addition to the referral power, the Draft Statute stipulated that the Council would have sole authority to determine the existence of an act of aggression. Furthermore, the court would be precluded from initiating a prosecution if the situation under investigation was simultaneously 'being dealt with' by the Security Council under Chapter VII.[12] This last provision was particularly contentious considering it essentially would have given the Security Council the power to prevent the commencement of court proceedings.[13]

In 1995 the UN General Assembly set up the Ad Hoc Committee on the Establishment of an International Criminal Court, which continued to deliberate on the role of the Security Council. Several delegations expressed 'serious reservations' about the powers granted to the Council

---

[8] 'Draft Code of Crimes against the Peace and Security of Mankind', *Report of the International Law Commission on the Work of Its Forty-Third Session*, 29 April–19 July 1991, UN Doc A/46/10 (1991) 243 ('1991 Draft Code of Crimes') Article 15.

[9] D Ruiz Verduzco, 'The Relationship between the ICC and the United Nations Security Council' in C Stahn (ed), *The Law and Practice of the International Criminal Court* (Oxford University Press, 2015) p. 33.

[10] 'Draft Code of Crimes Against the Peace and Security of Mankind', *Report of the International Law Commission on the Work of Its Forty-Sixth Session*, UN GAOR, 49th sess, Supp No 10, UN Doc A/49/10 (2 May–22 July 1994) 84–8 ('1994 Draft Statute') Article 23(1).

[11] Ibid., 44; W Schabas, and G Pecorella, 'Article 13 Exercise of Jurisdiction' in O Triffterer and K Ambos (eds), *Rome Statute of the International Criminal Court – A Commentary* 3rd ed, (CH Beck Hart Nomos, 2016) 690.

[12] 1994 Draft Statute, Articles 23(2) and (3).

[13] *Report of the International Law Commission on the Work of Its Forty-Sixth Session*, UN GAOR, 49th sess, Supp No 10, UN Doc A/49/10 (2 May–22 July 1994) 87–8.

under the Draft Statute.[14] They argued that giving the Security Council total authority over the crime of aggression and the power to block commencement of proceedings would undermine the credibility, independence and impartiality of the court.[15] From 1996 until the Rome Conference in 1998, the discussions continued in the Preparatory Committee, and questions surrounding the role of the Security Council remained highly contentious.[16] At Rome, there was resolute opposition from a small group of delegates who objected to any involvement of the Security Council whatsoever,[17] but the compromise reached in the final hours of the conference cemented the relationship between the Council and the new court.

The final text of the Rome Statute provides two avenues for Security Council involvement with the Court. Article 13(b) gives the Council the ability to refer situations to the ICC, regardless of whether the situation involves States not party to the Rome Statute. Because of the nature of the referral power as potentially extending the jurisdiction of the Court, it has become known as the 'positive pillar' of the Council's relationship with the Court.[18] Under Article 16 of the Statute, the Security Council has the power to defer an ICC investigation or prosecution for twelve months at a time. The deferral power is, conversely, known as the 'negative pillar' because it provides the Security Council with an ostensibly broad power that could significantly curtail the activities of the Court.[19]

Given the outwardly hostile position taken by the US towards the ICC in the early years of the Court's establishment, there was little expectation that the Security Council would be cooperating with the ICC any time

---

[14] *Report of the Ad Hoc Committee on the Establishment of an International Criminal Court*, UN GAOR, 50th sess, Supp No 22, UN Doc A/50/22 (1995) 27.

[15] Ibid., 278.

[16] See, eg, *Report of the Preparatory Committee on the Establishment of an International Criminal Court (Volume I)*, UN GAOR, 51st sess, Supp No 22, UN Doc A/51/22 (1996) 31–2; W Schabas, *The International Criminal Court: A Commentary on the Rome Statute*, 2nd ed (Oxford University Press, 2016) pp. 367–71.

[17] Triffterer, *Commentary on the Rome Statute of the International Criminal Court: Observers' Notes, Article by Article*, p. 695.

[18] F Berman, 'The Relationship between the International Criminal Court and the Security Council' in H von Hebel, JG Lammers and J Schukking (eds), *Reflections on the International Criminal Court: Essays in Honour of Adriaan Bos* (TMC Asser Press, 1999) pp. 173–80; Ruiz Verduzco, 'The Relationship between the ICC and the United Nations Security Council', p. 30.

[19] Berman, 'The Relationship between the International Criminal Court and the Security Council'; Ruiz Verduzco, 'The Relationship between the ICC and the United Nations Security Council', p. 30.

soon after its establishment. Yet in the first decade of the Court's operation, the Security Council invoked both its referral and deferral powers in ways that were not anticipated by the Statute's drafters.[20] In particular, Court watchers and commentators did not foresee the Security Council's attempts to restrict the Court's jurisdiction over nationals of non-States Parties by invoking Article 16.[21] The following sections explore the legal parameters of the Security Council's role under Articles 16 and 13(b) with a focus on how it affects the legal basis for the ICC's jurisdiction over nationals of non-States Parties.

5.3 The Negative Pillar: Excluding Jurisdiction

In this section I examine the power of the Security Council to defer ICC prosecutions under Article 16 as well as the creative ways in which the Council has actually deployed Article 16 in an attempt to limit the jurisdiction of the Court. I also explore whether the Security Council can lawfully exempt certain non-party nationals from the jurisdiction of the ICC simply by invoking Chapter VII of the UN Charter.

5.3.1 Article 16: The Deferral Power

Article 16 provides that

> [n]o investigation or prosecution may be commenced or proceeded with under this Statute for a period of 12 months after the Security Council, in a resolution adopted under Chapter VII of the Charter of the United Nations, has requested the Court to that effect; that request may be renewed by the Council under the same conditions.

Article 16 came about as an alternative proposal to the suggestion in the 1994 ILC Draft Statute that the Security Council should have the ability to prevent the Court from proceeding with a prosecution if the Council was already dealing with the matter.[22] Article 16 differs from the proposal first made in the Draft Statute in two important aspects. The first is that Article 16 puts the onus on the Security Council to make a request under Chapter VII of the Charter if the Council wants to prevent or halt ICC

---

[20] White and Cryer, 'The ICC and the Security Council', p. 466.
[21] Ibid.
[22] UN Diplomatic Conference of Plenipotentiaries on the Establishment of an International Court, *Draft Statute for the International Criminal Court*, UN Doc A/CONF.183/2/Add.1 (14 April 1998) Article 5. The original proposal was in Article 23(3) of the 1994 ILC Draft Statute.

proceedings for the sake of international peace and security. This means that it must adopt a resolution with the affirmative vote of nine Council members and there must be no veto from any of the permanent five. This mechanism is designed to stop any one of the permanent members from being able to disingenuously interfere with ICC proceedings.[23] The second difference between Article 16 and the proposed provision in the ILC Draft Statute is that Article 16 provides a time limit on the deferral request. Again, the onus is on the Security Council to reassess the situation every 12 months and adopt another Chapter VII resolution to keep the matter out of the ICC's jurisdiction.

Critics have suggested that without a limit on the number of times a deferral resolution can be adopted under Article 16, the Council could prevent an ICC investigation or prosecution from proceeding indefinitely.[24] This is theoretically true, but the fact that the Council must reconsider the deferral every twelve months and adopt a new resolution if it wants the stay to continue means that the odds of an indefinite deferral are significantly decreased. The Council is a political body subject to the ever-changing dynamics of international relations, meaning that the political will for ongoing deferrals will fluctuate. Furthermore, of the permanent five members, France and the UK are also States Parties to the Rome Statute and arguably have a vested interest in ensuring that the Security Council deferral power is not abused.

Article 16 does not, prima facie, raise any questions with respect to the ICC's jurisdiction over nationals of non-States Parties. But early on, the Security Council controversially attempted to use Article 16 to exempt nationals from non-States Parties from the jurisdiction of the Court.

5.3.1.1 Resolutions 1422 (2002) and 1487 (2003)

The Rome Statute entered into force on 1 July 2002. Just twelve days later the Security Council adopted Resolution 1422 in which it made a blanket request in the following terms:

> *Acting* under Chapter VII of the Charter of the United Nations [the Security Council],
>
> 1. *Requests,* consistent with the provisions of Article 16 of the Rome Statute, that the ICC, if a case arises involving current or former officials or personnel from a contributing State not a Party to the Rome Statute

---
[23] Schabas and Pecorella, 'Article 13 Exercise of Jurisdiction' p. 695.
[24] D Sarooshi, 'Aspects of the Relationship between the International Criminal Court and the United Nations' (2001) 32 *Netherlands Yearbook of International Law* 27 at 39.

5.3 NEGATIVE PILLAR: EXCLUDING JURISDICTION

over acts or omissions relating to a United Nations established or authorized operation, shall for a twelve-month period starting 1 July 2002 not commence or proceed with investigation or prosecution of any such case, unless the Security Council decides otherwise.[25]

In operative paragraph 2, the resolution expressed the Council's intention to renew this request every twelve months 'for as long as may be necessary'. The resolution did not refer to any specific countries or issues on the Council's agenda but nevertheless purported to exclude from the jurisdiction of the ICC any UN peacekeepers from States not party to the Rome Statute. Driven by the US threat to block future UN peacekeeping missions if its concerns were not addressed,[26] the resolution was a clear attempt to circumvent Article 12(2)(a) of the Rome Statute. If a situation were to arise in which UN peacekeepers were accused of committing Statute crimes on the territory of a State Party to the Rome Statute, Resolution 1422 intended to give those accused peacekeepers who are nationals of non-States Parties immunity from ICC jurisdiction. This is at odds with the jurisdiction granted to the ICC by Article 12(2)(a).

Of particular concern with Resolution 1422 was the fact that both Chapter VII of the Charter and Article 16 of the Statute were invoked for unspecified, future situations in which potential ICC cases would be deferred indefinitely based solely on the involvement of nationals of non-States Parties. The implied rationale for such a sweeping resolution was that those States not party to the Statute would be reluctant to contribute troops to UN peacekeeping operations if there was any risk that such forces might be prosecuted by the ICC.[27] Facilitating UN Member States' ability to contribute to such operations was therefore claimed to be 'in the interests of international peace and security'.[28]

Twelve months later, the provisions of Resolution 1422 were renewed by the adoption of Resolution 1487.[29] The renewal did not go ahead without

---

[25] SC Res 1422, UN SCOR, 4572nd mtg, UN Doc S/RES/1422 (12 July 2002).
[26] *Record of UN Security Council 4568th meeting*, UN SCOR, 57th sess, 4568th mtg, UN Doc S/PV.4568 (10 July 2002).
[27] SC Res 1422, UN SCOR, 4572nd mtg, UN Doc S/RES/1422 (12 July 2002), Preambular paragraphs 7 and 8 of Resolution 1422:
Determining that operations established or authorized by the United Nations Security Council are deployed to maintain or restore international peace and security,
Determining further that it is in the interests of international peace and security to facilitate Member States' ability to contribute to operations established or authorized by the United Nations Security Council.
[28] Ibid.
[29] SC Res 1487, UN SCOR, 4772nd mtg, UN Doc S/RES/1487 (12 June 2003).

issue, however, as the UN Secretary-General took the unusual step of addressing the Security Council in its chamber with a plea against making the resolution renewal 'an annual routine'.[30] The Secretary-General warned that ongoing renewals would create a permanent immunity that 'would undermine not only the authority of the ICC but also the authority of the Council and the legitimacy of United Nations peacekeeping'.[31]

Resolution 1422 was not renewed for a third time, as the US lost support for its cause after evidence of prisoner abuse by American soldiers at Abu Ghraib prison in Iraq came to light in the first half of 2004.[32] Despite the fact that the resolution was only in operation for two years and did not apply to any specific situation during that time period, it created a potential precedent for the notion that the Security Council has the ability to exempt nationals of non-States Parties from the jurisdiction of the ICC.[33]

It has been suggested that because an Article 16 deferral simply prevents the commencement or continuation of an investigation or prosecution, it 'does not mean that the ICC has lost jurisdiction regarding the case subject to the deferral'.[34] This is perhaps technically true, but if we conceive of jurisdiction as the right to exercise certain powers, a deferral essentially takes away the ICC's right to exercise its powers in particular circumstances, for a limited time. It is a temporary suspension of jurisdiction. Whether Resolution 1422 was a valid suspension of jurisdiction with respect to Article 16 is the focus of much of the post-resolution commentary.[35] I do not intend to review the arguments about the validity

---

[30] *UN Secretary-General address to the UN Security Council* in UN SCOR, 58th sess, 4772nd mtg, UN Doc S/PV.4772 (12 June 2003) 3.

[31] Ibid.

[32] White and Cryer, 'The ICC and the Security Council', p. 471.

[33] This issue will be discussed further in Section 5.4.

[34] A Mokhtar, 'The Fine Art of Arm-Twisting: The US, Resolution 1422 and Security Council Deferral Power under the Rome Statue' (2003) 3 *International Criminal Law Review* 295 at 310.

[35] See, eg, C Stahn, 'The Ambiguities of Security Council Resolution 1422 (2002)' (2003) 14 *European Journal of International Law* 85; N Jain, 'A Separate Law for Peacekeepers: The Clash between the Security Council and the International Criminal Court' (2005) 16 *European Journal of International Law* 239; R Lavalle, 'A Vicious Storm in a Teacup: The Action by the United Nations Security Council to Narrow the Jurisdiction of the International Criminal Court' (2003) 14 *Criminal Law Forum* 195; S Zappalà, 'The Reaction of the US to the Entry into Force of the ICC Statute: Comments on UN SC Resolution 1422 (2002) and Article 98 Agreements' (2003) 1 *Journal of International Criminal Justice* 114; Mokhtar, 'Fine Art of Arm-Twisting'; M El Zeidy, 'The United States Dropped the Atomic Bomb of Article 16 of the ICC Statute: Security Council Power of Deferrals and Resolution 1422' (2002) 35 *Vanderbilt Journal of Transnational Law* 1503.

of Resolution 1422 in any great detail, but it is worth summarising the main criticisms of the Council's first attempt to limit the operation of the Court.

5.3.1.2 The Validity of Resolution 1422

The issue of Resolution 1422's validity may be split into two separate questions. The first is whether the resolution was intra vires with respect to the UN Charter, and the second is whether the resolution was a properly constituted deferral within the terms of Article 16 of the Rome Statute.

Was Resolution 1422 intra vires the UN Charter? The chief complaint directed towards Resolution 1422 was that the Security Council did not draw a link to any threat to the peace or breach of the peace which is required by Article 39 of the Charter before the Council can take measures under Chapter VII. At most, the preamble of Resolution 1422 implies that the mere possibility of ICC prosecution is enough to discourage some UN Member States from contributing to UN peacekeeping operations, and that this could prevent the UN from addressing future conflicts.[36] The Council seemed to be drawing a very tenuous inference that the potential for ICC prosecution of peacekeepers from non-States Parties could exacerbate a threat to, or breach of, the peace. This reading of Resolution 1422 was considered entirely insufficient by many UN Member States and commentators to bring it intra vires the UN Charter.[37] Ultimately, however, the issue of whether Resolution 1422 is valid under the UN Charter is less relevant for the ICC than the question of whether the resolution conforms to the requirements of the Rome Statute.[38]

The Consistency of Resolution 1422 with the Rome Statute In operative paragraph 1 of Resolution 1422, the request for a deferral is prefaced

---

[36] Stahn, 'The Ambiguities of Security Council Resolution 1422 (2002)', 87.
[37] See, eg, Statements of the Representatives of Canada, New Zealand, Liechtenstein, Trinidad and Tobago, Greece and The Netherlands, UN SCOR, 58th sess, 4772nd mtg, UN Doc S/PV.4772 (12 June 2003). See also, Stahn, 'The Ambiguities of Security Council Resolution 1422 (2002)', 86–7; Mokhtar, 'Fine Art of Arm-Twisting', 314; R Cryer and ND White, 'The Security Council and the International Criminal Court: Who's Feeling Threatened' (2004) 8 *International Peacekeeping* 143 at 155–8.
[38] For further discussion of the limits of Security Council power under the UN Charter, see Section 5.4.3.2. For a more comprehensive analysis of this issue as it relates to Resolution 1422, see Mokhtar, 'Fine Art of Arm-Twisting', 317–26; Lavalle, 'A Vicious Storm in a Teacup', 200–6.

by a declaration that the terms of the request are 'consistent with the provisions of Article 16 of the Rome Statute'. Yet by attempting to defer future cases on uncertain grounds, critics argue that the Security Council's interpretation of Article 16 was inappropriately broad and incompatible with the purpose of the provision.[39] A number of States took to the floor of the Security Council to protest that the Council's interpretation of Article 16 did not reflect what was agreed upon by States Parties to the Rome Statute. They called attention to the negotiating history of the provision, which 'makes clear that recourse to Article 16 is on a case-by-case basis only, where a particular situation – for example the dynamic of a peace negotiation – warrants a 12-month deferral'.[40] The fact that there is no specific case or situation mentioned in the resolution lends credence to the argument that Resolution 1422 is not consistent with the provisions of Article 16. In order for a resolution to be compatible with Article 16, the Security Council would need to make a determination that a threat to the peace exists in relation to a particular situation before the ICC, and that a deferral of investigation or prosecution is therefore required in those circumstances.[41]

In light of Resolution 1422's apparent incompatibility with Article 16, some observers concluded that the Security Council was not merely trying to interpret Article 16 to suit its agenda, but was in fact attempting to 'amend the negotiated terms' of the Rome Statute.[42] Irrespective of what the Security Council actually intended, the perception that the Council was attempting to amend the terms of a treaty was roundly criticised:

> The Council cannot alter international agreements that have been duly negotiated and freely entered into by States parties. The Council is not vested with treaty-making and treaty-reviewing powers. It cannot create new obligations for the States parties to the Rome Statute, which is an international treaty that can be amended only through the procedures provided in articles 121 and 122 of the Statute.[43]

---

[39] Berman, 'The Relationship between the International Criminal Court and the Security Council', pp. 177–8; Stahn, 'The Ambiguities of Security Council Resolution 1422 (2002)', 88–91; Cryer and White, 'Security Council and the International Criminal Court', 149.

[40] Statement of the Representative of Canada, UN SCOR, 57th sess, 4568th mtg, UN Doc S/PV.4568 (10 July 2002). See also, statements of the Representatives of New Zealand, Liechtenstein, Brazil, Switzerland and Mexico. Under Article 32 of the VCLT, recourse may be had to *travaux préparatoires* as supplementary means of treaty interpretation.

[41] Cryer and White, 'Security Council and the International Criminal Court', 150.

[42] Mokhtar, 'Fine Art of Arm-Twisting', 328.

[43] Statement of the Representative of Brazil, UN SCOR, 57th sess, 4568th mtg, UN Doc S/PV.4568 (10 July 2002) 22. See also, statements of the Representatives of Canada, New

Even if there was some allowance for the Security Council to modify the terms of a treaty via a resolution, such action would only be binding on UN Member States and not on the ICC as an institution.[44] As discussed in Chapter 3, Article 4(1) of the Rome Statute establishes the ICC's international legal personality, and the ICC-UN Relationship Agreement further recognises the Court's independence from the UN system.[45] As an independent body, the ICC is only bound by the Rome Statute, not by Security Council resolutions.[46] Therefore, unless a Security Council resolution complies with the Statute, the ICC is not obliged to follow the terms of the resolution. The only conceivable way that the ICC would be bound by the Security Council's interpretation of Article 16, is if Resolution 1422 was read as obliging those UN Member States who also make up the Assembly of States Parties to the Rome Statute to amend Article 16 to bring it in line with Resolution 1422. This would be an extraordinary use (and arguably an abuse) of the Security Council's Chapter VII powers.

Perhaps as a consequence of the controversy surrounding the invocation of Article 16 in Resolution 1422, the Council's next attempt at limiting the jurisdiction of the ICC appeared to circumvent the Rome Statute entirely.

5.3.2 Excluding Jurisdiction without Reference to the Rome Statute

In August 2003, two months after the adoption of Resolution 1487 to extend the mandate of Resolution 1422, the Security Council adopted Resolution 1497, which authorised the establishment of a multinational force in Liberia.[47] Operative paragraph 7 of that resolution was included at the insistence of the US[48] and decides the following:

> [T]hat current or former officials or personnel from a contributing State, which is not a party to the Rome Statute of the International Criminal Court, shall be subject to the exclusive jurisdiction of the contributing

---

Zealand, France, the Islamic Republic of Iran, Mongolia, Liechtenstein and Switzerland, UN SCOR, 57th sess, 4568th mtg, UN Doc S/PV.4568 (10 July 2002).

[44] White and Cryer, 'The ICC and the Security Council', p. 458.
[45] ICC-UN Relationship Agreement, Article 2(1).
[46] Those States Parties that are also members of the UN are bound in their individual capacities by Security Council resolutions. But the ICC *as an institution* is not: Article 1 of the Rome Statute provides that '[t]he jurisdiction and functioning of the Court shall be governed by the provisions of this Statute'.
[47] SC Res 1497, UN SCOR, 4803rd mtg, UN Doc S/RES/1497 (1 August 2003).
[48] White and Cryer, 'The ICC and the Security Council', p. 471.

State for all alleged acts or omissions arising out of or related to the Multinational Force or United Nations stabilization force in Liberia, unless such exclusive jurisdiction has been expressly waived by that contributing State.

Resolution 1497 was directed at a specific situation in which there had been a clear determination of a threat to international peace and security, which immediately distinguishes it from Resolution 1422. What also sets Resolution 1497 apart from 1422 is the fact that there was no mention of Article 16. Instead, the resolution purported to exempt nationals of non-States Parties from any foreign criminal jurisdiction: domestic or international. There was a legitimate concern, raised by Germany, that Resolution 1497 would prevent States from asserting universal or passive personality jurisdiction over certain foreign nationals accused of committing *jus cogens* crimes in Liberia.[49] But the clear intention behind operative paragraph 7 was to prevent the ICC from exercising jurisdiction over nationals of non-States Parties without the constraints of Article 16. The result is that Resolution 1497 appeared to provide permanent immunity from ICC jurisdiction to peacekeepers from non-States Parties in Liberia despite the fact that there is no basis for such in the Rome Statute.

Unlike Resolution 1422, Resolution 1497's validity under the UN Charter was not in issue. Aside from its clear link to a threat to the peace, giving troop-contributing States exclusive jurisdiction over their personnel is not a novel arrangement for UN-sanctioned missions.[50] The chief controversy over Resolution 1497 was whether operative paragraph 7 would actually prevent the ICC from exercising jurisdiction over

---

[49] Statement of the Representative of Germany, UN SCOR, 58th sess, 4803rd mtg, UN Doc S/PV.4803 (1 August 2003) 4.

[50] See, eg, *Model status-of-forces agreement for peace-keeping operations*, UN GAOR, 45th sess, UN Doc A/45/594 (9 October 1990) clause 47(b); Jain, 'A Separate Law for Peacekeepers', 245. The issue of foreign immunity for members of national armed forces and UN peacekeepers is particularly complex and far beyond the scope of this book. To give a greatly simplified overview, members of armed forces have functional immunity from foreign domestic jurisdictions under customary international law and also usually enjoy personal immunity under bilateral and multilateral international agreements. As a starting point for further research on this issue, see generally R Burke, 'Status of Forces Deployed on UN Peacekeeping Operations: Jurisdictional Immunity' (2011) 16 *Journal of Conflict and Security Law* 63; A Sari, 'The Status of Armed Forces in Public International Law: Jurisdiction and Immunity' in A Orakhelashvili (ed), *Research Handbook on Jurisdiction and Immunities in International Law* (Edward Elgar Publishing, 2015) p. 319; RS Clark, 'Peacekeeping Forces, Jurisdiction and Immunity: A Tribute to George Barton' (2012) 43 *Victoria University of Wellington Law Review* 77.

5.3 NEGATIVE PILLAR: EXCLUDING JURISDICTION

nationals from non-States Parties for Statute crimes allegedly committed while part of the Liberian peacekeeping force.

Importantly, Liberia did not ratify the Rome Statute until September 2004. Consequently, when Resolution 1497 was adopted in August 2003, the only way the ICC could have exercised jurisdiction over nationals of non-States Parties for crimes committed on the territory of Liberia would have been if the Security Council had referred the situation under Article 13(b). It would thus appear that the inclusion of operative paragraph 7 at the insistence of the US was, at the time, entirely unnecessary. For the sake of analysis, however, the remainder of this part makes the hypothetical assumption that Liberia was a State Party to the Rome Statute when Resolution 1497 was adopted, meaning that under Article 12(2)(a), the ICC could have gained jurisdiction over accused nationals of non-States Parties.[51]

5.3.2.1 Resolution 1497 and Article 98(2) of the Rome Statute

As discussed previously, the ICC is an independent international institution not bound by Security Council resolutions. For Resolution 1497 to have an effect on the jurisdiction of the ICC, the source of any obligation on the Court would have to be found in the Rome Statute. Neha Jain posits that Article 98(2) could be used to require the ICC's compliance with operative paragraph 7 of Resolution 1497. Recalling the analysis in Chapter 4, Article 98(2) prevents the Court from proceeding with a request for surrender when that surrender would be at odds with the requested State's obligations under international agreements. Jain argues that because the Security Council acts on behalf of UN Member States when it carries out its duties related to the maintenance of international peace and security, any Chapter VII resolution is essentially an international agreement among all UN Member States.[52] More likely, in my view, is that the UN Charter itself is the relevant international agreement among UN Member States who are obliged by Article 25 of the Charter 'to accept and carry out the decisions of the Security Council'. Either way, UN Member States were bound by the terms of Resolution 1497, meaning that operative paragraph 7 would arguably have had the effect of

---

[51] The following hypothetical analysis assumes that crimes within the jurisdiction of the ICC were committed on the territory of Liberia by UN peacekeepers from States not party to the Rome Statute during the nearly fifteen-year UN Mission in Liberia. The jurisdiction of the ICC has been triggered under Article 13(a) or (c) and admissibility criteria have been satisfied.

[52] Jain, 'A Separate Law for Peacekeepers', 248.

preventing any UN Member State (and therefore any ICC States Parties)[53] from surrendering to the ICC a peacekeeper from a non-State Party accused of crimes committed in Liberia. But Article 98(2) would only prevent the ICC from proceeding with a request for surrender, and would not oblige the Court to respect the Security Council's decision to subject the non-party national peacekeepers to the exclusive jurisdiction of the contributing State. As I argued in Chapter 4, Article 98(2) would not prevent the ICC from exercising jurisdiction in accordance with Article 12(2)(a) if the Court somehow gained custody of an accused non-party national. The question of whether there is a legal basis for such jurisdiction requires further analysis.

5.3.2.2 Can Liberia Delegate Jurisdiction in Light of Resolution 1497?

Pursuant to Resolution 1497, the Security Council established the United Nations Mission in Liberia (UNMIL) in September 2003.[54] The effect of operative paragraph 7 of Resolution 1497 was to give procedural immunity from foreign domestic jurisdictions to all members of the UNMIL peacekeeping force who are from States not party to the Rome Statute.[55] Under Article 25 of the UN Charter, UN members 'agree to accept and carry out the decisions of the Security Council'.[56] This means that if a national from a non-State Party committed a Statute crime while he or she was part of UNMIL, no State aside from the State of nationality would have jurisdiction over that individual.[57] As mentioned above, this reflects the typical jurisdictional arrangement found in SOFAs regulating UN

---

[53] At the time of Resolution 1497's adoption, all members of the Assembly of States Parties were also UN members. In July 2008, the Cook Islands, a non-UN member, ratified the Rome Statute, and in January 2015, Palestine became a State Party to the Rome Statute but remains a non-member observer State at the UN. The effect of Palestine's status will be discussed in more detail in Section 5.4.3.2. For the purposes of the hypothetical discussion relating to Resolution 1497, the assumption is that all ICC States Parties are also UN members.

[54] SC Res 1509, UN SCOR, 4830th mtg, UN Doc S/RES/1509 (19 September 2003). The mission ended on 31 March 2018.

[55] The resolution also purports to give such individuals immunity from prosecution before international courts, but as discussed in Section 5.3.1.2, the ICC itself is not directly bound by Security Council resolutions.

[56] For general discussion on the binding nature of Security Council resolutions, see MD Öberg, 'The Legal Effects of Resolutions of the UN Security Council and General Assembly in the Jurisprudence of the ICJ' (2005) 16 *European Journal of International Law* 879 at 891.

[57] See discussion in Section 4.4.1.1 and in Section 5.3.2 for criticism of 'exclusive jurisdiction'.

5.3 NEGATIVE PILLAR: EXCLUDING JURISDICTION

peacekeeping missions. Such an agreement was concluded between the UN and the government of Liberia in November 2003, Article 51(b) of which provided that '[m]ilitary members of the military component of UNMIL shall be subject to the exclusive jurisdiction of their respective participating States in respect of any criminal offences which may be committed by them in Liberia'.[58] The effect of both Resolution 1497 and the UNMIL SOFA means that Liberia cannot lawfully exercise jurisdiction over UNMIL peacekeepers. At the same time, however, by ratifying the Rome Statute, Liberia has agreed that the ICC may have jurisdiction over any Statute crimes committed on Liberian territory, with no exceptions as to the nationality of the perpetrator.

Recalling the analysis in Chapter 4 with respect to the situation in Afghanistan, Liberia appears to be in a position similar to that of Afghanistan. Both States are obliged under their respective SOFAs to recognise the exclusive jurisdiction of troop-sending States, and yet Afghanistan and Liberia have both ratified the Rome Statute and agreed to ICC jurisdiction over their territory. In Chapter 4 I argued that it would be problematic if the ICC were to hold that its jurisdiction could be limited on an ad hoc basis by agreements to which the Court is not party.[59] Just because Liberia has agreed under the UNMIL SOFA not to exercise its domestic judicial jurisdiction over foreign peacekeepers does not mean that it cannot delegate its rights and powers of sovereign jurisdiction to the ICC. The ICC would therefore treat Liberia's ratification of the Rome Statute as a valid delegation of jurisdiction and any conflict of Liberia's obligations as a matter for Liberia. In Chapter 4 I concluded that Afghanistan would need to make a political decision as to which of its conflicting agreements it would uphold. The Liberian situation is slightly different given that the UNMIL SOFA is not a traditional bilateral or multilateral agreement between States.

The UN Security Council established the Liberian peacekeeping mission as a measure under Chapter VII of the UN Charter, and the UNMIL SOFA was an international agreement between Liberia and the UN.[60]

---

[58] Agreement Between Liberia and the United Nations Concerning the Status of the United Nations Mission in Liberia (6 November 2003) ('UNMIL SOFA').
[59] See generally, Section 4.4.1.
[60] Although UNMIL was established by a Security Council resolution, one of the three basic principles of UN peacekeeping is that such operations are deployed with the consent of the parties, meaning that Liberia directly consented to the terms of the UNMIL SOFA. For a critique of the role of consent in UN peacekeeping operations, see H Nasu, *International Law on Peacekeeping: A Study of Article 40 of the UN Charter* (Martinus Nijhoff Publishers, 2009) pp. 17–23.

The UN Charter is therefore the ultimate source of Liberia's obligations in both Resolution 1497 and the SOFA. Article 103 of the UN Charter provides that '[i]n the event of a conflict between the obligations of the Members of the United Nations under the present Charter and their obligations under any other international agreement, their obligations under the present Charter shall prevail'.[61] The only way that Liberia could prevent the ICC from potentially exercising jurisdiction over a situation on its territory involving UNMIL peacekeepers from States not party to the Rome Statute would be to withdraw from the Statute itself.[62] Theoretically, the combination of Resolution 1497, the UNMIL SOFA and the UN Charter would legally oblige Liberia to take such action. It is far more likely, however, that the ICC – not Liberia – would bear the brunt of any recriminations for going ahead with the prosecution of UN peacekeepers from non-States Parties, even if the Court has held that such prosecutions are intra vires the Rome Statute.

5.3.3 Unorthodox and Unintended

To date, the Security Council has yet to invoke Article 16 as it was intended to be used by the drafters of the Rome Statute.[63] With respect to the Council's unorthodox attempts in Resolutions 1422 and 1497 to limit the jurisdiction of the ICC in future cases, the Court has not had the opportunity to test whether these resolutions would actually prevent it from exercising jurisdiction over peacekeepers from States not party to the Rome Statute. But as I argue above, it is unlikely that Resolution 1422 would have been a valid invocation of Article 16 under the Rome Statute. It is also unlikely that Resolution 1497 would prevent the ICC from exercising delegated jurisdiction over nationals from non-States Parties. The ICC is not bound by Security Council resolutions or SOFAs, and where States Parties have limited their own jurisdiction under an

---

[61] See generally, R Liivoja, 'The Scope of the Supremacy Clause of the United Nations Charter' (2008) 57 *International and Comparative Law Quarterly* 583.

[62] Under Article 127(2) of the Rome Statute, the ICC would continue to have jurisdiction over any matter commenced prior to Liberia's withdrawal taking effect.

[63] In 2013 there was a significant push by the African Union to defer the ICC cases against Kenyan President Uhuru Kenyatta and Deputy President William Rutu. But there was little appetite in the Security Council for such a deferral, with only seven Council members voting in favour of the draft resolution. UN SCOR, 68th sess, 7060th mtg, UN Doc S/PV.7060 (15 November 2013). See P Gaeta and P Labuda, 'The African Union versus the ICC in the *Al Bashir* and *Kenyatta* Cases' in C Chernor Taylor and I Bantekas (eds), *The International Criminal Court and Africa* (Oxford University Press, 2017).

international agreement it does not affect the jurisdiction of the ICC. The next section continues exploring questions of ICC jurisdiction and non-States Parties in the context of the positive pillar of the Security Council's relationship with the ICC.

5.4 The Positive Pillar: Enabling Jurisdiction

In the following analysis I focus on the Security Council's role in referring situations to the ICC under Article 13(b) of the Rome Statute. I canvass the Council referrals in Sudan and Libya to review the legal relationship between non-States Parties and the ICC where the Security Council has triggered the Court's jurisdiction. This section argues that the legal basis for the ICC's jurisdiction over nationals of non-States Parties is grounded in implied State consent when the situation is referred by the Security Council. I conclude by briefly examining the source of the Security Council's referral power in the UN Charter to demonstrate how this could affect the legal basis for the ICC's jurisdiction in particular cases.

5.4.1 Article 13(b): The Referral Power

Article 13(b) of the Rome Statute provides that the Court may exercise its jurisdiction with respect to crimes listed in Article 5 if '[a] situation in which one or more of such crimes appears to have been committed is referred to the Prosecutor by the Security Council acting under Chapter VII of the Charter of the United Nations'. As mentioned in the introduction to this chapter, the decision of the Security Council to refer a situation to the ICC must be made by 'an affirmative vote of nine members including the concurring votes of the permanent members' in order to comply with Article 27 of the UN Charter. The Article 13(b) referral power is essentially the same as what was envisioned in Draft Article 23(1) of the 1994 ILC Draft Statute.

Unlike the other two trigger mechanisms – referral by a State Party and *proprio motu* initiation of an investigation by the Prosecutor – referral by the Security Council is not limited to situations involving States Parties to the Rome Statute.[64] In general, the notion that the Security Council can trigger the Court's jurisdiction over situations involving nationals of non-States Parties has been viewed as more palatable than the alternative

---

[64] Rome Statute, Article 12(2).

avenues for such jurisdiction.[65] Reasons for this vary, but a general theme that emerges among the views is that the near-universal membership of the UN means that the international community of States has granted the Security Council broad powers to fulfil its mandate to maintain international peace and security.[66] I examine this concept in more detail in Section 5.4.3, but first turn to look at the two situations that have been referred to the Court by the Security Council.

5.4.1.1 Resolution 1593: The Situation in Darfur

The Security Council confounded all expectations in 2005 when it invoked Article 13(b) of the Rome Statute to refer the situation in Darfur to the ICC prosecutor.[67] Both China and the US abstained from the final vote, and in return for allowing the referral to go ahead without a veto, the US demanded a number of important concessions. The first was an acknowledgment of the controversial bilateral agreements concluded by the US under Article 98(2); the second recalls the wording of Resolution 1497 by exempting nationals of non-States Parties (other than Sudan) from the jurisdiction of the ICC; and the third placed the financial burden for any costs associated with the referral solely on the Assembly of States Parties.[68]

Since the 2005 referral, the Court has opened five cases against six suspects in the Darfur situation. Pre-Trial Chamber I declined to confirm the charges in one of the cases, but warrants of arrest have been issued for

---

[65] Although there was some concern during the Preparatory Committee phase that giving the Security Council the power to refer situations to the Court would undermine judicial independence: *Report of the Preparatory Committee on the Establishment of an International Criminal Court (Volume I)*, UN GAOR, 51st sess, Supp No 22, UN Doc A/51/22 (1996) para 130. By the time of the Rome Conference, however, there was 'strong support for referral by the Security Council': Preparatory Committee on the Establishment of an International Criminal Court, 'Proposal by the United Kingdom of Great Britain and Northern Ireland: Trigger mechanism', UN Doc A/AC.249/1998/WG.3/DP.1 (25 March 1998) para 2. See also, Schabas, *The International Criminal Court: A Commentary*, pp. 369–70.

[66] See, eg, M Morris, 'High Crimes and Misconceptions: The ICC and Non-Party States' (2001) 64 *Law and Contemporary Problems* 13 at 14.

[67] SC Res 1593, UN SCOR, 5158th mtg, UN Doc S/RES/1593 (31 March 2005).

[68] I will briefly deal with the first two concessions at the end of this part, but it is beyond the scope of this book to address the third concession. For more information on the Security Council's literal passing of the buck to the Assembly of States Parties, see WM Reisman, 'Editorial Comment: On Paying the Piper: Financial Responsibility for Security Council Referrals to the International Criminal Court' (2005) 99 *American Journal of International Law* 615.

5.4 POSITIVE PILLAR: ENABLING JURISDICTION

the remaining five accused, all of whom are still at large at the time of writing.[69] This is despite the inclusion of operative paragraph 2 of Resolution 1593:

> The Security Council ...
> *Decides* that the Government of Sudan and all other parties to the conflict in Darfur, shall cooperate fully with and provide any necessary assistance to the Court and the Prosecutor pursuant to this resolution and, while recognizing that States not party to the Rome Statute have no obligation under the Statute, urges all States and concerned regional and other international organizations to cooperate fully.

As discussed in Chapter 4, not only is Sudan refusing to cooperate with the ICC, but former President Omar Al Bashir frequently travelled outside Sudan until he was overthrown in April 2019.[70] The Security Council has adopted numerous follow-up resolutions repeatedly affirming the continuing threat to peace created by the situation in Darfur,[71] but the Council has fallen short when it comes to enforcing the outstanding arrest warrants. The ICC Prosecutor has made repeated appeals to the Council for assistance with the arrest and transfer of the accused to no avail,[72] leaving the impression that 'the Council uses the ICC whenever it

---

[69] *Prosecutor v Ahmad Muhammad Harun and Ali Muhammad Ali Abd-Al-Rahman (Warrant of Arrest for Ahmad Harun and Ali Muhammad Ali Abd-Al-Rahman)* (International Criminal Court, Pre-Trial Chamber I, Case No ICC-02/05-01/07, 27 April 2007); *Prosecutor v Omar Hassan Ahmad Al Bashir (Warrant of Arrest for Omar Al Bashir)* (International Criminal Court, Pre-Trial Chamber I, Case No ICC-02/05-01/09, 4 March 2009); *Prosecutor v Abdallah Banda Abakaer Nourain (Warrant of Arrest for Abdallah Banda Abakaer Nourain)* (International Criminal Court, Trial Chamber IV, Case No ICC-02/05-03/09, 11 September 2014); *Prosecutor v Abdel Raheem Muhammad Hussein (Warrant of Arrest for Abdel Raheem Muhammad Hussein)* (International Criminal Court, Pre-Trial Chamber I, Case No ICC-02/05-01/12, 1 March 2012).

[70] See, eg, *Prosecutor v Al Bashir (Order Regarding Omar Al-Bashir's Potential Visit to the Republic of Chad and to the State of Libya)* (International Criminal Court, Pre-Trial Chamber II, Case No ICC-02/05-01/09, 15 February 2013); *Prosecutor v Al Bashir (Judgment in the Jordan Referral re Al-Bashir Appeal)* (International Criminal Court, Appeals Chamber, Case No ICC/02/05-01/09, 6 May 2019).

[71] A recent example is SC Res 2479, UN SCOR, 8566th mtg, UN Doc S/RES/2479 (27 June 2019) extending the mandate of the African Union-United Nations Mission Hybrid Operation in Darfur.

[72] See, eg, Office of the Prosecutor, *Eighteenth Report of the Prosecutor of the International Criminal Court to the United Nations Security Council Pursuant to UNSCR 1593 (2005)* (11 December 2013) in which the Prosecutor declared that '[t]he Council's silence and inaction contributes to the Sudan's continued determination to ignore the Council' and implored the Council to take 'stronger action', 12–13.

is convenient for Council members, while turning a blind eye on the Court when its mandate needs to be operationalized'.[73]

As mentioned above, the Security Council included a number of concessions in Resolution 1593, which were made in exchange for the US agreeing to abstain from, rather than veto, the referral.[74] For example, the resolution's preamble 'takes note' of the existence of Article 98(2) agreements, which was undoubtedly a reference to the Bush administration's systematic campaign of concluding bilateral non-surrender agreements with States Parties.[75] In the Security Council, Brazil abstained from the vote on Resolution 1593, expressing disappointment that Article 98(2) was even mentioned in a referral resolution.[76] Denmark tried to assuage concerns by describing the acknowledgment of Article 98(2) as 'purely factual ... the reference in no way impinges on the integrity of the ICC'.[77] While the inclusion of a reference to Article 98 raised eyebrows, more concerning was the inclusion of operative paragraph 6 in which the Security Council:

> *Decides* that nationals, current or former officials or personnel from a contributing State outside Sudan which is not a party to the Rome Statute of the International Criminal Court shall be subject to the exclusive jurisdiction of that contributing State for all alleged acts or omissions arising out of or related to operations in Sudan established or authorized by the Council or the African Union, unless such exclusive jurisdiction has been expressly waived by that contributing State.

This stipulation recalls the Council's efforts in Resolutions 1422 and 1497 to exclude non-State Party nationals from the jurisdiction of the ICC. This time, however, the Council was attempting to shape the Court's jurisdiction through a referral resolution, leading to accusations that the Council was interfering with the ICC's judicial independence.[78]

The drafters of the Statute purposely chose the term 'situation' in Article 13 to avoid the possibility that a referral might be 'improperly [targeted]'.[79] The Security Council's attempts to narrow the ICC's

---

[73] Ruiz Verduzco, 'The Relationship between the ICC and the United Nations Security Council', p. 50.
[74] *Reports of the Secretary-General on the Sudan*, UN SCOR, 60th sess, 5158th mtg, UN Doc S/PV.5158 (31 March 2005): Statement of the US, 4.
[75] See Section 4.4.1.2 for more information.
[76] *Reports of the Secretary-General on the Sudan*, UN SCOR, 60th sess, 5158th mtg, UN Doc S/PV.5158 (31 March 2005): Statement of Brazil, 11.
[77] Ibid., Statement of Denmark, 6.
[78] Ibid., Statement of Brazil, 11; Statement of the Philippines, 6.
[79] Schabas, *The International Criminal Court: A Commentary*, p. 373.

personal jurisdiction in the referred situations is at odds with the fact that the Prosecutor has continually maintained that referral of a 'situation' must be construed broadly.[80] In 2003, for example, the government of Uganda became the first State to trigger the Court's jurisdiction through Article 13(a), and attempted to limit the referral to the 'situation concerning the Lord's Resistance Army'.[81] The Prosecutor decided that the referral had to be interpreted in conformity with the principles of the Rome Statute and that to do so meant broadening its scope to include crimes committed by anyone in the situation in Northern Uganda.[82]

Operative paragraph 6 of Resolution 1593 has not had any effect in practice, so it is unknown whether the Prosecutor would excise or otherwise ignore it for not according with the provisions of the Rome Statute. However, the Security Council's attempts to exclude nationals from non-States Parties from the jurisdiction of the ICC[83] is at best 'bad practice, devoid of any precedential value'[84] and at worst a 'dangerous erosion of the principle of equality before the law and the judicial independence of the Court'.[85]

5.4.1.2 Resolution 1970: The Situation in Libya

The second time the Security Council invoked its Article 13(b) power was in 2011 when it adopted Resolution 1970 referring the situation in Libya.[86] This resolution was adopted unanimously, and included affirmative votes from five States not party to the Rome Statute, including the US.[87] Despite this positive – and seemingly cooperative – new attitude

---

[80] The only exception is the Iraq/UK situation in which the Prosecutor has limited the scope of the preliminary examination to crimes allegedly committed by UK nationals in Iraq because Iraq is not a party to the Statute.

[81] Letter of the Prosecutor to the Presidency dated 17 June 2004 appended to *Situation in Uganda (Decision Assigning the Situation in Uganda to Pre-Trial Chamber II)* (International Criminal Court, Presidency, Case No ICC-02/04, 5 July 2004).

[82] Ibid.

[83] The Security Council included a nearly identical provision in operative paragraph 6 of its referral of the situation in Libya: SC Res 1970, UN SCOR, 6491st mtg, UN Doc S/RES/1970 (26 February 2011). See also operative paragraph 7 of the failed draft resolution to refer the situation in Syria to the ICC: UN Doc S/2014/348 (22 May 2014).

[84] Claus Kreß, 'The International Criminal Court and the United States: Reflections on Resolution 1422 of the UN Security Council' (2003) 77 *Fikran Wa Fann Art & Thought* 70.

[85] Ruiz Verduzco, 'The Relationship between the ICC and the United Nations Security Council', p. 38.

[86] SC Res 1970, UN SCOR, 6491st mtg, UN Doc S/RES/1970 (26 February 2011).

[87] Along with affirmative votes by permanent Council members China, Russia and the US, non-permanent members India and Lebanon also voted to refer Libya to the ICC.

towards the ICC, Resolution 1970 contained two of the same caveats as the Council's previous referral. Namely, the exemption of nationals of non-States Parties (other than Libya) from the jurisdiction of the ICC, and the refusal to fund any ICC investigations or prosecutions that arise out of the referral.[88]

Almost immediately, the ICC opened three cases against three high-ranking Libyan officials, with arrest warrants issued for President Muammar Gaddafi, Saif Al-Islam Gaddafi and Abdullah Al-Senussi.[89] The case against Muammar Gaddafi was terminated in November 2011 following his death, and in 2013 Pre-Trial Chamber I held that the case against Al Senussi was inadmissible.[90] Despite two admissibility challenges in the case of Saif Gaddafi, the Court has ruled that his case remains admissible.[91] The ICC has issued arrest warrants for two more suspects accused of committing Statute crimes in the Libyan situation, but has yet to secure custody of any of the wanted individuals.[92]

Despite the fact that the suspects wanted for crimes in the Darfur and Libyan situations remain at large, there has been some judicial

---

[88] SC Res 1970, UN SCOR, 6491st mtg, UN Doc S/RES/1970 (26 February 2011), operative paragraphs 6 and 8.

[89] *Situation in the Libyan Arab Jamahiriya (Warrant of Arrest for Muammar Mohammed Abu Minyar Gaddafi)* (International Criminal Court, Pre-Trial Chamber I, Case No ICC-01/11, 27 June 2011); *Situation in the Libyan Arab Jamahiriya (Warrant of Arrest for Saif Al-Islam Gaddafi)* (International Criminal Court, Pre-Trial Chamber I, Case No ICC-01/11, 27 June 2011); *Situation in the Libyan Arab Jamahiriya (Warrant of Arrest for Abdullah Al Senussi)* (International Criminal Court, Pre-Trial Chamber I, Case No ICC-01/11, 27 June 2011).

[90] *Prosecutor v Saif Al-Islam Gaddafi and Abdullah Al-Senussi (Decision on the admissibility of the case against Abdullah Al-Senussi)* (International Criminal Court, Pre-Trial Chamber I, Case No ICC-01/11-01/11, 11 October 2013).

[91] *Prosecutor v Saif Al-Islam Gaddafi and Abdullah Al-Senussi (Decision on the admissibility of the case against Saif Al-Islam Gaddafi)* (International Criminal Court, Pre-Trial Chamber I, Case No ICC-01/11-01/11, 31 May 2013); *Prosecutor v Saif Al-Islam Gaddafi and Abdullah Al-Senussi (Judgment on the appeal of Libya against the decision of Pre-Trial Chamber I of 31 May 2013)* (International Criminal Court, Appeals Chamber, Case No ICC-01/11-01/11, 21 May 2014); *Prosecutor v Saif Al-Islam Gaddafi (Decision on the 'Admissibility Challenge by Dr Saif Al-Islam Gadafi pursuant to Articles 17(1)(c), 19 and 20(3) of the Rome Statute')* (International Criminal Court, Pre-Trial Chamber I, Case No ICC-01/11-01/11, 5 April 2019).

[92] *Situation in Libya (Warrant of Arrest for Al-Tuhamy Mohamed Khaled)* (International Criminal Court, Pre-Trial Chamber I, Case No ICC-01/11-01/13, 18 April 2013); *Situation in Libya (Warrant of Arrest for Mahmoud Mustafa Busayf Al-Werfalli)* (International Criminal Court, Pre-Trial Chamber I, Case No ICC-01/11-01/17, 15 August 2017); *Prosecutor v Mahmoud Mustafa Busayf Al-Werfalli (Second Warrant of Arrest)* (International Criminal Court, Pre-Trial Chamber I, Case No ICC-01/11-01/17, 4 July 2018).

consideration of jurisdictional issues pertinent to these situations. For example, the ICC has undertaken preliminary analysis of the legal nature of Security Council referrals in some of the Al Bashir non-compliance decisions[93] which will be discussed in the next sections. A number of questions remain, however, about the authority of both the ICC and the Security Council over such matters.

5.4.2 Do Sudan and Libya Have Rights and Obligations under the Rome Statute?

One of the questions that captivated scholars soon after the adoption of Resolution 1593 was whether Sudan could be considered to be in a position analogous to that of States Parties to the Rome Statute.[94] Both Sudan and Libya are obliged by the terms of their respective Security Council resolutions to cooperate with the ICC. What is less certain is the extent to which the Rome Statute applies to Sudan and Libya as non-States Parties, and how any legal obligations can be reconciled with the principle of *pacta tertiis nec nocent nec prosunt*.[95]

While ordinarily the Rome Statute does not create any rights or obligations for non-States Parties, Resolutions 1593 and 1970 each provide that Sudan and Libya 'shall cooperate fully with and provide any necessary assistance to the Court and the Prosecutor pursuant to this resolution'. The resolutions do not specify that the provisions of the Rome Statute are binding on Sudan and Libya, but the Rome Statute remains the primary source of law for any ICC investigation or prosecution. Pre-Trial Chamber I confirmed as much in its decision to issue an arrest warrant for Omar Al Bashir:

> [B]y referring the Darfur situation to the Court, pursuant to article 13(b) of the Statute, the Security Council of the United Nations has also accepted that the investigation into the said situation, as well as any prosecution arising therefrom, will take place in accordance with the

---

[93] See, eg, *Prosecutor v Al Bashir (Decision on the Cooperation of the Democratic Republic of the Congo Regarding Omar Al Bashir's Arrest and Surrender to the Court)* (International Criminal Court, Pre-Trial Chamber II, Case No ICC/02/05-01/09, 9 April 2014); *Prosecutor v Al Bashir (Judgment in the Jordan Referral re Al-Bashir Appeal)* (International Criminal Court, Appeals Chamber, Case No ICC/02/05-01/09, 6 May 2019).

[94] See, eg, D Akande, 'The Legal Nature of Security Council Referrals to the ICC and its Impact on Al Bashir's Immunities' (2009) 7 *Journal of International Criminal Justice* 333 at 340–2.

[95] See Chapter 2 for further discussion of the *pacta tertiis* principle.

statutory framework provided for in the Statute, the Elements of Crimes and the Rules as a whole.[96]

The main difference, therefore, between States Parties to the Rome Statute and Sudan and Libya, is the source and extent of the States' legal obligations to cooperate with the Court. Under Article 25 of the UN Charter, UN Member States are bound by decisions of the Security Council, meaning that Sudan and Libya are obliged to cooperate with the ICC because the Security Council resolutions create a legal obligation for them to do so.[97]

Beyond the explicit obligation for Sudan and Libya to cooperate with the ICC, the implicit notion that any investigation and prosecution will take place within the ICC's statutory framework also means that these two non-States Parties have certain legal rights under the Statute. For example, they have the right under Article 17 to challenge the admissibility of a case before the ICC which would otherwise fall within domestic jurisdiction. As mentioned earlier in this section, Libya was successful in challenging the admissibility of the case against Al Senussi, in which Pre-Trial Chamber I held that 'Libya is not unwilling or unable genuinely to carry out its proceedings in relation to the case against Mr Al-Senussi'.[98] Again, the Rome Statute avoids falling foul of the *pacta tertiis* principle because Libya's membership of the UN and Resolution 1970 essentially place Libya in a position analogous to that of States Parties.[99]

To summarise, the provisions of the Rome Statute apply to any ICC investigation and prosecution of cases in the Darfur and Libya situations. This means that Sudan and Libya have the same legal obligations and rights under the Statute as States Parties (with respect to the specific situations in Darfur and Libya). Unlike States Parties, the Rome Statute applies to Sudan and Libya not because they consented to it directly, but

---

[96] *Prosecutor v Omar Hassan Ahmad Al Bashir (Warrant of Arrest for Omar Al Bashir)* (International Criminal Court, Pre-Trial Chamber I, Case No ICC-02/05-01/09, 4 March 2009) para 45.

[97] States Parties are legally obliged to arrest and transfer suspects in the Darfur and Libya situations, by virtue of both the Rome Statute and the Security Council resolutions.

[98] *Prosecutor v Saif Al-Islam Gaddafi and Abdullah Al-Senussi (Decision on the admissibility of the case against Abdullah Al-Senussi)* (International Criminal Court, Pre-Trial Chamber I, Case No ICC-01/11-01/11, 11 October 2013) para 311.

[99] Akande, 'The Legal Nature of Security Council Referrals to the ICC and its Impact on Al Bashir's Immunities', 342; J Crawford, 'The ILC's Draft Statute for an International Criminal Tribunal' (1994) 88 *American Journal of International Law* 140 at 147; Sarooshi, 'Aspects of the relationship between the International Criminal Court and the United Nations', 31–2.

5.4 POSITIVE PILLAR: ENABLING JURISDICTION 139

because they agreed upon ratification of the UN Charter to be bound by decisions of the UN Security Council. The Security Council decided to refer the situations to the ICC in compliance with Article 13(b) of the Rome Statute and, in doing so, directed Sudan and Libya to 'cooperate fully' with the ICC. In the context of Resolution 1593, the Appeals Chamber has held that '"full cooperation" in accordance with the Statute encompasses all those obligations that States Parties owe to the Court and that are necessary for the effective exercise of jurisdiction by the Court'.[100] This explains how and why the Rome Statute can apply to Sudan and Libya, as non-States Parties.[101] But the implied application of the Rome Statute by virtue of a Security Council resolution does not, on its own, provide a legal basis for the ICC's jurisdiction over Sudanese and Libyan nationals in this situation.

5.4.3 What Is the Legal Basis for ICC Jurisdiction over Situations Referred by the Security Council?

Recalling the discussion in Chapter 2, one of the key objections to the ICC's jurisdiction over nationals of non-States Parties is that it ignores the importance of State consent in international law. The consent of the State of nationality is not traditionally required for prosecution in foreign domestic courts, so the fact that Article 12(2) of the Rome Statute requires either the territorial State or the State of nationality to accept ICC jurisdiction is generally considered to be sufficient preservation of State consent.[102] But Article 12(2) does not apply to situations triggered by a Security Council referral, which has given rise to a perception that no State consent is involved.[103] Indeed, Sudan has repeatedly rejected the

---

[100] *Prosecutor v Al Bashir (Judgment in the Jordan Referral re Al-Bashir Appeal)* (International Criminal Court, Appeals Chamber, Case No ICC/02/05-01/09, 6 May 2019) para 143.

[101] While Sudan and Libya may be obliged to cooperate with the jurisdiction, investigation and other cooperation regimes established by the Rome Statute, it would be incorrect to say that the Statute applies to them in its entirety. There are clearly parts of the Statute that would not be relevant, such as 'Part XI: Assembly of States Parties' and 'Part XII: Financing'.

[102] See Section 2.2.2 for further analysis of State consent issues.

[103] See, eg, MP Scharf, 'The ICC's Jurisdiction over the Nationals of Non-Party States: A Critique of the U.S. Position' (2001) 64 *Law and Contemporary Problems* 67 at 79; C Heyder, 'The UN Security Council's Referral of the Crimes in Darfur to the International Criminal Court in Light of US Opposition to the Court: Implications for the International Criminal Court's Functions and Status' 24 *Berkeley Journal of International Law* 650 at 653; GM Danilenko, 'The Statute of the International Criminal Court and Third States' (1999) 21 *Michigan Journal of International Law* 445 at 456.

jurisdiction of the ICC over Darfur on the grounds that Sudan has not consented to it.[104] In the following sections, I explore how the problem of State consent may be addressed by re-examining the delegation theory as the legal basis for ICC jurisdiction over situations in non-States Parties referred to the Court by the Security Council. I use the situation in Sudan as the primary example in my analysis.

5.4.3.1 The Security Council Empowers the Court

In February 2014, Pre-Trial Chamber II addressed the DRC's failure to arrest Omar Al Bashir, and held that his position as Head of State does not preclude him from the jurisdiction of the ICC.[105] The rationale for this conclusion was that 'the SC implicitly waived the immunities granted to Omar Al Bashir under international law and attached to his position as a Head of State'.[106] In 2019, the Appeals Chamber considered Jordan's failure to arrest Omar Al Bashir and in line with previous non-compliance decisions concluded that he could not invoke Head of State immunity before the ICC. However, the Appeals Chamber disagreed with the Pre-Trial Chamber's earlier interpretation that the Security Council had implicitly waived Al Bashir's immunities. Instead the Chamber held that 'the effect of paragraph 2 of Resolution 1593 is to bring Sudan under the cooperation regime applicable to States Parties to the Rome Statute, which does not recognise immunities'. In other words, no waiver of immunity was required, because Article 27 of the Statute is part of the broader 'cooperation regime' which applies to Sudan by virtue of the Security Council resolution.

This is further evidence for the notion that a Security Council referral implicitly activates the application of the Rome Statute to referred situations. For the situation in Darfur, the Security Council has obliged Sudan to cooperate fully with the Court, which essentially ensures the application of the Rome Statute to the situation. Article 27 of the Statute therefore applies as part of the broader cooperation regime to prevent customary immunities from applying before the ICC. Despite the Appeals Chamber's rejection of the idea that Resolution 1593 represents

---

[104] 'Sudan rejects ICC ruling on Darfur', *Al Jazeera* (28 February 2007); Statement of Sudan, *Report of the International Criminal Court*, UN GAOR, 73rd sess, 27th mtg, Agenda Item 77, UN Doc A/73/PV.27 (29 October 2018) 12.
[105] See Section 4.3.3 for more discussion of this issue.
[106] *Prosecutor v Al Bashir (Decision on the Cooperation of the Democratic Republic of the Congo Regarding Omar Al Bashir's Arrest and Surrender to the Court)* (International Criminal Court, Pre-Trial Chamber II, Case No ICC/02/05-01/09, 9 April 2014) para 29.

a waiver of immunities on Sudan's behalf, there is no reason why the Resolution could not be construed as an implicit waiver, especially if it can be said that for States Parties, Article 27 represents a waiver of all immunities by direct consent.[107] Whichever interpretation is preferred, the Security Council resolution allows the ICC to exercise its jurisdiction over the situation in Darfur and over any Sudanese individual who would otherwise be able to invoke personal immunity. But how does the Security Council empower the Court to exercise jurisdiction over situations in non-States Parties in the first place?

Dapo Akande writes that '[a]t a minimum, the referral of a situation to the ICC is a decision to confer jurisdiction on the Court (in circumstances where such jurisdiction may otherwise not exist)'.[108] This is not to say that the Security Council possesses criminal jurisdiction which it bestows upon the Court. Recalling the discussion in Chapter 3, the source of the ICC's powers of criminal justice is the Rome Statute, and the legal basis for these powers is delegation from States Parties. The source of the ICC's right to exercise its powers is a matter of which trigger mechanism is used. For example, the ICC has the right to exercise its powers when a State Party refers a situation to the Prosecutor under Article 13(a) or when the Prosecutor initiates an investigation *proprio motu* under Article 13(c). The legal basis for the right to exercise its powers in either situation may be conceived of as delegation of jurisdiction from States Parties. Where the Security Council refers a situation in a non-State Party to the ICC under Article 13(b), it gives the Court the right to exercise its powers over that situation. But to say that the Security Council has empowered the ICC to exercise jurisdiction over the situation in Darfur is not enough to explain how the Court can lawfully investigate and prosecute crimes committed in non-States Parties by non-party nationals. A Security Council referral may trigger the ICC's jurisdiction, but it does not, on its own, provide a legal basis for that jurisdiction.

5.4.3.2 What Empowers the Security Council?

To ascertain the legal basis for the ICC's jurisdiction over situations in non-States Parties referred by the Security Council, it is necessary to

---

[107] D Akande, 'International Law Immunities and the International Criminal Court' (2004) 98 *American Journal of International Law* 407 at 420.

[108] Akande, 'The Legal Nature of Security Council Referrals to the ICC and its Impact on Al Bashir's Immunities', 341. Other scholars have used similar language to describe the mechanics of a Security Council referral. See, eg, J Foakes, *The Position of Heads of State and Senior Officials in International Law* (Oxford University Press, 2014) p. 201.

determine what (beyond the Rome Statute) gives the Council the authority to trigger the ICC's jurisdiction. How is it that the Council can authorise a treaty-based court to exercise jurisdiction over a situation in a State that has not consented to the terms of that treaty? Answering this question involves an examination of the basis for the Security Council's powers under the UN Charter. It is beyond the scope of this book to discuss the actions and authority of the Council in any great depth; the following provides a cursory analysis of the UN Charter and the powers of the Security Council as they relate to an ICC referral.[109]

The Powers of the Security Council under the UN Charter   The organs of the UN, including the Security Council, derive their powers from the UN Charter. The UN Charter empowers the Security Council to refer situations to the ICC through a combination of Article 24(1) and Article 41 of the UN Charter. Article 24(1) provides that:

> In order to ensure prompt and effective action by the United Nations, its Members confer on the Security Council primary responsibility for the maintenance of international peace and security, and agree that in carrying out its duties under this responsibility the Security Council acts on their behalf.

Article 41 gives the Council the authority to decide 'what measures not involving the use of armed force are to be employed to give effect to its decisions'. As Article 24(1) suggests, the original source of the Security Council's powers is UN Member States, who have collectively conferred powers on the UN through ratification of the Charter.[110] In the ICJ's *Certain Expenses* case, Judge Bustamante affirmed that the Charter's

---

[109] There is a significant body of scholarship that examines the parameters of the Security Council's powers. See generally, H Kelsen, *The Law of the United Nations: A Critical Analysis of its Fundamental Problems* (FA Praeger, 1950); LM Goodrich, E Hambro and AP Simons, *Charter of the United Nations – Commentary and Documents*, 3rd ed (Columbia University Press, 1969); G Nolte, 'The Limits of the Security Council's Powers and its Functions in the International Legal System: Some Reflections' in M Byers (ed), *The Role of Law in International Politics* (Oxford University Press, 2001) p. 315; E de Wet, *The Chapter VII Powers of the United Nations Security Council* (Hart Publishing, 2004); D Sarooshi, *The United Nations and the Development of Collective Security: The Delegation by the UN Security Council of its Chapter VII Powers* (Clarendon Press, 1999); B Simma et al (eds), *The Charter of the United Nations: A Commentary*, 3rd ed (Oxford University Press, 2012).

[110] D Sarooshi, 'Some Preliminary Remarks on the Conferral by States of Powers on International Organizations' (2003) *Jean Monnet Working Paper* at 7. See also, Section 3.3.2.2 for more information about collective conferral.

5.4 POSITIVE PILLAR: ENABLING JURISDICTION

provisions 'imply on the part of Member States certain partial and contractual renunciations in respect of the exercise of their own sovereignty – which indeed is fully recognized by Article 2 (paras 1 and 7) – in the interests of international co-operation and peace'.[111] In other words, by conferring powers on the UN, UN Member States have tacitly consented to action taken by the Security Council as long as it is intra vires the Charter.

Since the Security Council's establishment of the ad hoc international criminal tribunals in the 1990s,[112] it has been widely accepted that the Council's powers under Article 41 of the Charter extend to implementing measures involving criminal justice.[113] In the *Tadić* decision, the Appeals Chamber of the ICTY held that the Security Council had significant discretion to determine what measures to take under Chapter VII of the Charter, and that the establishment of an international tribunal was 'squarely within the powers of the Security Council under Article 41'.[114] Specifically, the Appeals Chamber found that the Council had 'resorted to the establishment of a judicial organ in the form of an international criminal tribunal as an instrument for the exercise of its own principle function of maintenance of peace and security'.[115]

Similarly, the ICTR Trial Chamber responded to allegations that the Security Council's establishment of the tribunal violated the sovereignty of Rwanda by noting that:

> membership of the United Nations entail [sic] certain limitations upon the sovereignty of the member States. This is true in particular by virtue of the fact that all member States, pursuant to Article 25 of the UN Charter, have agreed to accept and carry out the decisions of the Security Council in accordance with the Charter.[116]

---

[111] *Certain Expenses of the United Nations (Advisory Opinion)* [1962] ICJ Rep 151, 295 (Judge Bustamante).

[112] The ICTY was established by SC Res 827, UN SCOR, 3217th mtg, UN Doc S/RES/827 (25 May 1993); the ICTR was established by SC Res 955, UN SCOR, 3453rd mtg, UN Doc S/RES/955 (8 November 1994).

[113] See, eg, S Williams, *Hybrid and Internationalised Criminal Tribunals: Selected Jurisdictional Issues* (Hart Publishing, 2012) p. 258; White and Cryer, 'The ICC and the Security Council', p. 460; Schabas, *The International Criminal Court: A Commentary*, p. 368.

[114] *Prosecutor v Tadić (Decision on the Defence Motion for Interlocutory Appeal on Jurisdiction)* (International Criminal Tribunal for the former Yugoslavia, Appeals Chamber II, Case No ICTY-94-1-AR72, 2 October 1995) paras 31–6, at para 36.

[115] Ibid., para 38.

[116] *Prosecutor v Kanyabashi (Decision on the Defence Motion on Jurisdiction)* (International Criminal Tribunal for Rwanda, Trial Chamber II, Case No ICTR-96-15T, 18 June 1997) para 13.

One of the rationales for giving the Security Council a role in triggering the jurisdiction of the ICC was to provide the Council with an alternative to establishing ad hoc tribunals.[117] It stands to reason that if the Security Council can lawfully establish a criminal tribunal as a measure to maintain international peace and security under Chapter VII of the Charter, then it can also activate the jurisdiction of an existing international criminal court.[118]

Applying the above reasoning to the situation in Darfur, the legal basis for the ICC's jurisdiction is grounded in the implied consent of Sudan to the powers given to the Security Council by the UN Charter. In ratifying the UN Charter, Sudan consented to the fact that the Security Council may take measures under Chapter VII to maintain international peace and security and agreed that such enforcement measures may include intervention in the sovereign domestic sphere.[119] In adopting Resolution 1593, the Security Council implemented a Chapter VII measure not involving the use of armed force by referring the situation in Darfur to the ICC. By virtue of its UN membership, Sudan has tacitly consented to the jurisdiction of the ICC over Darfur.

Is the Security Council's Power to Refer Situations Universal? A common description of the Article 13(b) Security Council trigger is that it gives the ICC universal jurisdiction.[120] This is not to say that the ICC has jurisdiction based on the principle of universality,[121] but the Security Council could theoretically refer situations in any one of the 193

---

[117] *Report of the International Law Commission,* UN GAOR, 49th sess, Supp No 10, UN Doc A/49/10 (1994) 44.

[118] But see, D. Jacobs, 'Libya and the ICC: On the Legality of any Security Council Referral to the ICC' on *Spreading the Jam* (28 February 2011).

[119] Article 2(7) of the UN Charter provides:

> Nothing contained in the present Charter shall authorise the United Nations to intervene in matters which are essentially within the domestic jurisdiction of any state or shall require the Members to submit such matters to settlement under the present Charter; *but this principle shall not prejudice the application of enforcement measures* under Chapter VII (emphasis added).

[120] See, eg, Danilenko, 'The Statute of the International Criminal Court and Third States', 452; JJ Paust, 'The Reach of ICC Jurisdiction over Non-Signatory Nationals' (2000) 33 *Vanderbilt Journal of Transnational Law* 1 at 7–8; Williams, *Hybrid and Internationalised Criminal Tribunals: Selected Jurisdictional Issues,* p. 250; Heyder, 'The UN Security Council's Referral of the Crimes in Darfur to the International Criminal Court in Light of US Opposition to the Court: Implications for the International Criminal Court's Functions and Status', 653.

[121] See Chapter 6 for further discussion on the ICC and universal jurisdiction.

5.4 POSITIVE PILLAR: ENABLING JURISDICTION

UN Member States to the ICC as there is no territorial limit on Security Council referrals in the Rome Statute. For those UN Member States that are not also States Parties to the Rome Statute, the legal basis for ICC jurisdiction is grounded in consent to the UN Charter and the powers of the Security Council. But what about States that are not UN members? Are there any territorial limitations to the Security Council's referral power?[122]

Under Chapter VII of the UN Charter, the Security Council has far-reaching enforcement powers and may take binding action against a particular State irrespective of whether that State consents to such action.[123] There are two schools of thought as to whether a State that is not a member of the UN is bound by enforcement measures taken against it by the Security Council. Hans Kelsen is often cited as a proponent of the notion that the UN Charter is binding on non-Member States, finding support for it in the text of Article 2(6) of the Charter which provides that '[t]he Organization shall ensure that States which are not Members of the United Nations act in accordance with these Principles so far as may be necessary for the maintenance of international peace and security'.[124] It is, however, a minority view that the UN Charter can override the *pacta tertiis* principle to impose obligations on non-Member States.[125] A more widely held interpretation is that enforcement action taken by the Security Council is legally binding on non-UN Member States on the basis that States have the right under customary international law to enact a 'universal system of collective security'.[126] Through the Council, States are therefore said to be exercising their collective right to take 'international police action'.[127] Depending on the scope of this

---

[122] Politically, it would be exceedingly unlikely for the Council to refer a situation in any of the five permanent members of the Security Council, for the simple fact that any one of them could veto the referring resolution. This essentially means that the ICC could not exercise jurisdiction over situations in China, Russia or the US without their express consent.

[123] N Krisch, 'Introduction to Chapter VII: The General Framework' in B Simma, DE Khan, G Nolte, AL Paulus and N Wessendorf (eds), *The Charter of the United Nations: A Commentary* (Oxford University Press, 2012) p. 1248.

[124] Kelsen, *The Law of the United Nations*, pp. 106–10.

[125] S Talmon, 'Ch.I Purposes and Principles, Article 2(6)' in B Simma, DE Khan, G Nolte, AL Paulus and N Wessendorf (eds), *The Charter of the United Nations: A Commentary* (Oxford University Press, 2012) p. 255.

[126] Talmon, 'Ch.I Purposes and Principles, Article 2(6)', pp. 255–6. See also, de Wet, *The Chapter VII Powers of the United Nations Security Council*, p. 98.

[127] Sarooshi, *The United Nations and the Development of Collective Security*, pp. 28–30; Williams, *Hybrid and Internationalised Criminal Tribunals: Selected Jurisdictional Issues*, p. 317.

customary right, it would theoretically allow the Security Council to lawfully exercise its Chapter VII enforcement powers on a truly universal scale, including referral to the ICC of situations on any territory, even where the status of UN membership or statehood is in doubt.

Yet there have been few examples of non-UN Member States on the receiving end of Security Council enforcement measures, and none of those States objected to the Council's actions on the basis of their non-UN Member status.[128] Other non-Member States have implemented Security Council-mandated sanctions against Member States, although not necessarily on the basis of a perceived legal obligation to do so. For example, prior to Switzerland becoming a UN Member in 2002 it consistently characterised its participation in Chapter VII collective enforcement measures as voluntary.[129] Any uncertainty with respect to the legal basis for the application of the Security Council's Chapter VII powers to non-UN Member States will likely affect the legal basis for the ICC's jurisdiction over such States in situations where it has been triggered by Article 13(b). There are very few situations in which such a scenario might even be possible, but it is worth undertaking a brief hypothetical analysis to better understand the parameters of the Security Council's referral power and the legal basis for the ICC's jurisdiction. The following sections assume circumstances in which Statute crimes have been committed on the territories of Palestine, Vatican City and Kosovo, and also assume that there is no legal basis for the Security Council to impose enforcement measures on non-UN Member States.

---

[128] In 1966, the Security Council first imposed sanctions against Southern Rhodesia (SC Res 409, UN SCOR, 2011th mtg, UN Doc SC/Res/409 (27 May 1977)) and against the Federal Republic of Yugoslavia during the 1990s (eg, SC Res 713, UN SCOR, 3009th mtg, UN Doc SC/Res/713 (25 September 1991)). It should be noted that such examples are disputed as evidence of Security Council enforcement measures against non-Member States because at the time of the sanctions, Rhodesia was considered to be under the administration of the UK, and the Federal Republic of Yugoslavia still considered itself to be a UN Member State. See Krisch, 'Introduction to Chapter VII: The General Framework', p. 1269.

[129] A Zimmermann and C Stahn, 'Yugoslav Territory, United Nations Trusteeship or Sovereign State? Reflections on the Current and Future Legal Status of Kosovo' (2001) 70 *Nordic Journal of International Law* 423 at 440. Zimmermann and Stahn write that 'while non-member states like Switzerland and Germany before 1974, have de facto always abided by sanctions inflicted under Chapter VII, both states have continuously indicated in the relevant situations that they only do so on a purely voluntary basis without feeling legally obliged to do so. It is therefore difficult to conclude that this practice has crystallized as customary law'.

Palestine

Palestine is a State Party to the Rome Statute, which means that the ICC's jurisdiction over a situation in Palestine could be triggered by a State Party referral or the initiation of a *proprio motu* investigation by the Prosecutor.[130] Palestine is not, however, a member of the UN, which would seem to preclude the Security Council from adopting a resolution under Chapter VII involving any kind of interference with Palestinian sovereignty. Palestine has not acceded to the UN Charter, meaning that it has not consented to the Security Council's activation of the ICC's jurisdiction as a measure to maintain international peace and security. As discussed earlier in this section, it is not certain that the Security Council can lawfully impose enforcement measures on non-UN Member States. If the Council were to nevertheless go ahead with a referral of a situation in Palestine to the ICC, the question of whether the ICC can exercise jurisdiction would depend on whether the Security Council referral is valid under Article 13(b).

Article 13(b) simply states that the ICC may exercise its jurisdiction if a situation is referred 'by the Security Council acting under Chapter VII of the Charter of the United Nations'. Prima facie, a Security Council referral of Palestine would fulfil this provision, even where the resolution is ultra vires the Charter. In determining the validity of the triggering referral, the ICC would need to decide if it has the power to review the legitimacy of the Security Council's resolution under the Charter. While such a 'judicial review' of the Security Council's actions would undoubtedly be controversial, it would not be exceptional. The ICTY Appeals Chamber decision in *Tadić* represents an important precedent for the ICC not only in regard to the Council's power to use measures involving criminal justice, but also as a model for judicial scrutiny of the limits of the Council's powers under the UN Charter. The Appeals Chamber affirmed that 'neither the text nor the spirit of the Charter conceives of the Security Council as *legibus solutus* (unbound by law)'.[131] The Chamber then engaged in a detailed analysis of the Security Council's

---

[130] See Section 4.4.2 for a more detailed discussion of Palestine's relationship with the ICC and acknowledgment of issues surrounding its statehood. Note that Palestine itself referred its situation to the ICC in May 2018, so the question of a Security Council referral is purely for illustrative purposes. Palestinian National Authority, *Referral by the State of Palestine Pursuant to Articles 13(a) and 14 of the Rome Statute* (15 May 2018).

[131] *Prosecutor v Tadić (Decision on the Defence Motion for Interlocutory Appeal on Jurisdiction)* (International Criminal Tribunal for the former Yugoslavia, Appeals Chamber II, Case No ICTY-94-1-AR72, 2 October 1995) para 28.

powers under the Charter to ascertain whether the Council had acted lawfully in establishing the ICTY.[132] The Chamber held that it had inherent jurisdiction under the principle of *compétence de la compétence* to 'examine the legality of its establishment by the Security Council, solely for the purpose of ascertaining its own "primary" jurisdiction over the case before it'.[133] Given the status of the ICC as an independent legal entity and the undertaking in the ICC–UN Relationship Agreement to 'respect each other's status and mandate',[134] the ICC may be more reluctant than the ICTY Appeals Chamber to examine the legality of Security Council action.[135]

Paradoxically, if a Security Council referral of Palestine was accepted as valid under Article 13(b) (despite its invalidity under the Charter), there would still be a legal basis for ICC jurisdiction, but it would not be based on the consent of Palestine to the UN Charter. Instead it would be based on Palestine's status as a State Party to the Rome Statute and its delegation of jurisdiction to the Court.

---

[132] Ibid., paras 28–40.

[133] Ibid', para 20. The Special Court for Sierra Leone also examined the powers of the Security Council to establish a special court by treaty: *Prosecutor v Fofana (Decision on Preliminary Motion on Lack of Jurisdiction Materiae: Illegal Delegation of Powers by the United Nations)* (Special Court for Sierra Leone, Appeals Chamber, Case No SCSL-2004-14-AR72(E), 25 May 2004) paras 18–29. The ICJ has not ruled out the possibility that it could review the merits of a Security Council resolution. See, eg, *Questions of Interpretation and Application of the 1971 Montreal Convention Arising from the Aerial Incident at Lockerbie (Libyan Arab Jamahiriya v United States of America) (Preliminary Objections)* [1998] ICJ Rep 115, paras 9–50.

[134] ICC–UN Relationship Agreement, Article 2(3).

[135] In 2012, the Appeals Chamber of the Special Tribunal for Lebanon came to the opposite conclusion to the one reached by the ICTY about its own competence to review Security Council action in establishing the Special Tribunal. The majority held that the Security Council's decision to establish the Special Tribunal for Lebanon 'is essentially political in nature, and as such not amenable to judicial review'. *Prosecutor v Ayyash (Decision on the Defence Appeals Against the Trial Chamber's 'Decision on the Defence Challenges to the Jurisdiction and Legality of the Tribunal'* (Special Tribunal for Lebanon, Appeals Chamber, Case No STL-11-01/PT/AC/AR90.1, 24 October 2012) para 52. Judge Baragwanath provided a partially dissenting opinion in which he stressed that the Security Council's 'power is limited in law by the Charter of the United Nations which conferred it' (at para 2) and held that '[w]hile there can be no claim to any general power of judicial review of Security Council resolutions, their legality may require judicial determination within a specific context against competing norms' (at para 79). For a detailed critique of the *Ayyash* decision, see JE Alvarez, 'Tadić Revisited: The Ayyash Decisions of the Special Tribunal for Lebanon' (2013) 11 *Journal of International Criminal Justice* 291.

Vatican City

Vatican City is the world's smallest State in terms of both territory and population and it is neither a member of the UN nor a State Party to the Rome Statute.[136] Given the Vatican's small size, it is highly unlikely that a situation involving the commission of Statute crimes would ever arise solely on the territory of Vatican City. If such an improbable situation did occur, it would be difficult to see how the Security Council could claim the authority to refer this situation to the ICC. If the Council adopted a referral resolution ultra vires the Charter, the ICC would technically have jurisdiction in accordance with the Statute. There would not, however, be any legal basis for this jurisdiction because of the fact that Vatican City has not consented to either the UN Charter or the Rome Statute.

Related to the above scenario are interesting jurisdictional questions that would arise if the Security Council decided to refer to the ICC a non-territorially specific situation involving the sexual abuse of children committed all over the world by members of the Catholic Church.[137] The Council could oblige all UN Member States – including States not party to the Rome Statute – to cooperate with the Court. The Court would have jurisdiction over nationals of non-States Parties by virtue of the fact that as UN members those States have implicitly conferred authority on the Security Council to impose international criminal justice measures for the maintenance of international peace and security. But the Council might not have any authority under the Charter to oblige the Holy See to cooperate with the Court, which would leave a significant impunity gap in any ICC prosecution attempts.[138]

---

[136] While there is little doubt that the Vatican City has separate international personality, there remains some uncertainty about the Vatican's statehood in international law. See generally, JR Morss, 'The International Legal Status of the Vatican/Holy See Complex' (2015) 26 *European Journal of International Law* 927.

[137] An argument can be made that such crimes might constitute crimes against humanity under Article 7: G Robertson, *The Case of the Pope: Vatican Accountability for Human Rights Abuse* (Penguin Books, 2010). Whether that would be sufficient to bring the situation into the Security Council's mandate to maintain international peace and security is less predictable.

[138] The complexity of this issue is far greater than I have indicated here, and would include, inter alia, questions of dual nationality, extradition and the application of the effects doctrine. See generally, BD Landry, 'The Church Abuse Scandal: Prosecuting the Pope before the International Criminal Court' (2011) 12 *Chicago Journal of International Law* 341; D Groome, 'The Church Abuse Scandal: Were Crimes against Humanity Committed?' (2010) 11 *Chicago Journal of International Law* 439.

Kosovo

Kosovo is neither a Member State of the UN, nor a State Party to the Rome Statute. Whether or not the Security Council could trigger the jurisdiction of the ICC over a situation in Kosovo would likely depend on whether Kosovo is an independent State or an autonomous province of Serbia.[139] In 1999 the ICTY dealt with a somewhat comparable situation when it indicted Slobodan Milosević and four other senior officials from the Federal Republic of Yugoslavia (FRY) for crimes committed in Kosovo, which was part of the FRY's territory at the time.[140] The FRY considered itself the successor State to the Socialist Federal Republic of Yugoslavia (SFRY) upon its break up in the early 1990s. But the Security Council and General Assembly made it clear that the FRY did not automatically take over the UN membership of its predecessor[141] and would need to apply to become a UN member in its own right.[142] In the case of *Milutinović*, the defence challenged the jurisdiction of the tribunal over the FRY officials on the basis that the FRY was not a UN Member State at the time the crimes were committed and therefore could not be subject to the jurisdiction of a court whose legal basis was grounded in the UN Charter.[143] The Trial Chamber held that 'the FRY retained sufficient indicia of United Nations membership to make it amenable to the regime of Chapter VII Security Council resolutions adopted for the maintenance of international peace and security'.[144] The Chamber ultimately based its conclusion on the fact that the Council had, in 1991, made a Chapter VII determination that the situation in the SFRY was

---

[139] Kosovo unilaterally declared independence in February 2008. See M Sterio, 'The Case of Kosovo: Self-Determination, Secession, and Statehood under International Law' (2010) 104 *Proceedings of the Annual Meeting (American Society of International Law)* 361.

[140] The accused were indicted for crimes committed from January 1999 onwards. *Prosecutor v Milosević (Indictment)* (Office of the Prosecutor, International Criminal Tribunal for the Former Yugoslavia, Case No IT-99-37, 22 May 1999).

[141] SC Res 777, UN SCOR, 3116th mtg, UN Doc S/RES/777 (19 September 1992); GA Res 47/1, UN GAOR, 7th plen mtg, UN Doc A/RES/47/1 (22 September 1992).

[142] The other newly independent States that emerged from the Socialist Federal Republic of Yugoslavia (Bosnia-Herzegovina, Croatia, Macedonia and Slovenia) all became members of the UN soon after they declared independence. FRY was eventually admitted to the UN in November 2000: GA Res 55/12, UN GAOR, 55th sess, 48th plen mtg, UN Doc A/RES/55/12 (1 November 2000).

[143] *Prosecutor v Milutinović (Decision on Motion Challenging Jurisdiction)* (International Criminal Tribunal for the Former Yugoslavia, Trial Chamber, Case No IT-99-37-PT, 6 May 2003).

[144] Ibid., para 38. For a critique of this, see Akande, 'The Legal Nature of Security Council Referrals to the ICC and its Impact on Al Bashir's Immunities', 629–31.

a threat to international peace and security, and that it would be institutionally ineffective if the Council was stopped from taking further measures in that situation because one country involved ceased to be a UN member.[145]

In a hypothetical Kosovo situation, the validity of any Security Council referral would depend on whether Kosovo is a State under international law.[146] If it is not, then Serbia's consent – to both the UN Charter and the Rome Statute – would provide a legal basis for ICC jurisdiction. If Kosovo is an independent State, then as a non-UN Member and a non-State Party to the Rome Statute, there would be no basis for either a Security Council referral or ICC jurisdiction over any crimes committed in Kosovo after it became independent in February 2008.

The conclusions drawn above are predicated on the assumption that UN Member States are, collectively, the ultimate source of the Security Council's powers to maintain international peace and security.[147] The discussion also assumes that the Security Council's Chapter VII powers are subject to the usual limitations of treaty law which would prevent the Council from imposing any obligations on non-UN Member States.[148]

Given the near universal membership of the UN, the question of whether the Security Council can bind non-UN Member States is unlikely to arise in the ICC context. Acknowledging the uncertainties, however minor they seem, serves to demonstrate the complexity of the legal arrangement between the ICC and the Security Council when it comes to the legal basis for the ICC's jurisdiction.

5.4.4 Implied Consent as a Legal Basis

The idea that non-States Parties Sudan and Libya are obliged to cooperate with the ICC by virtue of their ratification of the UN Charter is largely

---

[145] *Prosecutor v Milutinović (Decision on Motion Challenging Jurisdiction)* (International Criminal Tribunal for the Former Yugoslavia, Trial Chamber, Case No IT-99-37-PT, 6 May 2003) paras 45–8.

[146] In 2010, the ICJ held that Kosovo's unilateral declaration of independence 'did not violate international law' but declined to give an opinion on whether or not Kosovo was a State. *Accordance with International Law of the Unilateral Declaration of Independence in Respect of Kosovo (Advisory Opinion)* [2010] ICJ Rep 403, paras 51 and 122.

[147] Sarooshi, *The United Nations and the Development of Collective Security*, p. 27.

[148] See earlier discussion of the universality of the Security Council's powers. For a general analysis of the limits of the Security Council's powers, see K Doehring, 'Unlawful Resolutions of the Security Council and their Legal Consequences' (1997) 1 *Max Planck Yearbook of United Nations Law* 91.

uncontroversial. As UN Member States, they have agreed 'to accept and carry out the decisions of the Security Council' under Article 25 of the Charter. It is also accepted that the source of the ICC's right to prosecute in these situations is the Security Council's Chapter VII powers, which trigger the Court's jurisdiction under Article 13(b).[149] What is less clear, however, is the legal basis for the ICC's jurisdiction over non-party situations when the jurisdiction is triggered by the Security Council. A strong argument can be made that as UN Member States, Libya and Sudan have consented to the Security Council's role under the Charter to maintain international peace and security, and that this implicitly includes the triggering of ICC jurisdiction. Assuming that such action is within the Council's power, then the legal basis for such jurisdiction is indirectly grounded in the consent of Libya and Sudan.

The final section of this chapter examines what role the Security Council plays with respect to the ICC's jurisdiction over the crime of aggression.

5.5 The Hidden Pillar Revealed: The Crime of Aggression

At Rome, States were so deeply divided on the issue of the crime of aggression that it was nearly left out of the Statute entirely.[150] In the end, the crime was included in Article 5(1)(d) of the Statute, but the elements of the crime and conditions of ICC jurisdiction over it were deferred, leading Sir Franklin Berman to term this the 'hidden pillar' of the Council's relationship to the Court.[151] In 2010, the Assembly of States Parties convened for a review conference in Kampala, Uganda, with the objective of finalising the crime of aggression in the Rome Statute. In the adopted Kampala Amendments, Article 8 *bis*(1) defines the crime as:

> [T]he planning, preparation, initiation or execution, by a person in a position effectively to exercise control over or to direct the political or military action of a State, of an act of aggression which, by its character, gravity and scale, constitutes a manifest violation of the Charter of the United Nations.

---

[149] See, eg, *Prosecutor v Omar Hassan Ahmad Al Bashir (Warrant of Arrest for Omar Al Bashir)* (International Criminal Court, Pre-Trial Chamber I, Case No ICC-02/05-01/09, 4 March 2009) para 40.

[150] C McDougall, *The Crime of Aggression under the Rome Statute of the International Criminal Court* (Cambridge University Press, 2013) p. 10.

[151] Berman, 'The Relationship between the International Criminal Court and the Security Council', p. 178.

5.5 HIDDEN PILLAR REVEALED: CRIME OF AGGRESSION

The definition necessarily recognises that the UN Charter prohibits States from threatening or using force against other States (unless in self-defence).[152] Article 39 of the Charter gives the Security Council the power to determine the existence of an act of aggression; what role the Council would play with respect to the ICC's jurisdiction over the crime of aggression was therefore a key question at the Kampala negotiations.[153] The Kampala Amendments entered into force in 2018, but at the time of writing the jurisdiction of the ICC over the crime of aggression was still untested.[154]

The following discussion is limited to an overview of the Security Council's role as set out in the Kampala Amendments and the consequences of this for States that have not consented to the Court's jurisdiction over the crime of aggression. Further analysis of the jurisdictional intricacies of the crime of aggression before the ICC is beyond the scope of this book.[155]

5.5.1 The Jurisdiction Trigger

The jurisdiction of the ICC over the crime of aggression involves a complex interaction between the Kampala Amendments and the Rome Statute. Specifically, regard must be had to the Article 15*bis* and 15*ter*

---

[152] UN Charter, Articles 2(4) and 51.
[153] S Barriga and C Kreß, *The Travaux Préparatoires of the Crime of Aggression* (Cambridge University Press, 2011) pp. 30–3.
[154] International Criminal Court, *Activation of the jurisdiction of the Court over the crime of aggression*, Resolution ICC-ASP/16/Res.5 (adopted 14 December 2017). The Assembly of States Parties decided 'to activate the Court's jurisdiction over the crime of aggression as of 17 July 2018'.
[155] For a more comprehensive analysis of such issues, see, eg, D Akande, 'Prosecuting Aggression: The Consent Problem and the Role of the Security Council' (2010); McDougall, *The Crime of Aggression under the Rome Statute of the International Criminal Court*; C Kreß and L von Holtzendorff, 'The Kampala Compromise on the Crime of Aggression' (2010) 8 *Journal of International Criminal Justice* 1179; RS Clark, 'Amendments to the Rome Statute of the International Criminal Court Considered at the First Review Conference on the Court, Kampala, 31 May–11 June 2010' (2010) 2 *Goettingen Journal of International Law* 689; A Reisinger Coracini, 'The International Criminal Court's Exercise of Jurisdiction over the Crime of Aggression – At Last ... in Reach ... over Some' (2010) 2 *Goettingen Journal of International Law* 745; B Van Schaack, 'Par in Parem Imperium Non Habet Complementarity and the Crime of Aggression' (2012) 10 *Journal of International Criminal Justice* 133; A Zimmermann, 'Amending the Amendment Provisions of the Rome Statute: The Kampala Compromise on the Crime of Aggression and the Law of Treaties' (2012) 10 *Journal of International Criminal Justice* 209; M. Milanović, 'Aggression and Legality Custom in Kampala' (2012) 10 *Journal of International Criminal Justice* 165.

amendments; the existing jurisdiction provisions and preconditions in Articles 12 and 13 of the Statute; and Article 121 of the Statute which sets out the rules for implementing amendments.[156] The primary role for the Security Council is set out in Article 15*ter*(1) which provides that the ICC may exercise jurisdiction over the crime of aggression in accordance with the provisions of Article 13(b) of the Statute. In other words, the ICC may prosecute a crime of aggression when a situation has been referred to the Court by the Security Council. Annex III to the Kampala Amendments confirms that the ICC may exercise jurisdiction in such a situation 'irrespective of whether the State concerned has accepted the Court's jurisdiction in this regard'.[157] This reflects the scope of the Council's referral power already established in Article 13(b).

One of the unique features of the jurisdictional regime for the crime of aggression is Article 15*bis*(5) which provides that '[i]n respect of a State that is not a party to this Statute, the Court shall not exercise its jurisdiction over the crime of aggression when committed by that State's nationals or on its territory'. This limits the application of Article 12(2) of the Rome Statute which otherwise allows for nationals from non-States Parties to be prosecuted for crimes committed on the territory of States Parties. It also means that even where a non-State Party has accepted the jurisdiction of the ICC on an ad hoc basis, the Court cannot exercise jurisdiction over a crime of aggression in that situation.[158] The rationale for this departure from the Article 12(2) and (3) preconditions is that the crime of aggression is inescapably a 'crime of state',[159] which by its nature involves an aggressor State and a victim State. Any investigation and prosecution of a crime of aggression would inherently involve adjudication of an interstate dispute, and as discussed in Chapter 2, this would likely present an unacceptable infringement on State sovereignty where one of the States has not consented to the jurisdiction of the ICC. China,

---

[156] See, eg, R Clark, 'Ambiguities in Articles 5(2), 121 and 123 of the Rome Statute' (2009) 41 *Case Western Reserve Journal of International Law* 413; D Akande and A Tzanakopoulos, 'Treaty Law and ICC Jurisdiction over the Crime of Aggression' (2018) 29 *European Journal of International Law* 939.

[157] Kampala Amendments, Annex III, para 2.

[158] It also means that a non-State Party cannot simply accept the Kampala Amendments on an ad hoc basis: Akande and Tzanakopoulos, 'Treaty Law and ICC Jurisdiction over the Crime of Aggression', 954–5.

[159] Assembly of States Parties to the Rome Statute, 'Discussion Paper 1: The Crime of Aggression and Article 25, paragraph (3) of the Statute', ICC OR, 4th sess, ICC-ASP /4/32, Annex II B (9 December 2005) 378. See also, Barriga and Kreß, *The Travaux Préparatoires of the Crime of Aggression*, p. 88.

Russia and the US were particularly influential in securing this outcome for non-States Parties.[160] Ultimately the Kampala Amendments ensure that the only avenue through which the ICC can exercise jurisdiction over a crime of aggression involving non-State Party nationals or territory is a Security Council referral.

There is one final distinctive jurisdictional feature of the Kampala Amendments, which is that the ICC will not have jurisdiction over an aggressor State Party if it has not specifically ratified that Kampala Amendments. In its activation resolution, the Assembly of States Parties agreed that:

> in accordance with the Rome Statute, the amendments to the Statute regarding the crime of aggression adopted at the Kampala Review Conference enter into force for those States Parties which have accepted the amendments one year after the deposit of their instruments of ratification or acceptance and that in the case of a State referral or proprio motu investigation the Court shall not exercise its jurisdiction regarding a crime of aggression when committed by a national or on the territory of a State Party that has not ratified or accepted these amendments.[161]

In not allowing State referrals and *proprio motu* investigations for a crime of aggression committed by a State Party that has not opted in to the Amendments, the Assembly of States Parties has indirectly increased the importance of the role of the Security Council. Without a Security Council referral, the ICC will only be able to exercise jurisdiction over the crime of aggression if the aggressor State is a State Party to the Rome Statute *and* has ratified the Kampala Amendments. The Council, on the other hand, may refer a crime of aggression involving any State to the Court.

5.5.2 Determining the Existence of a Crime of Aggression

As well as the power to trigger the ICC's jurisdiction over the crime of aggression, the Kampala Amendments give the Security Council an additional role. Article 15*bis* governs the jurisdiction of the ICC over the crime of aggression in situations referred by States Parties or investigations initiated *proprio motu* by the Prosecutor. The amendment stipulates that where the Office of the Prosecutor intends to proceed with an investigation potentially involving a crime of aggression, it must first ascertain whether

---

[160] RS Clark, 'The Crime of Aggression' in C Stahn (ed), *The Law and Practice of the International Criminal Court* (Oxford University Press, 2015) p. 792.
[161] International Criminal Court, *Activation of the jurisdiction of the Court over the crime of aggression,* Resolution ICC-ASP/16/Res.5 (adopted 14 December 2017) para 2.

the Security Council has made a determination about the existence of an act of aggression in that situation.[162] Where the Council has made such a determination, the Prosecutor may go ahead with the investigation into the crime of aggression.[163] If the Council has not made such a determination within six months from when the Prosecutor notifies the UN of the intention to investigate, then the Prosecutor may nevertheless proceed with the investigation upon authorisation by the Pre-Trial Chamber.[164] Giving the Security Council the opportunity to make a pronouncement under Article 39 of the Charter on the existence of an act of aggression was a concession to the permanent five who argued during the negotiations that a Security Council determination should be a prerequisite for ICC jurisdiction over a crime of aggression.[165]

How these Article 15*bis* requirements will work in practice remains to be seen. They appear to offer the Security Council a somewhat superfluous role given that the Prosecutor can go ahead with an investigation into a crime of aggression, even where the Council has not declared the existence of an act of aggression.[166] The Office of the Prosecutor need only notify the UN of its intention to investigate and, in doing so, give the Security Council the opportunity to make an Article 39 determination within six months. Furthermore, it can be inferred from Article 15*bis* that the role envisioned for the Security Council is limited to the opportunity to make positive pronouncements on the existence of an act of aggression. There is nothing in the Kampala Amendments to suggest that the Prosecutor would be prevented from investigating a crime of aggression if the Council were to take the unlikely step of specifically declaring that an act of aggression has *not* occurred. The only way the Security Council could stop the ICC from going ahead with such an investigation would be via an Article 16 deferral.[167]

---

[162] Kampala Amendments, Article 15*bis*(6).
[163] Ibid., Article 15*bis*(7).
[164] Ibid., Article 15*bis*(8).
[165] See, eg, *Review Conference of the Rome Statute of the International Criminal Court (Kampala 31 May–11 June 2010)*, Official Records, ICC Doc RC/11 (2010): Statement by France 122; Statement by the UK 124; Statement by China 125; Statement by the US 126.
[166] As long as the Pre-Trial Chamber approves the opening of such an investigation. See, J Trahan, 'Revisiting the Role of the Security Council Concerning the International Criminal Court's Crime of Aggression' (2019) 17 *Journal of International Criminal Justice* 471 at 476–7.
[167] McDougall, *The Crime of Aggression under the Rome Statute of the International Criminal Court*, p. 270.

Interestingly, the requirement that the Prosecutor must first ascertain whether the Security Council has made a determination on the existence of an act of aggression is limited to situations referred to the Court by States Parties or investigations initiated by the Prosecutor. There are no equivalent requirements in Article 15*ter*, which is the provision dealing with Security Council referrals. This is perhaps due to an assumption that an Article 13(b) referral giving rise to an ICC investigation into a crime of aggression would presumably contain a Council determination that an act of aggression exists in that situation. But as discussed, the Prosecutor's discretion to decide what acts and persons to investigate in any given situation cannot be limited by the Security Council. If an Article 13(b) referral resolution does not contain a determination about the existence of an act of aggression, this does not preclude the ICC prosecutor from pursuing an investigation based on other evidence that a crime of aggression has taken place.[168] Conversely, if the Council's Article 13(b) referral does specifically declare the existence of an act of aggression, this does not create an obligation for the Prosecutor to investigate a crime of aggression.[169]

5.5.3 A Mixed Role for the Security Council

The Security Council has an important role to play with respect to the ICC's jurisdiction over the crime of aggression, as it is the only avenue through which States not party to the Statute can be subject to the Court's jurisdiction. Similarly, given the limitations on the Court's jurisdiction over aggressor States Parties, a Council referral is, at this stage, the only guaranteed way that the ICC will be able to prosecute a crime of

---

[168] 'A determination of an act of aggression by an organ outside the Court shall be without prejudice to the Court's own findings under this Statute': Kampala Amendments, Article 15*bis*(9). See also, N Blokker and S Barriga, 'Conditions for the Exercise of Jurisdiction Based on Security Council Referrals' in C Kreß, S Barriga (eds), *The Crime of Aggression – A Commentary* (Cambridge University Press, 2016) p. 651.

[169] For discussion on the distinction between the Security Council's political right to determine an act of aggression and the ICC's judicial prerogatives relating to the crime of aggression, see, generally McDougall, *The Crime of Aggression under the Rome Statute of the International Criminal Court*, pp. 209–34; MS Stein, 'The Security Council, the International Criminal Court, and the Crime of Aggression: How Exclusive is the Security Council's Power to Determine Aggression' (2005) 16 *Indiana International and Comparative Law Review* 1 at 8–11; R Schaeffer, 'The Audacity of Compromise: The UN Security Council and the Pre-Conditions to the Exercise of Jurisdiction by the ICC with Regard to the Crime of Aggression' (2009) 9 *International Criminal Law Review* 411.

aggression in all situations involving States Parties. Beyond extending the Council's Article 13(b) referral power to the crime of aggression, however, the Council otherwise has a relatively inconsequential role in determining whether an act of aggression has taken place. The ICC Prosecutor is obliged to check whether the Council has made such a determination before proceeding with an investigation, but the Kampala Amendments and the Statute give the Prosecutor significant discretion to go ahead with an investigation into a suspected crime of aggression regardless of what the Council decides.

5.6 Conclusion

In the years since the Rome Statute entered into force, the Security Council has been relatively active in interacting with the ICC. The Court's supporters were surprised, and pleased, that the Council used its Article 13(b) power to refer situations in both Sudan and Libya to the ICC, although the Council has not followed its referral decisions with the assistance that the Court desperately needs. Consent from Sudan and Libya can be implied by virtue of their UN membership and adherence to the UN Charter, but questions of whether referrals are intra vires the UN Charter may be beyond the competence of the ICC. At some stage soon, the Court will need to make a pronouncement on whether the Council's attempts to curtail the jurisdiction of the ICC by exempting UN peacekeepers from non-States Parties has any legal bearing on the Court. As argued above, the Council's action does not conform to the parameters of Article 16 or any other provision in the Rome Statute, meaning that it is unlikely to have any legal impact on the ICC's jurisdiction. If the Council continues to include such exemption clauses in its resolutions without response from the ICC, it runs the risk of setting an unfortunate precedent.

6

Universality as a Legal Basis for ICC Jurisdiction

6.1 Introduction

Chapters 3 and 4 focused on the legal basis for the ICC's jurisdiction in situations referred to the Court by a State Party or investigations initiated by the ICC Prosecutor. I explored the theory that States Parties are delegating territorial and nationality jurisdiction to the ICC and concluded that this provides a sound legal basis for the ICC's exercise of jurisdiction over nationals of non-States Parties, with the possible exception of incumbent Heads of State. Chapter 5 then analysed the legal basis for the ICC's jurisdiction over nationals of non-States Parties in situations referred to the Court by the UN Security Council. I argued that the ICC's jurisdiction in such situations is predicated on implied consent of the territorial State by virtue of that State's obligations under the UN Charter. In this chapter I examine an alternative theory that the legal basis for the ICC's jurisdiction over nationals of non-States Parties is founded upon the principle of universality.

The idea that the principle of universality provides a legal basis for the ICC's jurisdiction has its origins in the Article 13(b) Security Council referral mechanism. The potentially global reach of the ICC's jurisdiction in situations referred to the Court by the Security Council has led a number of commentators to claim that this gives the ICC universal jurisdiction.[1] This is an accurate assessment to the extent that the Court could, in limited circumstances, prosecute crimes committed in any State, by any national, irrespective of whether States involved are party

---

[1] See, eg, GM Danilenko, 'The Statute of the International Criminal Court and Third States' (1999) 21 *Michigan Journal of International Law* 445 at 452; JJ Paust, 'The Reach of ICC Jurisdiction over Non-Signatory Nationals' (2000) 33 *Vanderbilt Journal of Transnational Law* 1 at 7–8; S Williams, *Hybrid and Internationalised Criminal Tribunals: Selected Jurisdictional Issues* (Hart Publishing, 2012) p. 250; C Heyder, 'The UN Security Council's Referral of the Crimes in Darfur to the International Criminal Court in Light of US Opposition to the Court: Implications for the International Criminal Court's Functions and Status' (2006) 24 *Berkeley Journal of International Law* 650 at 653.

to the Statute.[2] But a Court with the potential to exercise its jurisdiction universally must be distinguished from jurisdiction based on the principle of universality. In previous chapters, I have largely assumed that only the principles of territoriality and nationality have any direct relevance to the legal basis for the ICC's jurisdiction, as those two principles reflect the limitations contained in the Article 12 preconditions. Yet the nature of the Rome Statute's subject matter jurisdiction and the preambular declaration that the Court will prosecute 'the most serious crimes of concern to the international community as a whole' evokes the rhetoric and rationale more often associated with universal jurisdiction.[3] It is perhaps not surprising that some scholars argue that the principle of universality is relevant for the ICC's jurisdiction, especially in situations involving nationals of non-States Parties.[4]

This chapter examines the issue of whether the principle of universality has any bearing on the legal basis for the ICC's jurisdiction.[5] I begin in Section 6.2 by providing an overview of how the term 'universal jurisdiction' is commonly used in international criminal law, by canvassing three different conceptualisations of universal jurisdiction. I conclude that the most relevant characterisation provides that a State has the right to prescribe laws concerning crimes defined in customary international law where such offences are committed extraterritorially with no link to the prosecuting State.

Section 6.3 then turns to deal with the fact that Article 12 appears to preclude universality as a legal basis for the ICC's jurisdiction. I argue that the preconditions requiring either the territorial State or the State of

---

[2] Although see the discussion in Section 5.4.3.2 for an analysis of whether the Security Council can in fact refer any situation to the ICC.

[3] Unless stated otherwise, throughout this chapter I use 'universal jurisdiction' as a term of art to mean jurisdiction exercised on the basis of universality.

[4] See, eg, MP Scharf, 'The ICC's Jurisdiction over the Nationals of Non-Party States: A Critique of the U.S. Position' (2001) 64 *Law and Contemporary Problems* 67; LN Sadat and SR Carden, 'The New International Criminal Court: An Uneasy Revolution' (1999) 88 *Georgetown Law Journal* 381.

[5] It is beyond the scope of this chapter to discuss how the existence and operation of the ICC affects the exercise of universal jurisdiction by States. Similarly, I do not address whether States asserting universal jurisdiction is sufficient to render a particular case inadmissible under Article 17. For an analysis of these issues, see generally, L Arbour, 'Will the ICC have an Impact on Universal Jurisdiction?' (2003) 1 *Journal of International Criminal Justice* 585; G Bottini, 'Universal Jurisdiction after the Creation of the International Criminal Court' (2003) 36 *New York University Journal of International Law and Politics* 503; M Langer, 'The Archipelago and the Wheel: The Universal Jurisdiction and the International Criminal Court Regimes' in CC True-Frost, M Minow and A Whiting (eds), *The First Global Prosecutor* (University of Michigan Press, 2015) p. 204.

nationality to have accepted the jurisdiction of the Court are not necessarily indicative of the legal basis for the Court's jurisdiction. Instead, it is necessary to determine whether the offences in the Rome Statute are crimes that attract universal jurisdiction under customary international law. I demonstrate that, by and large, the Statute crimes are customarily justiciable under universal jurisdiction.

The final substantive section of this chapter explores two theories that would allow for the ICC's jurisdiction to be based on the principle of universality. The first is that States are delegating universal jurisdiction to the Court, alongside territorial and nationality jurisdiction. The result is that the ICC's jurisdiction in any given situation would be based on a combination of the principles of territoriality, nationality and universality, and would remain anchored in delegation from States. The second theory conceptualises universal jurisdiction as inherent to the international community and exercisable by the ICC as an agent of this community. I argue that either theory would, at least in principle, provide a legal basis for the ICC's jurisdiction over nationals of non-States Parties in most circumstances prescribed by the Statute. But there are also some significant limitations to both universal jurisdiction theories, and I conclude that there is no advantage to characterising the legal basis for ICC jurisdiction over nationals of non-States Parties in terms of universality.

6.2 What is Universal Jurisdiction?

As mentioned in Chapter 3, universality is one of the four principles of international law under which States may exercise jurisdiction extraterritorially. There is an inordinate amount of scholarship devoted to the conceptualisation of universal jurisdiction and the dissection of relevant State practice.[6] In this section I canvass the main definitional

---

[6] See, eg, L Reydams, *Universal Jurisdiction: International and Municipal Legal Perspectives* (Oxford University Press, 2003); R O'Keefe, 'Universal Jurisdiction: Clarifying the Basic Concept' (2004) 2 *Journal of International Criminal Justice* 735; MC Bassiouni, 'Universal Jurisdiction for International Crimes: Historical Perspectives and Contemporary Practice' (2001) 42 *Virginia Journal of International Law* 81; KC Randall, 'Universal Jurisdiction under International Law' (1987) 66 *Texas Law Review* 785; T Einarsen, *The Concept of Universal Crimes in International Law* (Torkel Opsahl Academic EPublisher, 2012); D Hovell, 'The Authority of Universal Jurisdiction' (2018) 29 *European Journal of International Law* 427; E Kontorovich, 'The Parochial Uses of Universal Jurisdiction' (2018) 94 *Notre Dame Law Review* 1417. See also, International Law Association, *Final Report on the Exercise of Universal Jurisdiction in respect of Gross Human Rights Abuses*

and conceptual issues that frequently arise in analyses of universal jurisdiction with a view to ascertaining how the principle of universality might apply in the ICC context. A survey of the relevant literature reveals that 'confusion and uncertainty reigns'[7] over what universal jurisdiction actually is, with three relatively distinct versions of the concept emerging in the doctrine.

6.2.1 Three Types of Universal Jurisdiction

6.2.1.1 Representative or Vicarious Jurisdiction

The first version of universal jurisdiction is what Luc Reydams terms 'cooperative general universality' which has its origins in the practice of States prior to World War II.[8] Under this construction, a custodial State may prosecute a foreign national for a crime committed extraterritorially, with no other nexus between the prosecuting State and the crime. The crime itself does not have to be an international crime; it may be a serious crime common among domestic criminal jurisdictions. The rationale for such jurisdiction is that the custodial State may prosecute where it is not possible to extradite the offender to a State with jurisdiction based on territoriality, nationality, passive personality or the protective principle.[9] To the extent that there is no link between the prosecuting State and the offence (other than custody), the description of this type of situation as universal jurisdiction makes sense. But since the post-war evolution of international criminal law, such jurisdiction has become better known as representative jurisdiction or the vicarious exercise of jurisdiction.[10] It is essentially an example of the custodial State exercising jurisdiction delegated from a State that would otherwise have jurisdiction on the basis of territoriality or nationality.

6.2.1.2 Treaty-Based Universal Jurisdiction

There are a growing number of multilateral treaties that give States Parties criminal jurisdiction over certain crimes without regard to the

---

(2000); Princeton Project on Universal Jurisdiction, *The Princeton Principles on Universal Jurisdiction* (2001); Amnesty International, *Universal Jurisdiction – A Preliminary Survey of Legislation Around the World 2012 Update* (9 October 2012).

[7] A Cassese, 'Is the Bell Tolling for Universality? A Plea for a Sensible Notion of Universal Jurisdiction' (2003) 1 *Journal of International Criminal Justice* 589 at 590.
[8] Reydams, *Universal Jurisdiction*, pp. 28–35.
[9] Ibid.
[10] Reydams, *Universal Jurisdiction*, pp. 34–5; M Inazumi, *Universal Jurisdiction in Modern International Law: Expansion of National Jurisdiction for Prosecuting Serious Crimes under International Law* (Intersentia, 2005) pp. 111–12.

6.2 WHAT IS UNIVERSAL JURISDICTION? 163

nationality of the offender or the territory of the offence. For example, the anti-terrorism treaties discussed in Chapter 3 are often described as providing universal jurisdiction over certain acts of terrorism, hijacking and torture.[11] These treaties prescribe a list of States with primary jurisdiction over the relevant crimes but also oblige custodial States to extradite or prosecute the suspected offender.[12]

Commentators are divided as to whether such treaties can accurately be described as providing for universal jurisdiction. There are those who contend that treaties cannot be a source of universal jurisdiction for the simple fact that only States Parties to the treaty regime are entitled to exercise jurisdiction under it.[13] In accordance with the principle of *pacta tertiis nec nocent nec prosunt,* a custodial State not party to the treaty does not have the right to prosecute a foreign national for a treaty crime with no other nexus to the custodial State. In contrast, other scholars argue that the *pacta tertiis* limitation does not affect the universal nature of the jurisdiction provided for in certain treaties.[14] O'Keefe, for example, argues that universal jurisdiction is simply 'prescriptive jurisdiction in the absence of any other recognized jurisdictional nexus'.[15] Insofar as treaties allow (or oblige) States Parties to

---

[11] Examples of such treaties include the *Convention on Offences and Certain Other Acts Committed on Board Aircraft*, opened for signature 14 September 1963, 704 UNTS 219 (entered into force 4 December 1969); *Convention for Suppression of Unlawful Seizure of Aircraft,* opened for signature 16 December 1970, 860 UNTS 105 (entered into force 14 October 1971); *Convention against the Taking of Hostages,* opened for signature 17 December 1979, 1316 UNTS 205 (entered into force 3 June 1983); *Convention against Torture and Other Cruel, Inhuman or Degrading Treatment or Punishment,* opened for signature 10 December 1984, 1465 UNTS 85 (entered into force 26 June 1987).

[12] See the discussion in Section 3.2.1.1. See also, *Questions Relating to the Obligation to Prosecute or Extradite (Belgium v Senegal) (Judgment)* [2012] ICJ Rep 422, in which the ICJ held that Senegal, as the custodial State, was obliged by the Convention against Torture to either prosecute the accused former president of Chad under universal jurisdiction, or extradite him.

[13] Cassese, 'Is the Bell Tolling for Universality?', 594; S Yee, 'Universal Jurisdiction: Concept, Logic, and Reality' (2011) 10 *Chinese Journal of International Law* 503 at 509; C Kreß, 'Universal Jurisdiction over International Crimes and the Institut de Droit international' (2006) 4 *Journal of International Criminal Justice* 561 at 566; R Liivoja, 'Treaties, Custom and Universal Jurisdiction' in R Liivoja and J Petman (eds), *International Law-Making: Essays in Honour of Jan Klabbers* (Routledge, 2013) p. 299.

[14] O'Keefe, 'Universal Jurisdiction', 746–7; Randall, 'Universal Jurisdiction under International Law'; Inazumi, *Universal Jurisdiction in Modern International Law*, p. 103; MP Scharf, 'Application of Treaty-Based Universal Jurisdiction to Nationals of Non-Party States' (2001) 35 *New England Law Review* 363.

[15] O'Keefe, 'Universal Jurisdiction', 747.

prescribe jurisdiction in this way, such jurisdiction may be characterised as universal.[16]

6.2.1.3 Universal Jurisdiction in Customary International Law

The third version of universality is the idea that under customary international law, any State can exercise criminal jurisdiction over a limited category of international crimes with absolutely no link to the offence. Piracy *jure gentium* has long assumed the mantle as the classic customary crime of universal jurisdiction, subject to prosecution by any State because of the *terra nullius* nature of the high seas.[17] Since World War II, war crimes, crimes against humanity and genocide have widely been considered as subject to universal jurisdiction under customary international law.[18] The rationale for universality in this instance is that such crimes are offences against the international community as a whole.[19] In *Israel v Eichmann*, for example, the District Court of Jerusalem tried Eichmann for crimes against humanity and war crimes,[20] holding that:

> These crimes, which struck at the whole of mankind and shocked the conscience of nations, are grave offences against the law of nations itself (*delicta juris gentium*). Therefore, so far from international law negating

---

[16] It is unnecessary to evaluate the merits of the various arguments for and against treaty-based universal jurisdiction in this book. It is sufficient to acknowledge the divergence of opinion among scholars.
[17] R O'Keefe, *International Criminal Law* (Oxford University Press, 2015) pp. 18–22.
[18] Ibid., pp. 22–3; Yee, 'Universal Jurisdiction', 519; KJ Heller, 'What Is an International Crime? (A Revisionist History)' (2017) 28 *Harvard International Law Journal* 353 at 388.
[19] FA Mann, 'The Doctrine of Jurisdiction in International Law' (1964) 111 *Recueil des Cours de l'Academie de Droit Internationale* 1 at 95; Cassese, 'Is the Bell Tolling for Universality?', 591; Bassiouni, 'Universal Jurisdiction for International Crimes', 88; *Arrest Warrant of 11 April 2000 (Congo v Belgium)* [2002] ICJ Rep 2001 (Joint Separate Opinion of Judges Higgins, Kooijmans and Buergenthal) at 60–1. See also, *Restatement of the Law Third, Foreign Relations Law of the United States* (American Law Institute, 1987) 2. But see, A Sammons, 'The Under-Theorization of Universal Jurisdiction: Implications for Legitimacy on Trials of War Criminals by National Courts' (2003) 21 *Berkeley Journal of International Law* 111 at 128. Sammons argues that 'universal jurisdiction arises not because the crimes are "heinous" but because they are committed *terra nullius*', even when committed on State territory. See also, E Kontorovich, 'The Piracy Analogy: Modern Universal Jurisdiction's Hollow Foundation' (2004) 45 *Harvard International Law Journal* 185; Hovell, 'The Authority of Universal Jurisdiction', 438–55.
[20] Eichmann was also charged with crimes against the Jewish people as defined in the *Nazi and Nazi Collaborators (Punishment) Law*, 5710/1950.

6.2 WHAT IS UNIVERSAL JURISDICTION? 165

or limiting the jurisdiction of countries with respect to such crimes, international law is, in the absence of an International Court, in need of the judicial and legislative organs of every country to give effect to its criminal interdictions and to bring the criminals to trial. The jurisdiction to try crimes under international law is universal.[21]

Where scholars and jurists are divided on customary universal jurisdiction is over the issue of whether the accused must be in the custody of the prosecuting State, or whether States may exercise universal jurisdiction *in absentia*.

In the 2002 ICJ *Arrest Warrant* case, Belgium issued an arrest warrant for the Foreign Minister of the DRC for war crimes and crimes against humanity committed on Congolese territory, against Congolese nationals. At the time the arrest warrant was issued, the accused foreign minister was not in Belgium's custody. The primary issue before the ICJ was whether Belgium had violated the minister's immunity, but a number of judges took the opportunity to pronounce on Belgium's assertion of universal jurisdiction. In a separate opinion, President Guillaume found that Belgium did not have jurisdiction to try the Congolese foreign minister on the grounds that 'universal jurisdiction *in absentia* as applied in the present case is unknown to international law'.[22] Similarly, Judges Rezek and Ranjeva rejected the notion that a State with no connection to the crime may seek to extradite or arrest a foreign national on the basis of universal jurisdiction.[23]

In contrast, Judges Higgins, Kooijmans and Buergenthal found that although there is no established practice of States exercising universal jurisdiction *in absentia*, neither is there any practice to suggest that custody is a precondition to such jurisdiction.[24] Their Excellencies noted that if a State's domestic law allows for a trial to take place *in absentia,* such proceedings would likely contravene the accused's right to a fair trial, but this 'has little to do with bases of jurisdiction recognized under international law'.[25]

---

[21] *Attorney-General of the Government of Israel v Adolf Eichmann* (1962) 36 ILR 5, 26. Emphasis original.
[22] *Arrest Warrant of 11 April 2000 (Congo v Belgium) (Judgment)* [2002] ICJ Rep 2001 (Separate Opinion of President Guillaume) para 14.
[23] *Arrest Warrant of 11 April 2000 (Congo v Belgium) (Judgment)* [2002] ICJ Rep 2001 (Separate Opinion of Judge Rezek) para 6; (Declaration of Judge Ranjeva) paras 5–6.
[24] *Arrest Warrant of 11 April 2000 (Congo v Belgium) (Judgment)* [2002] ICJ Rep 2001 (Joint Separate Opinion of Judges Higgins, Kooijmans and Buergenthal) paras 54–6.
[25] Ibid., para 56.

It seems many scholars accept that universal jurisdiction may, at least in theory, be asserted without the need for custody of the accused.[26] Antonio Cassese agrees with Judges Higgins, Kooijmans and Buergenthal that universal jurisdiction *in absentia* is permitted in international law, but argues that it would nevertheless be 'inadvisable' on policy grounds for States to assert jurisdiction in this manner.[27] O'Keefe clarifies that technically there is no such thing as universal jurisdiction *in absentia* because universality is solely a principle of prescriptive jurisdiction:

> The fact is that prescription is logically independent of enforcement. On the one hand, there is universal jurisdiction, a head of prescriptive jurisdiction alongside territoriality, nationality, passive personality and so on. On the other hand, there is enforcement *in absentia*, just as there is enforcement *in personam*.[28]

As discussed in Chapter 3, a State may assert prescriptive jurisdiction extraterritorially on the basis of the permissive principles, but its jurisdiction to enforce is strictly territorial.[29]

6.2.2 'Universal Jurisdiction' in This Book

While universal jurisdiction remains a complex – and at times, convoluted – concept, for the purposes of the analysis in this chapter, I will use the term to mean a State's right to prescribe laws in relation to certain customary international crimes that are committed extraterritorially with

---

[26] Reydams, *Universal Jurisdiction*, p. 38; AJ Colangelo, 'The New Universal Jurisdiction: In Absentia Signaling over Clearly Defined Crimes' (2005) 36 *Georgetown Journal of International Law* 537 at 548–9; Yee, 'Universal Jurisdiction', 508; Inazumi, *Universal Jurisdiction in Modern International Law*, pp. 101–3; Kreß, 'Universal Jurisdiction over International Crimes and the Institut de Droit international', 576.

[27] A Cassese, 'When May Senior State Officials Be Tried for International Crimes? Some Comments on the Congo v. Belgium Case' (2002) 13 *European Journal of International Law* 853 at 857; Cassese, 'Is the Bell Tolling for Universality?', 592. See also, G Abi-Saab, 'The Proper Role of Universal Jurisdiction' (2003) 1 *Journal of International Criminal Justice* 596 at 601.

[28] O'Keefe, 'Universal Jurisdiction', 750. See also, O'Keefe, *International Criminal Law*, p. 17.

[29] A State may only enforce its jurisdiction extraterritorially if the territorial State consents. For example, the Scottish court established in the Netherlands to try Libyan suspects under Scots law for the 1988 bombing of Pan Am Flight 103: *Al Megrahi v Her Majesty's Advocate (Scotland)* [1999] HCJT 1475. See generally, M Plachta, 'The Lockerbie Case: The Role of the Security Council in Enforcing the Principle Aut Dedere Aut Judicare' (2001) 12 *European Journal of International Law* 125; MP Scharf, 'The Lockerbie Model of Transfer of Proceedings' in MC Bassiouni (ed), *International Criminal Law* (Martinus Nijhoff Publishers, 2008).

no other nexus to the prosecuting State. The rest of the chapter examines whether the principle of universality may have any bearing on the legal basis for the ICC's jurisdiction.

6.3 Universality and the Rome Statute

6.3.1 Is the Principle of Universality Precluded by the Statute?

At the Rome Conference, States had the opportunity to consider establishing a court with universal jurisdiction under a proposal put forward by the German delegation. Under the German proposal, the future court would have jurisdiction over genocide, crimes against humanity and war crimes irrespective of where and by whom they were committed.[30] Representing Germany at the 7th meeting of the Committee of the Whole, Hans-Peter Kaul clarified the objective of the proposal:

> Since the contracting parties to the Statute could individually exercise universal jurisdiction for the core crimes they could also, by ratifying the Statute, vest the Court with a similar power to exercise such universal jurisdiction on their behalf, though only of course with regard to the core crimes.[31]

Advocates for this proposal believed that any State consent requirements would hinder the effectiveness of the court and potentially undermine its very *raison d'être*.[32] Despite strong support from many delegations, the resistance of some States to giving the court universal jurisdiction was intense, and the German proposal was removed from consideration.[33]

The compromise reached on the final text of the Rome Statute's jurisdiction provisions makes it clear that the ICC does not have universal jurisdiction. Article 12 of the Rome Statute plainly requires either the territorial State or the State of nationality to consent to the authority

---

[30] Preparatory Committee on the Establishment of an International Criminal Court, *The Jurisdiction of the International Criminal Court, An informal discussion paper submitted by Germany*, UN Doc A/AC.249/1998/DP.2 (23 March 1998) para 2(b).

[31] United Nations Diplomatic Conference of Plenipotentiaries on the Establishment of an International Criminal Court, *Summary records of the plenary meetings and of the meetings of the Committee of the Whole*, 7th mtg, UN Doc A/CONF.183/C.1/SR.7 (19 June 1998) 184.

[32] W Schabas and G Pecorella, 'Article 12 Preconditions to the Exercise of Jurisdiction' in O Triffterer and K Ambos (eds), *Rome Statute of the International Criminal Court – A Commentary* (CH Beck Hart Nomos, 2016) pp. 676–7.

[33] HP Kaul, 'Preconditions to the Exercise of Jurisdiction' in A Cassese, P Gaeta and JRWD Jones (eds), *The Rome Statute of the International Criminal Court: A Commentary* (Oxford University Press, 2002) p. 599.

of the ICC before the Court can exercise jurisdiction. The only circumstance in which State consent to the Statute is not a precondition to jurisdiction occurs when the Security Council refers a situation to the ICC in accordance with Article 13(b). While the Statute's complex 'consent regime' restricts the Court's jurisdiction to certain persons and territory, it does not necessarily mean that the principle of universality is precluded as a basis for the Court's limited jurisdiction.

Leila Nadya Sadat and S Richard Carden argue that the uncertainty surrounding the applicability of the principle of universality to the ICC 'has been generated by a failure to separate the principles of jurisdiction upon which the Statute is premised from the regime governing the exercise of jurisdiction by the Court in particular cases'.[34] The idea that the ICC's jurisdiction is predicated on delegated territorial and nationality jurisdiction from States Parties assumes that the Article 12 preconditions are indicative of the legal basis for the Court's jurisdiction. An alternative interpretation of the consent regime in Articles 12 and 13 is that it is a procedural limitation on the Court's jurisdiction that was included in the Statute as a political compromise to gain the consensus needed for the adoption of the Statute. Michael Scharf argues that:

> the drafters did not view the consent of the state of territoriality or nationality as necessary as a matter of international law to confer jurisdiction on the court. Rather, they adopted the consent regime as a limit to the exercise of the court's inherent jurisdiction as a politically expedient concession to the sovereignty of states in order to garner broad support for the statute.[35]

These procedural preconditions would not necessarily disqualify the principle of universality from being a relevant component of the legal basis for the ICC's jurisdiction. Advocates of the theory that universality plays a role in the ICC's jurisdiction view the Statute as providing 'an explicit clue'[36] that the drafters did not intend to preclude universality entirely. In particular, proponents of this view cite the declaration in the Preamble that the ICC has 'jurisdiction over the most serious crimes of concern to the international community as a whole'.[37] Such language

---

[34] Sadat and Carden, 'New International Criminal Court', 412.
[35] MP Scharf, 'The ICC's Jurisdiction over the Nationals of Non-Party States: A Critique of the U.S. Position', 77. See also, Sadat and Carden, 'New International Criminal Court', 413.
[36] Sadat and Carden, 'New International Criminal Court', 408. See also, Paust, 'The Reach of ICC Jurisdiction over Non-Signatory Nationals', 8.
[37] Sadat and Carden, 'New International Criminal Court', 408.

reflects the rationale for universal jurisdiction over international crimes discussed in Section 6.2.

Accepting that the Statute preconditions are not necessarily determinative of the legal basis for the Court's authority, the question of whether the principle of universality is relevant for ICC jurisdiction cannot be answered by simply looking to Articles 12 and 13. Ascertaining the relevance of universality also requires an analysis of whether the offences listed in the Statute are crimes justiciable under universal jurisdiction.

6.3.2 Justiciability of Statute Crimes under Universal Jurisdiction

When the Rome Statute was being drafted, there was an understanding that the intent 'was not to create new substantive law, but only to include crimes already prohibited under international law'.[38] As O'Keefe explains, 'a crime under customary international law is a crime under customary international law regardless of where, by whom, and against whom it is committed and regardless of whether it threatens the fundamental interests of or has deleterious effects in any state'.[39] The Statute drafting and negotiation process eventually reduced the list of crimes to those that give rise to individual criminal responsibility under customary international law.[40] Commentators who reject universality as a legal basis for the ICC argue that not all of the specific offences listed in the Statute are crimes of customary international law, nor are they necessarily justiciable under universal jurisdiction.[41] Indeed, the viability of the theory that universality is applicable as a legal basis for ICC jurisdiction

---

[38] P Kirsch and JT Holmes, 'The Rome Conference on an International Court: The Negotiating Process' (1999) 93 *American Journal of International Law* 2 at 7 fn 19. See also, *Report of the Preparatory Committee on the Establishment of an International Criminal Court*, UN GAOR, 51st sess, Supp No 22, UN Doc A/51/22 (1996) 16.

[39] O'Keefe, *International Criminal Law*, p. 25. There is some disagreement as to which offences fall into this category. For example, the crime of piracy may be distinguished from war crimes, crimes against humanity and genocide in that piracy is not actually prohibited by customary international law. Instead customary international law gives States the right to criminalise acts of piracy under domestic law and prosecute on the basis of universality: O'Keefe, *International Criminal Law*, pp. 50–7.

[40] With the possible exception of the crime of aggression – see discussion in Section 6.3.2.4. For an overview of the negotiation process on the crimes within the jurisdiction of the Court, see W Schabas, *The International Criminal Court: A Commentary on the Rome Statute*, 2nd ed (Oxford University Press, 2016) pp. 111–22.

[41] M Morris, 'High Crimes and Misconceptions: The ICC and Non-Party States' (2001) 64 *Law and Contemporary Problems* 13 at 28; J Stephens, 'Don't Tread on Me: Absence of Jurisdiction by the International Criminal Court over the U.S. and Other Non-Signatory States' (2005) 52 *Naval Law Review* 151 at 162.

depends on whether the crimes in the Statute are crimes of universal jurisdiction. This section provides a brief overview of the status of each of the four categories of Statute crimes with respect to universal jurisdiction.[42]

6.3.2.1 Genocide

The inclusion of genocide as a crime in the Rome Statute was the least controversial addition to the Court's subject matter jurisdiction at the Rome Conference. The definition of genocide contained in Article 6 of the Statute replicates verbatim that which is set out in Article II of the Genocide Convention,[43] a definition considered to accurately reflect customary international law.[44] Despite the early acknowledgment of genocide as a customary crime, doubts remained about whether States could lawfully prosecute genocide under universal jurisdiction because such a right is not recognised explicitly in the Genocide Convention.[45]

Article VI of the Convention provides that individuals suspected of committing genocide shall be tried by either the territorial State or 'such international penal tribunal as may have jurisdiction'. In 1948, States Parties were not prepared to accept universal jurisdiction over genocide, as demonstrated by the Ad Hoc Committee on Genocide's rejection of a provision that would have provided for universal jurisdiction under the

---

[42] The ensuing analysis is necessarily limited for the purposes of determining whether there is a rudimentary foundation that would allow for the ICC's jurisdiction to be based on universal jurisdiction. The complexity and continuing uncertainty surrounding State practice in relation to universal jurisdiction can be seen in the work of the Sixth Committee of the UN General Assembly, which has been grappling with 'the scope and application of the principle of universal jurisdiction' annually since 2010 with little consensus: *Summary Record of the 33rd Meeting*, UN GAOR, 6th Comm, 73rd sess, 33rd mtg, Agenda item 87, UN Doc A/C.6/73/SR.33 (5 November 2018) para 23. In 2018, the International Law Commission decided to include the topic 'Universal criminal jurisdiction' in its long-term programme of work: *Report of the International Law Commission*, UN GAOR, 70th sess, UN Doc A/73/10 (30 April–1 June and 2 July–10 August 2018) para 37.

[43] *Convention on the Prevention and Punishment of the Crime of Genocide*, opened for signature 9 December 1948, 78 UNTS 277 (entered into force 12 January 1951).

[44] '[T]he principles underlying the [Genocide] Convention are principles which are recognized by civilized nations as binding on States, even without any Conventional obligation.' *Reservations to the Convention on the Prevention and Punishment of the Crime of Genocide (Advisory Opinion)* [1951] ICJ Rep 15, 23.

[45] William Schabas refers to this lack of recognition as the 'great shortcoming' of the Genocide Convention: W Schabas, *Genocide in International Law: The Crime of Crimes*, 2nd ed (Cambridge University Press, 2009) p. 426.

6.3 UNIVERSALITY AND THE ROME STATUTE 171

Genocide Convention.[46] But in the decades since the Convention was adopted, Article VI has come to be interpreted as establishing only the 'minimum jurisdictional obligation' on territorial states.[47] The jurisprudence[48] and *travaux préparatoires*[49] of international courts; academic writing;[50] and State legislative practice[51] and *opinio juris*[52] provide

---

[46] *Report of the Ad Hoc Committee on Genocide*, UN ESCOR, 7th Sess., Supp No. 6, UN Doc. E/794/Corr. 1 (1948) paras 11–12.

[47] Scharf, 'ICC's Jurisdiction over the Nationals of Non-Party States', 76. See also, *Arrest Warrant of 11 April 2000 (Congo v Belgium)* [2002] ICJ Rep 2001 (Joint Separate Opinion of Judges Higgins, Kooijmans and Buergenthal) para 27.

[48] See, eg, *Attorney-General of the Government of Israel v Adolf Eichmann* (1962) 36 ILR 5 para 25; *Prosecutor v Tadić (Decision on the Defence Motion for Interlocutory Appeal on Jurisdiction)* (International Criminal Tribunal for the former Yugoslavia, Appeals Chamber II, Case No ICTY-94-1-AR72, 2 October 1995) para 62; *Prosecutor v Furundzija, (Judgement)* (International Criminal Tribunal for the former Yugoslavia, Trial Chamber, Case No IT-95-17/I-T, 10 December 1998) para 156; *Prosecutor v Ntuyahaga, (Decision on the Prosecutor's Motion to Withdraw the Indictment)* (International Criminal Tribunal for Rwanda, Trial Chamber I, Case No ICTR-90-40-T, 18 March 1999); *Application of the Convention on the Prevention and Punishment of the Crime of Genocide (Bosnia and Herzegovina v Yugoslavia (Serbia and Montenegro)) (Preliminary Objections)* [1996] ICJ Rep 595, 616: The ICJ adopted the view that territorial limitations do not apply to rights and obligations which are *erga omnes*; it held that the rights and obligations of the Genocide Convention fall into this category.

[49] See, eg, *Final Report of the Commission of Experts Established Pursuant to Security Council Resolution 780* (1992), UN Doc S/1994/674, annex, 13; *Report of the International Law Commission on the Work of its Forty-Eighth Session*, UN Doc A/51/10 (6 May–26 July 1996) 42.

[50] See, eg, Schabas, *Genocide in International Law*, pp. 429–3; MC Bassiouni, 'The History of Universal Jurisdiction and its Place in International Law' in S Macedo (ed), *Universal Jurisdiction: National Courts and the Prosecution of Serious Crimes under International Law* (Pennsylvania University Press, 2004) p. 54; T Meron, 'International Criminalization of Internal Atrocities' (1995) 89 *American Journal of International Law* 554 at 570; CC Joyner, 'Arresting Impunity: The Case for Universal Jurisdiction in Bringing War Criminals to Accountability' (1996) 59 *Law and Contemporary Problems* 153 at 159–60; Randall, 'Universal Jurisdiction under International Law', 837; A Zimmermann, 'The Creation of a Permanent International Criminal Court' (1998) 2 *Max Planck Yearbook of United Nations Law* 169 at 206–11; Inazumi, *Universal Jurisdiction in Modern International Law*, pp. 65–6.

[51] Much of this State legislative practice has occurred since the Rome Statute came into existence. Currently, at least 94 States have provided for some form of universal jurisdiction over genocide in their national law, but much of this is as a result of treaty implementation rather than on a customary basis. See, Amnesty International, *Universal Jurisdiction – A Preliminary Survey of Legislation Around the World 2012 Update*. For a critique of the survey and its claims, see Hovell, 'The Authority of Universal Jurisdiction', 434–5.

[52] See State observations submitted to the UN Secretary-General on the scope and application of universal jurisdiction (Agenda Item 86 for each session of the Sixth Committee of the General Assembly). At the 75th session in 2010, for example, a number of States

evidence of a growing acceptance of genocide as a crime of universal jurisdiction.

6.3.2.2 Crimes Against Humanity

Since 'crimes against humanity' first appeared in the Nuremberg Charter,[53] there has been increasing recognition that the category of crimes is customarily justiciable under universal jurisdiction.[54] Article 7 of the Rome Statute lists 11 specific acts that constitute crimes against humanity when 'committed as part of a widespread or systematic attack directed against any civilian population, with knowledge of the attack'. The provision also contains a residual category for 'other inhumane acts of a similar character intentionally causing great suffering, or serious injury to body or to mental and physical health'.[55] At the Rome Conference there was general consensus with respect to the propriety of including crimes against humanity as a category in the Statute, although delegates disagreed over which acts should be included in the list of specific offences.[56]

---

submitted observations in which they recognised genocide as a crime justiciable by universal jurisdiction under customary international law: Australia, Bulgaria, Germany, Israel, Netherlands, Rwanda, Slovenia, South Africa, Switzerland and the US. Available at http://un.org/en/ga/sixth/65/ScopeAppUniJuri.shtml.

[53] *Agreement for the Prosecution and Punishment of the Major War Criminals of the European Axis and Charter of the International Military Tribunal*, 82 UNTS 279 (signed and entered into force 8 August 1945) Article 6(c).

[54] I Bantekas and S Nash, *International Criminal Law*, 4th ed (Oxford University Press, 2010) p. 122; MC Bassiouni, *Crimes Against Humanity in International Criminal Law*, 2nd ed (Kluwer Law International, 1999) pp. 227–41; Zimmermann, 'The Creation of a Permanent International Criminal Court', 211; Randall, 'Universal Jurisdiction under International Law', 800–15; Bassiouni, 'Universal Jurisdiction for International Crimes', 118. See also, *Affirmation of the Principles of International Law recognised by the Charter of the Nuremberg Tribunal*, GA Res 95, UN GAOR, 2nd sess, UN Doc A/Res 95 (1946); State observations recognising universal jurisdiction over crimes against humanity as a matter of customary international law (Agenda Item 86 at the 75th session of the Sixth Committee of the General Assembly): Australia, Belgium, Bulgaria, Cuba, Germany, Netherlands, Rwanda, Slovenia, South Africa and Switzerland. Available at http://un.org/en/ga/sixth/65/ScopeAppUniJuri.shtml.

[55] Rome Statute, Article 7(1)(k).

[56] H von Hebel and D Robinson, 'Crimes within the Jurisdiction of the Court' in RS Lee (ed), *The International Criminal Court – The Making of the Rome Statute* (Kluwer Law International, 1999) pp. 90–1; Sadat and Carden, 'New International Criminal Court', 407; TL McCormack, 'Crimes Against Humanity' in D McGoldrick, P Rowe and E Donnelly (eds), *The Permanent International Criminal Court: Legal and Policy Issues* (Hart Publishing, 2004) pp. 179–82.

The Rome Statute expanded the list of offences previously categorised as crimes against humanity in the ICTY and ICTR Statutes. Specifically it includes apartheid and enforced disappearance of persons; and expands the offences of torture, deportation, imprisonment and rape. There has been some speculation about whether these additional and extended offences attract universal jurisdiction under customary international law.[57] With respect to the crime of apartheid, for example, the 1973 Convention on the Suppression and Punishment of the Crime of Apartheid (Apartheid Convention) provides that States Parties are obliged to prosecute and punish those responsible for acts of apartheid regardless of whether there is any jurisdictional nexus to the prosecuting State.[58] This is a classic example of treaty-based universal jurisdiction, but as discussed in Section 6.3.2.1, a treaty obligation is not necessarily indicative of broader customary universal jurisdiction over the crime.[59] Nor does the existence of the Apartheid Convention mean that apartheid is recognised in and of itself as a crime against humanity under customary international law.[60] But the list of acts in the Rome Statute that may constitute crimes against humanity is not finite, as indicated by the inclusion of 'other inhuman acts' in Article 7(d). As long as the customary elements of a crime against humanity are satisfied there is no prescribed limit to what acts might be considered crimes against humanity.[61] If 'crimes against humanity' is a category of offences justiciable under universal jurisdiction in customary international law, it stands to reason that an act of apartheid that meets the customary requirements for a crime against humanity is most likely justiciable under universal

---

[57] Morris, 'High Crimes and Misconceptions: The ICC and Non-Party States', 42 fn 114.
[58] *Convention on the Suppression and Punishment of the Crime of Apartheid*, opened for signature 30 November 1973, 1015 UNTS 243 (entered into force 18 July 1976).
[59] Morris, 'High Crimes and Misconceptions: The ICC and Non-Party States', 42 fn 114.
[60] A. Cassese, 'Crimes against Humanity' in A Cassese, P Gaeta and JRWD Jones (eds), *The Rome Statute of the International Criminal Court: A Commentary* (Oxford University Press, 2002) p. 376; C Byron, *War Crimes and Crimes against Humanity in the Rome Statute of the International Criminal Court* (Manchester University Press, 2009) pp. 239–42; RS Clark, 'Apartheid' in MC Bassiouni (ed), *International Criminal Law* (Transnational Publishers, 1999) p. 643. The Apartheid Convention itself declares apartheid to be a crime against humanity: Article 1(1).
[61] See Bantekas and Nash, *International Criminal Law*, pp. 121–2; Cassese, 'Crimes against Humanity', pp. 373–6. For a discussion of the category of 'other inhumane acts', see *Prosecutor v Krnojelac (Judgement)* (International Criminal Tribunal for the former Yugoslavia, Trial Chamber, Case No IT-97-25, 15 March 2002) para 130; *Prosecutor v Vasiljevic (Judgement)* (International Criminal Tribunal for the former Yugoslavia, Trial Chamber, Case No IT-98-32-T, 29 November 2002) para 234.

jurisdiction. This reasoning can also be applied to enforced disappearances of persons and the other extended offences of crimes against humanity in the Rome Statute.

6.3.2.3 War Crimes

The 2005 International Committee of the Red Cross Study on Customary International Humanitarian Law ('the ICRC Customary IHL Study') concluded that 'States have the right to vest universal jurisdiction in their national courts over war crimes'.[62] While the ICRC Customary IHL Study is not without its critics,[63] there is a reasonable argument to be made that States may exercise universal jurisdiction over the category of war crimes under customary international law.[64] There is less certainty, however, about the customary definition of 'war crimes'. The ICRC Customary IHL Study claims that 'serious violations of international humanitarian law' constitute war crimes in both international and non-international armed conflict, but this leaves open the question of what conduct amounts to a 'serious violation' of international humanitarian law.[65]

The definition of war crimes and the list of offences in Article 8 of the Rome Statute were drawn from the Hague Regulations,[66] the

---

[62] JM Henckaerts and L Doswald-Beck (eds), *Customary International Humanitarian Law* (Cambridge University Press, 2005) vol I p. 604.

[63] See, eg, Y Dinstein, 'The ICRC Customary International Humanitarian Law Study' (2006) 82 *International Law Studies* 99; TLH McCormack, 'An Australian Perspective on the ICRC Customary International Humanitarian Law Study' (2006) 82 *International Law Studies* 81; JB Bellinger III and WJ Haynes II, 'A US Government Response to the International Committee of the Red Cross Study *Customary International Humanitarian Law*' (2007) 89 *International Review of the Red Cross* 443.

[64] C Garraway, 'War Crimes' in E Wilmshurst and S Breau (eds), *Perspectives on the ICRC Study on Customary International Humanitarian Law* (Cambridge University Press, 2007) p. 390. The ILC recognised universal jurisdiction for war crimes in its 1996 Draft Code of Crimes: International Law Commission, *Draft Code of Crimes against the Peace and Security of Mankind with commentaries,* 48th sess, 1996, 29.

[65] Henckaerts and Doswald-Beck, *Customary International Humanitarian Law,* pp. 568–603; Garraway, 'War Crimes', pp. 384–90.

[66] See, eg, *Convention with respect to the Laws and Customs of War on Land and its Annex: Regulations Concerning the Laws and Customs of War on Land,* opened for signature 29 July 1899, (1907) 1 *American Journal of International Law Supplement* 129 (entered into force 4 September 1900) ('1899 Hague Convention II and Regulations'); *Convention respecting the Laws and Customs of War on Land and its Annex: Regulations Concerning the Laws and Customs of War on Land,* opened for signature 18 October 1907 (1908) 2 *American Journal of International Law Supplement* 90 (entered into force 26 January 1910) ('1907 Hague Convention IV and Regulations').

Geneva Conventions[67] and the Protocols additional to the Geneva Conventions.[68] There is little doubt that serious violations of the Hague Regulations and grave breaches of the Geneva Conventions give rise to individual criminal responsibility under customary international law.[69] The customary basis of Article 8 of the Rome Statute has, however, been challenged on two main grounds. The first is that Additional Protocol I in its entirety does not constitute customary international law,[70] and the second is that war crimes committed during non-international armed conflict are not universally recognised as part of custom.[71]

With respect to the customary status of Additional Protocol I, there was extensive debate at the Rome Conference about the inclusion of Article 8(2)(b)(viii) on deportation and transfer of population.[72] Based on Article 49 of Geneva Convention IV, the act of an occupied power transferring part of its civilian population into the territory it occupies is

---

[67] *Convention for the Amelioration of the Condition of the Wounded and Sick in Armed Forces in the Field*, opened for signature 12 August 1949, 75 UNTS 31 (entered into force 21 October 1950) ('Geneva Convention I'); *Convention for the Amelioration of the Condition of the Wounded, Sick and Shipwrecked Members of Armed Forces at Sea*, opened for signature 12 August 1949, 75 UNTS 85 (entered into force 21 October 1950) ('Geneva Convention II'); *Convention Relative to the Treatment of Prisoners of War*, opened for signature 12 August 1949, 75 UNTS 135 (entered into force 21 October 1950) ('Geneva Convention III'); *Convention Relative to Protection of Civilian Persons in Time of War*, opened for signature 12 August 1949, 75 UNTS 287 (entered into force 21 October 1950) ('Geneva Convention IV').

[68] *Protocol additional to the Geneva Conventions of 12 August 1949 and relating to the Protection of Victims of International Armed Conflicts*, opened for signature 8 June 1977, 1125 UNTS 3 (entered into force 7 December 1978) ('Additional Protocol I'); *Protocol additional to the Geneva Conventions of 12 August 1949 and relating to the Protection of Victims of Non-International Armed Conflicts*, opened for signature 8 June 1977, 1125 UNTS 609 (entered into force 7 December 1978) ('Additional Protocol II'). See also, Schabas, *The International Criminal Court: A Commentary*, pp. 228–31.

[69] von Hebel and Robinson, 'Crimes within the Jurisdiction of the Court', p. 104.

[70] *UN Diplomatic Conference of Plenipotentiaries on the Establishment of an International Court*, 5th mtg, UN Doc A/CONF.183/C.1/SR.5 (18 June 1998) Statement of Israel, para 79; 35th mtg, UN Doc A/CONF.183/C.1/SR.35 (13 July 1998) Statement of Egypt, para 2.

[71] See, eg, *UN Diplomatic Conference of Plenipotentiaries on the Establishment of an International Court*, 4th mtg, UN Doc A/CONF.183/C.1/SR.4 (17 June 1998) Statement of China, para 65; 5th mtg, UN Doc A/CONF.183/C.1/SR.5 (18 June 1998) Statement of Sudan, para 101; 27th mtg, UN Doc A/CONF.183/C.1/SR.27 (8 July 1998) Statement of Iraq, para 2. See also, Scharf, 'ICC's Jurisdiction over the Nationals of Non-Party States', 91; von Hebel and Robinson, 'Crimes within the Jurisdiction of the Court', p. 104.

[72] This Article provides that '[t]he transfer, directly or indirectly, by the Occupying Power of parts of its own civilian population into the territory it occupies, or the deportation or transfer of all or parts of the population of the occupied territory within or outside this territory' is a war crime.

recognised as a grave breach in Article 85(4)(a) of Additional Protocol I. Israel is not a party to Additional Protocol I, and insisted that this aspect of the provision was not part of customary international law.[73] Despite Israel's objection, there is evidence of State practice to suggest that the act described in Article 8(2)(b)(viii) does in fact amount to a war crime in customary international law.[74]

In the same vein, the US objected to the inclusion of Article 8(2)(b)(xxvi), which provides that it is a war crime to conscript or enlist children under the age of fifteen years into the national armed forces.[75] Specifically, the US held that this provision did not reflect customary international law and that conscription and enlistment of child soldiers is a human rights concern rather than a war crime.[76] The ICRC Customary IHL Study notes, however, that the inclusion of the child soldiers provision in the Rome Statute was 'uncontroversial' given the extensive State practice prohibiting the conscription and use of children in armed forces.[77] Furthermore, the Special Court for Sierra Leone (SCSL) undertook an extensive analysis of this issue in *Prosecutor v Norman* and concluded that conscription and enlistment of children under the age of fifteen as a war crime has crystallised into customary international law.[78]

When the Security Council established the ICTR, it ensured that the ICTR Statute included war crimes committed in non-international

---

[73] *UN Diplomatic Conference of Plenipotentiaries on the Establishment of an International Court*, 5th mtg, UN Doc A/CONF.183/C.1/SR.5 (18 June 1998) Statement of Israel, para 79. See also, von Hebel and Robinson, 'Crimes within the Jurisdiction of the Court', pp. 112–13; Byron, *War Crimes and Crimes against Humanity in the Rome Statute of the International Criminal Court*, p. 107.

[74] Such conduct is prohibited in numerous military manuals, State legislation and other practice. For a comprehensive list, see Henckaerts and Doswald-Beck, *Customary International Humanitarian Law*, pp. 578–9.

[75] *UN Diplomatic Conference of Plenipotentiaries on the Establishment of an International Court*, 4th mtg, UN Doc A/CONF.183/C.1/SR.4 (17 June 1998) Statement of the US, para 54.

[76] Ibid.; von Hebel and Robinson, 'Crimes within the Jurisdiction of the Court', p. 117; Morris, 'High Crimes and Misconceptions: The ICC and Non-Party States', 28.

[77] Henckaerts and Doswald-Beck, *Customary International Humanitarian Law*, p. 584.

[78] *Prosecutor v Norman (Decision on Preliminary Motion Based on Lack of Jurisdiction (Child Recruitment))* (Special Court for Sierra Leone, Appeals Chamber, Case No SCSL 2004-14-AR72(E), 31 May 2004) paras 33–51. See also, *Prosecutor v Lubanga (Judgment pursuant to Article 74 of the Statute)* (International Criminal Court, Trial Chamber I, Case No ICC-01/04-01/06, 14 March 2012) (Separate and Dissenting Opinion of Judge Odio Benito) paras 6, 8; *Prosecutor v Lubanga (Decision on the Confirmation of Charges)* (International Criminal Court, Pre-Trial Chamber I, Case No ICC-01/04-01/06, 29 January 2007) paras 242–8.

armed conflict within the tribunal's subject matter jurisdiction. This was seen as 'a more expansive approach', which incorporated serious violations of Common Article 3 and of Additional Protocol II 'regardless of whether they were considered part of customary international law'.[79] In *Prosecutor v Tadić* the ICTY Appeals Chamber undertook a thorough examination of State practice and concluded that there is extensive support for the notion that serious violations of international humanitarian law committed during non-international armed conflicts amount to war crimes under customary international law.[80] In addition, there have been several domestic criminal cases in which suspected war criminals were tried under universal jurisdiction for crimes committed in non-international armed conflicts.[81]

In summary, it would appear that the war crimes listed in the Rome Statute were, for the most part, intended to reflect customary international law. Where doubt existed at the time of the Statute's drafting with respect to the customary status of a particular offence, it was understood that the Statute would take a progressive approach by codifying offences that would, in the future, crystallise into customary international law.[82] Whether such crimes are also justiciable under universal jurisdiction is less certain, with the vast majority of States preferring to rely on the Geneva Conventions or Rome Statute to implement jurisdiction over war crimes.[83]

6.3.2.4 Aggression

As discussed in Chapter 5, the crime of aggression is, in several ways, unique among the Rome Statute's core crimes. Unlike the other crimes in

---

[79] *Report of the Secretary-General Pursuant to Paragraph 5 of Security Council Resolution 955*, UN Doc S/1995/134 (1995) para 12.
[80] *Prosecutor v Tadić (Decision on the Defence Motion for Interlocutory Appeal on Jurisdiction)* (International Criminal Tribunal for the former Yugoslavia, Appeals Chamber, Case No IT-94-1, 2 October 1995) paras 96–137. See also, *Military and Paramilitary Activities in and against Nicaragua (Nicaragua v US) (Merits)* [1986] ICJ Rep 14, para 218.
[81] See, eg, *Prosecutor v Vincent Ntezimana, Alphonse Higaniro, Consolata Mukangango, and Julienne Mukabutera*, Belgium, Brussels *Cour d'Assise*, 8 June 2001; *Knezević*, Dutch Supreme Court, 11 November 1997, NederJ (1998) No 463; *Grabež*, Tribunal Militaire de Division I, 18 April 1997.
[82] von Hebel and Robinson, 'Crimes within the Jurisdiction of the Court', pp. 122–6.
[83] State observations on the scope and application of universal jurisdiction (Agenda Item 86 at the 75th session of the Sixth Committee of the General Assembly): Armenia, Austria, Azerbaijan, Belarus, Chile, Costa Rica, Czech Republic, Denmark, Kenya, Kuwait, Malta, New Zealand, Norway, Peru, Portugal, Tunisia. Available at http://un.org/en/ga/sixth/65/ScopeAppUniJuri.shtml.

the Statute, the crime of aggression was not defined until 2010 when the Assembly of States Parties adopted the Kampala Amendments. Article 8*bis*(1) defines the crime of aggression as:

> [T]he planning, preparation, initiation or execution, by a person in a position effectively to exercise control over or to direct the political or military action of a State, of an act of aggression which, by its character, gravity and scale, constitutes a manifest violation of the Charter of the United Nations.

Article 8*bis*(2) then specifies what is meant by 'an act of aggression' providing a list of seven acts that could constitute the *actus reus* in a crime of aggression. Although the Kampala Amendments specifically prevent the ICC from exercising jurisdiction over a crime of aggression committed by a national of a non-State Party or on the territory of a non-State Party,[84] it is nevertheless instructive to examine whether the crime of aggression exists in customary international law and is justiciable under universal jurisdiction.

Any analysis of a customary crime of aggression by necessity begins with the Nuremberg and Tokyo judgments. Article 6 of the Nuremberg Charter provides:

> The following acts, or any of them, are crimes coming within the jurisdiction of the Tribunal for which there shall be individual responsibility:
>
> (a) Crimes Against Peace: namely, planning, preparation, initiation, or waging of a war of aggression, or a war in violation of international treaties, agreements or assurances, or participation in a common plan or conspiracy for the accomplishment of any of the foregoing.[85]

The term 'war of aggression' is not defined in the Charter and it was left up to the judges to interpret the term's meaning. A reading of both the Nuremberg and Tokyo judgments reveals three scenarios that would each constitute a 'war of aggression':

(i) War with the object of the occupation or conquest of the territory of another State or part thereof;
(ii) War declared in support of a third party's war of aggression; and

---

[84] Except in a situation referred by the Security Council. See Section 5.5.1 for further discussion.
[85] *Agreement for the Prosecution and Punishment of Major War Criminals of the European Axis and the Charter of the International Military Tribunal*, signed and entered into force 8 August 1945, 82 UNTS 279, Article 6.

6.3 UNIVERSALITY AND THE ROME STATUTE

(iii) War with the object of disabling another State's capacity to provide assistance to (a) third State(s) victim of a war of aggression initiated by the aggressor.[86]

In December 1946 the UN General Assembly affirmed the principles of international law enumerated in the Nuremberg Charter and the Tribunal's judgment, which was followed by a resolution in 1947 entrusting formulation of the Nuremberg Principles to the ILC.[87] The 1951 Draft Code of Offences against the Peace and Security of Mankind and the positive views of States received in relation to the Draft Code further affirmed the existence of the crime against peace in international law.[88] In the decades since, additional evidence of State practice and *opinio juris* with respect to the recognition of crimes against peace can be found in the significant number of States that have adopted legislation that criminalises the waging of wars of aggression.[89]

In its 2006 decision of *R v Jones*, the UK House of Lords had occasion to consider whether the crime of aggression exists in customary international law. Lord Bingham of Cornhill held that:

> [it] may, I think be doubtful whether [aggressive] wars were recognised in customary international law as a crime when the 20th century began. But whether that be so or not, it seems to me clear that such a crime was recognised by the time the century ended.[90]

---

[86] C McDougall, *The Crime of Aggression under the Rome Statute of the International Criminal Court* (Cambridge University Press, 2013) p. 139. See also *International Military Tribunal (Nuremberg), Judgment and Sentences*, reproduced in 'Judicial Decisions' (1947) 41 *American Journal of International Law* 172; BVA Röling and CF Rüter (eds), *The Tokyo Judgment: The International Military Tribunal for the Far East (IMTFE) 29 April 1946 – 2 November 1948* (APA – University Press, 1977). Control Council Law No 10 also included 'initiation of invasions of other countries' as an act included in the definition of crimes against peace: Control Council Law No 10: Punishment of Persons Guilty of War Crimes, Crimes Against Peace and Against Humanity, adopted 20 December 1945, Official Gazette, Control Council for Germany, No 3, Berlin, 31 January 1946, Article II(1)(a).

[87] *Affirmation of the Principles of International Law recognised by the Charter of the Nuremberg Tribunal*, GA Res 95, UN GAOR, 2nd sess, UN Doc A/Res 95 (1946); *Resolution on the Formation of the Principles Recognised in the Charter of the Nuremberg Tribunal and in the Judgment of the Tribunal*, UN Doc A/Res/177 (1947).

[88] *Draft Code of Offences against the Peace and Security of Mankind*, UN Doc A/CN.4/44 (12 April 1951).

[89] For an overview of such legislation, see McDougall, *The Crime of Aggression under the Rome Statute of the International Criminal Court*, pp. 142–8.

[90] [2006] UKHL 16, para 12.

Lord Hoffman also found that 'there is no doubt that this is a recognised crime in international law'.[91] Such statements by a high profile domestic court add weight to the argument that a customary crime of aggression exists in international law.[92]

It appears, therefore, that the crime of aggression is recognised to some extent as existing in customary international law, but as Carrie McDougall observes, '[r]eferences to wars of aggression dominate'.[93] In other words, any customary definition of the crime is narrow and reflects the 'crimes against peace' World War II jurisprudence rather than the 'crime of aggression' contained in the Kampala Amendments. While there is an argument to be made that wars of aggression are criminalised in customary international law, State practice and *opinio juris* do not support the notion that all acts of aggression attract individual criminal responsibility under customary law.[94]

There is some State practice to suggest that a narrow customary version of the crime of aggression may be prosecutable under universal jurisdiction. For example, a number of States have enacted legislation to give domestic courts universal jurisdiction over crimes against peace,[95] and in one of the UK House of Lords' *Pinochet* decisions, Lord Millet affirmed that crimes against peace were in the category of international crimes that attract universal jurisdiction.[96] Scholarly commentary on this issue is more cautious, with some authors expressing doubt as to whether it is possible to state with any certainty that crimes against peace are

---

[91] Ibid., para 44.
[92] McDougall, *The Crime of Aggression under the Rome Statute of the International Criminal Court*, p. 150.
[93] Ibid., p. 46.
[94] Ibid., p. 161. See also, G Werle and F Jessberger, *Principles of International Criminal Law*, 3rd ed (TMC Asser Press, 2014) pp. 535–8.
[95] Including Bulgaria, Moldova, Croatia, Hungary, Portugal, Azerbaijan, Belarus, Czech Republic, Armenia, Estonia, Georgia, Kazakhstan and Tajikistan. See *Report of the Secretary-General prepared on the basis of comments and observations of Governments: The scope and application of the principle of universal jurisdiction*, 65th sess, Agenda Item 88, UN Doc A/65/181 (29 July 2010); *Report of the Secretary-General: The scope and application of the principle of universal jurisdiction*, 68th sess, Agenda Item 86, UN Doc A/68/113 (26 June 2013). See also, A Reisinger Coracini, 'Evaluating Domestic Legislation on the Customary Crime of Aggression under the Rome Statute's Complementarity Regime' in C Stahn and G Sluiter (eds), *The Emerging Practice of the International Criminal Court* (Martinus Nijhoff Publishers, 2009) pp. 751–2.
[96] *R v Bartle & the Commissioner of Police for the Metropolis & Ors, Ex parte Pinochet; R v Evans & Anor and the Commissioner of Police for the Metropolis & Ors, ex parte Pinochet* [1999] UKHL 17 (24 March 1999) para 34.

justiciable under customary international law.[97] Although Principle 2(1) of the Princeton Principles on Universal Jurisdiction provides for universal jurisdiction over crimes against peace, it is notable that crimes against peace or the crime of aggression are often not mentioned in lists of universal jurisdiction crimes.[98]

Ultimately, it is difficult to conclude that there is sufficient State practice or *opinio juris* to establish universal jurisdiction for the crime of aggression in customary international law. McDougall notes that even if there is enough evidence to suggest that the narrow customary definition of crimes against peace attracts universal jurisdiction, the additional acts of aggression set out in the Kampala Amendments would not be justiciable under universal jurisdiction at present.[99]

6.3.3 Conclusion to Section 6.3

There is considerable support among scholars for the existence of a customary right for States to exercise universal jurisdiction over genocide, crimes against humanity and war crimes. There is not, however, much in the way of States practice or widespread *opinio juris* to be able to conclusively say that States consider all Rome Statute crimes justiciable on the basis of universal jurisdiction under customary international law. It is worth noting, however, that States frequently distinguish between their own right to exercise universal jurisdiction over such crimes and the jurisdiction of international courts,[100] observing that 'the two [are] complementary but not interchangeable' and intimating that the latter is

---

[97] R Clark, 'Defining the Crime of Aggression, its Elements and the Conditions for the ICC Exercise of Jurisdiction Over It' (2010) 20 *European Journal of International Law* 1103 at 1108; BS Brown, 'The Evolving Concept of Universal Jurisdiction' (2001) 35 *New England Law Review* 383 at 384; F Jessberger, 'Universal Jurisdiction' in A Cassese (ed), *The Oxford Companion to International Criminal Justice* (Oxford University Press, 2009) p. 556; AL Zuppi, 'Aggression as International Crime: Unattainable Crusade or Finally Conquering the Evil?' (2007) 26 *Penn State International Law Review* 2 at 34–5.

[98] LN Sadat, 'Redefining Universal Jurisdiction' (2000) 35 *New England Law Review* 241 at 244; M Morris, 'Universal Jurisdiction in a Divided World: Conference Remarks' (2001) 35 *New England Law Review* 337 at 337; B Broomhall, 'Toward the Development of an Effective System of Universal Jurisdiction for Crimes under International Law' (2001) 35 *New England Law Review* 399 at 404–5.

[99] McDougall, *The Crime of Aggression under the Rome Statute of the International Criminal Court*, p. 320.

[100] See, eg, statements of Ecuador, Singapore, Qatar, Colombia, the UK and Kenya: *Summary Record of the 12th Meeting*, UN GAOR, 6th Comm, 70th sess, 12th mtg, Agenda item 86, UN Doc A/C.6/70/SR.12 (20 October 2015).

perhaps wider than the former.[101] This leaves open the question of how the principle of universality might play a role in the legal basis for the ICC's jurisdiction.

6.4 Universality as the Basis for ICC Jurisdiction

The remainder of this chapter examines whether the principle of universality could operate as an alternative legal basis for ICC jurisdiction in any situations authorised by the Rome Statute. First I discuss the theory that States have delegated universal jurisdiction to the Court, which is similar to the prevailing theory that States have delegated territorial and nationality jurisdiction. The analysis in this section is predicated on the idea that universality is not precluded by the Statute consent regime and the belief that most Statute crimes attract universal jurisdiction under customary international law. Second I examine another theory based on the idea that universal jurisdiction belongs to the international community and that the ICC acts as an agent of this community. Ultimately I conclude that neither of these theories is sufficiently persuasive as a legal basis for ICC jurisdiction.

6.4.1 *Universal Jurisdiction as Belonging to States*

6.4.1.1 Delegation of Universal Jurisdiction

The notion that the ICC's authority over nationals of non-States Parties has its legal basis in delegated universal jurisdiction is conceptually similar to delegation of territorial jurisdiction discussed in Chapters 3 and 4. Recall that States have the right, under international law, to exercise their prescriptive powers of criminal justice on the basis of the territoriality, nationality, passive personality, protective and universality principles. In addition, States have the right to exercise powers of enforcement on the basis of territoriality.[102] A common argument is that if States may lawfully delegate territorial and nationality jurisdiction to an international court, then they can also delegate universal jurisdiction.[103]

---

[101] *Report of the Secretary-General: The scope and application of the principle of universal jurisdiction*, 65th sess, Agenda Item 88, UN Doc A/65/181 (29 July 2010) para 23.
[102] See Section 3.4.1.
[103] D Akande, 'The Jurisdiction of the International Criminal Court over Nationals of Non-Parties: Legal Basis and Limits' (2003) 1 *Journal of International Criminal Justice* 618 at 626; Einarsen, *The Concept of Universal Crimes in International Law*, p. 64; O Bekou and R Cryer, 'The International Criminal Court and Universal Jurisdiction:

6.4 UNIVERSALITY AS THE BASIS FOR ICC JURISDICTION 183

Delegated universal jurisdiction would not supplant delegated territorial jurisdiction as a legal basis but instead would complement it in situations where delegation of territorial jurisdiction is uncertain.

A number of scholars contend that delegated universal jurisdiction would work as the legal basis for the ICC's authority over situations in non-States Parties referred by the Security Council.[104] Under this theory, States Parties have each delegated to the ICC their right to exercise universal jurisdiction, and the ICC is then able to exercise its jurisdiction based on universality in the same way that States can do so individually. For example, if any State has the right to exercise universal jurisdiction over acts of genocide and crimes against humanity committed in Darfur, then States Parties to the Rome Statute can be said to have delegated this right to the ICC. Delegation of universal jurisdiction would have the effect of simplifying the legal basis for the ICC's authority over situations in non-States Parties, particularly those referred by the Security Council.

6.4.1.2 The Limits of Delegated Universal Jurisdiction

Commentators opposed to the idea of delegated universal jurisdiction argue that there is no precedent for States to establish an international court on the basis of universal jurisdiction, and that to accept the ICC as having jurisdiction based on universality would set a dangerous precedent itself.[105] As I argued in Chapter 3, the historical and contemporary international criminal tribunals have limited precedential value for the ICC when it comes to the legal basis for its jurisdiction. But to accept that universal jurisdiction can be delegated *sui generis* to an international

---

A Close Encounter' (2007) 56 *International and Comparative Law Quarterly* 49 at 51; Paust, 'The Reach of ICC Jurisdiction over Non-Signatory Nationals', 5; Scharf, 'ICC's Jurisdiction over the Nationals of Non-Party States', 77; Kaul, 'Preconditions to the Exercise of Jurisdiction', p. 587. But Morris argues that States may not delegate universal jurisdiction because the consequences of an international court exercising universal jurisdiction would be far greater than the consequences of a State exercising such jurisdiction. Morris, 'High Crimes and Misconceptions: The ICC and Non-Party States', 29–30.

[104] See, eg, Scharf, 'ICC's Jurisdiction over the Nationals of Non-Party States', 76; Sadat and Carden, 'New International Criminal Court', 412; Bekou and Cryer, 'International Criminal Court and Universal Jurisdiction', 50–1. For additional analysis on the idea that the ICC could be exercising delegated universal jurisdiction, see also, A Chehtman, *The Philosophical Foundations of Extraterritorial Punishment* (Oxford University Press, 2010) p. 132; Heller, 'What Is an International Crime? (A Revisionist History)', 388.

[105] Morris, 'High Crimes and Misconceptions: The ICC and Non-Party States', 29–35; Stephens, 'Don't Tread on Me', 163–5; D Scheffer, 'The International Criminal Court: The Challenge of Jurisdiction' (1999) 93 *American Society of International Law Proceedings* 68 at 70–1.

court does raise questions about the potential for States' misuse of this power. What, for example, would prevent two States from setting up an international criminal tribunal on the basis of delegated universal jurisdiction?

Hypothetically, Australia and New Zealand could adopt a treaty to establish a trans-Tasman criminal tribunal with authority to prosecute individuals of any nationality for crimes of universal jurisdiction committed anywhere in the world. Establishing an international court imbued with authority to exercise criminal jurisdiction on the basis of universality would be a clear case of States doing 'together what any one of them might have done singly'.[106] Such a tribunal might be accused of illegitimacy for its excessive reach, but if States can delegate universal jurisdiction to the ICC, it stands to reason that they can delegate universal jurisdiction to other treaty-based international tribunals as well.[107]

However, a trans-Tasman criminal tribunal exercising jurisdiction on the basis of delegated universal jurisdiction would be significantly restricted in what it could lawfully accomplish compared with the ICC, because of the fact that universality is a principle of prescriptive jurisdiction only. A trans-Tasman criminal tribunal would have no power to investigate, collect evidence, arrest suspects, compel testimony or enforce its jurisdiction in any way outside of Australian or New Zealand territory. It could theoretically issue subpoenas or arrest warrants *in absentia* but, even if lawful, such action would be entirely symbolic and unenforceable. The ICC, on the other hand, is able to rely on delegated territorial jurisdiction as a legal basis for its limited enforcement jurisdiction. Delegated universal jurisdiction on its own would not provide a legal basis for the ICC's enforcement jurisdiction, even in situations referred by the Security Council. It is only because the Security Council

---

[106] International Military Tribunal (Nuremberg), Judgment and Sentences, reproduced in 'Judicial Decisions' (1947) 41 *American Journal of International Law* 172, 216. See Section 3.2.1.2 for a discussion of the Nuremberg Tribunal's judgment. See also, the ICC Appeals Chamber's consideration of the definition of an international court in *Prosecutor v Al Bashir (Joint Concurring Opinion of Judges Eboe-Osuji, Morrison, Hofmański and Bossa)* (International Criminal Court, Appeals Chamber, Case No ICC/02/05-01/09, 6 May 2019) paras 56–60.

[107] For an interesting hypothetical scenario, see Heller, 'What Is an International Crime? (A Revisionist History)', 384–6. Claus Kreß disagrees that State practice and *opinio juris* supports the establishment of a bilateral international criminal court exercising jurisdiction 'even if the subject-matter jurisdiction of such a court would be limited to crimes under international law': C Kreß, 'Preliminary Observations on the ICC Appeals Chamber's Judgment of 6 May 2019 in the Jordan Referral re Al-Bashir Appeal' (Occasional Paper Series No 8, Torkel Opsahl Academic Epublisher, May 2019) 15.

has adopted resolutions under Chapter VII of the UN Charter to oblige Sudan and Libya to cooperate with the ICC that the Court can lawfully investigate, issue arrest warrants and otherwise enforce its jurisdiction over these situations.[108]

6.4.2 Universal Jurisdiction as Inherent to the International Community

There is a different conceptualisation of universal jurisdiction which purports to provide an alternative basis upon which the Court can prosecute nationals of non-States Parties without relying on delegation of jurisdiction from States. As discussed above, one of the main rationales for universal jurisdiction over international crimes is that certain conduct amounts to an offence against the international community. Explanations for why this is the case almost always involve rhetoric about how such crimes 'threaten the peace and security of mankind' or 'shock the conscience of humanity' and that their perpetrators are 'enemies of all mankind'.[109] The notion that these crimes have an intangible global effect has given rise to the argument that the right to prosecute such crimes belongs to the international community as a whole. States exercising universal jurisdiction are not acting merely on behalf of a community of States but as agents of the international community more broadly.[110] Under this conceptualisation of universal jurisdiction,

---

[108] Even in a situation where the ICC has prescriptive jurisdiction on the basis of delegated nationality, the Court's ability to exercise its enforcement jurisdiction is restricted to territory of States Parties. In the preliminary examination into the Iraq/UK situation, for example, the Prosecutor is assessing evidence of war crimes committed on Iraqi territory by UK nationals. The ICC has personal prescriptive jurisdiction over accused UK soldiers because the UK is a State Party to the Rome Statute, but it does not have territorial jurisdiction over Iraq because Iraq is not a party. This means that the ICC does not have the power to, inter alia, collect evidence in Iraq or to request Iraq's cooperation in any investigation. The Court's enforcement jurisdiction in this situation is instead limited to the territory of the UK and other States Parties where relevant, exercisable on the basis of delegated territorial jurisdiction. For more information on the preliminary examination in the situation in Iraq, see Office of the Prosecutor, *Report on Preliminary Examination Activities (2018)* (International Criminal Court, 5 December 2018) 49–54.

[109] See, eg, *Attorney-General of the Government of Israel v Adolf Eichmann* (1962) 36 ILR 5, 26.

[110] Ibid., 15. 'The State prosecuting [international crimes] acts as agent of the international community, administering international law'. See also, Hovell, 'The Authority of Universal Jurisdiction', 436–7.

international courts are also agents of the international community and their jurisdiction is not dependent upon delegation from States.

To recognise this theory as a legal basis for the ICC's jurisdiction requires a conceptual shift away from the Westphalian view of jurisdiction and sovereignty. The idea that universal jurisdiction is inherent to the international community – exercisable by States and international courts as agents of this international community – assumes what Martti Koskenniemi terms the 'descending approach' to sovereignty.[111] As I discussed in Chapter 2, Koskenniemi identifies oscillating 'ascending' and 'descending' views on statehood and sovereignty to explain the existence of conflicting perspectives on international law.[112] The argument that the ICC is exercising jurisdiction as an agent of the international community rests on the assumption that States must defer to certain global community norms surrounding criminal jurisdiction.

While the ICC's very existence and its relatively broad personal jurisdiction reflects changes to the State-centric system of international relations, the delegation theory of jurisdiction ensures that State consent retains a central role in the legal basis for ICC jurisdiction. To accept that the legal basis for ICC jurisdiction is universal jurisdiction belonging to the international community significantly reduces the role of the State in the authority of the Court.

6.4.2.1 The ICC as an Agent of the International Community

A number of scholars subscribe to the notion that there is a universal jurisdiction that exists independently of States and that the ICC is a mechanism through which the international community can exercise such jurisdiction.[113] Sadat and Carden, for example, posit:

> a theory of universal international jurisdiction which would permit the international community as a whole, in certain limited circumstances, to supplement, or even displace, ordinary national laws of territorial

---

[111] M Koskenniemi, *From Apology to Utopia: The Structure of International Legal Argument: Reissue with a New Epilogue* (Cambridge University Press, 2005) pp. 225–30.

[112] See also, Heller, 'What Is an International Crime? (A Revisionist History)', 355. Heller makes a distinction between 'a naturalist and positivist approach to international law'.

[113] See, eg, Rüdiger Wolfrum who argues that when States prosecute on the basis of universal jurisdiction they are 'acting instead of international organs ... as instruments of the decentralized enforcement of international law': R Wolfrum, 'The Decentralized Prosecution of International Offences through National Courts' in Y Dinstein and M Tabory (eds), *War Crimes in International Law* (Martinus Nijhoff Publishers, 1996) p. 236.

6.4 UNIVERSALITY AS THE BASIS FOR ICC JURISDICTION

application with international laws that are universal in their thrust and unbounded in their geographic scope.[114]

Such 'universal international jurisdiction' is exercisable by international courts, and provides the basis for the ICC's authority and its 'political legitimacy'.[115] Sadat contends that despite the shared goals and rationales between universal jurisdiction exercised by States and jurisdiction exercised by international courts, the practical differences in application and effect are significant enough to warrant a conceptual division between the two.[116]

This view is shared by Mitsue Inazumi, who argues that universal jurisdiction exercised by States should be distinguished from what she calls the 'inherent-jurisdiction' of international courts.[117] She writes that:

> [t]he crimes subject to the ICC are those whose prosecution and punishment relate to the interests of the international community as a whole, therefore it is this community that has to deal with these kinds of crimes in the first place. Under this inherent-jurisdiction theory, ICC jurisdiction exists irrespective of the consent or absence thereof, of the states.[118]

Other scholars refer to the existence of a supranational *ius puniendi*.[119] Claus Kreß argues that it is this *ius puniendi*, not delegation, that provides the legal basis for the ICC's jurisdiction:

> [T]he ICC has been established to exercise the *ius puniendi* of the international community with respect to crimes under international law. The ICC Statute has not created this *ius puniendi* and the latter can also not be properly conceived of as having resulted from a delegation of national criminal jurisdiction titles. Instead, the *ius puniendi* of the international community has come into existence through the ordinary process of the formation of a rule of (general) customary international law.[120]

---

[114] Sadat and Carden, 'New International Criminal Court', 407.
[115] Sadat, 'Redefining Universal Jurisdiction', 246.
[116] Ibid., 263.
[117] M Inazumi, 'The Meaning of the State Consent Precondition in Article 12(2) of the Rome Statute of the International Criminal Court: A Theoretical Analysis of the Source of International Criminal Jurisdiction' (2002) 49 *Netherlands International Law Review* 159 at 166; Inazumi, *Universal Jurisdiction in Modern International Law*, p. 115.
[118] Inazumi, 'The Meaning of the State Consent Precondition in Article 12(2) of the Rome Statute of the International Criminal Court', 166.
[119] K Ambos, 'Punishment without a Sovereign? The *Ius Puniendi* Issue of International Criminal Law: A First Contribution towards a Consistent Theory of International Criminal Law' (2013) 33 *Oxford Journal of Legal Studies* 293.
[120] Kreß, 'Preliminary Observations on the ICC Appeals Chamber's Judgment of 6 May 2019 in the Jordan Referral re Al-Bashir Appeal', 19.

The SCSL characterised its jurisdiction in similar terms. In 2004 the Appeals Chamber found that the international crimes listed in the Special Court's Statute are crimes subject to universal jurisdiction and held that the Special Court 'does not operate on the basis of transferred jurisdiction but is a new jurisdiction operating in the sphere of international law'.[121] The Chamber went on to describe this new jurisdiction as 'reflecting the interests of the international community'.[122]

The next section revisits some of the case studies from previous chapters to ascertain whether this alternative conceptualisation of the Court's legal basis can overcome some of the challenges faced by the delegation of jurisdiction theory. As a shorthand, I refer to this legal basis as 'inherent universal jurisdiction', in reference to the contention that universal jurisdiction is inherent to the international community.[123]

6.4.2.2 Inherent Universal Jurisdiction as a Legal Basis for ICC Jurisdiction over Nationals of Non-States Parties

Situations Involving Immunities Recalling the analysis in Chapter 4, Heads of State retain absolute personal immunity from prosecution in foreign and international courts for the duration of their tenure in office, unless waived by the official's State of nationality. Although Article 98(1) of the Rome Statute precludes the ICC from requesting States to arrest and transfer an accused non-party Head of State to the Court, this is a separate issue from the legal basis for the ICC's jurisdiction. As I concluded in Chapter 4, there is not yet a customary exemption to Head of State immunity before international courts.[124] This means that even if the basis for the ICC's authority is inherent universal jurisdiction, without a Security Council referral, accused Heads of State from non-

---

[121] *Prosecutor v Gbao (Decision on the Preliminary Motion on the Invalidity of the Agreement between the United Nations and the Government of Sierra Leone on the Establishment of the Special Court)* (Special Court for Sierra Leone, Appeals Chamber, Case No SCSL-2004-15-AR72(E), 25 May 2004) para 6; *Prosecutor v Kallon and Kamara (Decision on Challenge to Jurisdiction: Lomé Accord Amnesty)* (Special Court for Sierra Leone, Appeals Chamber, Case No SCSL-2004-15-AR72(E), 13 March 2004) paras 68–70.

[122] *Prosecutor v Gbao (Decision on the Preliminary Motion on the Invalidity of the Agreement between the United Nations and the Government of Sierra Leone on the Establishment of the Special Court)* (Special Court for Sierra Leone, Appeals Chamber, Case No SCSL-2004-15-AR72(E), 25 May 2004) para 6.

[123] This should not be confused with the ICC's inherent jurisdiction of *compétence de la compétence*.

[124] See generally, Section 4.3.

6.4 UNIVERSALITY AS THE BASIS FOR ICC JURISDICTION 189

States Parties can continue to rely on their personal immunity and are exempt from the Court's jurisdiction as a matter of procedure.[125]

The situation is different in the case of procedural immunities granted by international agreements. Returning to the example of the US–Afghanistan SOFA, conceptualising the basis for ICC jurisdiction as inherent universal jurisdiction would not be dissimilar to the conclusion reached via delegated territorial jurisdiction. The only effect that the SOFA would have is under Article 98(2) of the Statute which prevents the ICC from requesting States to arrest and transfer a suspect to the ICC if to do so would violate an existing international agreement. In the Afghanistan situation, the existence of the SOFA would mean that the ICC could not request Afghanistan to arrest and transfer any US suspects, but this has no bearing on the legal basis for the ICC's jurisdiction should the Court somehow otherwise gain custody.

Inherent universal jurisdiction as a legal basis would also remove any potential obstacles to the ICC's jurisdiction over Israeli nationals accused of committing Statute crimes on Palestinian territory. Any uncertainties surrounding Palestine's statehood or the status of the Oslo Accords would have no impact on the ICC's jurisdiction if the Court's legal basis is not dependent on delegation.[126]

Situations involving a Security Council Referral Inherent universal jurisdiction would arguably also provide a more straightforward basis for the ICC's jurisdiction over situations in non-States Parties referred to the Court by the Security Council. Once the Court's jurisdiction is properly triggered under Article 13(b) of the Statute, inherent universal jurisdiction would provide a legal basis for the ICC to exercise its powers over situations in non-States Parties such as Sudan and Libya. There would still be a question about the Security Council's power to trigger the jurisdiction of a treaty-based Court over States that have not agreed to be bound by the terms of the Statute. But as discussed in Chapter 5, this is a matter of UN membership and States' agreement to be bound by the terms of the UN Charter, which includes an obligation to accept decisions of the Security Council. As a UN member, Sudan, for example, has consented to the Security Council's power to take measures under Chapter VII of the Charter for the maintenance of international peace and security. There is established precedent that such measures include

---

[125] See Section 4.3.3.2 and Section 5.4.3.1.
[126] See Section 4.4.2 for background and analysis of the situation in Palestine.

the implementation of criminal justice mechanisms. The jurisdiction of the ICC, once triggered, would then be based on inherent universal jurisdiction rather than the non-State Party's implied consent by virtue of its UN membership and the Security Council resolution.[127]

6.4.2.3 The Limits of Inherent Universal Jurisdiction

Jurisdiction is Inherent to States Critics of the inherent universal jurisdiction theory argue that such jurisdiction does not and cannot exist.[128] Sarah Williams, for example, denounces the very idea of universal jurisdiction without delegation:

> This conjures the image of a 'floating' universal jurisdiction, once a tribunal is created to try crimes giving rise to universal jurisdiction under customary international law, that jurisdiction simply exists and is vested in the tribunal with no need for a delegation of jurisdiction from states. This simply cannot be the case: universal jurisdiction is exercised by *states*. States may delegate their own competencies for crimes subject to universal jurisdiction to an international or internationalised tribunal.[129]

Williams uses an interesting hypothetical example to demonstrate her argument against inherent universal jurisdiction: what if two non-governmental organisations (NGOs) established an international court to try individuals accused of crimes of universal jurisdiction? Williams contends that it is 'highly unlikely' that such a court would be accepted in the absence of any State approval.[130] But if inherent universal jurisdiction exists, an NGO court could, at least in theory, exercise jurisdiction over certain crimes without individual State consent as an agent of the international community. David Luban writes that the legitimacy of international courts derives 'not from the shaky political authority that

---

[127] And perhaps implied consent by virtue of Sudan's membership of the international community. See the section 'Is the ICC an Agent of the International Community?' for a critique of the concept of 'the international community'.

[128] See, eg, submissions made by Roger O'Keefe: Transcript of Proceedings, *Prosecutor v Al Bashir (Judgment in the Jordan Referral re Al-Bashir Appeal)* (International Criminal Court, Appeals Chamber, Case No ICC/02/05-01/09, 14 September 2018) 56; D Jacobs, 'You have just entered Narnia: ICC Appeals Chamber adopts the worst possible solution on immunities in the Bashir case', *Spreading the Jam* (6 May 2019).

[129] Williams, *Hybrid and Internationalised Criminal Tribunals: Selected Jurisdictional Issues*, p. 315. Similarly Frédéric Mégret rejects the notion that jurisdiction, even universal jurisdiction, can be separated from States: F Mégret, 'Epilogue to an Endless Debate: The International Criminal Court's Third Party Jurisdiction and the Looming Revolution of International Law' (2001) 12 *European Journal of International Law* 247 at 251 fn 16.

[130] Williams, *Hybrid and Internationalised Criminal Tribunals: Selected Jurisdictional Issues*, p. 316.

creates them, but from manifested fairness of their procedures and punishments'.[131] If Amnesty International or Human Rights Watch decided to establish a special court for international crimes vested with sound rules of procedure, humane punishments and experienced judges of the highest quality, such a court could theoretically operate on the basis of inherent universal jurisdiction.[132]

As discussed above, acceptance of inherent universal jurisdiction as a conceivable basis for the ICC's jurisdiction is predicated on a descending perspective of jurisdiction and sovereignty. Outright rejections of inherent universal jurisdiction are firmly anchored in an ascending perspective. Rather than framing criticisms of inherent universal jurisdiction in terms of blanket assertions that jurisdiction unequivocally belongs to States, a more useful critique raises the question of what it means to say that universal jurisdiction can be inherent to the international community and exercised by an international court.

Is the ICC an Agent of the International Community? The term 'international community' is ubiquitous (it appears twice in the Rome Statute preamble alone), but its meaning remains elusive.[133] As Dino Kritsiotis observes, 'it is almost as if there exists a subliminal and pervasive appreciation of the meaning of this term – of what forms and frames this community – that eliminates the need for further detail or consideration'.[134] A conservative view would be that the international community refers simply to the community of States. But does this mean that acts or principles attributed to the international community reflect

---

[131] D Luban, 'Fairness to Rightness: Jurisdiction, Legality and the Legitimacy of International Criminal Law' in S Besson and J Tasioulas (eds), *The Philosophy of International Law* (Oxford University Press, 2010) p. 579.

[132] At least insofar as prescriptive jurisdiction is concerned. Without acceptance by States, such a court would lack any type of enforcement jurisdiction.

[133] David Luban describes the international community as 'something of a gaseous invertebrate': Luban, 'Fairness to Rightness: Jurisdiction, Legality and the Legitimacy of International Criminal Law', p. 577. See also, A Addis, 'Imagining the International Community: The Constitutive Dimension of Universal Jurisdiction' (2009) 31 *Human Rights Quarterly* 129; D Kritsiotis, 'Imagining the International Community' (2002) 13 *European Journal of International Law* 961; GI Hernández, 'A Reluctant Guardian: The International Court of Justice and the Concept of "International Community"' (2013) 83 *British Yearbook of International Law* 13; A Duff, 'Authority and Responsibility in International Criminal Law' in S Besson and J Tasioulas (eds), *The Philosophy of International Law* (Oxford University Press, 2010) p. 604; United Nations Secretary-General, 'Secretary-General examines "meaning of international community" in address to DPI/NGO conference' (Press Release, SG/SM/7133, 15 September 1999).

[134] Kritsiotis, 'Imagining the International Community', 964.

the acquiescence of every member of this community? Or is it sufficient that the 'vast majority' of States are in agreement?[135] As discussed in Chapter 3, the ambiguity of what constitutes a majority of States risks contravening the principle of *res inter alios acta*.

Proponents of the inherent jurisdiction theory might argue that the will of the international community can be ascertained by looking to customary international law, which develops through uniform, consistent and general State practice.[136] To the extent that certain universal jurisdiction crimes are offences against customary international law, it reflects a consensus by the international community. But in this instance, customary international law is only an indicator of (a) the existence and scope of certain crimes and (b) the right of States to prescribe criminal conduct on the basis of universal jurisdiction.[137] At present, there is not sufficient State practice and *opinio juris* to suggest that customary international law gives international courts the right to exercise jurisdiction on the basis of universality.[138]

While the ICC skated close to characterising its legal basis for jurisdiction as a supranational *ius puniendi* in the 2019 Jordan Appeal decision, the Appeals Chamber stopped short of clearly articulating an inherent universal basis for its jurisdiction. The Chamber took care to point out that the ICC exercises its jurisdiction 'in no other circumstances than on behalf of the international community'; a description which is perfectly appropriate for an international court exercising powers based on delegated territorial and nationality jurisdiction. Nevertheless, there were pronouncements in this judgment and joint concurring opinion which suggest the Chamber intended a more expansive view of its jurisdictional basis. For example, as mentioned in Chapter 4, the Chamber held that States Parties executing a request under Article 59 'should not be seen as exercising their own criminal jurisdiction' because in doing so they are 'merely acting as jurisdictional surrogates of the ICC'.[139] This is akin to

---

[135] *Reparation for Injuries Suffered in the Service of the United Nations (Advisory Opinion)* [1949] ICJ Rep 174, 185. See discussion in Section 3.2.2.

[136] With accompanying *opinio juris*. See J Crawford and I Brownlie, *Brownlie's Principles of Public International Law*, 8th ed (Oxford University Press, 2012) pp. 24–30.

[137] As discussed in Section 6.3.2, there is considerable uncertainty as to precisely which crimes States may exercise universal jurisdiction over as a matter of customary international law.

[138] *Report of the Secretary-General: The scope and application of the principle of universal jurisdiction*, 70th sess, Agenda Item 86, UN Doc A/70/125 (1 July 2015).

[139] *Prosecutor v Al Bashir (Joint Concurring Opinion of Judges Eboe-Osuji, Morrison, Hofmański and Bossa)* (International Criminal Court, Appeals Chamber, Case No ICC/02/05-01/09, 6 May 2019) para 445.

conceptualising a State Party's jurisdiction in such circumstances as delegated by the ICC, which would only make sense if the Court's jurisdiction was not based on delegation from States Parties. Furthermore, in holding that customary international law does not recognise Head of State immunities before an international court, the Appeals Chamber stressed the 'fundamentally different nature of an international court' meant that a customary exception to immunity did not have to be established, further hinting at a jurisdictional legal basis as separate from its States Parties.[140]

If the ICC's membership was universal, or near-universal, this would likely overcome any objections to the idea that the Court is acting as an agent of the international community. Perhaps if the ICC had been established by the Security Council the idea that the Court is exercising jurisdiction as an agent of the international community could be sustained. As a treaty-body without universal membership, however, it is a bridge too far to accept that the legal basis for the ICC's jurisdiction is universal jurisdiction inherent to the international community.

6.4.3 Two Shortcomings

No matter which theory is preferred – delegated or inherent universal jurisdiction – universality as a legal basis for the ICC's jurisdiction suffers from two basic shortcomings. The first is that there is still uncertainty surrounding which acts can be prosecuted as crimes of universal jurisdiction under customary international law. While there is a sound argument to be made that acts meeting the customary requirements of a crime against humanity or a war crime should attract universal jurisdiction, there remains some contention over whether certain offences are, in fact, universally justiciable. Furthermore, the crime of aggression as defined in the Kampala Amendments is not yet a customary crime of universal jurisdiction, which would automatically preclude inherent universal jurisdiction as a basis for ICC prosecution in such cases.[141]

---

[140] *Prosecutor v Al Bashir (Judgment in the Jordan Referral re Al-Bashir Appeal)* (International Criminal Court, Appeals Chamber, Case No ICC/02/05-01/09, 6 May 2019) para 116. See also, Kreß, 'Preliminary Observations on the ICC Appeals Chamber's Judgment of 6 May 2019 in the Jordan Referral re Al-Bashir Appeal', 17–20.

[141] Given that the Kampala Amendments prevent the ICC from exercising jurisdiction over acts of aggression involving non-States Parties in all circumstances other than a Security Council referral, it may not matter that delegated universal jurisdiction would not

The second shortcoming with the universal jurisdiction theory has to do with the fact that universality is a principle of prescriptive jurisdiction only. Even conceding the possibility that universal jurisdiction exercisable by an international court is something that can be distinguished from universal jurisdiction exercisable by States, this cannot overcome the fact that jurisdiction to enforce is exclusively territorial. Without the cooperation of States to gather evidence, arrest and incarcerate offenders, an international court would be significantly limited in what it can actually achieve.

6.5 Conclusion

Some scholars have suggested that the principle of universality remains applicable to ICC jurisdiction even in a situation involving only a State Party. Sadat and Carden maintain that in such a case, 'the universality principle does not disappear, layered upon it is a State consent regime based on two additional principles (which are disjunctive) of jurisdiction: the territorial principle and the nationality principle'.[142] As I have argued in this chapter, however, there is no substantial advantage to characterising the legal basis for the ICC's jurisdiction as either delegated or inherent universal jurisdiction. In situations involving a Security Council referral, for example, universality potentially simplifies the basis for ICC jurisdiction over nationals of non-States Parties. But in such a situation, the Court would still need to rely on delegated territorial jurisdiction for its powers to enforce, and universal jurisdiction cannot overcome the personal immunities of incumbent Heads of State from States not party to the Rome Statute. On balance, given the shortcomings in both the delegated and inherent universal jurisdiction theories, the principle of universality as a legal basis for ICC jurisdiction does not work as well as delegated territorial jurisdiction and implied consent, which provide an adequate basis for ICC authority in the same situations.

This does not mean that the principle of universality is immaterial for the ICC. The Court has a legitimate interest in casting its jurisdictional net as wide as possible if it is to fulfil its promise that 'the most

---

provide a legal basis for the Court's jurisdiction over the crime of aggression. The legal basis would remain delegated territorial or nationality jurisdiction.

[142] Sadat and Carden, 'New International Criminal Court', 413.

serious crimes of concern to the international community as a whole must not go unpunished'.[143] To the extent that the aims and objectives of the ICC align with the rationale for universal jurisdiction, the Court does represent certain universal norms and values of the international community.

---

[143] Rome Statute, Preamble.

7

Concluding Remarks

'[A]ll jurisdictional claims need a basis in international law.'[1]

The central argument in this book is that the ICC needs to carefully articulate the legal basis for its jurisdiction over nationals of non-States Parties. Contrary to what some States and commentators have claimed, the key concern is less a question of whether a legal basis exists, and more a question of what form such a basis should take. Conceiving of the legal basis for such jurisdiction as individual delegation of territorial jurisdiction from States Parties,[2] or as a matter of implied consent by virtue of UN membership,[3] is a way of grounding the legal basis for the Court's jurisdiction over nationals of non-States Parties in State consent.

The positivist tradition in international legal scholarship views States as the primary subjects of international law and State consent as foundational.[4] States themselves continue to use rhetoric espousing the fundamental importance of Westphalian sovereignty,[5] which explains why the principle of State consent underpins many of the legal arguments against

---

[1] F Berman, 'Jurisdiction: The State' in SV Konstadinidis, MD Evans and P Capps (eds), *Asserting Jurisdiction: International and European Legal Approaches* (Hart Publishing, 2003) 3, 3.

[2] For situations that come before the Court via Article 13(a) and (c) avenues.

[3] For situations that come before the Court via Article 13(b).

[4] MN Shaw, *International Law*, 7th ed (Cambridge University Press, 2014) pp. 35–9; B Simma and AL Paulus, 'The Responsibility of Individuals for Human Rights Abuses in Internal Conflicts: A Positivist View' (1999) 93 *American Journal of International Law* 302; F Lachenmann, 'Legal Positivism' *Max Planck Encyclopedia of Public International Law* (Oxford University Press, 2011).

[5] See, eg, 'Trial of Sayf-al-Islam in Libya is question of sovereignty – NTC official' *BBC Monitoring Middle East* (9 April 2012); Statement of Vestine Nahimana Ambassador of Burundi, *Fifteenth Session of the Assembly of States Parties to the Rome Statute* (16–24 November 2016) in which the ICC preliminary examination into the situation in Burundi is described as 'a betrayal of the sovereignty of Burundi'.

ICC jurisdiction over nationals of non-States Parties. Acknowledging the primacy of this worldview among States allows for greater scope to challenge such arguments. By framing the legal basis for the ICC's jurisdiction in a way that prioritises State consent, certain objections to the Court's prosecution of nationals of non-States Parties can be minimised. This is not to say that the State-centrism of international law should be accepted uncritically, and as I discussed in Chapter 2, the concept of sovereignty is evolving to accommodate cosmopolitan ideals.[6] The primacy of sovereignty and State consent must be reconciled with the aims and values of international criminal justice, and the Rome Statute's jurisdiction regime represents an example of how the two can be balanced. By necessity, this means that the Statute and activities of the ICC can and do affect the sovereignty of non-States Parties. But any perceived infringements can be mitigated by underpinning the Statute's jurisdiction framework with a legal basis that tacitly recognises the ascending model of sovereignty. The ICC's right to exercise its powers under the Statute ultimately reflects the rights of States themselves to exercise their powers of criminal justice in accordance with recognised international legal principles of territoriality and nationality.

The delegation and implied consent theories allow the Court to proceed with investigations and prosecutions within the framework of the Rome Statute in nearly all circumstances envisaged by the framers. As I argued in Chapter 4, however, at present there is insufficient State practice to conclude customary international law allows international courts to prosecute incumbent Heads of States. Without a customary exception to Head of State immunity at the international court level, delegation of jurisdiction as a legal basis cannot overcome this limitation on the ICC's competence. Without a Security Council referral to anchor the Court's jurisdiction in implied consent, the ICC will not be able to lawfully prosecute a Head of State from a non-State Party until customary international law allows it. The vexed issue of Head of State immunity has not been helped by the ICC's piecemeal and contradictory jurisprudence in the Al Bashir arrest warrant decisions. While the Appeals Chamber finally gave some detailed consideration to the immunities question in

---

[6] Indeed, modern positivism in international law has evolved from its association with absolute State voluntarism: Simma and Paulus, 'The Responsibility of Individuals for Human Rights Abuses in Internal Conflicts: A Positivist View', 304.

the Jordan Appeal decision,[7] it missed an opportunity to consider how its reasoning would apply to a Head of State from a non-State Party in a situation not involving the Security Council.

As I have demonstrated throughout this book, however, the legal uncertainties surrounding the ICC's jurisdiction over nationals of non-States Parties go beyond the issue of Head of State immunity. What the ICC needs is a foundational, *Tadić*-style decision in which it sets out the legal basis for its jurisdiction and explains how this allows the Court to exercise jurisdiction over nationals of non-States Parties in the circumstances provided for by the Rome Statute.[8] In the Jordan Appeal decision, the Appeals Chamber seemed to come close to identifying the legal basis for its jurisdiction as akin to a *ius puniendi*, but it ultimately did not go further than declaring that the Court exercises its jurisdiction 'on behalf of the international community'.[9] Basing the ICC's jurisdiction on the principle of universality unmoored from States would conceivably explain how and why the ICC can exercise its powers over nationals of non-States Parties. As I explained in Chapter 6, however, this theory has some important shortcomings, not least of which is the uncertainty surrounding which acts can be prosecuted as crimes of universal jurisdiction.

Delegation of jurisdiction and implied consent provide a sound legal basis for the Court to proceed with investigations and prosecutions in accordance with the framework of the Rome Statute. However the Court decides to characterise its legal basis, it should aim for coherence and consistency in its decisions on jurisdiction and it should pay due regard to the principle of State consent. By conceptualising the legal basis for the Court's jurisdiction as delegated territorial and nationality jurisdiction from States Parties, the ICC will be able to lawfully exercise jurisdiction over nationals of non-States Parties in most situations allowed by the Rome Statute.

Going forward, concern about the jurisdiction of the ICC over nationals of non-States Parties is only going to intensify and new legal issues will arise. State withdrawals from the Statute, for example, raise

---

[7] *Prosecutor v Al Bashir (Judgment in the Jordan Referral re Al-Bashir Appeal)* (International Criminal Court, Appeals Chamber, Case No ICC/02/05–01/09, 6 May 2019).

[8] *Prosecutor v Tadić (Decision on the Defence Motion for Interlocutory Appeal on Jurisdiction)* (International Criminal Tribunal for the former Yugoslavia, Appeals Chamber II, Case No ICTY-94-1-AR72, 2 October 1995).

[9] *Prosecutor v Al Bashir (Judgment in the Jordan Referral re Al-Bashir Appeal)* (International Criminal Court, Appeals Chamber, Case No ICC/02/05–01/09, 6 May 2019) para 115.

further questions about the legal basis for the Court's jurisdiction where the territorial State has withdrawn its consent.[10] I anticipate that it is only a matter of time before a significant test of the Court's jurisdiction over nationals of non-States Parties takes place in circumstances where the Security Council is not involved. While the ICC may be facing multiple and multifaceted challenges to its credibility and legitimacy, as I have argued throughout this book, the legal basis for its jurisdiction over nationals of non-States Parties does not have to be one of them.

---

[10] Burundi's withdrawal took effect in October 2017 and The Philippines' in March 2019. Situations in both States were before the ICC at the time of their withdrawals.

BIBLIOGRAPHY

Books, Chapters and Articles

Abass, Ademola, 'The Competence of the Security Council to Terminate the Jurisdiction of the International Criminal Court' (2004) 40 *Texas International Law Journal* 263

Abass, Ademola, 'The International Criminal Court and Universal Jurisdiction' (2006) 6 *International Criminal Law Review* 349

Abi-Saab, Georges, 'The Proper Role of Universal Jurisdiction' (2003) 1(3) *Journal of International Criminal Justice* 596

Abtahi, Hirad, 'The Islamic Republic of Iran and the ICC' (2005) 3 *Journal of International Criminal Justice* 635

Aceves, William J, 'Murphy v Netherland' (1998) 92(1) *American Journal of International Law* 87

Addis, Adeno, 'Imagining the International Community: The Constitutive Dimension of Universal Jurisdiction' (2009) 31(1) *Human Rights Quarterly* 129

Addo, Michael K, 'Vienna Convention on Consular Relations (Paraguay v. United States of America) ("Breard") and Lagrand (Germany v. United States of America), Applications for Provisional Measures' (1999) 48(3) *International & Comparative Law Quarterly* 673

Akande, Dapo, 'The Jurisdiction of the International Criminal Court over Nationals of Non-Parties: Legal Basis and Limits' (2003) 1 *Journal of International Criminal Justice* 618

Akande, Dapo, 'International Law Immunities and the International Criminal Court' (2004) 98 *American Journal of International Law* 407

Akande, Dapo, 'The Legal Nature of Security Council Referrals to the ICC and Its Impact on Al Bashir's Immunities' (2009) 7(2) *Journal of International Criminal Justice* 333

Akande, Dapo, 'Prosecuting Aggression: The Consent Problem and the Role of the Security Council' (Working Paper, Oxford Institute for Ethics, Law and Armed Conflict, May 2010) papers.ssrn.com/abstract=1762806

Akande, Dapo, 'The Effect of Security Council Resolutions and Domestic Proceedings on State Obligations to Cooperate with the ICC' (2012) 10(2) *Journal of International Criminal Justice* 299

Akande, Dapo and Sangeeta Shah, 'Immunities of State Officials, International Crimes, and Foreign Domestic Courts' (2010) 21 *European Journal of International Law* 815

Akande, Dapo and Antonios Tzanakopoulos, 'Treaty Law and ICC Jurisdiction over the Crime of Aggression' (2018) 29 *European Journal of International Law* 939

Akehurst, Michael, 'Jurisdiction in International Law' (1972) 46 *British Year Book of International Law* 145

Alter, Karen J, 'Delegating to International Courts: Self-Binding vs. Other-Binding Delegation' (2008) 71 *Law and Contemporary Problems* 37

Altman, Andrew and Christopher Heath Wellman, *A Liberal Theory of International Justice* (Oxford University Press, 2009)

Alvarez, José E, 'Nuremberg Revisited: The Tadić Case' (1996) 7 *European Journal of International Law* 245

Alvarez, José E, 'Tadić Revisited: The Ayyash Decisions of the Special Tribunal for Lebanon' (2013) 11(2) *Journal of International Criminal Justice* 291

Ambos, Kai, 'Punishment without a Sovereign? The *Ius Puniendi* Issue of International Criminal Law: A First Contribution towards a Consistent Theory of International Criminal Law' (2013) 33(2) *Oxford Journal of Legal Studies* 293

Amerasinghe, Chittharanjan Felix, *Jurisdiction of International Tribunals* (Kluwer Law International, 2003)

Amerasinghe, Chittharanjan Felix, *Principles of the Institutional Law of International Organizations* (Cambridge University Press, 2nd ed, 2005)

Amerasinghe, Chittharanjan Felix, *Jurisdiction of Specific International Tribunals* (Martinus Nijhoff Publishers, 2009)

Arbour, Louise, 'Will the ICC Have an Impact on Universal Jurisdiction?' (2003) 1(3) *Journal of International Criminal Justice* 585

Armstead Jr, J Holmes, 'The International Criminal Court: History, Development and Status' (1997) 38 *Santa Clara Law Review* 745

Aust, Anthony, *Modern Treaty Law and Practice* (Cambridge University Press, 3rd ed, 2013)

Banerjee, Rishav, 'Rome Statute and India: An Analysis of India's Attitude towards the International Criminal Court' (2011) 4 *Journal of East Asia and International Law* 457

Bantekas, Ilias, 'Head of State Immunity in the Light of Multiple Legal Regimes and Non–Self-Contained System Theories: Theoretical Analysis of ICC Third Party Jurisdiction Against the Background of the 2003 Iraq War' (2005) 10(1) *Journal of Conflict and Security Law* 21

Bantekas, Ilias and Susan Nash, *International Criminal Law* (Oxford University Press, 4th ed, 2010)

Barker, J Craig, Colin Warbrick and Dominic McGoldrick, 'The Future of Former Head of State Immunity after Ex Parte Pinochet' (1999) 48(4) *The International and Comparative Law Quarterly* 937

Barriga, Stefan and Claus Kreß, *The Travaux Préparatoires of the Crime of Aggression* (Cambridge University Press, 2011)

Bassiouni, M Cherif, 'International Crimes: Jus Cogens and Obligatio Erga Omnes Accountability for International Crime and Serious Violations of Fundamental Human Rights' (1996) 59 *Law and Contemporary Problems* 63

Bassiouni, M Cherif, *Crimes Against Humanity in International Criminal Law* (Kluwer Law International, 2nd ed, 1999)

Bassiouni, M Cherif, 'Universal Jurisdiction for International Crimes: Historical Perspectives and Contemporary Practice' (2001) 42 *Virginia Journal of International Law* 81

Bassiouni, M Cherif, 'The Permanent International Criminal Court' in Mark Lattimer and Philippe Sands (eds), *Justice for Crimes Against Humanity* (Hart Publishing, 2003) 190

Bassiouni, M Cherif, 'The History of Universal Jurisdiction and Its Place in International Law' in Stephen Macedo (ed), *Universal Jurisdiction: National Courts and the Prosecution of Serious Crimes under International Law* (Pennsylvania University Press, 2004) 39

Bassiouni, M Cherif, *The Legislative History of the International Criminal Court* (Transnational Publishers, 2005)

Bassiouni, M Cherif (ed), *International Criminal Law* (Martinus Nijhoff Publishers, 3rd ed, 2008)

Bassiouni, M Cherif, 'Introduction to Transfer of Criminal Proceedings' in M Cherif Bassiouni (ed), *International Criminal Law* (Martinus Nijhoff Publishers, 3rd ed, 2008) vol II 515

Bassiouni, M Cherif, *Introduction to International Criminal Law* (Martinus Nijhoff Publishers, 2nd ed, 2012)

Beale, Joseph H, 'The Jurisdiction of a Sovereign State' (1922) 36 *Harvard Law Review* 241

Beale, Joseph H, *A Treatise on the Conflict of Laws* (Baker, Voorhis & Co, 1935)

Beckett, Jason A, 'Rebel without a Cause – Martti Koskenniemi and the Critical Legal Project' (2006) 7 *German Law Journal* 1045

Beckett, WE, 'Criminal Jurisdiction over Foreigners' (1927) 8 *British Year Book of International Law* 108

Bederman, David J, 'Third Party Rights and Obligations in Treaties' in Duncan B Hollis (ed), *The Oxford Guide to Treaties* (Oxford University Press, 2012) 328

Bekou, Olympia and Robert Cryer, 'The International Criminal Court and Universal Jurisdiction: A Close Encounter' (2007) 56 *International and Comparative Law Quarterly* 49

Bellinger III, JB, and WJ Haynes II, 'A US government response to the International Committee of the Red Cross study *Customary International Humanitarian Law*' (2007) 89 *International Review of the Red Cross* 443

Benzing, Markus, 'The Complementarity Regime of the International Criminal Court: International Criminal Justice between State Sovereignty and the Fight against Impunity' (2003) 7 *Max Planck Yearbook of United Nations Law* 591

Benzing, Markus, 'U.S. Bilateral Non-Surrender Agreements and Article 98 of the Statute of the International Criminal Court: An Exercise in the Law of Treaties' (2004) 8(1) *Max Planck Yearbook of United Nations Law Online* 181

Benzing, Markus, 'Sovereignty and the Responsibility to Protect in International Criminal Law' in Doris König, Peter-Tobias Stoll, Volker Röben and Nele Matz-Lück (eds), *International Law Today: New Challenges and the Need for Reform?* (Springer Berlin Heidelberg, 2008) 17

Berg, Bradley E, 'The 1994 ILC Draft Statute for an International Criminal Court: A Principled Appraisal of Jurisdictional Structure' (1996) 28 *Case Western Reserve Journal of International Law* 221

Bergsmo, Morten, 'Occasional Remarks on Certain State Concerns about the Jurisdictional Reach of the International Criminal Court, and Their Possible Implications for the Relationship between the Court and the Security Council' (2000) 69 *Nordic Journal of International Law* 87

Bergsmo, Morten (ed), *Complementarity and the Exercise of Universal Jurisdiction for Core International Crimes* (Torkel Opsahl Academic EPublisher, 2010)

Bergsmo, Morten and Yan LING (eds), *State Sovereignty and International Criminal Law* (Torkel Opsahl Academic EPublisher, 2012)

Berman, Franklin, 'Jurisdiction: The State' in Stratos V Konstadinidis, Malcolm D Evans and Patrick Capps (eds), *Asserting Jurisdiction: International and European Legal Approaches* (Hart Publishing, 2003) 3

Bing Bing Jia, 'The International Criminal Court and Third States' in Antonio Cassese (ed), *The Oxford Companion to International Criminal Justice* (Oxford University Press, 2009) 160

Birdsall, Andrea, *The International Politics of Judicial Intervention: Creating a More Just Order* (Routledge, 2009)

Bishop, Anna, 'Failure of Complementarity: The Future of the International Criminal Court Following the Libyan Admissibility Challenge' (2013) 22 *Minnesota Journal of International Law* 388

Bitti, Gilbert, 'Article 21 of the Statute of the International Criminal Court and the Treatment of Sources of Law in the Jurisprudence of the ICC' in Göran Sluiter and Carsten Stahn (eds), *The Emerging Practice of the International Criminal Court* (Brill, 2008) 281

Blakesley, Christopher L, 'Jurisdiction Ratione Personae or the Personal Reach of the Court's Jurisdiction' in Jośe Doria, Hans-Peter Gasser and M Cherif Bassiouni (eds), *The Legal Regime of the International Criminal Court: Essays in Honour of Professor Igor Blishchenko* (Martinus Nijhoff Publishers, 2009) 423

Blokker, Niels, 'The Crime of Aggression and the United Nations Security Council' (2007) 20(4) *Leiden Journal of International Law* 867

Blokker, Niels and Stefan Barriga, 'Conditions for the Exercise of Jurisdiction Based on Security Council Referrals' in Claus Kreß, Stefan Barriga (eds), *The Crime of Aggression – A Commentary* (Cambridge University Press, 2016)

Boas, Gideon, William Schabas and Michael Scharf, *International Criminal Justice: Legitimacy and Coherence* (Edward Elgar Publishing, 2012)

Bogdan, Attila, 'The United States and the International Criminal Court: Avoiding Jurisdiction through Bilateral Agreements in Reliance on Article 98' (2008) 8 *International Criminal Law Review* 1

Boister, Neil, 'The ICJ in the Belgian Arrest Warrant Case: Arresting the Development of International Criminal Law' (2002) 7(2) *Journal of Conflict and Security Law* 293

Bolton, John R, 'The Risks and the Weaknesses of the International Criminal Court from America's Perspective' (2000) 41 *Virginia Journal of International Law* 186

Borgen, Christopher J, 'Treaty Conflicts and Normative Fragmentation' in Duncan B Hollis (ed), *The Oxford Guide to Treaties* (Oxford University Press, 2012) 448

Boschiero, Nerina, 'The ICC Judicial Finding on Non-Cooperation against the DRC and No Immunity for Al-Bashir Based on UNSC Resolution 1593' (2015) 13(3) *Journal of International Criminal Justice* 625

Bosco, David, *Rough Justice: The International Criminal Court in a World of Power Politics* (Oxford University Press, 2014)

Bottini, Gabriel, 'Universal Jurisdiction after the Creation of the International Criminal Court' (2003) 36 *New York University Journal of International Law and Politics* 503

Bourgon, S, 'Jurisdiction Ratione Loci' in Antonio Cassese, Paola Gaeta and John RWD Jones (eds), *The Rome Statute of the International Criminal Court: A Commentary* (Oxford University Press, 2002) 559

Bowett, DW, 'Jurisdiction: Changing Patterns of Authority over Activities and Resources' (1983) 53(1) *British Yearbook of International Law* 1

Bradley, Curtis A and Judith G Kelley (eds), 'Special Issue: The Law and Politics of International Delegation' (2008) 71 *Law and Contemporary Problems* 1

Bradley, Curtis A and Judith G Kelley, 'The Concept of International Delegation' (2008) 71 *Law and Contemporary Problems* 1

Brölmann, Catherine, 'Specialized Rules of Treaty Interpretation: International Organizations' in Duncan B Hollis (ed), *The Oxford Guide to Treaties* (Oxford University Press, 2012) 507

Broomhall, Bruce, 'Toward the Development of an Effective System of Universal Jurisdiction for Crimes under International Law' (2001) 35 *New England Law Review* 399

Broomhall, Bruce, *International Justice and the International Criminal Court: Between Sovereignty and the Rule of Law* (Oxford University Press, 2003)

Brown, Bartram, 'Primacy or Complementarity: Reconciling the Jurisdiction of National Courts and International Criminal Tribunals' (1998) 23 *Yale Journal of International Law* 383

Brown, Bartram S, 'US Objections to the Statute of the International Criminal Court: A Brief Response' (1999) 31 *International Law and Politics* 855

Brown, Bartram S, 'The Evolving Concept of Universal Jurisdiction' (2001) 35 *New England Law Review* 383

Brown, Chester, 'The Inherent Powers of International Courts and Tribunals' (2006) 76(1) *British Yearbook of International Law* 195

Bull, Hedley, *The Anarchical Society: A Study of Order in World Politics* (Columbia University Press, 1977)

Burke, Róisín, 'Status of Forces Deployed on UN Peacekeeping Operations: Jurisdictional Immunity' (2011) 16(1) *Journal of Conflict and Security Law* 63

Buzzard, Lucas, 'Holding an Arsonist's Feet to the Fire – The Legality and Enforceability of the ICC's Arrest Warrant for Sudanese President Omar Al-Bashir' (2008) 24 *American University International Law Review* 897

Buzzini, Gionata, 'Lights and Shadows of Immunities and Inviolability of State Officials in International Law: Some Comments on the Djibouti v. France Case' (2009) 22(3) *Leiden Journal of International Law* 455

Byers, Michael, *The Role of Law in International Politics* (Oxford University Press, 2001)

Byron, Christine, *War Crimes and Crimes against Humanity in the Rome Statute of the International Criminal Court* (Manchester University Press, 2009)

Cameron, Iain, 'Jurisdiction and Admissibility Issues under the ICC Statute' in Dominic McGoldrick, Peter Rowe and Eric Donnelly (eds), *The Permanent International Criminal Court: Legal and Policy Issues* (Hart Publishing, 2004) 65

Caron, David D, 'The Legitimacy of the Collective Authority of the Security Council' (1993) 87 *American Journal of International Law* 552

Carty, Anthony, 'The Black Hole of Modernity: From Sovereignty to International Legal Order and Back Again!' (2006) 1(1) *Journal of the Philosophy of International Law* 7

Casey, Lee A and David B Rivkin Jr, 'The Limits of Legitimacy: The Rome Statute's Unlawful Application to Non-State Parties' (2003) 44 *Virginia Journal of International Law* 63

Cash, Heather, 'Security Council Resolution 1593 and Conflicting Principles of International Law: How the Future of the International Criminal Court is at Stake' (2006) 45 *Brandeis Law Journal* 573

Cassese, Antonio, 'Crimes against Humanity' in Antonio Cassese, Paola Gaeta and John RWD Jones (eds), *The Rome Statute of the International Criminal Court: A Commentary* (Oxford University Press, 2002) 353

Cassese, Antonio, 'When May Senior State Officials Be Tried for International Crimes? Some Comments on the Congo v. Belgium Case' (2002) 13(4) *European Journal of International Law* 853

Cassese, Antonio, 'Is the Bell Tolling for Universality? A Plea for a Sensible Notion of Universal Jurisdiction' (2003) 1(3) *Journal of International Criminal Justice* 589

Cassese, Antonio, *International Law* (Oxford University Press, 2nd ed, 2005)

Cassese, Antonio, 'The Legitimacy of International Criminal Tribunals and the Current Prospects of International Criminal Justice' (2012) 25(2) *Leiden Journal of International Law* 491

Cassese, Antonio and Paola Gaeta (eds), *Cassese's International Criminal Law* (Oxford University Press, 3rd ed, 2013)

Cassese, Antonio, Paola Gaeta and John RWD Jones (eds), *The Rome Statute of the International Criminal Court: A Commentary* (Oxford University Press, 2002)

Chehtman, Alejandro, *The Philosophical Foundations of Extraterritorial Punishment* (Oxford University Press, 2010)

Chehtman, Alejandro, 'Jurisdiction' in Markus D Dubber and Tatjana Hörnle (eds), *The Oxford Handbook of Criminal Law* (Oxford University Press, 2014) 399

Chibueze, Remigius, 'United States Objection to the International Criminal Court: A Paradox of Operation Enduring Freedom' (2003) 9 *Annual Survey of International & Comparative Law* 19

Chinkin, Christine, *Third Parties in International Law* (Oxford University Press, 1993)

Clapham, Andrew, 'National Action Challenged: Sovereignty, Immunity and Universal Jurisdiction before the International Court of Justice' in Mark Lattimer and Philippe Sands (eds), *Justice for Crimes against Humanity* (Hart Publishing, 2003) 303

Clark, Roger S, 'The Laws of Armed Conflict and the Use or Threat of Use of Nuclear Weapons' (1996) 7(2) *Criminal Law Forum* 265

Clark, Roger S, 'Apartheid' in M Cherif Bassiouni (ed), *International Criminal Law* (Transnational Publishers, 2nd ed, 1999) 643

Clark, Roger S, 'The ICC Statute: Protecting the Sovereign Rights of Non-Parties' in Dinah Shelton (ed), *International Crimes, Peace, and Human Rights: The Role of the International Criminal Court* (Transnational Publishers, 2000) 207

Clark, Roger S, 'Nuremberg and the Crime Against Peace' (2007) 6 *Washington University Global Studies Law Review* 527

Clark, Roger S, 'Ambiguities in Articles 5(2), 121 and 123 of the Rome Statute' (2009) 41 *Case Western Reserve Journal of International Law* 413

Clark, Roger S, 'Amendments to the Rome Statute of the International Criminal Court Considered at the First Review Conference on the Court, Kampala, 31 May–11 June 2010' (2010) 2 *Goettingen Journal of International Law* 689

Clark, Roger S, 'Defining the Crime of Aggression, Its Elements and the Conditions for the ICC Exercise of Jurisdiction Over It' (2010) 20 *European Journal of International Law* 1103

Clark, Roger S, 'Peacekeeping Forces, Jurisdiction and Immunity: A Tribute to George Barton' (2012) 43 *Victoria University of Wellington Law Review* 77

Clark, Roger S, 'The Crime of Aggression' in Carsten Stahn (ed), *The Law and Practice of the International Criminal Court* (Oxford University Press, 2015) 778

Colangelo, Anthony J, 'The New Universal Jurisdiction: In Absentia Signaling over Clearly Defined Crimes' (2005) 36 *Georgetown Journal of International Law* 537

Collins, Richard and Nigel D White (eds), *International Organizations and the Idea of Autonomy: Institutional Independence in the International Legal Order* (Routledge, 2011)

Combs, Nancy Amoury, 'Establishing the International Criminal Court' (2003) 5 (1) *International Law FORUM du droit international* 77

Condorelli, Luigi and Annalisa Ciampi, 'Comments on the Security Council Referral of the Situation in Darfur to the ICC' (2005) 3(3) *Journal of International Criminal Justice* 590

Cormier, Monique, 'Can the ICC Exercise Jurisdiction over US Nationals for Crimes Committed in the Afghanistan Situation?' (2018) 5 *Journal of International Criminal Justice* 1043

Cowles, Willard B, 'Universality of Jurisdiction over War Crimes' (1945) 33 *California Law Review* 177

Crawford, James, 'The ILC's Draft Statute for an International Criminal Tribunal' (1994) 88 *American Journal of International Law* 140

Crawford, James R, *The Creation of States in International Law* (Oxford University Press, 2nd ed, 2006)

Crawford, James, 'Sovereignty as a Legal Value' in James Crawford and Martti Koskenniemi (eds), *The Cambridge Companion to International Law* (2012) 117

Crawford, James and Ian Brownlie, *Brownlie's Principles of Public International Law* (Oxford University Press, 8th ed, 2012)

Cronin, Bruce, *The UN Security Council and the Politics of International Authority Law, Politics and Power* (Taylor & Francis, 2008)

Cryer, Robert, 'International Criminal Law vs State Sovereignty: Another Round?' (2005) 16 *European Journal of International Law* 979

Cryer, Robert, 'Sudan, Resolution 1593, and International Criminal Justice' (2006) 19(1) *Leiden Journal of International Law* 195

Cryer, Robert, 'Royalism and the King: Article 21 of the Rome Statute and the Politics of Sources' (2009) 12(3) *New Criminal Law Review* 390

Cryer, Robert, 'The International Criminal Court and Its Relationship to Non-Party States' in Göran Sluiter and Carsten Stahn (eds), *The Emerging Practice of the International Criminal Court* (Martinus Nijhoff Publishers, 2009) 260

Cryer, Robert, 'Immunities and International Criminal Tribunals' in Alexander Orakhelashvili (ed), *Research Handbook on Jurisdiction and Immunities in International Law* (Edward Elgar Publishing, 2015) 468

Cryer, Robert, 'The ICC and Its Relationship to Non-States Parties' in Carsten Stahn (ed), *The Law and Practice of the International Criminal Court* (Oxford University Press, 2015) 260

Cryer, Robert and Nigel D White, 'The Security Council and the International Criminal Court: Who's Feeling Threatened' (2004) 8 *International Peacekeeping* 143

Cullen, Holly, Philipp Kastner and Sean Richmond, 'Introduction: The Politics of International Criminal Law' (2018) 18 *International Criminal Law Review* 907

Currie, Robert J, 'Abducted Fugitives before the International Criminal Court: Problems and Prospects' (2007) 18(3) *Criminal Law Forum* 349

Danilenko, Gennady M, 'The Statute of the International Criminal Court and Third States' (1999) 21 *Michigan Journal of International Law* 445

Daphna Shraga, 'Politics and Justice: The Role of the Security Council' in Antonio Cassese (ed), *The Oxford Companion to International Criminal Justice* (Oxford University Press, 2009) 168

de Wet, Erika, *The Chapter VII Powers of the United Nations Security Council* (Hart Publishing, 2004)

Deen-Racsmany, Zsuzsanna, 'The Nationality of the Offender and the Jurisdiction of the International Criminal Court' (2001) 95 *American Journal of International Law* 606

Dietz, Jeffrey S, 'Protecting the Protectors: Can the United States Successfully Exempt U.S. Persons from the International Criminal Court with U.S. Article 98 Agreements?' (2004) 27(1) *Houston Journal of International Law* 137

Dinstein, Yoram, 'The ICRC Customary International Humanitarian Law Study' (2006) 82 *International Law Studies* 99

Doehring, Karl, 'Unlawful Resolutions of the Security Council and Their Legal Consequences' (1997) 1 *Max Planck Yearbook of United Nations Law* 91

Drumbl, Mark A, 'A Hard Look at the Soft Theory of International Criminal Law' in Leila Sadat and Michael Scharf (eds), *The Theory and Practice of International Criminal Law* (Brill, 2008) 1

Duff, Antony, 'Authority and Responsibility in International Criminal Law' in Samantha Besson and John Tasioulas (eds), *The Philosophy of International Law* (Oxford University Press, 2010) 604

Eckelmans, Franziska C, 'The First Jurisprudence of the Appeals Chamber of the ICC' in Göran Sluiter and Carsten Stahn (eds), *The Emerging Practice of the International Criminal Court* (Brill, 2008) 525

Einarsen, Terje, *The Concept of Universal Crimes in International Law* (Torkel Opsahl Academic EPublisher, 2012)

El Zeidy, Mohamed, 'The United States Dropped the Atomic Bomb of Article 16 of the ICC Statute: Security Council Power of Deferrals and Resolution 1422' (2002) 35 *Vanderbilt Journal of Transnational Law* 1503

Engström, Viljam, 'Reasoning on Powers of Organizations' in Jan Klabbers and Åsa Wallendahl (eds), *Research Handbook on the Law of International Organizations* (Edward Elgar, 2011) 56

Engström, Viljam, *Constructing the Powers of International Institutions* (Brill, 2012)

Epstein, David and Sharyn O'Halloran, 'Sovereignty and Delegation in International Organizations' (2008) 71 *Law and Contemporary Problems* 77

Eseed, Jennifer Nimry, 'The International Criminal Court's Unjustified Jurisdiction Claims Libya as a Case Study' (2012) 88 *Chicago-Kent Law Review* 567

Fassbender, Bardo, 'Reflections on the International Legality of the Special Tribunal for Lebanon' (2007) 5 *Journal of International Criminal Justice* 1091

Fitzmaurice, Malgosia, 'Third Parties and the Law of Treaties' (2002) 6 *Max Planck Yearbook of United Nations Law* 37

Fitzmaurice, Malgosia and Olufemi Elias, *Contemporary Issues in the Law of Treaties* (Eleven International Publishing, 2005)

Fitzpatrick, Joan, 'Sovereignty, Territoriality, and the Rule of Law' (2001) 25 *Hastings International and Comparative Law Review* 303

Foakes, Joanne, *The Position of Heads of State and Senior Officials in International Law* (Oxford University Press, 2014)

Ford, Richard T, 'Law's Territory (A History of Jurisdiction)' (1999) 97(4) *Michigan Law Review* 843

Fox, Hazel, 'The Objections to Transfer of Criminal Jurisdiction to the UN Tribunal' (1997) 46(2) *The International and Comparative Law Quarterly* 434

Fox, Hazel, 'The Resolution of the Institute of International Law on the Immunities of Heads of State and Government' (2002) 51(1) *International and Comparative Law Quarterly* 119

Franck, Thomas M, *Fairness in International Law and Institutions* (Clarendon Press; Oxford University Press, 1995)

Franck, Thomas M (ed), *Delegating State Powers: The Effect of Treaty Regimes on Democracy and Sovereignty* (Transnational Publishers, 2000)

Franey, Elizabeth Helen, 'Immunity from the Criminal Jurisdiction of National Courts' in Alexander Orakhelashvili (ed), *Research Handbook on Jurisdiction and Immunities in International Law* (Edward Elgar Publishing, 2015) 205

Freeland, Steven, 'How Open Should the Door Be? – Declarations by Non-States Parties under Article 12(3) of the Rome Statute of the International Criminal Court' (2006) 75(2) *Nordic Journal of International Law* 211

French, Duncan (ed), *Statehood and Self-Determination: Reconciling Tradition and Modernity in International Law* (Cambridge University Press, 2013)

Gaeta, Paola, 'Inherent Powers of International Courts and Tribunals' in Lal Chand Vohrah, Fausto Pocar, Yvonne Featherstone, Olivier Fourmy, Christine Graham, John Hocking and Nicholas Robson (eds), *Man's Inhumanity to Man: Essays on International Law in Honour of Antonio Cassese* (Kluwer Law International, 2003) 353

Gaeta, Paola, 'Does President Al Bashir Enjoy Immunity from Arrest?' (2009) 7(2) *Journal of International Criminal Justice* 315

Gaeta, Paola and Patryk Labuda, 'The African Union versus the ICC in the *Al Bashir* and *Kenyatta* Cases' in Charles Chernor Taylor and Ilias Bantekas (eds), *The International Criminal Court and Africa* (Oxford University Press, 2017) 138

Gallant, Kenneth S, 'The International Criminal Court in the System of States and International Organizations' (2003) 16(3) *Leiden Journal of International Law* 553

Garraway, Charles, 'War Crimes' in Elizabeth Wilmshurst and Susan Breau (eds), *Perspectives on the ICRC Study on Customary International Humanitarian Law* (Cambridge University Press, 2007) 377

Ginsberg, Tom, 'The Clash of Commitments at the International Criminal Court' (2008) 9 *Chicago Journal of International Law* 499

Ginsburgs, George and VN Kudriavtsev (eds), *The Nuremberg Trial and International Law* (Martinus Nijhoff Publishers, 1990)

Goodrich, Leland M, Edvard Hambro and Anne Patricia Simons, *Charter of the United Nations – Commentary and Documents*, 3rd ed (Columbia University Press, 1969)

Grimm, Dieter, *Sovereignty: The Origin and Future of a Political Concept* (Belinda Cooper trans, Columbia University Press, 2015) [trans of Souveränität: Herkunft und Zukunft eines Schlüsselbegriffs, first published 2009]

Groome, Dermot, 'The Church Abuse Scandal: Were Crimes against Humanity Committed?' (2010) 11 *Chicago Journal of International Law* 439

Guzman, Andrew T, 'Against Consent' (2011) 52 *Virginia Journal of International Law* 747

'Harvard Research in International Law, Jurisdiction with Respect to Crime' (1935) 29 *Supplement to the American Journal of International Law* 435

Hashmi, Sohail H (ed), *State Sovereignty: Change and Persistence in International Relations* (Pennsylvania State University Press, 1997)

Hawkins, Darren G, David A Lake, Daniel L Nielson and Michael J Tierney (eds), *Delegation and Agency in International Organizations* (Cambridge University Press, 2006)

Heller, Kevin Jon and Markus D Dubber (eds), *Handbook of Comparative Criminal Law* (Stanford University Press, 2010)

Heller, Kevin Jon, *The Nuremberg Military Tribunals and the Origins of International Criminal Law* (Oxford University Press, 2011)

Heller, Kevin Jon, 'What Is an International Crime? (A Revisionist History)' (2017) 28 *Harvard International Law Journal* 353

Henckaerts, Jean-Marie and Louise Doswald-Beck (eds), *Customary International Humanitarian Law* (Cambridge University Press, 2005) vol I

Hernández, Gleider I, 'A Reluctant Guardian: The International Court of Justice and the Concept of "International Community"' (2013) 83(1) *British Yearbook of International Law* 13

Hessler, Kristen, 'State Sovereignty as an Obstacle to International Criminal Law' in Larry May and Zachary Hoskins (eds), *International Criminal Law and Philosophy* (Cambridge University Press, 2010) 39

Heyder, Corrina, 'The UN Security Council's Referral of the Crimes in Darfur to the International Criminal Court in Light of US Opposition to the Court: Implications for the International Criminal Court's Functions and Status' (2006) 24 *Berkeley Journal of International Law* 650

Higgins, Rosalyn, 'The Legal Bases of Jurisdiction' in Cecil J Olmstead (ed), *Extra-Territorial Application of Laws and Responses Thereto* (International Law Association in association with ESC Publishers, 1984) 3

Higgins, Rosalyn, *Problems and Process: International Law and How We Use It* (Clarendon, 2000)

Hirst, Michael, *Jurisdiction and the Ambit of the Criminal Law* (Oxford University Press, 2003)

Hobbs, Harry Orr, 'The Security Council and the Complementary Regime of the International Criminal Court: Lessons from Libya' (2012) 9 *Eyes on the ICC* 19

Hoover, Dalila, 'Universal Jurisdiction Not So Universal: Time to Delegate to the International Criminal Court' (2011) 8 *Eyes on the ICC* 73

Hovell, Devika, 'The Authority of Universal Jurisdiction' (2018) 29 *European Journal of International Law* 427

Huikuri, S, 'Empty Promises: Indonesia's Non-Ratification of the Rome Statute of the International Criminal Court' (2017) 30 *The Pacific Review* 74

Inazumi, Mitsue, 'The Meaning of the State Consent Precondition in Article 12(2) of the Rome Statute of the International Criminal Court: A Theoretical Analysis of the Source of International Criminal Jurisdiction' (2002) 49(2) *Netherlands International Law Review* 159

Inazumi, Mitsue, *Universal Jurisdiction in Modern International Law: Expansion of National Jurisdiction for Prosecuting Serious Crimes under International Law* (Intersentia, 2005)

Ireland-Piper, Danielle, 'Extraterritorial Criminal Jurisdiction: Does the Long Arm of the Law Undermine the Rule of Law' (2012) 13 *Melbourne Journal of International Law* 1

Jacobs, Dov, 'The Frog That Wanted to Be an Ox: The ICC's Approach to Immunities and Cooperation' in Carsten Stahn (ed), *The Law and Practice of the International Criminal Court* (Oxford University Press, 2015) 281

Jacobsen, Trudy, CJG Sampford and Ramesh Chandra Thakur (eds), *Re-Envisioning Sovereignty: The End of Westphalia?* (Ashgate, 2008)

Jain, Neha, 'A Separate Law for Peacekeepers: The Clash between the Security Council and the International Criminal Court' (2005) 16(2) *European Journal of International Law* 239

Jescheck, Hans-Heinrich, 'The General Principles of International Criminal Law Set Out in Nuremberg, as Mirrored in the ICC Statute' (2004) 2 *Journal of International Criminal Justice* 38

Jessberger, Florian, 'Universal Jurisdiction' in Antonio Cassese (ed), *The Oxford Companion to International Criminal Justice* (Oxford University Press, 2009) 555

Jianping, Lu and Wang Zhixiang, 'China's Attitude Towards the ICC' (2005) 3(3) *Journal of International Criminal Justice* 608

Jöbstl, Hannes, 'An Unlikely Day in Court? Legal Challenges for the Prosecution of Israeli Settlements under the Rome Statute' (2018) 51(3) *Israel Law Review* 339

Johnson, Larry D, 'The Lubanga Case and Cooperation between the UN and the ICC Disclosure Obligation v. Confidentiality Obligation' (2012) 10(4) *Journal of International Criminal Justice* 887

Joyner, Christopher C, 'Arresting Impunity: The Case for Universal Jurisdiction in Bringing War Criminals to Accountability' (1996) 59 *Law and Contemporary Problems* 153

Kastner, Philipp, 'The ICC in Darfur – Savior or Spoiler' (2007) 14 *ILSA Journal of International & Comparative Law* 145

Kaul, Hans-Peter, 'Preconditions to the Exercise of Jurisdiction' in Antonio Cassese, Paola Gaeta and John RWD Jones (eds), *The Rome Statute of the International Criminal Court: A Commentary* (Oxford University Press, 2002) 583

Kaul, Hans-Peter, 'The International Criminal Court – Its Relationship to Domestic Jurisdictions' in Göran Sluiter and Carsten Stahn (eds), *The Emerging Practice of the International Criminal Court* (Brill, 2008) 31

Kaul, Hans-Peter and Claus Kreß, 'Jurisdiction and Cooperation in the Statute of the International Criminal Court: Principles and Compromises' (1999) 2 *Yearbook of International Humanitarian Law* 143

Kelsen, Hans, 'The Legal Status of Germany According to the Declaration of Berlin' (1945) 39 *American Journal of International Law* 518

Kelsen, Hans, 'Will the Judgment in the Nuremberg Trial Constitute a Precedent in International Law' (1947) 1 *International Law Quarterly* 153

Kelsen, Hans, *The Law of the United Nations: A Critical Analysis of Its Fundamental Problems* (FA Praeger, 1950)

Kielsgard, Mark D, 'War on the International Criminal Court' (2005) 8 *New York City Law Review* 2

King, Henry T Jr, 'The Limitations of Sovereignty from Nuremberg to Sarajevo' (1994) 20 *Canada-United States Law Journal* 167

Kirsch, Philippe and John T Holmes, 'The Rome Conference on an International Court: The Negotiating Process' (1999) 93 *American Journal of International Law* 2

Kirsch, Philippe and Darryl Robinson, 'Reaching Agreement at the Rome Conference' in Antonio Cassese, Paola Gaeta and John RWD Jones (eds), *The Rome Statute of the International Criminal Court: A Commentary* (Oxford University Press, 2002) 67

Kiyani, Asad G, 'Al-Bashir & the ICC: The Problem of Head of State Immunity' (2013) 12(3) *Chinese Journal of International Law* 467

Klabbers, Jan, *An Introduction to International Institutional Law* (Cambridge University Press, 2nd ed, 2009)

Klabbers, Jan, *Treaty Conflict and the European Union* (Cambridge University Press, 2009)

Klabbers, Jan, *International Law* (Cambridge University Press, 2013)

Knop, Karen, 'Statehood: Territory, People, Government' in James Crawford and Martti Koskenniemi (eds), *The Cambridge Companion to International Law* (2012) 95

Knottnerus, Abel S, 'The AU, the ICC, and the Prosecution of African Presidents' in Kamari M Clarke, Abel S Knottnerus and Eefje de Volder (eds), *Africa and the ICC – Perceptions of Justice* (Cambridge University Press, 2016)

Kolb, Robert, 'The Jurisprudence of the Yugoslav and Rwandan Criminal Tribunals on Their Jurisdiction and on International Crimes' (2001) 71(1) *British Yearbook of International Law* 259

Kontorovich, Eugene, 'The Piracy Analogy: Modern Universal Jurisdiction's Hollow Foundation' (2004) 45(1) *Harvard International Law Journal* 185

Kontorovich, Eugene, 'Israel/Palestine – The ICC's Uncharted Territory' (2013) 11(5) *Journal of International Criminal Justice* 979

Koremenos, Barbara, 'When, What, and Why Do States Choose to Delegate' (2008) 71 *Law and Contemporary Problems* 151

Koshy, Ninan, 'International Criminal Court and India' (2004) 39(24) *Economic and Political Weekly* 2439

Koskenniemi, Martti, 'The Politics of International Law' (1990) 1 *European Journal of International Law* 4

Koskenniemi, Martti, 'Legitimacy, Rights, and Ideology – Notes Towards a Critique of the New Moral Internationalism' (2003) 7(2) *Associations: Journal for Legal and Social Theory* 349

Koskenniemi, Martti, *From Apology to Utopia: The Structure of International Legal Argument: Reissue with a New Epilogue* (Cambridge University Press, 2005)

Kreß, Claus, 'The International Criminal Court and the United States: Reflections on Resolution 1422 of the UN Security Council' (2003) 77 *Fikran Wa Fann Art & Thought* 70

Kreß, Claus, 'Universal Jurisdiction over International Crimes and the Institut de Droit International' (2006) 4(3) *Journal of International Criminal Justice* 561

Kreß, Claus, 'Preliminary Observations on the ICC Appeals Chamber's Judgment of 6 May 2019 in the Jordan Referral re Al-Bashir Appeal (Occasional Paper Series No 8, Torkel Opsahl Academic Epublisher, May 2019)

Kreß, Claus and Flavia Lattanzi, (eds), *The Rome Statute and Domestic Legal Orders* (Nomos, 2000)

Kreß, Claus and Kimberly Prost, 'Article 98 Cooperation with Respect to Waiver of Immunity and Consent to Surrender' in O Triffterer, K Ambos (eds), *Rome Statute of the International Criminal Court – A Commentary* (CH Beck Hart Nomos, 3rd ed, 2016)

Kreß, Claus and Leonie von Holtzendorff, 'The Kampala Compromise on the Crime of Aggression' (2010) 8(5) *Journal of International Criminal Justice* 1179

Krisch, Nico, 'Introduction to Chapter VII: The General Framework' in Bruno Simma, Daniel-Erasmus Khan, Georg Nolte, Andreas L Paulus and Nikolai Wessendorf (eds), *The Charter of the United Nations: A Commentary* (Oxford University Press, 2012)

Kritsiotis, Dino, 'Imagining the International Community' (2002) 13(4) *European Journal of International Law* 961

Kuhn, Arthur K, 'International Criminal Jurisdiction' (1947) 41 *American Journal of International Law* 430

La Haye, Eve, 'The Jurisdiction of the International Criminal Court: Controversies over the Preconditions for Exercising Its Jurisdiction' (1999) 46 *Netherlands International Law Review* 1

Lachenmann, Frauke, 'Legal Positivism' *Max Planck Encyclopedia of Public International Law* (Oxford University Press, 2011)

Landry, Benjamin David, 'The Church Abuse Scandal: Prosecuting the Pope before the International Criminal Court' (2011) 12 *Chicago Journal of International Law* 341

Langer, Maximo, 'The Archipelago and the Wheel: The Universal Jurisdiction and the International Criminal Court Regimes' in Cora C True-Frost, Martha Minow and Alex Whiting (eds), *The First Global Prosecutor* (University of Michigan Press, 2015) 204

Lantto, Megan E, 'The United States and the International Criminal Court: A Permanent Divide' (2007) 31 *Suffolk Transnational Law Review* 619

Lattanzi, Flavia, 'The Rome Statute and State Sovereignty: ICC Competence, Jurisdictional Links, Trigger Mechanism' in Flavia Lattanzi and William Schabas (eds), *Essays on the Rome Statute of the International Criminal Court* (Il Sirente, 1999) 51

Lavalle, Roberto, 'A Vicious Storm in a Teacup: The Action by the United Nations Security Council to Narrow the Jurisdiction of the International Criminal Court' (2003) 14(2) *Criminal Law Forum* 195

Lee, Hyeyoung, 'Defining "State" for the Purpose of the International Criminal Court: The Problem Ahead after the Palestine Decision' (2016) 77 *University of Pittsburgh Law Review* 345

Lee, Win-chiat, 'International Crimes and Universal Jurisdiction' in Larry May and Zachary Hoskins (eds), *International Criminal Law and Philosophy* (Cambridge University Press, 2010) 15

Leigh, M, 'The United States and the Statute of Rome' (2001) 95 *American Journal of International Law* 124

Lietzau, William K, 'International Criminal Law after Rome: Concerns from a U.S. Military Perspective' (2001) 64 *Law and Contemporary Problems* 119

Liivoja, Rain, 'The Scope of the Supremacy Clause of the United Nations Charter' (2008) 57 *International and Comparative Law Quarterly* 583

Liivoja, Rain, 'The Criminal Jurisdiction of States – A Theoretical Primer' (2010) 7 *No Foundations* 27

Liivoja, Rain, 'Treaties, Custom and Universal Jurisdiction' in Rain Liivoja and Jarna Petman (eds), *International Law-Making: Essays in Honour of Jan Klabbers* (Routledge, 2013) 298

Liivoja, Rain, *Criminal Jurisdiction over Armed Forces Abroad* (Cambridge University Press, 2017)

Luban, David, 'A Theory of Crimes against Humanity' (2004) 29 *Yale Journal of International Law* 85

Luban, David, 'Fairness to Rightness: Jurisdiction, Legality and the Legitimacy of International Criminal Law' in Samantha Besson and John Tasioulas (eds), *The Philosophy of International Law* (Oxford University Press, 2010) 584

Luban, David, 'Hannah Arendt as a Theorist of International Criminal Law' (2011) 11 *International Criminal Law Review* 621

Mann, Frederick A, 'The Present Legal Status of Germany' (1947) 1 *International Law Quarterly* 314.

Mann, Frederick A, 'The Doctrine of Jurisdiction in International Law' (1964) 111 *Recueil des Cours de l'Academie de Droit Internationale* 1

Mann, Frederick A, 'The Doctrine of International Jurisdiction Revisited After Twenty Years' (1984) 186 *Recueil des Cours de l'Academie de Droit Internationale* 9

Maogoto, Jackson Nyamuya, *State Sovereignty and International Criminal Law: Versailles to Rome* (Transnational Publishers, 2003)

Martenczuk, Bernd, 'The Security Council, the International Court and Judicial Review: What Lessons from Lockerbie?' (1999) 10(3) *European Journal of International Law* 517

Martines, Francesca, 'Legal Status and Powers of the Court' in Antonio Cassese, Paola Gaeta and John RWD Jones (eds), *The Rome Statute of the International Criminal Court: A Commentary* (Oxford University Press, 2002) 203

May, Larry, *Crimes Against Humanity: A Normative Account* (Cambridge University Press, 2004)

McCormack, Timothy LH, 'Crimes Against Humanity' in Dominic McGoldrick, Peter Rowe and Eric Donnelly (eds), *The Permanent International Criminal Court: Legal and Policy Issues* (Hart Publishing, 2004) 198

McCormack, Timothy LH, 'An Australian Perspective on the ICRC Customary International Humanitarian Law Study' (2006) 82 *International Law Studies* 81

McCormack, Timothy LH and Sue Robertson, 'Jurisdictional Aspects of the Rome Statute for the New International Criminal Court' (1999) 23 *Melbourne University Law Review* 635

McDougall, Carrie, *The Crime of Aggression under the Rome Statute of the International Criminal Court* (Cambridge University Press, 2013)

McEvoy, Patrick, 'Reflections on US Opposition to the International Criminal Court' (2006) 6 *Hibernian Law Journal* 33

Meessen, Karl M, 'International Law Limitations on State Jurisdiction' in Cecil J Olmstead (ed), *Extra-Territorial Application of Laws and Responses Thereto* (International Law Association in association with ESC Publishing, 1984) 38

Meessen, Karl M (ed), *Extraterritorial Jurisdiction in Theory and Practice* (Kluwer Law International, 1996)

Mégret, Frédéric, 'Epilogue to an Endless Debate: The International Criminal Court's Third Party Jurisdiction and the Looming Revolution of International Law' (2001) 12(2) *European Journal of International Law* 247

Mégret, Frédéric, 'In Search of the "Vertical": Towards an Institutional Theory of International Criminal Justice's Core' in Carsten Stahn and Larissa van den Herik (eds), *Future Perspectives on International Criminal Justice* (TMC Asser Press, 2010) 178

Meron, Theodor, 'International Criminalization of Internal Atrocities' (1995) 89 *American Journal of International Law* 554

Meyer, Jurgen, 'The Vicarious Administration of Justice: An Overlooked Basis of Jurisdiction' (1990) 31 *Harvard International Law Journal* 108

Milanović, Marko, 'From Compromise to Principle: Clarifying the Concept of State Jurisdiction in Human Rights Treaties' (2008) 8 *Human Rights Law Review* 411

Milanović, Marko, 'Is the Rome Statute Binding on Individuals? (And Why We Should Care)' (2011) 9(1) *Journal of International Criminal Justice* 25

Milanović, Marko, 'Aggression and Legality Custom in Kampala' (2012) 10(1) *Journal of International Criminal Justice* 165

Militello, Vincenzo, 'The Personal Nature of Individual Criminal Responsibility and the ICC Statute' (2007) 5(4) *Journal of International Criminal Justice* 941

Mokhtar, Aly, 'The Fine Art of Arm-Twisting: The US, Resolution 1422 and Security Council Deferral Power under the Rome Statue' (2003) 3 *International Criminal Law Review* 295

Morris, Madeline H, 'The Trials of Concurrent Jurisdiction: The Case of Rwanda' (1996) 7 *Duke Journal of Comparative & International Law* 349

Morris, Madeline, 'The Jurisdiction of the International Criminal Court over Nationals of Non-Party States (Conference Remarks)' (1999) 6 *ILSA Journal of International & Comparative Law* 363

Morris, Madeline, 'High Crimes and Misconceptions: The ICC and Non-Party States' (2001) 64 *Law and Contemporary Problems* 13

Morris, Madeline, 'Universal Jurisdiction in a Divided World: Conference Remarks' (2001) 35 *New England Law Review* 337

Morss, John R, 'The International Legal Status of the Vatican/Holy See Complex' (2015) 26 *European Journal of International Law* 927

Muller, AS, 'Setting up the International Criminal Court: Not One Moment but a Series of Moments' (2004) 1 *International Organizations Law Review* 189

Naqvi, Yasmin, *Impediments to Exercising Jurisdiction over International Crimes* (TMC Asser Press, 2010)

Nasu, Hitoshi, *International Law on Peacekeeping: A Study of Article 40 of the UN Charter* (Martinus Nijhoff Publishers, 2009)

Nesi, Giuseppe and Mauro Politi (eds), *The Rome Statute of the International Criminal Court: A Challenge to Impunity* (Ashgate, 2001)

Newton, Michael A, 'How the International Criminal Court Threatens Treaty Norms' (2016) 49 *Vanderbilt Journal of Transnational Law* 371

Nikolova, Mariya and Manuel J Ventura, 'The Special Tribunal for Lebanon Declines to Review UN Security Council Action Retreating from Tadić's Legacy in the Ayyash Jurisdiction and Legality Decisions' (2013) 11(3) *Journal of International Criminal Justice* 615

Nolte, Georg, 'The Limits of the Security Council's Powers and Its Functions in the International Legal System: Some Reflections' in Michael Byers (ed), *The Role of Law in International Politics* (Oxford University Press, 2001) 315

Nolte, Georg, 'The Fourth Restatement of Foreign Relations Law of the United States' (2014) 108 *Proceedings of the Annual Meeting-American Society of International Law* 27

Nouwen, Sarah MH, *Complementarity in the Line of Fire: The Catalysing Effect of the International Criminal Court in Uganda and Sudan* (Cambridge University Press, 2013)

O'Keefe, Roger, 'Universal Jurisdiction: Clarifying the Basic Concept' (2004) 2(3) *Journal of International Criminal Justice* 735

O'Keefe, Roger, 'The United States and the ICC: The Force and Farce of the Legal Arguments' (2011) 24(3) *Cambridge Review of International Affairs* 335

O'Keefe, Roger, 'An "International Crime" Exception to the Immunity of State Officials from Foreign Criminal Jurisdiction: Not Currently, Not Likely' (2015) 109 *AJIL Unbound* 167

O'Keefe, Roger, *International Criminal Law* (Oxford University Press, 2015)

O'Keefe, Roger, 'Quid Not Quantum: A Comment on How the International Criminal Court Threatens Treaty Norms' (2016) 49 *Vanderbilt Journal of Transnational Law* 433

O'Neill, Kerry Creque, 'A New Customary Law of Head of State Immunity? Hirohito and Pinochet' (2002) 38 *Stanford Journal of International Law* 289

Öberg, Marko Divac, 'The Legal Effects of Resolutions of the UN Security Council and General Assembly in the Jurisprudence of the ICJ' (2005) 16(5) *European Journal of International Law* 879

Olásolo, Héctor, *The Triggering Procedure of the International Criminal Court* (Martinus Nijhoff Publishers, 2005)

Oosthuizen, Gabriël H, 'Playing the Devil's Advocate: The United Nations Security Council is Unbound by Law' (1999) 12(3) *Leiden Journal of International Law* 549

Orentlicher, Diane F, 'Universal Jurisdiction: A Pragmatic Strategy in Pursuit of a Moralist's Vision' in Leila Sadat and Michael P Scharf (eds), *The Theory and Practice of International Criminal Law* (Brill, 2008) 127

Orford, Anne, *International Authority and the Responsibility to Protect* (Cambridge University Press, 2011)

Pace, William R, 'The ICC Review Conference and Changing U.S. Policy toward the Court: Remarks' (2010) 104 *American Society of International Law Proceedings* 517

Papillon, Sophie, 'Has the United Nations Security Council Implicitly Removed Al Bashir's Immunity?' (2010) 10(2) *International Criminal Law Review* 275

Paust, Jordan J, 'The Reach of ICC Jurisdiction over Non-Signatory Nationals' (2000) 33 *Vanderbilt Journal of Transnational Law* 1

Pedretti, Ramona, *Immunity of Heads of State and State Officials for International Crimes* (Brill Nijhoff, 2015)

Pichon, Jakob, 'The Principle of Complementarity in the Cases of the Sudanese Nationals Ahmad Harun and Ali Kushayb before the International Criminal Court' (2008) 8 *International Criminal Law Review* 185

Pikis, Georghios M, *The Rome Statute for the International Criminal Court – Analysis of the Statute, the Rules of Procedure and Evidence, the Regulations of the Court and Supplementary Instruments* (Martinus Nijhoff Publishers, 2010)

Plachta, Michael, 'The Lockerbie Case: The Role of the Security Council in Enforcing the Principle *Aut Dedere Aut Judicare*' (2001) 12 *European Journal of International Law* 125

Ralph, Jason G, *Defending the Society of States: Why America Opposes the International Criminal Court and Its Vision of World Society* (Oxford University Press, 2007)

Ramanathan, Usha, 'India and the ICC' (2005) 3 *Journal of International Criminal Justice* 627

Ramsden, Michael and Isaac Yeung, 'Head of State Immunity and the Rome Statute: A Critique of the PTC's Malawi and DRC Decisions' (2016) 16 *International Criminal Law Review* 1

Randall, Kenneth C, 'Universal Jurisdiction under International Law' (1987) 66 *Texas Law Review* 785

Ranganathan, Surabhi, *Strategically Created Treaty Conflicts and the Politics of International Law* (Cambridge University Press, 2014)

Rastan, Rod, 'The Jurisdictional Scope of Situations Before the International Criminal Court' (2012) 23 *Criminal Law Forum* 1

Rastan, Rod, 'Jurisdiction' in Carsten Stahn (ed), *The Law and Practice of the International Criminal Court* (Oxford University Press, 2015) 142

Reisinger Coracini, Astrid, '"Amended Most Serious Crimes": A New Category of Core Crimes within the Jurisdiction but out of the Reach of the International Criminal Court?' (2008) 21(03) *Leiden Journal of International Law* 699

Reisinger Coracini, Astrid, 'Evaluating Domestic Legislation on the Customary Crime of Aggression under the Rome Statute's Complementarity Regime' in Carsten Stahn and Goran Sluiter (eds), *The Emerging Practice of the International Criminal Court* (Martinus Nijhoff Publishers, 2009) 726

Reisinger Coracini, Astrid, 'The International Criminal Court's Exercise of Jurisdiction over the Crime of Aggression – At Last ... in Reach ... over Some' (2010) 2 *Goettingen Journal of International Law* 745

Reisman, W Michael, 'Editorial Comment: On Paying the Piper: Financial Responsibility for Security Council Referrals to the International Criminal Court' (2005) 99 *American Journal of International Law* 615

Restatement of the Law Third, Foreign Relations Law of the United States (American Law Institute, 1987)

Restatement of the Law Fourth, Foreign Relations Law of the United States (American Law Institute, 2017)

Reydams, Luc, *Universal Jurisdiction: International and Municipal Legal Perspectives* (Oxford University Press, 2003)

Roach, Steven C, 'Should the International Criminal Court Impose Justice?' (2012) *Yale Journal of International Affairs* 64

Roberts, Ivor, 'Privileges and Immunities of Diplomatic Agents' in Ivor Roberts (ed), *Satow's Diplomatic Practice* (Oxford University Press, 6th ed, 2009) 121

Robertson, Geoffrey, *The Case of the Pope: Vatican Accountability for Human Rights Abuse* (Penguin Books, 2010)

Robinson, Darryl, 'The Controversy over Territorial State Referrals and Reflections on ICL Discourse' (2011) 9(2) *Journal of International Criminal Justice* 355

Ronen, Yaël, 'ICC Jurisdiction over Acts Committed in the Gaza Strip Article 12(3) of the ICC Statute and Non-State Entities' (2010) 8(1) *Journal of International Criminal Justice* 3

Ronen, Yaël, 'Israel, Palestine and the ICC – Territory Uncharted but Not Unknown' (2014) 12(1) *Journal of International Criminal Justice* 7

Ronen, Yaël, 'Recognition of the State of Palestine: Still Too Much Too Soon?' in Christine Chinkin and Freya Baetens (eds), *Sovereignty, Statehood and State Responsibility: Essays in Honour of James Crawford* (Cambridge University Press, 2015) 229

Rosenfeld, Erik, 'Application of U.S. Status of Forces Agreements to Article 98 of the Rome Statute' (2003) 2(1) *Washington University Global Studies Law Review* 273

Ruiz Verduzco, Deborah, 'The Relationship between the ICC and the United Nations Security Council' in Carsten Stahn (ed), *The Law and Practice of the International Criminal Court* (Oxford University Press, 2015) 30

Rutigliano Jr, Joseph A, 'Fundamental Concerns: Why the US Government Should Not Accede to the Rome Statute' (2014) 63 *Naval Law Review* 92

Ryngaert, Cedric, *Jurisdiction in International Law* (Oxford University Press, 2nd ed, 2015)

Ryngaert, Cedric and Sven Sobrie, 'Recognition of States: International Law or Realpolitik? The Practice of Recognition in the Wake of Kosovo, South Ossetia, and Abkhazia' (2011) 24(2) *Leiden Journal of International Law* 467

Sadat, Leila N, 'Unpacking the Complexities of International Criminal Tribunal Jurisdiction' (Social Science Research Network, 31 March 2010) papers.ssrn.com/abstract=1583105

Sadat, Leila Nadya (ed), *Forging a Convention for Crimes Against Humanity* (Cambridge University Press, 2011)

Sadat, Leila Nadya, 'Heads of State and Other Government Officials Before the International Criminal Court: The Uneasy Revolution Continues' (Research Paper No 19-01-12, Washington University in St Louis School of Law, January 2019)

Sadat, Leila Nadya and S Richard Carden, 'The New International Criminal Court: An Uneasy Revolution' (1999) 88 *Georgetown Law Journal* 381

Sadat, Leila and Michael Scharf (eds), *The Theory and Practice of International Criminal Law* (Brill, 2008)

Sammons, Anthony, 'The Under-Theorization of Universal Jurisdiction: Implications for Legitimacy on Trials of War Criminals by National Courts' (2003) 21 *Berkeley Journal of International Law* 111

Sands, Philippe (ed), *From Nuremberg to the Hague: The Future of International Criminal Justice* (Cambridge University Press, 2003)

Sands, Philippe and Pierre Klein, *Bowett's Law of International Institutions* (Sweet & Maxwell, 6th ed, 2009)

Sari, Aurel, 'The Status of Foreign Armed Forces Deployed in Post-Conflict Environments: A Search for Basic Principles' in Carsten Stahn, Jennifer S Easterday and Jens Iverson (eds), *Jus Post Bellum: Mapping the Normative Foundations* (Oxford University Press, 2014) 467

Sari, Aurel, 'The Status of Armed Forces in Public International Law: Jurisdiction and Immunity' in Alexander Orakhelashvili (ed), *Research Handbook on Jurisdiction and Immunities in International Law* (Edward Elgar Publishing, 2015) 319

Sarooshi, Danesh, *The United Nations and the Development of Collective Security: The Delegation by the UN Security Council of Its Chapter VII Powers* (Clarendon Press; Oxford University Press, 1999)

Sarooshi, Dan, 'Aspects of the Relationship between the International Criminal Court and the United Nations' (2001) 32 *Netherlands Yearbook of International Law* 27

Sarooshi, Dan, 'Some Preliminary Remarks on the Conferral by States of Powers on International Organizations' [2003] *Jean Monnet Working Paper* jeanmon netprogram.org/archive/papers/03/030401.rtf

Sarooshi, Dan, 'The Essentially Contested Nature of the Concept of Sovereignty: Implications for the Exercise by International Organizations of Delegated Powers of Government' (2003) 25 *Michigan Journal of International Law* 1107

Sarooshi, Dan, 'Conferrals by States of Powers on International Organizations: The Case of Agency' (2004) 74(1) *British Yearbook of International Law* 291

Sarooshi, Dan, 'The Peace and Justice Paradox: The International Criminal Court and the UN Security Council' in Dominic McGoldrick, Peter Rowe and Eric Donnelly (eds), *The Permanent International Criminal Court: Legal and Policy Issues* (Hart Publishing, 2004) 96

Sarooshi, Danesh, *International Organizations and Their Exercise of Sovereign Powers* (Oxford University Press, 2005)

Sarooshi, Dan, 'The Role of Domestic Public Law Analogies in the Law of International Organizations' (2008) 5(2) *International Organizations Law Review* 237

Saxum, Erica J, 'The ICC versus Sudan: How Does the Darfur Case Impact the Principle of Complementarity' (2009) 6 *Eyes on the ICC* 1

Schabas, William, *An Introduction to the International Criminal Court* (Cambridge University Press, 4th ed, 2011)

Schabas, William, *The International Criminal Court: A Commentary on the Rome Statute* (Oxford University Press, 2nd ed, 2016)

Schabas, William and Giulia Pecorella, 'Article 12 Preconditions to the Exercise of Jurisdiction' in Otto Triffterer and Kai Ambos (eds), *Rome Statute of the International Criminal Court – A Commentary* (CH Beck Hart Nomos, 3rd ed, 2016) 672

Schabas, William and Giulia Pecorella, 'Article 13 Exercise of Jurisdiction' in Otto Triffterer and Kai Ambos (eds), *Rome Statute of the International Criminal Court – A Commentary* (CH Beck Hart Nomos, 3rd ed, 2016) 690

Schaeffer, Robert, 'The Audacity of Compromise: The UN Security Council and the Pre-Conditions to the Exercise of Jurisdiction by the ICC with Regard to the Crime of Aggression' (2009) 9(2) *International Criminal Law Review* 411

Scharf, Michael P, 'Application of Treaty-Based Universal Jurisdiction to Nationals of Non-Party States' (2001) 35 *New England Law Review* 363

Scharf, Michael P, 'The ICC's Jurisdiction over the Nationals of Non-Party States: A Critique of the U.S. Position' (2001) 64 *Law and Contemporary Problems* 67

Scharf, Michael P, 'The Lockerbie Model of Transfer of Proceedings' in M Cherif Bassiouni (ed), *International Criminal Law* (Martinus Nijhoff Publishers, 3rd ed, 2008) vol II

Scharf, Michael P, 'Introductory Note to the International Criminal Court's Arrest Warrant for Omar Al Bashir, President of the Sudan' (2009) 48 *International Legal Materials* 463

Scharf, Michael P, 'Universal Jurisdiction and the Crime of Aggression' (2012) 53 *Harvard International Law Journal* 357

Scharf, Michael P and Thomas C Fischer, 'Foreword' (2000) 35 *New England Law Review* 227

Scheffer, David, 'The International Criminal Court: The Challenge of Jurisdiction' (1999) 93 *American Society of International Law Proceedings* 68

Scheffer, David, 'The United States and the International Criminal Court' (1999) 93 *American Journal of International Law* 12

Scheffer, David, 'Opening Address' (2000) 35 *New England Law Review* 233

Scheffer, David, 'Letter to the Editors' (2001) 95 *American Journal of International Law* 624

Scheffer, David J, 'Staying the Course with the International Criminal Court' (2001) 35 *Cornell International Law Journal* 47

Scheffer, David, 'Article 98(2) of the Rome Statute: America's Original Intent' (2005) 3(2) *Journal of International Criminal Justice* 333

Scheffer, David, 'The Complex Crime of Aggression under the Rome Statute' (2011) 43 *Studies in Transnational Legal Policy* 173

Scheipers, Sibylle, *Negotiating Sovereignty and Human Rights: International Society and the International Criminal Court* (Manchester University Press, 2009)

Schermers, Henry G and Niels Blokker, *International Institutional Law: Unity within Diversity* (Brill Nijhoff, 6th ed, 2018)

Schmitt, Carl, *Political Theology: Four Chapters on the Concept of Sovereignty* (MIT Press, 1985)

Schwarzenberger, Georg, 'The Problem of an International Criminal Law' (1950) 3 (1) *Current Legal Problems* 263

Scobbie, Iain, 'New Wine in Old Bottles or Old Wine in New Bottles or Only Old Wine in Old Bottles? Reflections on the Assertion of Jurisdiction in Public International Law' in Stratos V Konstadinidis, Malcolm D Evans and Patrick Capps (eds), *Asserting Jurisdiction: International and European Legal Approaches* (Hart Publishing, 2003) 17

Seyersted, Finn, *Common Law of International Organizations* (Martinus Nijhoff Publishers, 2008)

Shany, Yuval, *The Competing Jurisdictions of International Courts and Tribunals* (Oxford University Press, 2003)

Shany, Yuval, *Regulating Jurisdictional Relations between National and International Courts* (Oxford University Press, 2007)

Shany, Yuval, 'In Defence of Functional Interpretation of Article 12(3) of the Rome Statute: A Response to Yaël Ronen' (2010) 8(2) *Journal of International Criminal Justice* 329

Shany, Yuval, *Assessing the Effectiveness of International Courts* (Oxford University Press, 2014)

Shany, Yuval, *Questions of Jurisdiction and Admissibility before International Courts* (Cambridge University Press, 2016)

Shaw, Malcolm N, 'The Article 12(3) Declaration of the Palestinian Authority, the International Criminal Court and International Law' (2011) 9(2) *Journal of International Criminal Justice* 301

Shaw, Malcolm N, *International Law* (Cambridge University Press, 7th ed, 2014)

Shearer, Ivan, 'Jurisdiction' in Sam Blay, Martin Tsamenyi and Ryszard Piotrowicz (eds), *Public International Law: An Australian Perspective* (Oxford University Press, 2nd ed, 2005) 154

Shelton, Dinah (ed), *International Crimes, Peace, and Human Rights: The Role of the International Criminal Court* (Transnational Publishers, 2000)

Simbeye, Yitiha, *Immunity and International Criminal Law* (Ashgate, 2004)

Simma, Bruno, Daniel-Erasmus Khan, Georg Nolte, Andreas Paulus and Nikolai Wessendorf (eds), *The Charter of the United Nations: A Commentary* (Oxford University Press, 3rd ed, 2012)

Simma, Bruno and Andreas L Paulus, 'The Responsibility of Individuals for Human Rights Abuses in Internal Conflicts: A Positivist View' (1999) 93 *American Journal of International Law* 302

Simmons, David, 'The Caribbean Court of Justice: A Unique Institution of Caribbean Creativity' (2004) 29 *Nova Law Review* 171

Simons, Wiliam B, 'The Jurisdictional Bases of the International Military Tribunal at Nuremberg' in George Ginsburgs and VN Kudriavtsev (eds), *The Nuremberg Trial and International Law* (Martinus Nijhoff Publishers, 1990) 39

Sivakumaran, Sandesh, 'Identifying An Armed Conflict Not of an International Character' in Göran Sluiter and Carsten Stahn (eds), *The Emerging Practice of the International Criminal Court* (Brill, 2008) 361

Sluiter, Göran, 'Obtaining Cooperation from Sudan – Where Is the Law?' (2008) 6(5) *Journal of International Criminal Justice* 871

Ssenyonjo, Manisuli, 'The International Criminal Court Arrest Warrant Decision for President Al Bashir of Sudan' (2010) 59(1) *International & Comparative Law Quarterly* 205

Stahn, Carsten, 'The Ambiguities of Security Council Resolution 1422 (2002)' (2003) 14(1) *European Journal of International Law* 85

Stahn, Carsten and Jann K Kleffner (eds), *Jus Post Bellum: Towards a Law of Transition from Conflict to Peace* (TMC Asser; Cambridge University Press, 2008)

Stahn, Carsten and Mohamed El Zeidy (eds), *The International Criminal Court and Complementarity: From Theory to Practice* (Cambridge University Press, 2011)

Stein, Mark S, 'The Security Council, the International Criminal Court, and the Crime of Aggression: How Exclusive Is the Security Council's Power to Determine Aggression' (2005) 16 *Indiana International and Comparative Law Review* 1

Stephens, Jon, 'Don't Tread on Me: Absence of Jurisdiction by the International Criminal Court over the U.S. and Other Non-Signatory States' (2005) 52 *Naval Law Review* 151

Sterio, Milena, 'The Case of Kosovo: Self-Determination, Secession, and Statehood under International Law' (2010) 104 *Proceedings of the Annual Meeting (American Society of International Law)* 361

Stone, Christopher D, 'Common but Differentiated Responsibilities in International Law' (2004) 98 *American Journal of International Law* 276

Strapatsas, Nicolaos, 'Universal Jurisdiction and the International Criminal Court' (2002) 29 *Manitoba Law Journal* 1

Takemura, Hitomi, 'Reconsidering the Meaning and Actuality of the Legitimacy of the International Criminal Court' (2012) 4(2) *Amsterdam Law Forum* 3

Takemura, Hitomi, 'The Asian Region and the International Criminal Court' in Y Nakanishi (ed), *Contemporary Issues in Human Rights Law – Europe and Asia* (Springer Open, 2018) 107

Tallman, David A, 'Catch 98(2): Article 98 Agreements and the Dilemma of Treaty Conflict' (2004) 92 *Georgetown Law Journal* 1033

Talmon, Stefan, 'Ch.I Purposes and Principles, Article 2(6)' in Bruno Simma, Daniel-Erasmus Khan, Georg Nolte, Andreas L Paulus and Nikolai Wessendorf (eds), *The Charter of the United Nations: A Commentary* (Oxford University Press, 2012)

Thirawat, J, 'To Join or Not to Join the International Criminal Court: The Thai Dilemma' (2005) 1 *Asia-Pacific Yearbook of International Humanitarian Law* 168

Tladi, Dire, 'The ICC Decisions on Chad and Malawi' (2013) 11(1) *Journal of International Criminal Justice* 199

Tofan, Claudia (ed), *The Long and Winding Road to ... Rome: A Brief History of the ICC* (International Courts Association by Wolf Legal Publishers, 2011)

Trahan, Jennifer, 'Revisiting the Role of the Security Council Concerning the International Criminal Court's Crime of Aggression' (2019) 17 *Journal of International Criminal Justice* 471

Triffterer, Otto, '"Irrelevance of Official Capacity" – Article 27 Rome Statute Undermined by Obligations under International Law or by Agreement (Article 98)?' in Isabelle Buffard, James Crawford, Alain Pellet and Stephan Wittich (eds), *International Law between Universalism and Fragmentation* (Martinus Nijhoff Publishers, 2008) 571

Triffterer, Otto and Kai Ambos (eds), *The Rome Statute of the International Criminal Court – A Commentary* (CH Beck Hart Nomos, 3rd ed, 2016)

Triffterer, Otto and Christoph Burchard, 'Article 27 Irrelevance of Official Capacity' in Otto Triffterer and Kai Ambos (eds), *Rome Statute of the International Criminal Court – A Commentary* (CH Beck Hart Nomos, 3rd ed, 2016) 1037

Triggs, Gillian D, *International Law: Contemporary Principles and Practices* (LexisNexis Butterworths, 2006)

Tunks, Michael A, 'Diplomats or Defendants? Defining the Future of Head-of-State Immunity' (2002) 52(3) *Duke Law Journal* 651

Tzanakopoulos, Antonios, *Disobeying the Security Council* (Oxford University Press, 2011)

Vagias, Michail, 'The Territorial Jurisdiction of the International Criminal Court – A Jurisdictional Rule of Reason for the ICC?' (2012) 59(1) *Netherlands International Law Review* 43

Vagias, Michail, *The Territorial Jurisdiction of the International Criminal Court* (Cambridge University Press, 2014)

van Alebeek, Rosanne, *The Immunity of States and Their Officials in International Criminal Law and International Human Rights Law* (Oxford University Press, 2008)

Van Panhuys, HF, 'In the Borderland between the Act of State Doctrine and Questions of Jurisdictional Immunities' (1964) 13 *International and Comparative Law Quarterly* 1193

Van Schaack, Beth, 'Negotiating at the Interface of Power and Law: The Crime of Aggression' (2011) 49(3) *Columbia Journal of Transnational Law* 505

Van Schaack, Beth, 'Par in Parem Imperium Non Habet Complementarity and the Crime of Aggression' (2012) 10(1) *Journal of International Criminal Justice* 133

Van Sliedregt, Elise, 'International Crimes before Dutch Courts: Recent Developments' (2007) 20 *Leiden Journal of International Law* 895

Vattel, Emer de, *The Law of Nations, Or, Principles of the Law of Nature Applied to the Conduct and Affairs of Nations and Sovereigns: A Work Tending to Display the True Interest of Powers* (Printed by TM Pomroy for S & E Butler, 1805)

Vidmar, Jure, 'International Legal Responses to Kosovo's Declaration of Independence' [2009] *Vanderbilt Journal of Transnational Law* 779

von Hebel, Herman and Darryl Robinson, 'Crimes within the Jurisdiction of the Court' in Roy S Lee (ed), *The International Criminal Court – The Making of the Rome Statute* (Kluwer Law International, 1999) 79

Wagner, Markus, 'The ICC and Its Jurisdiction – Myths, Misperceptions and Realities' (2003) 7 *Max Planck Yearbook of United Nations Law* 409

Walker, Andrew J, 'When a Good Idea Is Poorly Implemented: How the International Criminal Court Fails to Be Insulated from International Politics and to Protect Basic Due Process Guarantees' (2003) 106 *West Virginia Law Review* 245

Wallerstein, Shlomit, 'Delegation of Powers and Authority in International Criminal Law' (2015) 9 *Criminal Law and Philosophy* 124

Watson, Geoffrey R, *The Oslo Accords: International Law and the Israeli–Palestinian Peace Agreements* (Oxford, Oxford University Press, Tokyo, Oxford University Press, 2000)

Watts, Sir Arthur, 'The Legal Position in International Law of Heads of State, Heads of Government and Foreign Ministers' (1994) 247 *Recueil des Cours de l'Academie de Droit Internationale* 9

Wedgwood, Ruth, 'The International Criminal Court: An American View' (1999) 10(1) *European Journal of International Law* 93

Wedgwood, Ruth, 'The Irresolution of Rome' (2001) 64 *Law and Contemporary Problems* 193

Wedgwood, Ruth, 'Justice & Sovereignty: Implications of the International Criminal Court' (2003) 8 *UCLA Journal of International Law and Foreign Affairs* 45

Weil, Prosper, 'International Law Limitations on State Jurisdiction' in Cecil J Olmstead (ed), *Extra-Territorial Application of Laws and Responses Thereto* (International Law Association in association with ESC, 1984) 32

Weiler, JHH, 'The Geology of International Law – Governance, Democracy and Legitimacy' (2004) 64 *Heidelberg Journal of International Law* 547

Wellman, Christopher Heath, 'Piercing Sovereignty: A Rationale for International Jurisdiction Over Crimes That Do Not Cross International Borders' in RA Duff and Stuart Green (eds), *Philosophical Foundations of Criminal Law* (Oxford University Press, 2011) 462

Werle, Gerhard, 'Individual Criminal Responsibility in Article 25 ICC Statute' (2007) 5(4) *Journal of International Criminal Justice* 953

Werle, Gerhard and Florian Jessberger, *Principles of International Criminal Law* (TMC Asser Press, 3rd ed, 2014)

Wexler, Ian, 'A Comfortable Sofa: The Need for an Equitable Foreign Criminal Jurisdiction Agreement with Iraq' (2008) 56 *Naval Law Review* 43

White, Nigel D, *The Law of International Organisations* (Manchester University Press, 2nd ed, 2005)

White, Nigel and Robert Cryer, 'The ICC and the Security Council: An Uncomfortable Relationship' in José Doria, Hans-Peter Gasser and M Cherif Bassiouni (eds), *The Legal Regime of the International Criminal Court* (Martinus Nijhoff Publishers, 2009) 455

Wickremasinghe, Chanaka, 'Immunities Enjoyed by Officials of States and International Organizations' in Malcolm D Evans (ed), *International Law* (Oxford University Press, 3rd ed, 2010)

Wilke, Christiane, 'A Particular Universality: Universal Jurisdiction for Crimes Against Humanity in Domestic Courts' (2005) 12(1) *Constellations* 83

Williams, Sarah, *Hybrid and Internationalised Criminal Tribunals: Selected Jurisdictional Issues* (Hart Publishing, 2012)

Williams, Sharon A, 'The Rome Statute on the International Criminal Court – Universal Jurisdiction or State Consent – To Make or Break the Package Deal' (2000) 75 *International Law Studies* 539

Wilmshurst, Elizabeth, 'Jurisdiction of the Court' in Roy S Lee (ed), *The International Criminal Court – The Making of the Rome Statute* (Kluwer Law International, 1999) 127

Wilmshurst, Elizabeth and Susan Breau (eds), *Perspectives on the ICRC Study on Customary International Humanitarian Law* (Cambridge University Press, 2007)

Wirth, Steffen, 'Immunities, Related Problems, and Article 98 of the Rome Statute' (2001) 12(4) *Criminal Law Forum* 429

Wirth, Steffen, 'Immunity for Core Crimes? The ICJ's Judgment in the Congo v. Belgium Case' (2002) 13(4) *European Journal of International Law* 877

Woetzel, Robert K, *The Nuremberg Trials in International Law with a Postlude on the Eichmann Case* (Steven & Sons Ltd, 1962)

Wolf, Willem-Jan van der, *Prosecution and Punishment of International Crimes by National Courts* (International Courts Association, 2011)

Wolfrum, Rüdiger, 'The Decentralized Prosecution of International Offences through National Courts' in Yoram Dinstein and Mala Tabory (eds), *War Crimes in International Law* (Martinus Nijhoff Publishers, 1996) 233

Worster, William Thomas, 'The Exercise of Jurisdiction by the International Criminal Court over Palestine' (2010) 26 *American University International Law Review* 1153

Wuerth, Ingrid, 'Pinochet's Legacy Reassessed' (2012) 106 *American Journal of International Law* 731

Yee, Sienho, 'Universal Jurisdiction: Concept, Logic, and Reality' (2011) 10(3) *Chinese Journal of International Law* 503

Zappalà, Salvatore, 'Do Heads of State in Office Enjoy Immunity from Jurisdiction for International Crimes? The Ghaddafi Case Before the French Cour de Cassation' (2001) 12(3) *European Journal of International Law* 595

Zappalà, Salvatore, 'The Reaction of the US to the Entry into Force of the ICC Statute: Comments on UN SC Resolution 1422 (2002) and Article 98 Agreements' (2003) 1(1) *Journal of International Criminal Justice* 114

Zimmermann, Andreas, 'Amending the Amendment Provisions of the Rome Statute: The Kampala Compromise on the Crime of Aggression and the Law of Treaties' (2012) 10 *Journal of International Criminal Justice* 209

Zimmermann, Andreas and Carsten Stahn, 'Yugoslav Territory, United Nations Trusteeship or Sovereign State? Reflections on the Current and Future Legal Status of Kosovo' (2001) 70 *Nordic Journal of International Law* 423

Zimmermann, Andreas, Christian J Tams, Karin Oellers-Frahm and Christian Tomuschat (eds), *The Statute of the International Court of Justice: A Commentary* (Oxford Commentaries on International Law, 2nd ed, 2012)

Zuleeg, Manfred, 'Vertragskonkurrenz im Völkerrecht. Teil I: Verträge zwischen souveränen Staaten' (1977) 20 *German Yearbook of International Law* 246
Zuppi, Alberto L, 'Aggression as International Crime: Unattainable Crusade or Finally Conquering the Evil?' (2007) 26 *Penn State International Law Review* 2

United Nations Documents

Affirmation of the Principles of International Law recognised by the Charter of the Nuremberg Tribunal, GA Res 95, UN GAOR, 2nd sess, UN Doc A/Res 95 (1946)
Final Report of the Commission of Experts Established Pursuant to Security Council Resolution 780 (1992), UN Doc S/1994/674 (27 May 1994)
GA Res 47/1, UN GAOR, 7th plen mtg, UN Doc A/RES/47/1 (22 September 1992)
GA Res 55/12, UN GAOR, 48th plen mtg, UN Doc A/RES/55/12 (1 November 2000)
Hernández, Concepción Escobar, Special Rapporteur, *Fifth report on the immunity of State officials from foreign criminal jurisdiction*, UN Doc A/CN.4/701 (14 June 2016)
International Law Commission, *Draft articles on immunity of State officials from foreign criminal jurisdiction*, UN Doc A/CN.4/L.814 (4 June 2014)
Kolodkin, Roman Anatolevich, Special Rapporteur, *Second report on the immunity of State officials from foreign criminal jurisdiction*, UN Doc A/CN.4/631 (10 June 2010)
Memorandum submitted by the Secretary-General, *Historical Survey of the Question of International Criminal Jurisdiction*, UN Doc A/Cn.4/7/Rev.1 (1949)
Memorandum submitted by the Secretary-General, *The Charter and Judgment of the Nürnberg Tribunal History and Analysis*, UN Doc A/CN.4/5 (1949)
Model status-of-forces agreement for peace-keeping operations, UN GAOR, 45th sess, UN Doc A/45/594 (9 October 1990)
Official Records of the United Nations Diplomatic Conference of Plenipotentiaries on the Establishment of an International Criminal Court (Summary records of the plenary meetings and of the meetings of the Committee of the Whole) UN Doc A/CONF.183/C.1/SR (15 June–17 July 1998)
'Proposal by the United Kingdom of Great Britain and Northern Ireland: Trigger mechanism' UN Doc A/AC.249/1998/WG.3/DP.1 (25 March 1998)
Record of the 4568th meeting of the United Nations Security Council, UN SCOR, 57th sess, 4568th mtg, UN Doc S/PV.4568 (10 July 2002)
Record of the 4772nd meeting of the United Nations Security Council, UN SCOR, 58th sess, 4772nd mtg, UN Doc S/PV.4772 (12 June 2003)
Record of the 4803rd meeting of the United Nations Security Council, UN SCOR, 58th sess, 4803rd mtg, UN Doc S/PV.4803 (1 August 2003)
Record of the 7060th meeting of the United Nations Security Council, UN SCOR, 68th sess, 7060th mtg, UN Doc S/PV.7060 (15 November 2013)

Report of the Ad Hoc *Committee on Genocide*, UN ESCOR, 7th sess, Supp No 6, UN Doc E/794/Corr. 1 (1948)

Report of the Ad Hoc *Committee on the Establishment of an International Criminal Court*, UN GAOR, 50th sess, Supp No 22, UN Doc A/50/22 (6 September 1995)

Report of the International Criminal Court, UN GAOR, 63rd sess, 35th mtg, Agenda Item 69, UN Doc A/63/PV.35 (31 October 2008)

Report of the International Criminal Court, UN GAOR, 64th sess, 29th mtg, Agenda Item 75, UN Doc A/64/PV.29 (29 October 2009)

Report of the International Criminal Court, UN GAOR, 65th sess, 41st mtg, Agenda Item 73, UN Doc A/65/PV.41 (29 October 2010)

Report of the International Criminal Court, UN GAOR, 68th sess, 42nd mtg, Agenda Item 75, UN Doc A/68/PV.42 (31 October 2013)

Report of the International Criminal Court, UN GAOR, 72nd sess, 37th mtg, Agenda Item 76, UN Doc A/72/PV.37 (30 October 2017)

Report of the International Criminal Court, UN GAOR, 73rd sess, 27th mtg, Agenda Item 77, UN Doc A/73/PV.27 (29 October 2018)

Report of the International Law Commission on the Work of Its Forty-Third Session, 29 April–19 July 1991, UN Doc A/46/10 (1991)

Report of the International Law Commission on the Work of Its Forty-Sixth Session, 2 May–21 July 1994, UN Doc A/49/10 (1994)

Report of the International Law Commission on the Work of Its Forty-Sixth Session, 2 May–21 July 1994, Addendum, UN Doc A/CN.4/464/Add.1 (22 February 1995)

Report of the International Law Commission on the Work of Its Forty-Eighth Session, 6 May–26 July 1996, UN Doc A/51/10 (1996)

Report of the International Law Commission, UN GAOR, 70th sess, UN Doc A/73/10 (30 April–1 June and 2 July–10 August 2018)

Report of the Preparatory Committee on the Establishment of an International Criminal Court (Volume I), UN GAOR, 51st sess, Supp No 22, UN Doc A/51/22 (Proceedings of the Preparatory Committee during March–April and August 1996)

Report of the Secretary-General on the Establishment of a Special Court for Sierra Leone, UN Doc S/2000/915 (4 October 2000)

Reports of the Secretary-General on the Sudan and South Sudan, UN SCOR, 70th sess, 7478th mtg, UN Doc S/PV.7478 (15 June 2015)

Reports of the Secretary-General on the Sudan and South Sudan, UN SCOR, 72nd sess, 7963rd mtg, UN Doc S/PV.7963 (8 June 2017)

Reports of the Secretary-General on the Sudan and South Sudan, UN SCOR, 73rd sess, 8425th mtg, UN Doc S/PV.8425 (14 December 2018)

Report of the Secretary-General prepared on the basis of comments and observations of Governments: The scope and application of the principle of universal jurisdiction, 65th sess, Agenda Item 88, UN Doc A/65/181 (29 July 2010)

Report of the Secretary-General Pursuant to Paragraph 5 of Security Council Resolution 955, UN Doc S/1995/134 (13 February 1995)

Report of the Secretary-General: The scope and application of the principle of universal jurisdiction, UN GAOR, 6th Comm, 65th sess, Agenda Item 88, UN Doc A/65/181 (29 July 2010)

Report of the Secretary-General: The scope and application of the principle of universal jurisdiction, 68th sess, Agenda Item 86, UN Doc A/68/113 (26 June 2013)

Report of the Secretary-General: The scope and application of the principle of universal jurisdiction, 70th sess, UN Doc A/70/125 (1 July 2015)

Reports of the Secretary-General on the Sudan, UN SCOR, 5158th mtg, UN Doc S/PV.5158 (31 March 2005)

Reports of the Secretary-General on the Sudan and South Sudan, UN SCOR, 8554th mtg, UN Doc S/PV.8554 (19 June 2019)

Resolution on the Formation of the Principles Recognised in the Charter of the Nuremberg Tribunal and in the Judgment of the Tribunal, UN Doc A/Res/177 (21 November 1947)

Spiropoulos, Jean, Special Rapporteur, *Second report on a draft code of offences against the peace and security of mankind*, UN Doc A/CN.4/44 (12 April 1951)

Status of Palestine in the United Nations, GA Res 67/19, UN GAOR, 44th mtg, UN Doc A/Res/67/19 (29 November 2012)

Summary Record of the 9th Meeting, UN GAOR, 6th Comm, 53rd sess, 9th mtg, Agenda Item 153, UN Doc A/C.6/53/SR.9 (4 November 1998)

Summary Record of the 10th Meeting, UN GAOR, 6th Comm, 53rd sess, 10th mtg, Agenda Item 153, UN Doc A/C.6/53/SR.10 (11 December 1998)

Summary Record of the 11th Meeting, UN GAOR, 6th Comm, 53rd sess, 11th mtg, Agenda Item 153, UN Doc A/C.6/53/SR.11 (3 November 1998)

Summary Record of the 12th Meeting, UN GAOR, 6th Comm, 53rd sess, 12th mtg, Agenda Item 153, UN Doc A/C.6/53/SR.12 (19 December 1998)

Summary Record of the 12th Meeting, UN GAOR, 6th Comm, 70th sess, 12th mtg, Agenda Item 86, UN Doc A/C.6/70/SR.12 (20 October 2015)

Summary Record of the 14th Meeting, UN GAOR, 6th Comm, 54th sess, 14th mtg, Agenda Item 158, UN Doc A/C.6/54/SR.14 (10 November 1999)

Summary Record of the 33rd Meeting, UN GAOR, 6th Comm, 73rd sess, 33rd mtg, Agenda Item 87, UN Doc A/C.6/73/SR.33 (5 November 2018)

Syria ICC Resolution Draft Referral, UN Doc S/ 192014/348 (22 May 2014)

Statement by Mr Dilip Lahiri, Head of the Indian Delegation at the United Nations Diplomatic Conference of Plenipotentiaries on the Establishment of an International Criminal Court (Rome, 16 June 1998) 'The Jurisdiction of the International Criminal Court, An informal discussion paper submitted by Germany' UN Doc A/AC.249/1998/DP.2 (23 March 1998)

The Situation in Libya, UN SCOR, 73rd sess, 8250th mtg, UN Doc S/PV.8250 (9 May 2018)

Thiam, Doudou, Special Rapporteur, *Eighth report on the draft code of crimes against the peace and security of mankind*, UN Doc A/CN.4/430 (8 March 1990)

Thiam, Doudou, Special Rapporteur, *Ninth report on the draft code of crimes against the peace and security of mankind*, UN Doc A/CN.4/435 (8 February 1991)

Thiam, Doudou, Special Rapporteur, *Tenth report on the draft code of crimes against the peace and security of mankind*, UN Doc A/CN.4/449 (20 March 1992)

Thiam, Doudou, Special Rapporteur, *Eleventh report on the draft code of crimes against the peace and security of mankind*, UN Doc A/CN.4/442 (25 March 1993)

UN Diplomatic Conference of Plenipotentiaries on the Establishment of an International Court, *Draft Statute for the International Criminal Court*, UN Doc A/CONF.183/2/Add.1 (14 April 1998)

United Nations, 'Conflict between Security Council powers, international court, discussed in preparatory committee' (Press Release, L/2777, 4 April 1996)

United Nations, 'Role of Security Council in triggering prosecution discussed in preparatory committee for international criminal court' (Press Release, L/2776, 4 April 1996)

United Nations Secretary-General, 'Secretary-General examines "meaning of international community" in address to DPI/ NGO conference'; (Press Release, SG/SM/7133, 15 September 1999)

International Criminal Court Documents

Assembly of States Parties to the Rome Statute, 'Discussion Paper 1: The Crime of Aggression and Article 25, paragraph (3) of the Statute', ICC OR, 4th sess, ICC-ASP/4/32, Annex II B (9 December 2005)

Delegations to the Review Conference of the Rome Statute of the International Criminal Court, ICC Doc RC/INF.1 (26 August 2010)

International Criminal Court, *Activation of the jurisdiction of the Court over the crime of aggression*, Resolution ICC-ASP/16/Res.5 (adopted 14 December 2017)

International Criminal Court Press and Media, 'ICC Trial Chamber I acquits Laurent Gbagbo and Charles Blé Goudé from all charges' (Press release, ICC-CPI-1920190115-PR1427, 15 January 2019)

International Criminal Court Press and Media, 'President of the Assembly of States Parties visit to Ukraine' (Press release, ICC-ASP-1920141009-PR1048, 9 October 2014)

International Criminal Court Press and Media, 'The State of Palestine accedes to the Rome Statute' (Press release, ICC-ASP-1920150107-PR1082, 7 January 2015)

International Criminal Court Press and Media, 'Trial of Laurent Gbagbo and Charles Blé Goudé opens at International Criminal Court' (Press Release, ICC-CPI- 1920160128-PR1184, 28 January 2016)

International Criminal Court Press and Media, 'Ukraine accepts ICC jurisdiction over alleged crimes committed between 21 November 2013 and 22 February 2014' (Press Release, ICC-CPI-20140417-PR997, 17 April 2014)

Letter of the Prosecutor to the Presidency dated 17 June 2004 appended to *Situation in Uganda (Decision Assigning the Situation in Uganda to Pre-Trial Chamber II)* (International Criminal Court, Presidency, Case No ICC-02/04, 5 July 2004)

Office of the Prosecutor, 'ICC Prosecutor receives referral by the authorities of the Union of the Comoros in relation to the events of May 2010 on the vessel 'MAVI MARMARA' (Statement, 14 May 2013)

Office of the Prosecutor, 'Prosecutor of the International Criminal Court, Fatou Bensouda, re-opens the preliminary examination of the situation in Iraq' Office of the Prosecutor, 'Situation in Palestine' (Statement, 3 April 2012)

Office of the Prosecutor, 'Statement of the Prosecutor of the International Criminal Court, Fatou Bensouda, on opening a Preliminary Examination into the situation in Burundi' (Statement, 25 April 2016)

Office of the Prosecutor, 'Statement of the Prosecutor of the International Criminal Court, Fatou Bensouda, on the conclusion of the preliminary examination of the situation in the Republic of Korea' (Statement, 23 June 2014)

Office of the Prosecutor, 'The determination of the Office of the Prosecutor on the communication received in relation to Egypt' (Press Release, ICC-OTP-1920140508-PR1003, 8 May 2014)

Office of the Prosecutor, *Eighteenth Report of the Prosecutor of the International Criminal Court to the United Nations Security Council Pursuant to UNSCR 1593 (2005)* (11 December 2013)

Office of the Prosecutor, *Eighteenth Report of the Prosecutor of the International Criminal Court to the United Nations Security Council Pursuant to UNSCR 1970 (2011)* (6 November 2019)

Office of the Prosecutor, 'The Prosecutor of the International Criminal Court, Fatou Bensouda, opens a preliminary examination of the situation in Palestine' (Press Release, ICC-OTP-1920150116-PR1083, 16 January 2015)

Office of the Prosecutor, *Report on Preliminary Examination Activities (2018)* (International Criminal Court, 5 December 2018)

Office of the Prosecutor, *Situation on Registered Vessels of Comoros, Greece and Cambodia Article 53(1) Report* (6 November 2014)

Office of the Prosecutor, *Twelfth Report of the Prosecutor of the International Criminal Court to the United Nations Security Council Pursuant to UNSCR 1970 (2011)* (9 November 2016)

Palestinian National Authority, *Declaration recognizing the Jurisdiction of the International Criminal Court* (21 January 2009)

Palestinian National Authority, *Referral by the State of Palestine Pursuant to Articles 13(a) and 14 of the Rome Statute* (15 May 2018) icc-cpi.int/itemsDocuments/2018-05-22_ref-palestine.pdf.

Prosecutor v Al Bashir (Observations by Professor Paola Gaeta as amicus curiae on the merits of the legal questions presented in Jordan's appeal against the 'Decision under Article 87(7) of the Rome Statute on the non-compliance by Jordan with the request by the Court for the arrest and surrender of Omar Al-Bashir' of 12 March 2018) (International Criminal Court, Appeals Chamber, Case No ICC/02/05-01/09 OA2, 18 June 2018)

Prosecutor v Saif Al-Islam Gaddafi and Abdullah Al-Senussi (Document in support of the Government of Libya's Appeal against the 'Decision on the admissibility of the case against Saif Al-Islam Gaddafi') (International Criminal Court, Appeals Chamber, Case No ICC-01/11–01/11, 24 June 2013)

Review Conference of the Rome Statute of the International Criminal Court (Kampala 31 May–11 June 2010), Official Records, ICC Doc RC/11 (2010)

Situation in the State of Palestine (Prosecution request pursuant to article 19(3) for a ruling on the Court's territorial jurisdiction in Palestine) (International Criminal Court, Office of the Prosecutor, Case No ICC-01/18, 20 December 2019)

Situation on the Registered Vessels of the Union of the Comoros, the Hellenic Republic and the Kingdom of Cambodia (Final decision of the Prosecutor concerning the 'Article 53(1) Report' (ICC-01/13–6-AnxA), dated 6 November 2014) (International Criminal Court, Office of the Prosecutor, Case No ICC-01/13, 2 December 2019)

Statement by HE Mrs Soraya Alvarez Núñez, Ambassador of Cuba in the Kingdom of the Netherlands, *Eighteenth Session of the Assembly of the States Parties to the Rome Statute of the International Criminal Court* (2–7 December 2019)

Statement by Mr Hu Bin, Head of the Chinese Observer Delegation and Deputy Director-General of the Department of Treaty and Law, Ministry of Foreign Affairs of China, *Eighteenth Session of the Assembly of States Parties to the Rome Statute of the International Criminal Court* (The Hague, 3 December 2019)

Statement by Mr Issaskar Ndjoze, Permanent Secretary, Republic of Namibia Ministry of Justice, *Fifteenth Meeting of the Assembly of States Parties to the International Criminal Court* (16–24 November 2016)

Statement of Vestine Nahimana Ambassador of Burundi, *Fifteenth Session of the Assembly of States Parties to the Rome Statute of the International Criminal Court* (16–24 November 2016)

Transcript of Proceedings, *Prosecutor v Al Bashir (Judgment in the Jordan Referral re Al-Bashir Appeal)* (International Criminal Court, Appeals Chamber, Case No ICC/02/05–01/09, 14 September 2018)

UK Statement by Andrew Murdoch, Legal Director to the International Criminal Court Assembly of States Parties, *Seventeenth Session of the Assembly of States*

Parties to the Rome Statute of the International Criminal Court (5 December 2018)

Ukraine, *Declaration by Ukraine lodged under Article 12(3) of the Rome Statute* (8 September 2015)

United States of America, *Statement on behalf of the United States of America*, 16th Session of the Assembly of States Parties (8 December 2017)

News Articles and Blog Posts

Akande, Dapo, 'ICC Issues Detailed Decision on Bashir's Immunity (... At Long Last ...) But Gets the Law Wrong', *EJIL: Talk!* (15 December 2011)

Akande, Dapo, 'An International Court of Justice Advisory Opinion on the ICC Head of State Immunity Issue' *EJIL: Talk!* (31 March 2016)

Akande, Dapo, 'ICC Appeals Chamber Holds that Heads of State Have No Immunity Under Customary International Law Before International Tribunals' *EJIL: Talk!* (6 May 2019)

Anderson, Keilin, 'ICC Appeals Chamber Resurrects Controversial Customary International Law Argument to find Al-Bashir Has No Immunity before International Courts' *ILA Reporter* (May 2019)

Baker, Peter, 'Donald Trump's Victory Promises to Upend the International Order' *New York Times* (9 November 2016)

Batros, Ben, 'A Confusing ICC Appeals Judgment on Head-of-State Immunity' *Just Security* (7 May 2019)

de Hoogh, André and Abel Knottnerus, 'ICC Issues New Decision on Al Bashir's Immunities – But Gets the Law Wrong ... Again', *EJIL: Talk!* (18 April 2014)

Doherty, Ben, 'Aung San Suu Kyi Cannot Be Prosecuted in Australia, Christian Porter Says' *The Guardian* (17 March 2018)

'Full Text of John Bolton's Speech to the Federalist Society', *Al Jazeera* (11 September 2018)

'Gaddafi's Son Saif al-Islam Sentenced to Death' *Al Jazeera* (28 July 2015)

Gaeta, Paola, 'Guest Post: The ICC Changes Its Mind on the Immunity from Arrest of President Al Bashir, But It Is Wrong Again', *Opinio Juris* (23 April 2014)

Gettleman, Jeffrey, 'Rebel Leader in Congo Is Flown to The Hague' *New York Times* (22 March 2013)

Gladstone, Rick and Jodi Rudoren, 'Mahmoud Abbas, at UN, Says Palestinians Are No Longer Bound by Oslo Accords' *New York Times* (30 September 2015)

Heller, Kevin Jon, 'Thoughts on the Ukraine Ad Hoc Self-Referral' *Opinio Juris* (18 April 2014)

'In the Name of the Palestinian People: Court Abrogates Oslo Accords' *The Legal Agenda* (24 February 2015)

'Italian Diplomat Faces Child Abuse Charges in Philippines' *Agence France Presse* (26 May 2014)
Jacobs, Dov, 'Libya and the ICC: On the Legality of any Security Council Referral to the ICC' *Spreading the Jam* (28 February 2011)
Jacobs, Dov, 'You Have Just Entered Narnia: ICC Appeals Chamber Adopts the Worst Possible Solution on Immunities in the Bashir Case' *Spreading the Jam* (6 May 2019)
Kershner, Isabel, 'Israeli Government Watchdog Investigates Military's Conduct in Gaza War' *New York Times* (20 January 2015)
Kiyani, Asad, 'Elisions and Omissions: Questioning the ICC's Latest Bashir Immunity Ruling' *Just Security* (8 May 2019)
Knottnerus, Abel, 'The Immunity of al-Bashir: The Latest Turn in the Jurisprudence of the ICC', *EJIL: Talk!* (15 November 2017)
Lamony, Stephen, 'Rwanda and the ICC: Playing Politics with Justice', *African Arguments* (21 October 2013)
'Letter to the Editor from former Deputy Legal Adviser to Israel's Permanent Mission to the United Nations' *Just Security* (8 April 2014)
Luban, David, 'Palestine and the ICC – Some Legal Questions' *Just Security* (2 January 2015)
Magid, Jacob, 'Attorney General: ICC Can't Rule on Conflict as There Is No Palestinian State' *The Times of Israel* (27 November 2018)
Nazzal, Nasouh, 'Jenin Judge Reassigned over Unilateral Move' *Gulf News* (19 January 2015)
Rudoren, Jodi, 'What the Oslo Accords Accomplished' *New York Times* (30 September 2015)
Sayigh, Yezid and Saeb Erekat, 'Who Killed the Oslo Accords?' *Al Jazeera* (1 October 2015)
Schabas, William A, 'Obama, Medvedev and Hu Jintao May Be Prosecuted by International Criminal Court, Pre-Trial Chamber Concludes', *PhD Studies in Human Rights* (15 December 2011)
'Sudan Rejects ICC Arrest Warrants', *Sudan Tribune* (2 May 2007)
'Sudan Rejects ICC Ruling on Darfur' *Al Jazeera* (28 February 2007)
'Sudan's Military Seizes Power from President Omar al-Bashir' *Al Jazeera* (12 April 2019)
'Trial of Sayf-al-Islam in Libya Is Question of Sovereignty – NTC Official' *BBC Monitoring Middle East* (9 April 2012)
Wuthnow, Joel, 'China and the ICC' *The Diplomat* (7 December 2012)

Other

Ambassador Anne W Patterson, Acting US Representative to the United Nations, *Explanation of Vote on the Sudan Accountability Resolution*, in the Security Council, 31 March 2005

American Non-Governmental Organizations Coalition for the International Criminal Court, *Countries Concluding Bilateral Immunity Agreements* amicc.org/usicc/bialist

American Servicemembers' Protection Act, 22 USC §§7421–7433 (2002) [United States]

Amnesty International, *Universal Jurisdiction – A Preliminary Survey of Legislation Around the World 2012 Update* (9 October 2012)

Amnesty International, *Universal Jurisdiction – Strengthening This Essential Tool of International Justice* (2012) amnesty.org/download/Documents/24000/ior530202012en.pdf

Assembly of the African Union, *Decision on Africa's Relationship with the International Criminal Court*, Extraordinary Session, Ext/Assembly/AU/Dec.1 (12 October 2013)

Barbour, Emily C and Matthew C Reid, *The International Criminal Court (ICC): Jurisdiction, Extradition, and US Policy* (Congressional Research Service Report for Congress, 16 March 2010) fas.org/sgp/crs/row/R41116.pdf

Control Council Law No 10: Punishment of Persons Guilty of War Crimes, Crimes Against Peace and Against Humanity, (adopted 20 December 1945, Official Gazette, Control Council for Germany, No 3, Berlin, 31 January 1946)

Crawford, James, Philippe Sands and Ralph Wilde, 'In the Matter of the Statute of the International Criminal Court and In the Matter of Bilateral Agreements Sought by the United States Under Article 98(2) of the Statute' (Joint Legal Opinion, 5 June 2003) amicc.org/docs/Art98-14une03FINAL.pdf

Crimes Act 1914 (Cth) [Australia]

Criminal Code Act 1995 (Cth) [Australia]

European Union Guiding Principles concerning Arrangements between a State Party to the Rome Statute of the International Criminal Court and the United States Regarding the Conditions to Surrender of Persons to the Court [2002] 12488/1/02 COJUR 10 USA 37 PESC 374

Explanation of vote by Mr Dilip Lahiri, Head of Delegation of India, on the adoption of the Statute of the International Criminal Court (17 July 1998) legal-tools.org/en/go-to-database/record/9f86d4/

Explanatory Report to the European Convention on the Transfer of Proceedings in Criminal Matters, ETS 73 (1972)

Georgetown Law Library, *International Criminal Court – Article 98 Agreements Research Guide* (31 January 2017) guides.ll.georgetown.edu/article_98

Government of the Republic of the Union of Myanmar Ministry of the Office of the State Counsellor (Press Release, 9 August 2018)

Hostage Taking Act, 18 USC §1203 (1985) [United States]

International Commission on Intervention and State Sovereignty, *The Responsibility to Protect* (International Development Research Centre, December 2001) responsibilitytoprotect.org/ICISS%20Report.pdf

International Law Association Committee on Human Rights Law and Practice, 'Final Report on the Exercise of Universal Jurisdiction in Respect of Gross Human Rights Abuses', *Report of the 69th Conference of the International Law Association* (2000)

International Law Commission, 'Commentary to Article 16 (Articles on State Responsibility)' [2001] II(2) *Yearbook of the International Law Commission*

'Is a UN International Criminal Court in the US National Interest?' *Hearing before the Subcommittee on International Operations of the Committee on Foreign Relations of the United States Senate*, S HRG 105–724 (23 July 1998)

Israel Ministry of Foreign Affairs, 'Palestinian Authority joins the ICC – Israel's response' (Statement, 1 April 2015)

Letter from John R Bolton, US Under Secretary of State for Arms Control and International Security to Kofi Annan, UN Secretary General (6 May 2002)

Marty, D, Rapporteur, Council of Europe Parliamentary Assembly Committee on Legal Affairs and Human Rights, *Secret detentions and illegal transfers of detainees involving Council of Europe member states: second report*

Ministry of Foreign Affairs of the Russian Federation, 'Statement by the Russian Foreign Ministry' (Statement, 2111-16-11-2016, 16 November 2016)

Nazi and Nazi Collaborators (Punishment) Law, 5710/1950 [Israel]

Office of General Counsel Department of Defense, *Department of Defense Law of War Manual* (June 2015) dod.mil/dodgc/images/law_war_manual15.pdf

Permanent Observer Mission of the State of Palestine to the United Nations, 'Statement by HE Mr Mahmoud Abbas President of the State of Palestine at the General Debate of the United Nations General Assembly at Its 70th Session' (30 September 2015)

Princeton Project on Universal Jurisdiction, *The Princeton Principles on Universal Jurisdiction* (2001) lapa.princeton.edu/hosteddocs/unive_jur.pdf

Regional and Country Information, Coalition for the International Criminal Court iccnow.org/?mod=world

Scheffer, David, Ambassador-At-Large for War Crimes Issues, *Remarks before the 6th Committee of the 53rd General Assembly* (21 October 1998) state.gov/documents/organization/7095.doc

Statement of David Scheffer, Hearing Before the Subcommittee on International Operations of the Senate Committee on Foreign Relations of the United States Senate, 23 July 1998, 105th Congress, 2nd sess, S Rep No 105 724

State of Israel Office of the Attorney General, 'The International Criminal Court's lack of jurisdiction over the so-called "situation in Palestine"' (20 December 2019)

US Department of State, *One-Year Follow-Up Response of the United States of America to Recommendations of the Committee Against Torture on Its Combined Third to Fifth Periodic Reports* (27 November 2015) state.gov/j/drl/rls/250342.htm

US Department of State, *Daily Briefing*, 15 November 2016 (Elizabeth Trudeau) state.gov/r/pa/prs/dpb/2016/11/264350.htm

US Department of State, *Treaties in Force – A List of Treaties and Other International Agreements of the United States in Force on January 1, 2016* state.gov/documents/organization/264509.pdf

INDEX

active personality principle. *See*
 jurisdiction, extraterritorial,
 permissive principles,
 nationality
admissibility, 24, 100
 challenges to, 25–8, 35, *See also*
 Gaddafi, Saif Al-Islam
Afghanistan situation, 94–106, 129, 189
aggression, crime of, 152–8, 177–81
 customary international law, under,
 178–80
 universal jurisdiction, under, 180–1
Akande, Dapo, 37, 47, 48, 141
Al Bashir decisions, 84–91, 197
 arrest warrant PTC I, 84, 137
 DRC non-cooperation PTC II,
 86, 140
 Jordan appeal decision AC, 87, 89,
 140, 192, 198
 Jordan non-cooperation PTC II, 87
 Malawi and Chad non-cooperation
 PTC I, 85
 South Africa non-compliance
 PTC II, 86
Al Bashir, Omar, 82, 133
Al-Senussi, Abdullah, 20, 136, 138
American Servicemembers' Protection
 Act, 16
anti-terrorism treaties, 42, 65, 163
Apartheid Convention, 173
Article 98 agreements. *See* bilateral
 non-surrender agreements
aut dedere aut judicare, 42, 163

Bangladesh/Myanmar situation, 62, 76
Bassiouni, M. Cherif, 29, 31

bilateral non-surrender agreements,
 98, 132
Blokker, Niels, 51
Broomhall, Bruce, 29
Burundi, 55

Carden, S Richard, 168, 186,
 194
Cassese, Antonio, 30, 67
China, 17, 18, 24, 90
Comoros, Greece and Cambodia,
 registered vessels of, 4, 62
complementarity, 24–8, 100, *See also*
 admissibility
 State sovereignty, and, 24–8
conferral of powers. *See also*
 international organisation
 collective, 55, 93,
 142
 individual, 55
 typology, 54–5
 agency, 54
 delegation, 54
 transfer, 54
consent. *See* State consent
consent principle, 23
Convention against the Taking of
 Hostages, 43
cooperation of non-States Parties with
 the ICC. *See* International
 Criminal Court
Crawford, James, 67, 109
crimes against humanity, 94,
 172–4
Cryer, Robert, 30
Cuba, 18

customary international law
  and crimes of universal jurisdiction, 169–82
  and immunities, 78

Darfur situation, 84, 132–4, 144
delegation of jurisdiction
  among States
    lawfulness of, 40–4
  institutional law, in, 50
  legal basis for the ICC's jurisdiction, as a. *See* separate entry
  limitations on, 71–6, 96, 109, 128
  meaning of, 38, 50–7
  to international courts
    lawfulness of, 44–50
    precedents, 44–8
  transfer and agency, distinguished, 55
  without consent of the State of nationality, 40
Democratic Republic of the Congo, 5
Draft Code of Crimes against the Peace and Security of Mankind, 117
Draft Statute for an International Criminal Court, 117, 119, 131

Eichmann decision, 66, 164
European Convention on the Transfer of Proceedings in Criminal Matters, 41

France, 90

Gaddafi, Muammar, 83, 136
Gaddafi, Saif Al-Islam, 20, 136
  challenges to ICC admissibility, 25–6, 34, 136
Gbagbo, Laurent, 82
Geneva Conventions, 175
genocide, 170–2
  customary international law, as a crime under, 170
  universal jurisdiction, as a crime under, 170
Genocide Convention, 170
Georgia situation, 27, 76

Hart, HLA, 32
Heads of State. *See also* immunities
  ICC jurisdiction over, 82
  prosecution of, 77
Heads of State (non-States Parties)
  arrest and transfer to the ICC, 91–3
  ICC jurisdiction over, 84–94, 197

ICC Statute. *See* Rome Statute
ICC-UN Relationship Agreement, 114, 148
immunities
  exceptions to, 79, 81, 85
  Foreign Ministers, 80
  functional (ratione materiae), 78
  Heads of Government, 80
  Heads of State, 21, 76
  international courts, before, 81
  International Criminal Court, 81
    Article 27, 81
    Article 98, 81
  jurisprudence on, 84–91
  personal (ratione personae), 78, 80, 93
  waiver of, implied, 86, 140
Inazumi, Mitsue, 187
indeterminacy, 33, 34, 105
India, 14, 17, 24
Indonesia, 24
international community, 56, 185
  meaning of, 191
International Court of Justice (ICJ)
  Arrest Warrant case, 73, 165
  Certain Expenses case, 142
  Legality of the Use of Nuclear Weapons Advisory Opinion, 53
  Monetary Gold case, 23
  Reparations for Injuries case, 56
International Criminal Court
  agent of the international community, as an, 186–8
  as adjudicator of interstate disputes, 22
  challenges to admissibility, 25–8, 34
  cooperation obligations
    of non-States Parties, 26, 137, 140
    of States Parties, 85–8, 98, 99

cooperation of non-States Parties, 17
international legal personality, 52, 57
international organisation, as an,
    51–2, 57
jurisdiction
  immunities, and, 188
  objections to, 1, 14–28, 139
  over Heads of State from
      non-States Parties, 82
  personal, 2, 4, 135, 186
  preconditions to, 3, 154, 168
  State consent to, 33
  trigger, 4, 115, 131, 141, 153
political consequences of
    prosecution by, 21, 35
preliminary examination, 2
prosecution of a State by proxy, 22, 35
prosecution of Heads of State and
    senior State officials, 21, See
    Heads of State
review of national decisions. See
    admissibility
review of Security Council referral
    resolution, 147
Security Council referrals. See UN
    Security Council
Security Council resolutions, not
    bound by, 130
International Criminal Tribunal for
    Rwanda (ICTR), 47, 143, 176
International Criminal Tribunal for the
    former Yugoslavia
    (ICTY), 47
  Milutinović decision, 150
  Tadić decision, 143, 147, 177
International Law Commission (ILC),
    79, 116
International Military Tribunal. See
    Nuremberg Tribunal; Tokyo
    Tribunal
international organisation
  constituent treaty of, 52
  defining features of, 51
  establishment of, on a functional
      basis, 52
  powers
    acquisition of, 52–4
    express, 53

implied, 53
the ICC, as an. See International
    Criminal Court
Iraq/UK situation, 27, 185
Israel, 17, 22, 77, 176, See also Palestine
    situation
ius puniendi, 187, 192

jurisdiction
  delegation of. See separate entry
  extraterritorial, 63–9
    permissive principles, 166
    nationality, 64, 97
    passive personality, 65, 101
    protective, 66
    universality, 66, 159
  judicial, 59, 72, 97, 109, 129
  meaning of, 57–9
  personal, 64
  powers of, 59, 73, 109
  sovereign, 59, 97, 109, 129
  territorial, 61–3, 97
  to adjudicate, 60
  to enforce, 59–61, 166, 182
  to prescribe, 59–61, 166, 182, 185

Kampala Amendments. See Rome
    Statute
Kaul, Hans-Peter, 167
Kelsen, Hans, 32, 145
Kenyatta, Uhuru, 83, 130
Klabbers, Jan, 105
Korea, Republic of, 4
Koskenniemi, Martti, 32, 33, 67, 186
Kosovo, 150–1
Kreβ, Claus, 187
Kritsiotis, Dino, 191

legal basis for the ICC's jurisdiction,
    141, 182, 196
  delegation, 36, 71, 93, 111
  nationality jurisdiction, 168
  territorial jurisdiction, 6, 94, 168
  implied consent by virtue of UN
      membership, 7, 115, 131, 139,
      144, 151, 158, 189
  universal jurisdiction
    delegation of, 182–5, 193

legal basis (cont.)
    inherent to the international
        community, 185–94
lex loci, 65, 73–5
Liberia, 125, 128
Libya, 20, 33, 34
Libya situation, 25–6, 135
Lithuania, 102
Lotus case, 49, 63–4, 67–8
Lozano case, 101
Luban, David, 108, 190

Mann, Frederick A, 58
Mavi Marmara. *See* Comoros, Greece
    and Cambodia, registered
    vessels of
McDougall, Carrie, 180–1
Mégret, Frédéric, 49
Morris, Madeline, 21, 22, 23,
    41, 45
Myanmar, 15, 77

nationality principle of jurisdiction. *See*
    jurisdiction, extraterritorial
Newton, Michael, 96, 99, 102
North Atlantic Treaty Organization
    (NATO), 95
Nuremberg Tribunal, 44–7, 178

O'Keefe, Roger, 60, 97, 163, 166, 169
Oslo Accords, 109–12

pacta tertiis, 14–16, 137–8, 145, 163
Palestine, 17, 147–8
    statehood, 106–9
Palestine situation, 22, 76, 106–12, 189
passive nationality principle. *See*
    jurisdiction, extraterritorial
passive personality principle of
    jurisdiction. *See* jurisdiction,
    extraterritorial
peacekeepers, exempt from ICC
    jurisdiction. *See* UN Security
    Council
Permanent Court of International
    Justice (PCIJ), 49, 63
permissive rules of jurisdiction. *See*
    jurisdiction, extraterritorial

Philippines, The, 55
Poland, 102
powers
    conferral of. *See* conferral of
        powers
    of States, 58, 60, 97
    of the ICC, 69
    right to exercise. *See* jurisdiction
preconditions to jurisdiction. *See*
    International Criminal Court
Princeton Principles on Universal
    Jurisdiction, 181
protective principle of jurisdiction. *See*
    jurisdiction, extraterritorial

Responsibility to Protect doctrine, 31
Reydams, Luc, 162
Romania, 102
Rome Conference, 2, 118, 152, 167, 172
Rome Statute
    application to non-States Parties,
        137, 138, 140
    Article 6, 170
    Article 7, 172
    Article 8, 174
    Article 12(2), 3, 121, 139, 154
    Article 12(3), 4, 75, 107, 154
    Article 13(a), 4, 135, 141
    Article 13(b), 4, 115, 118, 131–52,
        154, 189
    Article 13(c), 4, 141
    Article 16, 119–25
    Article 17, 24, 100, 138
    Article 19, 27, 34
    Article 21, 74
    Article 27, 22, 81, 104, 140
    Article 88, 18
    Article 98(1), 82, 90, 188
    Article 98(2), 98–100, 127–8,
        134, 189
    Article 120, 101
    Article 121, 154
    Article 127, 55
    conflict with, 98, 101, 111
    effects on the interests of non-States
        Parties, 16–18, 23, 28
    Kampala Amendments
        Article 8bis, 152, 178

INDEX 243

Article 15bis, 153, 155
Article 15ter, 153, 157
normative consequences of, 18
objections of non-States Parties to, 13
potential to generate customary international law, 18
Preamble, 114, 160, 168, 195
rights and obligations of non-States Parties under, 16, 28, 87, 137–9
sovereignty
  infringement on. *See* sovereignty
universality, and, 167–9
withdrawal from, 55
Russian Federation, 17, 27, 77
Rwanda, 5, *See also* International Criminal Tribunal for Rwanda (ICTR)
Ryngaert, Cedric, 63, 66, 68

Sadat, Leila, 30, 168, 186, 194
Sarooshi, Dan, 54, 102
Scharf, Michael, 41, 44, 49, 168
Scheffer, David, 14
Schermers, Henry, 51
Schmitt, Carl, 32
Schwarzenberger, Georg, 32
Security Council. *See* UN Security Council
situation, meaning of, 134
sovereignty, 68, 197
  absolute, 12, 32
  as responsibility, 31
  contradictions inherent in, 29, 35
  cosmopolitanism, 12
  criminal jurisdiction, and, 28
  external interference, freedom from, 11
  ICC effect on, 13
  ICC infringement on, 11, 13, 28, 29–32, 33–5, 154
  international law, subject to, 12
  interpretations of, 28, 33
    as control, 31
    ascending, 32–4, 68, 191, 197
    descending, 32, 34, 186, 191
  limitations on, 31, 34
  powers of, 58

reconceptualisation of, 31
theoretical foundations of, 32–3
Westphalian model, 12, 30, 33, 186, 196
Special Court for Sierra Leone (SCSL), 47, 176, 188
State consent, 5–7, 18–23, 139, 196
  implied. *See* legal basis for the ICC's jurisdiction
  limits of, 21
  under customary international law, 21
status of forces agreements (SOFAs), 95–106, 128–30, 189
  exclusive jurisdiction of sending State, 96, 100
Sudan, 15, 20, 33, 139, *See* Darfur situation; Al Bashir decisions

territorial jurisdiction. *See* jurisdiction
Tokyo Tribunal, 47, 178
treaty conflict, 105
  political decision principle, 105, 112, 129

Uganda situation, 135
UK House of Lords
  Pinochet, 180
  R v Jones, 179
Ukraine, 74
UN Charter
  Article 2(6), 145
  Article 2(7), 144
  Article 24(1), 142
  Article 25, 115, 127, 152
  Article 27, 131
  Article 103, 130
  Chapter VII, 145
    Article 41, 142
    Article 39, 153
UN Security Council
  aggression, determining an act of, 155–7
  attempt to amend the Rome Statute, 124

UN Security Council (cont.)
  exempting nationals of non-States Parties from ICC jurisdiction, 120–8, 132, 134, 136
  ICC jurisdiction and
    deferral power, 118, 119–25
    referral power, 4, 6, 118, 131–52, 189
  non-UN Member States, and, 145–51
  permanent members, 115, 120, 145, 156
  powers under the UN Charter, 142–51
  resolutions
    1422, 120–5
    1497, 125–30
    1593, 132–5
    1970, 137
  role in the Rome Statute, 116–19
United Kingdom, 27
United Nations Mission in Liberia (UNMIL), 128–30
United States, 33, 43, 77, 132, 176
  Afghanistan situation. *See* separate entry
  armed forces, 94–106
  attitudes towards the ICC, 1, 14, 15, 17, 19, 90, 118
  bilateral non-surrender agreements. *See* separate entry
  Bush administration, 16, 104, 134
  Central Intelligence Agency (CIA), 94, 102–4
  Obama administration, 19
  Trump administration, 19
universal jurisdiction
  and the ICC, 144, 159
  customary international law, in, 164–6
  defined, 161–7
  in absentia, 165
  inherent to the international community, 185–8
  treaty-based, 162
  vicarious, 162
US v Ali, 43

Vatican City, 149
Vienna Convention on Diplomatic Relations, 80
Vienna Convention on the Law of Treaties
  Article 34, 14
  Article 46, 75
  Article 5, 52

war crimes, 73, 94, 103, 174–7
Weil, Prosper, 68
Williams, Sarah, 190